The Best AMERICAN SPORTS WRITING 1997

The Best AMERICAN SPORTS WRITING 1997

EDITED AND WITH
AN INTRODUCTION BY

George Plimpton

Glenn Stout, *Series Editor*

HOUGHTON MIFFLIN COMPANY
BOSTON • NEW YORK 1997

ISSN: 1056-8034
ISBN: 0-395-79762-4

Printed in the United States of America

QUM 10 9 8 7 6 5 4 3 2 1

Contents

represented in these pages the past seven years and, I suspect, those who will reside here sometime in the future.

I went to college in the glorious late '70s, a time period much maligned today but that I remember during which you could do just about any damn thing you wanted without being bothered by anyone, a kind of a suspended magnetic field between the disparate excesses of the '60s and the '80s. What this meant for me was that I somehow managed to spend my five years of undergraduate study completing four years of work without ever pausing, for even a moment, to consider what I was going to do to earn a living. This is, undoubtedly, the reason why within about a week of graduation I was back to pouring concrete and tying re-bar and wanting to write, precisely what I had been doing a week before my higher education started — only now I used bigger words, cursed my fate ever more creatively, and owed the federal government ten thousand dollars.

So I quit. But what to do?

Well, I had spent the bulk of my time at Bard College in upstate New York playing softball and writing poetry. I even tried to combine the two whenever I could get away with it, subtitling my senior project, a collection of poetry, "More Poems about Baseball and Fish." So it made perfect sense that when I went looking for work I got a job selling minor league baseball tickets over the phone.

I was singularly unsuccessful pitching group buys for a spurious "Business Night" at the ballpark and never made more than seventy dollars a week commission, although I did get free tickets to the games. The only groups that I demonstrated any facility at all selling to were motorcycle gangs and Catholic priests. That's because I cheated. I departed from my script and told the motorcycle gangs that such and such gang from across town had bought tickets, and challenged them to prove their toughness by attending the same game. To the priests, I casually mentioned that the local Methodist, Lutheran, or Baptist church had also bought tickets, leading the dear Father to conclude that his gang wasn't about to back down either. But I eventually ran out of both insecure motorcycle gangs and gullible priests. When I did, I quit that job, too.

And went back to pouring concrete and tying re-bar and wanting to write. But now I started looking at the want ads.

I found one from a small weekly newspaper in a county seat in eastern Ohio that wanted a sports editor. I typed up a résumé,

Foreword

ON A RACK in my junior high school library was a selection of vocational pamphlets, all bearing titles that began "So You Want to Be a . . ." To the best of my recollection, most of the career choices were on the order of "Farmer," "Nurse," and "Engineer." I do not believe there was a pamphlet entitled "So You Want to Be a . . . Sports Writer."

That's just as well, because I really can't ever recall a time when I really ever wanted to be a sports writer. At age thirteen or fourteen, I still held out the hope of someday filling the shoes of Roberto Clemente or Bob Gibson or any of a number of my other adolescent heroes. By the time it became obvious that that simply wasn't going to happen, at about age fifteen, I had discovered new heroes named Jack Kerouac and James Wright. I decided to become a writer. The adjective "sports" had yet to work its way into the phrase.

I mention this for two reasons. When an acquaintance first learns that I am a sports writer, the next question is inevitably, "What paper do you write for?" And ever since I became editor of this series, I am occasionally asked by those who feel compelled to address me as "Mr." or "Sir" how I became a sports writer.

I was reminded of this as I considered the selections Guest Editor George Plimpton made in this volume. Unlike some earlier editions of this series, there's only one selection from a newspaper, and hardly a "sports writer" to be found. I suppose that's fine. It keeps this book from becoming too predictable and allows me to go off on the route that has brought me here, one that I think is not all that dissimilar from the paths of many other writers who have been hedged on the Wite-Out, and applied. Obviously impressed by my impeccable typing, superb academic credentials, and my recent position as group ticket sales manager for the Columbus Clippers triple A baseball team, they gave me an interview.

So I drove out between the abandoned strip mines to the depressed little hamlet and within ten minutes of meeting the editor was offered the job. All I had to do was meet with the publisher after lunch. Only a formality, I was told. I scoped out an apartment above the Sears catalog center on the town square and met with the great man.

Unfortunately, the publisher was not from Ohio. Reeking of grease from his recent lunch and sweating ever more profusely with each word, he explained to me that he was from upstate New York and knew all about me and people like me, and by god no graduate of godless goddamn Bard College was gonna cut his hair and get a job working for him. No sir.

I looked winsomely at the apartment above the Sears catalog center as I left town. My career as an official sports writer was over.

So I went back to pouring concrete and tying re-bar. And writing. I eventually quit the first two tasks while becoming, in turn, unemployed, a security guard, a janitor, a painter, and a library assistant, although I earned the best money after I sold my trombone and moved to Boston by writing papers for nitwit undergrads attending Harvard and Boston University.

But I kept writing and the pages kept piling up, a fact that eventually made each move from one crummy apartment to another more and more problematic. I was out of options. I either had to start making money writing, stop writing, or never move again.

That's when I figured it out. Sports and writing. It didn't matter that I had two thousand poems screaming from the bottom of my file cabinet. They were never going to earn me a nickel (well, reading in the street one time I did get a dollar, but I think the guy thought I was panhandling and schizophrenic). Fine by me. I was spending half my time with the box scores anyway. So I started writing about it. People bought it. I concluded that I didn't need a newspaper behind me.

That was fine, because I had convinced myself that writing about sports was not only fun, but a cut above other journalisms, like writing about what the local sewer commission was up to, or the hair-care industry, or writing software manuals, or the thousand other kinds of writing I could do. It wasn't literature, but then again, the more I thought of it, well . . . sometimes it was. I reread the great stories I remembered from the old Best Sports Stories series and the Fireside baseball books. These led me to seek out the great sports writers of the past, like Ring Lardner, Paul Gallico, and a host of others. I started paying more attention to those who were writing now, and then discovered, or remembered, the great writing on sports that other non-sports writers had done. My beloved James Wright wrote a poem about football. Kerouac was a gridiron star and also wrote of baseball, boxing, and horse racing. Even Theodore Roethke had once taught tennis. Sports and literature were not strangers. They hung out on the side, after hours, in secret, swapping stories late into the night. They didn't always go home together but they had a certain respect for one another. There was a way I could do this.

Over the next decade I made that most delicate transformation, changing from someone who had a job and wrote to someone who had to write or else sell their belongings. I became a freelancer, which I once described to someone, stealing the metaphor from Red Smith, as the "ability to freely lance one's arm, causing a flow of words in the hope that someone might offer one or more green Band-Aids to staunch the flood."

Today I've written some hundred articles, four books under my own name and eight under some else's, have edited this series since its inception, and am not embarrassed by hardly any of it. I like sports, and still play. I like poems, and still write them. My chances of making the major leagues and winning the Nobel Prize in Literature are roughly similar. But what really gets me is being handed the ball. Writing what I want to about sports is just as real as any other kind of writing is, and sometimes even more so. I mean, let's face it, we all know the score ahead of time.

I bring all this up because I suspect that a number of the writers who have been represented in this book have followed similar paths to reach their destination here. Sports can be some kind of equalizer, and I think that's true of those who write about sports, too. I don't care what anybody's name is, who they write for or where. It never ceases to amaze me that as soon as someone reaches the bestseller list with a book about something else they decide to become a sports writer, and the next thing I see with their byline is a personal account of the world tiddly-winks tournament. Art is one thing, but free tickets, autographs, and press passes are another. Still, the writing I like is the writing I like.

That's the reason why this book isn't called *The Best Sports Reporting* or *The Best-Known Sports Writers in America* or *The Best Sports Writers Who Now Usually Appear on Television and Just Talk*. All of which, I guess, is a roundabout way of saying that sports writing need not be confined to certain topics or publications, or certain styles or approaches, and that there is no strict career track to follow to become a sports writer. As far as I know, most of us attended junior high school. Many of us spent the rest of our formal education cutting class in favor of the library or tavern, some have missed most important morning events to stay up late to get the scores from the West Coast, and a few have just plain quit jobs we hate no matter how far in debt we were. I can form and pour concrete, and have heard rumors that there are some among us who have actually attended journalism school. But fortunately, you usually can't tell which is which — er — whom is whom.

Each year, I read each and every issue of some three hundred sports and general interest magazines in search of stories that I believe might merit inclusion in *The Best American Sports Writing*. I also look at the Sunday magazines from about fifty daily newspapers and read as many newspapers as I can. I try not to miss anything, so each year I send requests to the editors of more than three hundred magazines and three hundred newspapers asking them to submit stories for my consideration, or better yet, provide me with a complimentary subscription to their publication. These really help. Otherwise submissions risk being overlooked in the glut of material I receive each January. Writers and readers are likewise encouraged to send me stories they've written or read that they would like to see in this series. Writers, in particular, should feel welcome to submit their own work. Believe me, your editor may not bother submitting anything, especially from newspapers, and those who do don't always submit the best stuff. Besides, won't it feel great to go up to him or her and say, "Hey, remember that story I wrote that you hated?" Then subtly push this book under his or her nose, coyly opened to the page upon which your story begins. There's nothing better, so I've been told.

Each year, I submit the best seventy-five stories to the guest editor, who makes the final selection. This year's guest editor, George

Plimpton, supplemented my choices with a few of his own. To be considered for inclusion in next year's volume, each nonfiction story must have been published in 1997 in either the United States or Canada and must be column length or longer. Reprints or book excerpts are not eligible. I must receive all stories by February 1, 1998. This is a real deadline, and I hate telling this to people in mid-March.

All submissions must include author's name, date of publication, publication name, and address. Photocopies, tearsheets, or clean copies are fine. Submissions from on-line publications must be made in hard copy. Submissions cannot be returned, and I don't feel it is appropriate for me to comment on or critique any submissions. Publications that want to make 100 percent certain their contributions are considered should provide a complimentary subscription to the' address listed below. Those that already do so should make sure to extend the subscription for another couple of years.

Please send subscriptions or submissions to this exact address: Glenn Stout, Series Editor, The Best American Sports Writing, P.O. Box 381, Uxbridge, MA 01569.

You may also communicate your thoughts to me by e-mail at ChinMusic@compuserve.com. I'll answer if or when I have the time. However, *no submissions of material will be accepted electronically.* There is simply no way to make certain any such submissions were really published, so please respect this request.

Copies of previous editions of this book can be ordered through most bookstores. Earlier volumes may be available from out-of-print book dealers you can find in the yellow pages. I do not have copies of earlier editions, nor can I be of any assistance in helping you acquire any.

My thanks go out to the usual suspects, including my editor, Marnie Patterson Cochran, George Plimpton, and Siobhan and my daughter Saorla, who thinks I am made of paper. Still, like every other year, those who deserve the most credit are those of you who write and make my job vastly more enjoyable than pouring concrete and tying re-bar.

GLENN STOUT

Introduction

MY FATHER NEVER THOUGHT much about sports literature. A lawyer and late in his life an ambassador to the United Nations, he had a considerable library, hundreds of volumes, but I recall only one with a sports background, P. C. Wodehouse's hilarious book on golf, *Divots*. He added my books from time to time, setting them in on the shelf next to the Greek dramatists. At the breakfast table he never read the sports pages, considering them a waste of time. And yet for all of this he was an excellent athlete — football, hockey, and tennis at Amherst, a tennis doubles champion at the local country club playing with my mother, and a windmilling softball pitcher in the Sunday pickup games on the lawn behind Charles Ames's house in Laurel Hollow. He batted from the left side of the plate with his feet together, lifting the forward leg off the ground in the style made famous by Mel Ott of the New York Giants. I think the style came naturally to him, since I doubt he had ever seen Mel Ott play, much less read about him. If he had gone to the Polo Grounds one day and seen Ott at the plate lifting a forward leg as if fending off a dog, he would have turned to my mother and whispered, "That chap must have passed by Laurel Hollow that Sunday and seen me hit the ball out into Charlie's rose garden."

I never succumbed to father's attitude about sports writing. I read the sports pages and I knew the lineups and the batting averages of the teams I favored, the Giants and the Boston Red Sox, and in later years I thought Willie Mays was God's greatest creation. Still, I never imagined that I would do any writing about sports. In fact, for many years I didn't foresee doing any kind of writing at all. Too many of my peers at college, especially at Cambridge University, wrote with style and grace and with an ease as simple as breathing. Putting ideas on paper, even in letters to my parents, was an embarrassing cross-stitching process . . . with words, even sentences abandoned in their making and penciled out. The best I could imagine for myself in the communications field was that I might become an editor — that is, fiddling with words already put to paper by someone else.

My sports-writing career began in my mid-twenties on the Long Island Railroad somewhere near the town of Syosset, chatting with a friend of mine, Whitney Tower, who was a writer on the recently founded *Sports Illustrated.* I was back from Paris with a part-time job teaching at Barnard College while editing the *Paris Review* from New York. As we slowed for the station, Whitney asked me if I would consider doing a story for *Sports Illustrated* on Harold S. Vanderbilt, the successful defender of the America's Cup in the great J-Boats of the 1930s, as well as being (which I learned later) the inventor of contract bridge. Whitney explained that Vanderbilt was an extremely shy gentleman of the school which firmly believes that mention in the press should be restricted to birth, marriage, and death, and that the magazine was having trouble finding someone with whom Vanderbilt would be willing to share the particulars of his sports career. It so happened that Vanderbilt was a member of a club at Harvard which engenders a strong bond between its members whatever their differences in age. So, in fact, it was a relatively easy assignment to visit Vanderbilt and talk with him. The story ran through four issues of *Sports Illustrated.* The fact that my words — a bit stiff and pedantic as I look back at them — had appeared in a national magazine gave me enough courage to quit teaching and to start writing about sports part-time.

Almost as important as my chance meeting with Whitney Tower on the Syosset train was reading Paul Gallico's *Farewell to Sport* and its famous chapter entitled "The Feel," in which he states how important it had been to his sports writing to experience professional sports firsthand and at their highest level . . . catching major league curve balls, getting in the ring with the heavyweight champion (Jack Dempsey), playing golf and tennis with the best in the world . . . so impressed by all of this was I that I was inspired to go to Sidney James, the editor-in-chief of *Sports Illustrated,* to see if he would allow me to do very much the same kind of "participatory journalism." I remember what he said to me as he nodded and agreed to the project: "I would advise getting in shape."

The final epiphany — if these events can be referred to as such — occurred just outside a classroom at the Cranbrook School near Bloomfield Hills in Michigan. The Detroit Lions held their training camp in these somewhat sylvan grounds — a campus of ivy-flanked dormitories and lawns with sprinklers endlessly ticking back and forth. I was there for one of my participatory journalistic stints. The third day, the team was lined up to receive their playbooks — large, stiff-backed ledgers with snap-rings to hold the play diagrams. Getting the playbook is symbolic of becoming a team member; the playbook is taken back when a player is dropped from the roster . . . the knock on the dormitory door and the dreaded words from an assistant, "Coach wants to see you. Bring your playbook." The procedure always reminded me of the ceremony of cashiering an officer in the French army — a senior officer approaching the poor soul on the parade ground and physically ripping away his shoulder epaulettes.

Thus the importance of the playbook, piles of them on a table by the classroom door, must have been very much on my mind as we approached. I held out my hand. George Wilson, the head coach, was standing behind the table. He said quite sharply, "No, no, hold on now. You can't go in there. The room's closed to the press."

I must have gasped. "But, coach, don't you see what I want to do? Stick with the rookies throughout, the classes, the scrimmages, all of it . . . just as if I were one of them."

I could see him turning it over in his mind. After all, it was surely risky to let a journalist in amongst his players where he would be privy to everything going on — a fox in a hen coop if he ungraciously chose to write about the less felicitous aspects of professional football. Vince Lombardi told me years later that it wouldn't have crossed his mind to allow such a thing. "Hell, no," he said.

It seemed like an eternity before Wilson, rather abruptly, as if he didn't want to spend too much time considering the consequences, waved me into the classroom and a bit later on walked over and handed me a playbook . . . such a simple act, but it meant that I then belonged to a sacrosanct group. I was eventually able to write about my experiences with the team, *Paper Lion,* an account which caught the public's attention and made further participatory adventures less disturbing to managements.

Because I only wrote about sports part-time, though, I never truly felt myself a member of the sportswriting fraternity. I was barely on nodding terms with the daily columnists, though I idolized them and tended to stare if I recognized them at work in the press boxes. At Arlington Raceway outside Chicago I remember Red Smith at the press desk down the line, slamming away with two fingers at a little portable typewriter, absorbed in a cocoon of concentration. We were both on the same assignment, the great horse Secretariat's last race before being retired, and seeing Red Smith at work tempted one to snap the top back on one's pen and hope for an assignment the next time that didn't involve him. My copy was due the next morning at *Sports Illustrated.* The coeds had come out by the hundreds that spring to watch Secretariat run his last race, leaning against the rail to watch him go by, probably the handsomest horse ever, Big Red they called him, big-haunched and powerful, about the only truly honest thing in the country just then, and when I looked over, quite a few of the co-eds were crying as he went by. It seemed awfully slim stuff to put to paper at the time and I haven't the courage to look back in the files for an affirmation. Come to think of it, I didn't look at Red Smith's column the following morning either.

Another one of my idols was Jimmy Cannon, a tough Runyan-esque character who wrote syndicated columns for the *New York Post* and the *New York Journal-American* through the '40s, '50s, and '60s. My favorite columns were entitled "Nobody Asked Me, but . . ." which listed one- or two-sentence observations, often of a curious koanlike quality: "Men with high freckled foreheads favor small knots in their ties," or, "In every man's private club there is a dentist who is a big horse player." The quips were easy to parody and on some occasions ("Men who eat a lot of candy don't do much boasting" or "I never met a man from Sandusky, Ohio") one wondered if Cannon had phoned a big-time parodist (E. B. White or Roger Angell), having run out of ideas of his own.

He was city-bred, and he wrote of boyhood fishing with a line baited with chewing gum and dropped through the subway gratings in the hope of fetching out the occasional dime dropped in error by a passing pedestrian. He couldn't drive, or perhaps he had once and forgotten, so I drove him around Lewiston, Maine, when we were covering the Ali–Liston fight. The countryside seemed utterly foreign to him. "What's that?" he asked in alarm. "A water tower," I said.

Oddly, Cannon, Smith, and other popular sports columnists of the day were not regular contributors to *Sports Illustrated*. Conditioned as they were to turn out exactly the same number of words five times a week, they didn't seem to relish the freedom of length and the languor enjoyed by magazine writers. In the metaphor of the track, they were dash men, sub-ten-second champions at 100 yards, but not equipped to handle the mile or the ten thousand meters. They understood the power of the haiku. Both of them could have taken my four-issue Harold Vanderbilt piece and bottled it up nicely in 799 words.

Over the years, reading as much sports literature as I did, I developed a theory about sports writing — actually two of them. The first is the Small Ball Theory. It states that the quality of the writing seems to depend on the size of the ball. The smaller the ball, the more distinguished the writing. Compare Mark Twain's famous story "The Celebrated Jumping Frog of Calaveras County," in which an important ingredient is birdshot — very small balls indeed! There are splendid books about golf (Bernard Darwin, P. G. Wodehouse, Herbert Warren Wind, Dan Jenkins, Don Marquis, John Updike), then a great baseball shelf (Roger Angell, Mark Harris, Pat Jordan, Ring Lardner, Philip Roth, among many), but diminishing returns as one moves up through soccer balls, bowling balls, footballs, volleyballs, basketballs, and finally medicine balls, about which in the files I can find only a frayed photograph. It shows a medicine ball on the front lawn of the White House. Herbert Hoover is standing behind it. From his slightly glazed look, it looks as if the ball has tumbled from the heavens and he has been asked out of the Oval Office, as chief executive, to see what should be done with it.

The second theory is referred to as the Uh-Oh! (often the Look Out Below!) and it embraces sports which do not involve the use of balls — wrestling, crew, white-water rafting, climbing, fishing, and so on. Here, it would seem that the quality of the work depends on the degree of danger involved. There are superb books about mountaineering, big-game hunting, bullfighting, boxing, automobile racing — all of which are based on the possibility of disaster . . . a dreadful outcome caused by the slightest slip. Conversely, there is not much of a shelf of literary distinction about weightlifting, the tug-of-war, canoeing, and so forth. Admittedly, the Uh-Oh is not as trustworthy as the Small Ball Theory . . . in that fiṣhing (to pick one nonball example) has a magnificent library of high-quality material, going back to Isaak Walton and indeed long before that, to *The Book of Life* (1490).

The contents of this edition of *The Best American Sports Writing* would appear to bear one out, though I should hasten to add that the selections were not made to conform to any theory other than general excellence. There are three pieces on golf (my associates at *Sports Illustrated* consider the Gary Smith piece on Tiger Woods, "The Chosen One," one of the finest stories to appear in the magazine in years), three on baseball, one on tennis (I would hope that David Foster Wallace, a remarkable writer, the author of "The String Theory," tries his hand at other sports), one on football, and two on basketball, one of which is David Remnick's portrait of Dennis Rodman, a matter unto itself. As for the Uh-Oh Theory, it is amply sustained by Jon Krakauer's remarkable account ("Into Thin Air") of the ill-fated Everest expedition in 1996, Tony Hendra's report on bullfighting in Spain ("Man and Bull"), and three stories on boxing. Linda Robertson writes about the perils of platform diving.

It is worth noting that many of the authors in this volume would not be considered sports writers, which is indeed a trend if one looks at the annual sports anthologies over the years. In 1971, E. P. Dutton's annual sports anthology (entitled Best Sports Stories) included fifty entries, forty-seven of them written by either sports editors or sports writers. Thirty-seven came directly from the sports pages. Compare the first edition of this series, *The Best American Sports Writing 1991*. Of the twenty-four selections, fifteen were from magazines and only nine from the sports pages, with only seven of the writers identified as sports writers by the daily press. In subsequent annuals there were only five such sports writers selected in 1992, two in 1993, and three in 1994. The last two editions have showed a surprising turnaround. Dan Jenkins and John Feinstein, the guest editors in 1995 and 1996, must have felt a compassion for the old-time profession of sports writing.

Why does sport have such a hold on contemporary writing? It has always been an axiom (surely my father would have believed it so) that no serious high-minded player in the Quality Lit Game would engage in writing about a pursuit in which, say, the object is to carry a pigskin across a goal line or hit a horsehide over a fence. In fact, it is a relatively new phenomenon. The great writers of the past have on occasion written of sport but only as a background for their stories. Tolstoy wrote about wolf hunting and steeplechasing (in *War and Peace* and *Anna Karenina*), Thomas Mann touched on skiing in *The Magic Mountain*. F. Scott Fitzgerald wrote a short story called "The Bowl" about football. The great exception would be Hemingway, of course, who, guided by his principle of portraying his characters under pressure, wrote about bullfighting, boxing, and big-game hunting. It is not easy to imagine any of these men sent out to do a sports story or to interview a great athlete of the times. Would that it had happened!

In fact, some years ago *Sports Illustrated* asked William Faulkner to cover the Kentucky Derby. His piece, somewhat to the bewilderment of the editors, came in laced with such arcane words as excrescent, surpiration, parterns, lambence, and fiacre (my father would have been delighted) and took a gentle dig at the *Time*-ese practice of reversing common usage ("Said Roosevelt . . .") by starting off the story with a description of the bluegrass country: "This saw Boone:"

In more recent times James Baldwin has written about boxing; so has Joyce Carol Oates. Norman Mailer, of course. Philip Roth and Bernard Malamud on baseball. John Updike on golf. Don de Lillo on football and baseball. Stanley Elkin on wrestling. Tom Wolfe on red-dirt automobile racing. William Kennedy's character Billy Phelan from his Albany novels is a bowler. And then, of course, we have the contributors to this present volume.

Surely the reason for the abiding interest in sport lies in the sentiment expressed in the lines written by William Hazlitt (1778–1830) in his tribute to John Cavanaugh, a famous fives player of that time: "When a person dies who does one thing better than anyone else in the world, which so many others are trying to do well, it leaves a gap in society." Why would one not want to write about such people and the sports they play? I have no doubt that if I could have persuaded my father to read the contents of this edition of *The Best American Sports Writing* he would have been pleased to settle it in alongside the Greek dramatists . . .

GEORGE PLIMPTON

The Best AMERICAN SPORTS WRITING 1997

JON KRAKAUER

Into Thin Air

FROM OUTSIDE

STRADDLING THE TOP of the world, one foot in Tibet and the
other in Nepal, I cleared the ice from my oxygen mask, hunched a
shoulder against the wind, and stared absently at the vast sweep
of earth below. I understood on some dim, detached level that it
was a spectacular sight. I'd been fantasizing about this moment,
and the release of emotion that would accompany it, for many
months. But now that I was finally here, standing on the summit of
Mount Everest, I just couldn't summon the energy to care.

It was the afternoon of May 10. I hadn't slept in fifty-seven hours.
The only food I'd been able to force down over the preceding three
days was a bowl of Ramen soup and a handful of peanut M&M's.
Weeks of violent coughing had left me with two separated ribs,
making it excruciatingly painful to breathe. Twenty-nine thousand
twenty-eight feet up in the troposphere, there was so little oxygen
reaching my brain that my mental capacity was that of a slow child.
Under the circumstances, I was incapable of feeling much of anything except cold and tired.

I'd arrived on the summit a few minutes after Anatoli Boukreev, a
Russian guide with an American expedition, and just ahead of
Andy Harris, a guide with the New Zealand–based commercial
team that I was a part of and someone with whom I'd grown to be
friends during the last six weeks. I snapped four quick photos of
Harris and Boukreev striking summit poses, and then turned and
started down. My watch read 1:17 P.M. All told, I'd spent less than
five minutes on the roof of the world.

After a few steps, I paused to take another photo, this one looking down the Southeast Ridge, the route we had ascended. Training my lens on a pair of climbers approaching the summit, I saw something that until that moment had escaped my attention. To the south, where the sky had been perfectly clear just an hour earlier, a blanket of clouds now hid Pumori, Ama Dablam, and the other lesser peaks surrounding Everest.

Days later — after six bodies had been found, after a search for two others had been abandoned, after surgeons had amputated the gangrenous right hand of my teammate Beck Weathers — people would ask why, if the weather had begun to deteriorate, had climbers on the upper mountain not heeded the signs? Why did veteran Himalayan guides keep moving upward, leading a gaggle of amateurs, each of whom had paid as much as $65,000 to be ushered safely up Everest, into an apparent death trap?

Nobody can speak for the leaders of the two guided groups involved, for both men are now dead. But I can attest that nothing I saw early on the afternoon of May 10 suggested that a murderous storm was about to bear down on us. To my oxygen-depleted mind, the clouds drifting up the grand valley of ice known as the Western Cwm looked innocuous, wispy, insubstantial. Gleaming in the brilliant midday sun, they appeared no different than the harmless puffs of convection condensation that rose from the valley almost daily. As I began my descent, I was indeed anxious, but my concern had little to do with the weather. A check of the gauge on my oxygen tank had revealed that it was almost empty. I needed to get down, fast.

The uppermost shank of the Southeast Ridge is a slender, heavily corniced fin of rock and wind-scoured snow that snakes for a quarter-mile toward a secondary pinnacle known as the South Summit. Negotiating the serrated ridge presents few great technical hurdles, but the route is dreadfully exposed. After fifteen minutes of cautious shuffling over a 7,000-foot abyss, I arrived at the notorious Hillary Step, a pronounced notch in the ridge named after Sir Edmund Hillary, the first Westerner to climb the mountain, and a spot that does require a fair amount of technical maneuvering. As I clipped into a fixed rope and prepared to rappel over the lip, I was greeted by an alarming sight.

Thirty feet below, some twenty people were queued up at the base of the Step, and three climbers were hauling themselves up the rope that I was attempting to descend. I had no choice but to unclip from the line and step aside.

The traffic jam comprised climbers from three separate expeditions: the team I belonged to, a group of paying clients under the leadership of the celebrated New Zealand guide Rob Hall; another guided party headed by American Scott Fischer; and a nonguided team from Taiwan. Moving at the snail's pace that is the norm above 8,000 meters, the throng labored up the Hillary Step one by one, while I nervously bided my time.

Harris, who left the summit shortly after I did, soon pulled up behind me. Wanting to conserve whatever oxygen remained in my tank, I asked him to reach inside my backpack and turn off the valve on my regulator, which he did. For the next ten minutes I felt surprisingly good. My head cleared. I actually seemed less tired than with the gas turned on. Then, abruptly, I felt like I was suffocating. My vision dimmed and my head began to spin. I was on the brink of losing consciousness.

Instead of turning my oxygen off, Harris, in his hypoxically impaired state, had mistakenly cranked the valve open to full flow, draining the tank. I'd just squandered the last of my gas going nowhere. There was another tank waiting for me at the South Summit, 250 feet below, but to get there I would have to descend the most exposed terrain on the entire route without benefit of supplemental oxygen.

But first I had to wait for the crowd to thin. I removed my now useless mask, planted my ice ax into the mountain's frozen hide, and hunkered on the ridge crest. As I exchanged banal congratulations with the climbers filing past, inwardly I was frantic: "Hurry it up, hurry it up!" I silently pleaded. "While you guys are screwing around here, I'm losing brain cells by the millions!"

Most of the passing crowd belonged to Fischer's group, but near the back of the parade two of my teammates eventually appeared: Hall and Yasuko Namba. Girlish and reserved, the 47-year-old Namba was forty minutes away from becoming the oldest woman to climb Everest and the second Japanese woman to reach the highest point on each continent, the so-called Seven Summits.

Later still, Doug Hansen — another member of our expedition, a postal worker from Seattle who had become my closest friend on the mountain — arrived atop the Step. "It's in the bag!" I yelled over the wind, trying to sound more upbeat than I felt. Plainly exhausted, Doug mumbled something from behind his oxygen mask that I didn't catch, shook my hand weakly, and continued plodding upward.

The last climber up the rope was Fischer, whom I knew casually from Seattle, where we both lived. His strength and drive were legendary — in 1994 he'd climbed Everest without using bottled oxygen — so I was surprised at how slowly he was moving and how hammered he looked when he pulled his mask aside to say hello. "Bruuuuuuce!" he wheezed with forced cheer, employing his trademark, fratboyish greeting. When I asked how he was doing, Fischer insisted he was feeling fine: "Just dragging ass a little today for some reason. No big deal." With the Hillary Step finally clear, I clipped into the strand of orange rope, swung quickly around Fischer as he slumped over his ice ax, and rappelled over the edge.

It was after 2:30 when I made it down to the South Summit. By now tendrils of mist were wrapping across the top of 27,890-foot Lhotse and lapping at Everest's summit pyramid. No longer did the weather look so benign. I grabbed a fresh oxygen cylinder, jammed it onto my regulator, and hurried down into the gathering cloud. Moments after I dropped below the South Summit, it began to snow lightly and the visibility went to hell.

Four hundred vertical feet above, where the summit was still washed in bright sunlight under an immaculate cobalt sky, my compadres were dallying, memorializing their arrival at the apex of the planet with photos and high-fives — and using up precious ticks of the clock. None of them imagined that a horrible ordeal was drawing nigh. None of them suspected that by the end of that long day, every minute would matter.

In May of 1963, when I was 9 years old, Tom Hornbein and Willi Unsoeld made the first ascent of Everest's daunting West Ridge, one of the great feats in the annals of mountaineering. Late in the day on their summit push, they climbed a stratum of steep, crumbly limestone — the infamous Yellow Band — that they didn't think they'd be able to descend. Their best shot for getting off the mountain alive, they reckoned, was to go over the top and down the Southeast Ridge, an extremely audacious plan, given the late hour and the unknown terrain. Reaching the summit at sunset, they

were forced to spend the night in the open above 28,000 feet —
at the time, the highest bivouac in history — and to descend the
Southeast Ridge the next morning. That night cost Unsoeld his
toes, but the two survived to tell their tale.

Unsoeld, who hailed from my hometown in Oregon, was a close
friend of my father's. I climbed my first mountain in the company
of my dad, Unsoeld, and his oldest son, Regon, a few months before
Unsoeld departed for Nepal. Not surprisingly, accounts of the 1963
Everest epic resonated loud and long in my preadolescent imagination. While my friends idolized John Glenn, Sandy Koufax, and
Johnny Unitas, my heroes were Hornbein and Unsoeld.

Secretly, I dreamed of climbing Everest myself one day; for more
than a decade it remained a burning ambition. It wasn't until my
mid 20s that I abandoned the dream as a preposterous boyhood
fantasy. Soon thereafter I began to look down my nose at the
world's tallest mountain. It had become fashionable among alpine
cognoscenti to denigrate Everest as a "slag heap," a peak lacking
sufficient technical challenge or aesthetic appeal to be a worthy
objective for a "serious" climber, which I desperately aspired to be.

Such snobbery was rooted in the fact that by the early 1980s,
Everest's easiest line — the South Col/Southeast Ridge, or the so-
called Yak Route — had been climbed more than a hundred times.
Then, in 1985, the floodgates were flung wide open when Dick
Bass, a wealthy 55-year-old Texan with limited climbing experience,
was ushered to the top of Everest by an extraordinary young climber named David Breashears. In bagging Everest, Bass became the
first person to ascend all of the so-called Seven Summits, a feat that
earned him worldwide renown and spurred a swarm of other amateur climbers to follow in his guided bootprints.

"To aging Walter Mitty types like myself, Dick Bass was an inspira-
tion," Seaborn Beck Weathers explained during the trek to Everest
Base Camp last April. A 49-year-old Dallas pathologist, Weathers
was one of eight paying clients on my expedition. "Bass showed that
Everest was within the realm of possibility for regular guys. Assuming you're reasonably fit and have some disposable income, I think
the biggest obstacle is probably taking time off from your job and
leaving your family for two months."

For a great many climbers, the record shows, stealing time away
from the daily grind has not been an insurmountable obstacle, nor

has the hefty outlay of cash. Over the past half-decade, the traffic on all of the Seven Summits, and especially Everest, has grown at an astonishing rate. And to meet demand, the number of commercial enterprises peddling guided ascents of these mountains has multiplied correspondingly. In the spring of 1996, thirty separate expeditions were on the flanks of Everest, at least eight of them organized as moneymaking ventures.

Even before last season's calamitous outcome, the proliferation of commercial expeditions was a touchy issue. Traditionalists were offended that the world's highest summit was being sold to rich parvenus who, if denied the services of guides, would have difficulty making it to the top of a peak as modest as Mount Rainier. Everest, the purists sniffed, had been debased and profaned.

Such critics also point out that, thanks to the commercialization of Everest, the once hallowed peak has now even been dragged into the swamp of American jurisprudence. Having paid princely sums to be escorted up Everest, some climbers have then sued their guides after the summit eluded them. "Occasionally you'll get a client who thinks he's bought a guaranteed ticket to the summit," laments Peter Athans, a highly respected guide who's made eleven trips to Everest and reached the top four times. "Some people don't understand that an Everest expedition can't be run like a Swiss train."

Sadly, not every Everest lawsuit is unwarranted. Inept or disreputable companies have on more than one occasion failed to deliver crucial logistical support — oxygen, for instance — as promised. On some expeditions guides have gone to the summit without any of their clients, prompting the bitter clients to conclude that they were brought along simply to pick up the tab. In 1995, the leader of one commercial expedition absconded with tens of thousands of dollars of his clients' money before the trip even got off the ground.

To a certain degree, climbers shopping for an Everest expedition get what they pay for. Expeditions on the northern, Tibetan side of the mountain are considerably cheaper — the going rate there is $20,000 to $40,000 per person — than those on the south, in part because China charges much less for climbing permits than does Nepal. But there's a tradeoff: until 1995, no guided client had ever reached the summit from Tibet.

This year, Hall charged $65,000 a head, not including airfare or personal equipment, to take people up the South Col/Southeast Ridge route. Although no commercial guide service charged more, Hall, a lanky 35-year-old with a biting Kiwi wit, had no difficulty booking clients, thanks to his phenomenal success rate: He'd put thirty-nine climbers on the summit between 1990 and 1995, which meant that he was responsible for three more ascents than had been made in the first twenty years after Hillary's inaugural climb. Despite the disdain I'd expressed for Everest over the years, when the call came to join Hall's expedition, I said yes without even hesitating to catch my breath. Boyhood dreams die hard, I discovered, and good sense be damned.

On April 10, after ten days of hiking through the steep, walled canyons and rhododendron forests of northern Nepal, I walked into Everest Base Camp. My altimeter read 17,600 feet.

Situated at the entrance to a magnificent natural amphitheater formed by Everest and its two sisters, Lhotse and Nuptse, was a small city of tents sheltering 240 climbers and Sherpas from fourteen expeditions, all of it sprawled across a bend in the Khumbu Glacier. The escarpments above camp were draped with hanging glaciers, from which calved immense serac avalanches that thundered down at all hours of the day and night. Hard to the east, pinched between the Nuptse wall and the West Shoulder of Everest, the Khumbu Icefall spilled to within a quarter-mile of the tents in a chaos of pale blue shards.

In stark contrast to the harsh qualities of the environment stood our campsite and all its creature comforts, including a nineteen-person staff. Our mess tent, a cavernous canvas structure, was wired with a stereo system and solar-powered electric lights; an adjacent communications tent housed a satellite phone and fax. There was a hot shower. A cook boy came to each client's tent in the mornings to serve us steaming mugs of tea in our sleeping bags. Fresh bread and vegetables arrived every few days on the backs of yaks.

In many ways, Rob Hall's Adventure Consultants site served as a sort of town hall for Base Camp, largely because nobody on the mountain was more respected than Hall, who was on Everest for his eighth time. Whenever there was a problem — a labor dispute with the Sherpas, a medical emergency, a critical decision about climbing strategy — people came to him for advice. And Hall, always generous, dispensed his accumulated wisdom freely to the very rivals who were competing with him for clients, most notably Fischer.

Fischer's Mountain Madness camp, distinguished by a huge Starbucks Coffee banner that hung from a chunk of granite, was a mere five minutes' walk down the glacier. Fischer and Hall were competitors, but they were also friends, and there was a good deal of socializing between the two teams. His mess tent wasn't as well appointed as ours, but Fischer was always quick to offer a cup of fresh-brewed coffee to any climber or trekker who poked a head inside the door.

The 40-year-old Fischer was a strapping, gregarious man with a blond ponytail and manic energy. He'd grown up in New Jersey and had fallen in love with climbing after taking a NOLS course as a 14-year-old. In his formative years, during which he became known for a damn-the-torpedoes style, he'd survived a number of climbing accidents, including twice cratering into the ground from a height of more than 70 feet. Fischer's infectious, seat-of-the-pants approach to his own life was reflected in his improvisational approach to guiding Everest. In striking contrast to Hall — who insisted that his clients climb as a group at all times, under the close watch of his guides — Fischer encouraged his clients to be independent, to move at their own pace, to go wherever they wanted, whenever they wanted.

Both men were under considerable pressure this season. The previous year, Hall had for the first time failed to get anybody to the top. Another dry spell would be very bad for business. Meanwhile Fischer, who had climbed the peak without oxygen but had never guided the mountain, was still trying to get established in the Everest business. He needed to get clients to the summit, especially a high-profile one like Sandy Hill Pittman, the Manhattan boulevardier-cum-writer who was filing daily diaries on an NBC World Wide Web site.

Despite the many trappings of civilization at Base Camp, there was no forgetting that we were more than three miles above sea level. Walking to the mess tent at mealtime left me wheezing to catch my breath. If I sat up too quickly, my head reeled and vertigo set in. I developed a dry, hacking cough that would steadily worsen over the next six weeks. Cuts and scrapes refused to heal. I was rarely hungry, a sign that my oxygen-deprived stomach had shut down and my body had begun to consume itself for sustenance. My arms and legs gradually began to wither to toothpicks, and by expedition's end I would weigh twenty-five pounds less than when I left Seattle.

Some of my teammates fared even worse than I in the meager air. At least half of them suffered from various intestinal ailments that kept them racing to the latrine. Hansen, 46, who'd paid for the expedition by working at a Seattle-area post office by night and on construction jobs by day, was plagued by an unceasing headache for most of his first week at Base Camp. It felt, as he put it, "like somebody's driven a nail between my eyes." This was Hansen's second time on Everest with Hall. The year before, he'd been forced to turn around 330 vertical feet below the summit because of deep snow and the late hour. "The summit looked *sooooo* close," Hansen recalled with a painful laugh. "Believe me, there hasn't been a day since that I haven't thought about it." Hansen had been talked into returning this year by Hall, who felt sorry that Hansen had been denied the summit and who had significantly discounted Hansen's fee to entice him to give it another try.

A rail-thin man with a leathery, prematurely furrowed face, Hansen was a single father who spent a lot of time in Base Camp writing faxes to his two kids, ages 19 and 27, and to an elementary school in Kent, Washington, that had sold T-shirts to help fund his climb. Hansen bunked in the tent next to mine, and every time a fax would arrive from his daughter, Angie, he'd read it to me, beaming. "Jeez," he'd announce, "how do you suppose a screw-up like me could have raised such a great kid?"

As a newcomer to altitude — I'd never been above 17,000 feet — I brooded about how I'd perform higher on the mountain, especially in the so-called Death Zone above 25,000 feet. I'd done some fairly extreme climbs over the years in Alaska, Patagonia, Canada, and the Alps. I'd logged considerably more time on technical rock and ice than most of the other clients and many of the guides. But technical expertise counted for very little on Everest, and I'd spent less time at high altitude — none, to be precise — than virtually every other climber here. By any rational assessment, I was singularly unqualified to attempt the highest mountain in the world.

This didn't seem to worry Hall. After seven Everest expeditions he'd fine-tuned a remarkably effective method of acclimatization. In the next six weeks, we would make three trips above Base Camp, climbing about two thousand feet higher each time. After that, he insisted, our bodies would be sufficiently adapted to the altitude to permit safe passage to the 29,028-foot summit. "It's worked thirty-nine times so far, pal," Hall assured me with a wry grin.

Three days after our arrival in Base Camp, we headed out on our first acclimatization sortie, a one-day round-trip to Camp One, perched at the upper lip of the Icefall, two thousand vertical feet above. No part of the South Col route is more feared than the Icefall, a slowly moving jumble of huge, unstable ice blocks: We were all well aware that it had already killed nineteen climbers. As I strapped on my crampons in the frigid predawn gloom, I winced with each creak and rumble from the glacier's shifting depths.

Long before we'd even got to Base Camp, our trail had been blazed by Sherpas, who had fixed more than a mile of rope and installed about sixty aluminum ladders over the crevasses that crisscross the shattered glacier. As we shuffled forth, three-quarters of the way to Camp One, Hall remarked glibly that the Icefall was in better shape than he'd ever seen it: "The route's like a bloody freeway this season."

But only slightly higher, at about 19,000 feet, the fixed ropes led us beneath and then over a twelve-story chunk of ice that leaned precariously off kilter. I hurried to get out from beneath its wobbly tonnage and reach its crest, but my fastest pace was no better than a crawl. Every four or five steps I'd stop, lean against the rope, and suck desperately at the thin, bitter air, searing my lungs.

We reached the end of the Icefall about four hours after setting out, but the relative safety of Camp One didn't supply much peace of mind: I couldn't stop thinking about the ominously tilted slab and the fact that I would have to pass beneath its frozen bulk at least seven more times if I was going to make it to the top of Everest.

Most of the recent debate about Everest has focused on the safety of commercial expeditions. But the least experienced, least qualified climbers on the mountain this past season were not guided clients; rather, they were members of traditionally structured, noncommercial expeditions.

While descending the lower Icefall on April 13, I overtook a pair of slower climbers outfitted with unorthodox clothing and gear.

Almost immediately it became apparent that they weren't very familiar with the standard tools and techniques of glacier travel. The climber in back repeatedly snagged his crampons and stumbled. Waiting for them to cross a gaping crevasse bridged by two rickety ladders lashed end to end, I was shocked to see them go across together, almost in lockstep, a needlessly dangerous act. An awkward attempt at conversation revealed that they were members of a Taiwanese expedition.

The reputation of the Taiwanese had preceded them to Everest. In the spring of 1995, the team had traveled to Alaska to climb Mount McKinley as a shakedown for their attempt on Everest in 1996. Nine climbers reached the summit of McKinley, but seven of them were caught by a storm on the descent, became disoriented, and spent a night in the open at 19,400 feet, initiating a costly, hazardous rescue by the National Park Service.

Five of the climbers — two of them with severe frostbite and one dead — were plucked from high on the peak by helicopter. "If we hadn't arrived right when we did, two others would have died, too," says American Conrad Anker, who with his partner Alex Lowe climbed to 19,400 feet to help rescue the Taiwanese. "Earlier, we'd noticed the Taiwanese group because they looked so incompetent. It really wasn't any big surprise when they got into trouble."

The leader of the expedition, Ming Ho Gau — a jovial photographer who answers to "Makalu" — had to be assisted down the upper mountain. "As they were bringing him down," Anker recalls, "Makalu was yelling, 'Victory! Victory! We made summit!' to everyone he passed, as if the disaster hadn't even happened." When the survivors of the McKinley debacle showed up on Everest in 1996, Makalu Gau was again their leader.

In truth, their presence was a matter of grave concern to just about everyone on the mountain. The fear was that the Taiwanese would suffer a calamity that would compel other expeditions to come to their aid, risking further lives and possibly costing climbers a shot at the summit. Of course, the Taiwanese were by no means the only group that seemed egregiously unqualified. Camped beside us at Base Camp was a 25-year-old Norwegian climber named Petter Neby, who announced his intention to make a solo ascent of the Southwest Face, an outrageously difficult route, despite the fact that his Himalayan experience consisted of two easy ascents of neighboring Island Peak, a 20,270-foot bump.

And then there were the South Africans. Lavishly funded, sponsored by a major newspaper, the source of effusive national pride, their team had received a personal blessing from Nelson Mandela prior to their departure. The first South African expedition ever to be granted a permit to climb Everest, they were a mixed-race group that hoped to put the first black person on the summit. They were led by a smooth-talking former military officer named Ian Woodall. When the team arrived in Nepal it included three very strong members, most notably a brilliant climber named Andy de Klerk, who happened to be a good friend of mine.

But almost immediately, four members, including de Klerk, defected. "Woodall turned out to be a total control freak," said de Klerk. "And you couldn't trust him. We never knew when he was talking bullshit or telling the truth. We didn't want to put our lives in the hands of a guy like that. So we left."

Later de Klerk would learn that Woodall had lied about his climbing record. He'd never climbed anywhere near 8,000 meters, as he claimed. In fact, he hadn't climbed much of anything. Woodall had also allegedly lied about expedition finances and even lied about who was named on the official climbing permit.

After Woodall's deceit was made public, it became an international scandal, reported on the front pages of newspapers throughout the Commonwealth. When the editor of the Johannesburg *Sunday Times,* the expedition's primary sponsor, confronted Woodall in Nepal, Woodall allegedly tried to physically intimidate him and, according to de Klerk, threatened, "I'm going to rip your fucking head off!"

In the end, Woodall refused to relinquish leadership and insisted that the climb would proceed as planned. By this point none of the four climbers left on the team had more than minimal alpine experience. At least two of them, says de Klerk, "didn't even know how to put their crampons on."

The solo Norwegian, the Taiwanese, and especially the South Africans were frequent topics of discussion around the dinner table in our mess tent. "With so many incompetent people on the mountain," Hall frowned one evening in late April, "I think it's pretty unlikely that we'll get through this without something bad happening."

*

For our third and final acclimatization excursion, we spent four nights at 21,300-foot Camp Two and a night at 24,000-foot Camp Three. Then on May 1 our whole team descended to Base Camp to recoup our strength for the summit push. Much to my surprise, Hall's acclimatization plan seemed to be working: After three weeks, I felt like I was finally adapting to the altitude. The air at Base Camp now seemed deliciously thick.

From the beginning, Hall had planned that May 10 would be our summit day. "Of the four times I've summited," he explained, "twice it was on the tenth of May. As the Sherps would put it, the tenth is an 'auspicious' date for me." But there was also a more down-to-earth reason for selecting this date: The annual ebb and flow of the monsoon made it likely that the most favorable weather of the year would fall on or near May 10.

For all of April, the jet stream had been trained on Everest like a fire hose, blasting the summit pyramid with nonstop hurricane-force winds. Even on days when Base Camp was perfectly calm and flooded with sunshine, an immense plume of wind-driven snow was visible over the summit. But if all went well, in early May the monsoon approaching from the Bay of Bengal would force the jet stream north into Tibet. If this year was like past years, between the departure of the wind and the arrival of the monsoon storms we would be presented with a brief window of clear, calm weather during which a summit assault would be possible.

Unfortunately, the annual weather patterns were no secret, and every expedition had its sights set on the same window. Hoping to avoid dangerous gridlock on the summit ridge, Hall held a pow-wow in the mess tent with leaders of the expeditions in Base Camp. The council, as it were, determined that Göran Kropp, a young Swede who had ridden a bicycle all the way to Nepal from Stockholm, would make the first attempt, alone, on May 3. Next would be a team from Montenegro. Then, on May 8 or 9, it would be the turn of the IMAX expedition, headed by David Breashears, which hoped to wrap up a large-format film about Everest with footage from the top.

Our team, it was decided, would share a summit date of May 10 with Fischer's group. An American commercial team and two British-led commercial groups promised to steer clear of the top of the mountain on the tenth, as did the Taiwanese. Woodall, however,

declared that the South Africans would go to the top whenever they
pleased, probably on the tenth, and anyone who didn't like it could
"bugger off."

Hall, ordinarily extremely slow to rile, flew into a rage over Woodall's refusal to cooperate. "I don't want to be anywhere near the
upper mountain when those punters are up there," he seethed.

"It feels good to be on our way to the summit, yeah?" Harris in-
quired as we pulled into Camp Two. The midday sun was reflecting
off the walls of Nuptse, Lhotse, and Everest, and the entire ice-
coated valley seemed to have been transformed into a huge solar
oven. We were finally ascending for real, headed straight toward
the top, Harris and me and everybody else.

Harris — Harold to his friends — was the junior guide on the
expedition and the only one who'd never been to Everest (indeed,
he'd never been above 23,000 feet). Built like an NFL quarterback
and preternaturally good-natured, he was usually assigned to the
slower clients at the back of the pack. For much of the expedition,
he had been laid low with intestinal ailments, but he was finally
getting his strength back, and he was eager to prove himself to his
seasoned colleagues. "I think we're actually gonna knock this big
bastard off," he confided to me with a huge smile, staring up at the
summit.

Harris worked as a much-in-demand heli-skiing guide in the an-
tipodal winter. Summers he guided climbers in New Zealand's
Southern Alps and had just launched a promising heli-hiking business. Sipping tea in the mess tent back at Base Camp, he'd shown
me a photograph of Fiona McPherson, the pretty, athletic doctor
with whom he lived, and described the house they were building
together in the hills outside Queenstown. "Yeah," he'd marveled,
"it's kind of amazing, really. My life seems to be working out pretty
well."

Later that day, Kropp, the Swedish soloist, passed Camp Two on
his way down the mountain, looking utterly worked. Three days
earlier, under clear skies, he'd made it to just below the South
Summit and was no more than an hour from the top when he decided to turn around. He had been climbing without supplemental
oxygen, the hour had been late — 2 P.M., to be exact — and he'd
believed that if he'd kept going, he'd have been too tired to descend safely.

"To turn around that close to the summit," Hall mused, shaking his head. "That showed incredibly good judgment on young Göran's part. I'm impressed." Sticking to your predetermined turnaround time — that was the most important rule on the mountain. Over the previous month, Rob had lectured us repeatedly on this point. Our turn-around time, he said, would probably be 1 P.M., and no matter how close we were to the top, we were to abide by it. "With enough determination, any bloody idiot can get up this hill," Hall said. "The trick is to get back down alive."

Cheerful and unflappable, Hall's easygoing facade masked an intense desire to succeed — which to him was defined in the fairly simple terms of getting as many clients as possible to the summit. But he also paid careful attention to the details: the health of the Sherpas, the efficiency of the solar-powered electrical system, the sharpness of his clients' crampons. He loved being a guide, and it pained him that some celebrated climbers didn't give his profession the respect he felt it deserved.

On May 8 our team and Fischer's team left Camp Two and started climbing the Lhotse Face, a vast sweep of steel-hard ice rising from the head of the Western Cwm. Hall's Camp Three, two-thirds of the way up this wall, was set on a narrow ledge that had been chopped into the face by our Sherpas. It was a spectacularly perilous perch. A hundred feet below, no less exposed, were the tents of most of the other teams, including Fischer's, the South Africans, and the Taiwanese.

It was here that we had our first encounter with death on the mountain. At 7:30 A.M. on May 9, as we were pulling on our boots to ascend to Camp Four, a 36-year-old steelworker from Taipei named Chen Yu-Nan crawled out of his tent to relive himself, with only the smooth-soled liners of his mountaineering boots on his feet — a rather serious lapse of judgment. As he squatted, he lost his footing on the slick ice and went hurtling down the Lhotse Face, coming to rest, headfirst, in a crevasse. Sherpas who had seen the incident lowered a rope, pulled him out of the slot, and carried him back to his tent. He was bruised and badly rattled, but otherwise he seemed unharmed. Chen's teammates left him in a tent to recover and departed for Camp Four. That afternoon, as Chen tried to descend to Camp Two with the help of the Sherpas, he keeled over and died.

Over the preceding six weeks there had been several serious accidents: Tenzing Sherpa, from our team, fell 150 feet into a crevasse and injured a leg seriously enough to require helicopter evacuation from Base Camp. One of Fischer's Sherpas nearly died of a mysterious illness at Camp Two. A young, apparently fit British climber had a serious heart attack near the top of the Icefall. A Dane was struck by a falling serac and broke several ribs. Until now, however, none of the mishaps had been fatal.

Chen's death cast a momentary pall over the mountain. But 33 climbers at the South Col would be departing for the summit in a few short hours, and the gloom was quickly shoved aside by nervous anticipation of the challenge to come. Most of us were simply wrapped too tightly in the grip of summit fever to engage in thoughtful reflection about the death of someone in our midst. There would be plenty of time for reflection later, we assumed, after we all had summited — and got back down.

Climbing with oxygen for the first time, I had reached the South Col, our launching pad for the summit assault, at one o'clock that afternoon. A barren plateau of bulletproof ice and windswept boulders, the Col sits at 26,000 feet above sea level, tucked between the upper ramparts of Lhotse, the world's fourth-highest mountain, and Everest. Roughly rectangular, about four football fields long by two across, the Col is bounded on the east by the Kangshung Face, a 7,000-foot drop-off, and on the west by the 4,000-foot Lhotse Face. It is one of the coldest, most inhospitable places I have ever been.

I was the first Western climber to arrive. When I got there, four Sherpas were struggling to erect our tents in a 50-mph wind. I helped them put up my shelter, anchoring it to some discarded oxygen canisters wedged beneath the largest rocks I could lift. Then I dove inside to wait for my teammates.

It was nearly 5 P.M. when the last of the group made camp. The final stragglers in Fischer's group came in even later, which didn't augur well for the summit bid, scheduled to begin in six hours. Everyone retreated to their nylon domes the moment they reached the Col and did their best to nap, but the machine-gun rattle of the flapping tents and the anxiety over what was to come made sleep out of the question for most of us.

Surrounding me on the plateau were some three dozen people,

huddled in tents pitched side by side. Yet an odd sense of isolation hung over the camp. Up here, in this godforsaken place, I felt distressingly disconnected from everyone around me — emotionally, spiritually, physically. We were a team in name only, I'd sadly come to realize. Although we would leave camp in a few hours as a group, we would ascend as individuals, linked to one another by neither rope nor any deep sense of loyalty. Each client was in it for himself or herself, pretty much. And I was no different: I really hoped Doug Hansen would get to the top, for instance, yet if he were to turn around, I knew I would do everything in my power to keep pushing on. In another context this insight would have been depressing, but I was too preoccupied with the weather to dwell on it. If the wind didn't abate, the summit would be out of the question for all of us.

At 7 P.M. the gale abruptly ceased. The temperature was 15 below zero, but there was almost no wind. Conditions were excellent; Hall, it appeared, had timed our summit bid perfectly. The tension was palpable as we sipped tea, delivered to us in our tents by Sherpas, and readied our gear. Nobody said much. All of us had suffered greatly to get to this moment. I had eaten little and slept not at all since leaving Camp Two two days earlier. Damage to my thoracic cartilage made each cough feel like a stiff kick between the ribs and brought tears to my eyes. But if I wanted a crack at the summit, I had no choice but to ignore my infirmities as much as possible and climb.

Finally, at 11:35, we were away from the tents. I strapped on my oxygen mask and ascended into the darkness. There were fifteen of us in Hall's team: guides Hall, Harris, and Mike Groom, an Australian with impressive Himalayan experience; Sherpas Ang Dorje, Lhakpa Chhiri, Nawang Norbu, and Kami; and clients Hansen, Namba, Weathers, Stuart Hutchison (a Canadian doctor), John Taske (an Australian doctor), Lou Kasischke (a lawyer from Michigan), Frank Fischbeck (a publisher from Hong Kong), and me.

Fischer's group — guides Fischer, Boukreev, and Neal Beidleman; five Sherpas; and clients Charlene Fox, Tim Madsen, Klev Schoening, Sandy Pittman, Lene Gammelgaard, and Martin Adams — left the South Col at midnight. Shortly after that, Makalu Gau started up with three Sherpas, ignoring his promise that no Taiwanese would make a summit attempt on May 10. Thankfully, the

South Africans had failed to make it to Camp Four and were nowhere in sight.

The night had a cold, phantasmal beauty that intensified as we
ascended. More stars than I had ever seen smeared the frozen sky.
Far to the southeast, enormous thunderheads drifted over Nepal,
illuminating the heavens with surreal bursts of orange and blue
lightning. A gibbous moon rose over the shoulder of 27,824-foot
Makalu, washing the slope beneath my boots in ghostly light, obvi-
ating the need for a headlamp. I broke trail throughout the night
with Ang Dorje — our *sirdar,* or head Sherpa — and at 5:30, just as
the sun was edging over the horizon, I reached the crest of the
Southeast Ridge. Three of the world's five highest peaks stood out
in jagged relief against the pastel dawn. My altimeter read 27,500
feet.

Hall had instructed us to climb no higher until the whole group
gathered at this level roost known as the Balcony, so I sat down on
my pack to wait. When Hall and Weathers finally arrived at the back
of the herd, I'd been sitting for more than ninety minutes. By now
Fischer's group and the Taiwanese team had caught and passed us.
I was peeved over wasting so much time and at falling behind everybody else. But I understood Hall's rationale, so I kept quiet and
played the part of the obedient client. To my mind, the rewards of
climbing come from its emphasis on self-reliance, on making critical decisions and dealing with the consequences, on personal responsibility. When you become a client, I discovered, you give up all
that. For safety's sake, the guide always calls the shots.

Passivity on the part of the clients had thus been encouraged
throughout our expedition. Sherpas put in the route, set up the
camps, did the cooking, hauled the loads; we clients seldom carried
more than daypacks stuffed with our personal gear. This system
conserved our energy and vastly increased our chances of getting to
the top, but I found it hugely unsatisfying. I felt at times as if I
wasn't really climbing the mountain — that surrogates were doing
it for me. Although I had willingly accepted this role in order to
climb Everest, I never got used to it. And I was happy as hell when,
at 7:10 A.M., Hall gave me the O.K. to continue climbing.

One of the first people I passed when I started moving again
was Fischer's sirdar, Lobsang Jangbu, kneeling in the snow over a
pile of vomit. Both Lobsang and Boukreev had asked and been

granted permission by Fischer to climb without supplemental oxygen, a highly questionable decision that significantly affected the performance of both men, but especially Lobsang. His feeble state, moreover, had been compounded by his insistence on "short-roping" Pittman on summit day.

Lobsang, 25, was a gifted high-altitude climber who'd summited Everest twice before without oxygen. Sporting a long black ponytail and a gold tooth, he was flashy, self-assured, and very appealing to the clients, not to mention crucial to their summit hopes. As Fischer's head Sherpa, he was expected to be at the front of the group this morning, putting in the route. But just before daybreak, I'd looked down to see Lobsang hitched to Pittman by her three-foot safety tether; the Sherpa, huffing and puffing loudly, was hauling the assertive New Yorker up the steep slope like a horse pulling a plow. Pittman was on a widely publicized quest to ascend Everest and thereby complete the Seven Summits. She'd failed to make it to the top on two previous expeditions; this time she was determined to succeed.

Fischer knew that Lobsang was short-roping Pittman, yet did nothing to stop it; some people have thus concluded that Fischer ordered Lobsang to do it, because Pittman had been moving slowly when she started out on summit day, and Fischer worried that if Pittman failed to reach the summit, he would be denied a marketing bonanza. But two other clients on Fischer's team speculate that Lobsang was short-roping her because she'd promised him a hefty cash bonus if she reached the top. Pittman has denied this and insists that she was hauled up against her wishes. Which begs a question: Why didn't she unfasten the tether, which would have required nothing more than reaching up and unclipping a single carabiner?

"I have no idea why Lobsang was short-roping Sandy," confesses Beidleman. "He lost sight of what he was supposed to be doing up there, what the priorities were." It didn't seem like a particularly serious mistake at the time. A little thing. But it was one of many little things — accruing slowly, compounding imperceptibly, building steadily toward critical mass.

A human plucked from sea level and dropped on the summit of Everest would lose consciousness within minutes and quickly die. A

well-acclimatized climber can function at that altitude with supplemental oxygen — but not well, and not for long. The body becomes far more vulnerable to pulmonary and cerebral edema, hypothermia, frostbite. Each member of our team was carrying two
orange, seven-pound oxygen bottles. A third bottle would be waiting for each of us at the South Summit on our descent, stashed
there by Sherpas. At a conservative flow rate of two liters per minute, each bottle would last between five and six hours. By 4 or 5
P.M., about eighteen hours after starting to climb, everyone's gas
would be gone.

Hall understood this well. The fact that nobody had summited
this season prior to our attempt concerned him, because it meant
that no fixed ropes had been installed on the upper Southeast
Ridge, the most exposed part of the climb. To solve this problem,
Hall and Fischer had agreed before leaving Base Camp that on
summit day the two sirdars — Ang Dorje from Hall's team and
Lobsang from Fischer's — would leave Camp Four 90 minutes
ahead of everybody else and put in the fixed lines before any clients
reached the upper mountain. "Rob made it very clear how important it was to do this," recalls Beidleman. "He wanted to avoid a
bottleneck at all costs."

For some reason, however, the Sherpas hadn't set out ahead of us
on the night of May 9. When Ang Dorje and I reached the Balcony,
we were an hour in front of the rest of the group, and we could have
easily moved on and installed the ropes. But Hall had explicitly
forbidden me to go ahead, and Lobsang was still far below, short-
roping Pittman. There was nobody to accompany Ang Dorje.

A quiet, moody young man who regarded Lobsang as a showboat
and a goldbrick, Ang Dorje had been working extremely hard, well
beyond the call of duty, for six long weeks. Now he was tired of
doing more than his share. If Lobsang wasn't going to fix ropes,
neither was he. Looking sullen, Ang Dorje sat down with me to wait.

Sure enough, not long after everybody caught up with us and we
continued climbing up, a bottleneck occurred when our group
encountered a series of giant rock steps at 28,000 feet. Clients
huddled at the base of this obstacle for nearly an hour while Beidleman, standing in for the absent Lobsang, laboriously ran the
rope out.

Here, the impatience and technical inexperience of Namba

nearly caused a disaster. A businesswoman who liked to joke that her husband did all the cooking and cleaning, Namba had become famous back in Japan for her Seven Summits globe-trotting, and her quest for Everest had turned into a minor cause célèbre. She was usually a slow, tentative climber, but today, with the summit squarely in her sights, she seemed energized as never before. She'd been pushing hard all morning, jostling her way toward the front of the line. Now, as Beidleman clung precariously to the rock one hundred feet above, the overeager Namba clamped her ascender onto the dangling rope before the guide had anchored his end of it. Just as she was about to put her full body weight on the rope — which would have pulled Beidleman off — guide Mike Groom intervened and gently scolded her.

The line continued to grow longer, and so did the delay. By 11:30 A.M., three of Hall's clients — Hutchison, Taske, and Kasischke — had become worried about the lagging pace. Stuck behind the sluggish Taiwanese team, Hutchison now says, "It seemed increasingly unlikely that we would have any chance of summiting before the 1 P.M. turn-around time dictated by Rob."

After a brief discussion, they turned their back on the summit and headed down with Kami and Lhakpa Chhiri. Earlier, Fischbeck, one of Hall's strongest clients, had also turned around. The decision must have been supremely difficult for at least some of these men, especially Fischbeck, for whom this was a fourth attempt on Everest. They'd each spent as much as $70,000 to be up here and had endured weeks of misery. All were driven, unaccustomed to losing and even less to quitting. And yet, faced with a tough decision, they were among the few who made the right one that day.

There was a second, even worse, bottleneck at the South Summit, which I reached at about 11 A.M. The Hillary Step was just a stone's throw away, and slightly beyond that was the summit itself. Rendered dumb with awe and exhaustion, I took some photos and sat down with Harris, Beidleman, and Boukreev to wait for the Sherpas to fix ropes along the spectacularly corniced summit ridge.

A stiff breeze raked the ridge crest, blowing a plume of spindrift into Tibet, but overhead the sky was an achingly brilliant blue. Lounging in the sun at 28,700 feet inside my thick down suit, gazing across the Himalayas in a hypoxic stupor, I completely lost track of time. Nobody paid much attention to the fact that Ang Dorje and Nawang Norbu were sharing a thermos of tea beside us and seemed to be in no hurry to go higher. Around noon, Beidleman finally asked, "Hey, Ang Dorje, are you going to fix the ropes, or what?"

Ang Dorje's reply was a quick, unequivocal "No" — perhaps because neither Lobsang nor any of Fischer's other Sherpas was there to share the work. Shocked into doing the job ourselves, Beidleman, Boukreev, Harris, and I collected all the remaining rope, and Beidleman and Boukreev started stringing it along the most dangerous sections of the summit ridge. But by then more than an hour had trickled away.

Bottled oxygen does not make the top of Everest feel like sea level. Ascending above the South Summit with my regulator delivering two liters of oxygen per minute, I had to stop and draw three or four heaving lungfuls of air after each ponderous step. The systems we were using delivered a lean mix of compressed oxygen and ambient air that made 29,000 feet feel like 26,000 feet. But they did confer other benefits that weren't so easily quantified, not the least of which was keeping hypothermia and frostbite at bay.

Climbing along the blade of the summit ridge, sucking gas into my ragged lungs, I enjoyed a strange, unwarranted sense of calm. The world beyond the rubber mask was stupendously vivid but seemed not quite real, as if a movie were being projected in slow motion across the front of my goggles. I felt drugged, disengaged, thoroughly insulated from external stimuli. I had to remind myself over and over that there was seven thousand feet of sky on either side, that everything was at stake here, that I would pay for a single bungled step with my life.

Plodding slowly up the last few steps to the summit, I had the sensation of being underwater, of moving at quarter-speed. And then I found myself atop a slender wedge of ice adorned with a discarded oxygen cylinder and a battered aluminum survey pole, with nowhere higher to climb. A string of Buddhist prayer flags snapped furiously in the wind. To the north, down a side of the mountain I had never seen, the desiccated Tibetan plateau stretched to the horizon.

Reaching the top of Everest is supposed to trigger a surge of intense elation; against long odds, after all, I had just attained a goal I'd coveted since childhood. But the summit was really only the halfway point. Any impulse I might have felt toward self-congratulation was immediately extinguished by apprehension about the long, dangerous descent that lay ahead. As I turned to go down, I experienced a moment of alarm when a glance at my regulator showed that my oxygen was almost gone. I started down the ridge as fast as I could move but soon hit the traffic jam at the Hillary Step, which was when my gas ran out. When Hall came by, I masked my rising panic and thanked him for getting me to the top of Everest. "Yeah, it's turned out to be a pretty good expedition," he replied. "I only wish we could have gotten more clients to the top." Hall was clearly disappointed that five of his eight clients had turned back earlier in the day, while all six of Fischer's clients were still plugging toward the summit.

Soon after Hall passed, the Hillary Step finally cleared. Dizzy, fearing that I would black out, I made my way tenuously down the fixed lines. Then, fifty feet above the South Summit, the rope ended, and I balked at going farther without gas.

Over at the South Summit I could see Harris sorting through a pile of oxygen bottles. "Yo, Andy!" I yelled. "Could you bring me a fresh bottle?"

"There's no oxygen here!" the guide shouted back. "These bottles are all empty!" I nearly lost it. I had no idea what to do. Just then, Groom came past on his way down from the summit. He had climbed Everest in 1993 without supplemental oxygen and wasn't overly concerned about going without. He gave me his bottle, and we quickly scrambled over to the South Summit.

When we got there, an examination of the oxygen cache revealed right away that there were six full bottles. Harris, however, refused to believe it. He kept insisting that they were all empty, and nothing Groom or I said could convince him otherwise. Right then it should have been obvious that Harris was acting irrationally and had slipped well beyond routine hypoxia, but I was so impeded myself that it simply didn't register. Harris was the invincible guide, there to look after me and the other clients; the thought never entered my own crippled mind that he might in fact be in dire straits — that a guide might urgently need help from me.

As Harris continued to assert that there were no full bottles,

Groom looked at me quizzically. I looked back and shrugged. Turning to Harris, I said, "No big deal, Andy. Much ado about nothing." Then I grabbed a new oxygen canister, screwed it onto my regulator, and headed down the mountain. Given what unfolded over the next three hours, my failure to see that Harris was in serious trouble was a lapse that's likely to haunt me for the rest of my life.

At 3 P.M., within minutes of leaving the South Summit, I descended into clouds ahead of the others. Snow started to fall. In the flat, diminishing light, it became hard to tell where the mountain ended and where the sky began. It would have been very easy to blunder off the edge of the ridge and never be heard from again. The lower I went, the worse the weather became.

When I reached the Balcony again, about 4 P.M., I encountered Beck Weathers standing alone, shivering violently. Years earlier, Weathers had undergone radial keratotomy to correct his vision. A side effect, which he discovered on Everest and consequently hid from Hall, was that in the low barometric pressure at high altitude, his eyesight failed. Nearly blind when he'd left Camp Four in the middle of the night but hopeful that his vision would improve at daybreak, he stuck close to the person in front of him and kept climbing.

Upon reaching the Southeast Ridge shortly after sunrise, Weathers had confessed to Hall that he was having trouble seeing, at which point Hall declared, "Sorry, pal, you're going down. I'll send one of the Sherpas with you." Weathers countered that his vision was likely to improve as soon as the sun crept higher in the sky; Hall said he'd give Weathers thirty minutes to find out — after that, he'd have to wait there at 27,500 feet for Hall and the rest of the group to come back down. Hall didn't want Weathers descending alone. "I'm dead serious about this," Hall admonished his client. "Promise me that you'll sit right here until I return."

"I crossed my heart and hoped to die," Weathers recalls now, "and promised I wouldn't go anywhere." Shortly after noon, Hutchison, Taske, and Kasischke passed by with their Sherpa escorts, but Weathers elected not to accompany them. "The weather was still good," he explains, "and I saw no reason to break my promise to Rob."

By the time I encountered Weathers, however, conditions were turning ugly. "Come down with me," I implored. "I'll get you down, no problem." He was nearly convinced, until I made the mistake of mentioning that Groom was on his way down, too. In a day of many mistakes, this would turn out to be a crucial one. "Thanks anyway," Weathers said. "I'll just wait for Mike. He's got a rope; he'll be able to short-rope me." Secretly relieved, I hurried toward the South Col, 1,500 feet below.

These lower slopes proved to be the most difficult part of the descent. Six inches of powder snow blanketed outcroppings of loose shale. Climbing down them demanded unceasing concentration, an all but impossible feat in my current state. By 5:30, however, I was finally within two hundred vertical feet of Camp Four, and only one obstacle stood between me and safety: a steep bulge of rock-hard ice that I'd have to descend without a rope. But the weather had deteriorated into a full-scale blizzard. Snow pellets borne on 70-mph winds stung my face; any exposed skin was instantly frozen. The tents, no more than two hundred horizontal yards away, were only intermittently visible through the whiteout. There was zero margin for error. Worried about making a critical blunder, I sat down to marshal my energy.

Suddenly, Harris appeared out of the gloom and sat beside me. At this point there was no mistaking that he was in appalling shape. His cheeks were coated with an armor of frost, one eye was frozen shut, and his speech was slurred. He was frantic to reach the tents. After briefly discussing the best way to negotiate the ice, Harris started scooting down on his butt, facing forward. "Andy," I yelled after him, "it's crazy to try it like that!" He yelled something back, but the words were carried off by the screaming wind. A second later he lost his purchase and was rocketing down on his back.

Two hundred feet below, I could make out Harris's motionless form. I was sure he'd broken at least a leg, maybe his neck. But then he stood up, waved that he was O.K., and started stumbling toward camp, which was for the moment in plain sight, 150 yards beyond.

I could see three or four people shining lights outside the tents. I watched Harris walk across the flats to the edge of camp, a distance he covered in less than ten minutes. When the clouds closed in a moment later, cutting off my view, he was within 30 yards of the tents. I didn't see him again after that, but I was certain that he'd reached the security of camp, where Sherpas would be waiting with hot tea. Sitting out in the storm, with the ice bulge still standing between me and the tents, I felt a pang of envy. I was angry that my guide hadn't waited for me.

Twenty minutes later I was in camp. I fell into my tent with my crampons still on, zippered the door tight, and sprawled across the frost-covered floor. I was drained, more exhausted than I'd ever been in my life. But I was safe. Andy was safe. The others would be coming into camp soon. We'd done it. We'd climbed Mount Everest.

It would be many hours before I learned that everyone had in fact not made it back to camp — that one teammate was already dead and that twenty-three other men and women were caught in a desperate struggle for their lives.

Neal Beidleman waited on the summit from 1:25 until 3:10 as Fischer's clients appeared over the last rise, one by one. The lateness of the hour worried him. After Gammelgaard, the last of them, arrived with Lobsang, "I decided it was time to get the hell out of there," Beidleman says, "even though Scott hadn't shown yet." Twenty minutes down the ridge, Beidleman — with Gammelgaard, Pittman, Madsen, and Fox in tow — passed Fischer, still on his way up. "I didn't really say anything to him," Beidleman recalls. "He just sort of raised his hand. He looked like he was having a hard time, but he was Scott, so I wasn't particularly worried. I figured he'd tag the summit and catch up to us pretty quick to help bring the clients down. But he never showed up."

When Beidleman's group got down to the South Summit, Pittman collapsed. Fox, the most experienced client on the peak, gave her an injection of a powerful steroid, dexamethasone, which temporarily negates the symptoms of altitude sickness. Beidleman grabbed Pittman by her harness and started dragging her down behind him.

"Once I got her sliding," he explains, "I'd let go and glissade down in front of her. Every fifty meters I'd stop, wrap my hands around the fixed rope, and brace myself to arrest her slide with a body block. The first time Sandy came barrelling into me, the points of her crampons sliced into my down suit. Feathers went flying everywhere." Fortunately, after about twenty minutes the injection revived Pittman, and she was able to resume the descent under her own power.

As darkness fell and the storm intensified, Beidleman and five of Fischer's clients overtook Groom, who was bringing down Weathers, on a short rope, and Namba. "Beck was so hopelessly blind," Groom reports, "that every ten meters he'd take a step into thin air and I'd have to catch him with the rope. It was bloody nerveracking."

Five hundred feet above the South Col, where the steep shale gave way to a gentler slope of snow, Namba's oxygen ran out and the diminutive Japanese woman sat down, refusing to move. "When I tried to take her oxygen mask off so she could breathe more easily," says Groom, "she'd insist on putting it right back on. No amount of persuasion could convince her that she was out of oxygen, that the mask was actually suffocating her."

Beidleman, realizing that Groom had his hands full with Weathers, started dragging Namba down toward Camp Four. They reached the broad, rolling expanse of the South Col around 8 P.M., but by then it was pitch black, and the storm had grown into a hurricane. The wind-chill was in excess of 70 below. Only three or four headlamps were working, and everyone's oxygen was long gone. Visibility was down to a few meters. No one had a clue how to find the tents. Two Sherpas materialized out of the darkness, but they were lost as well.

For the next two hours, Beidleman, Groom, the two Sherpas, and seven clients staggered blindly around in the storm, growing ever more exhausted and hypothermic, hoping to blunder across the camp. "It was total chaos," says Beidleman. "People are wandering all over the place; I'm yelling at everyone, trying to get them to follow a single leader. Finally, probably around ten o'clock, I walked over this little rise, and it felt like I was standing on the edge of the earth. I could sense a huge void just beyond."

The group had unwittingly strayed to the easternmost edge of the Col, the opposite side from Camp Four, right at the lip of the 7,000-foot Kangshung Face. "I knew that if we kept wandering in the storm, pretty soon we were going to lose somebody," says Beidleman. "I was exhausted from dragging Yasuko. Charlotte and Sandy were barely able to stand. So I screamed at everyone to huddle up right there and wait for a break in the storm."

The climbers hunkered in a pathetic cluster on a windswept patch of ice. "By then the cold had about finished me off," says Fox.

"My eyes were frozen. The cold was so painful, I just curled up in a ball and hoped death would come quickly."

Three hundred and fifty yards to the west, while this was going on, I was shivering uncontrollably in my tent, even though I was zipped into my sleeping bag and wearing my down suit and every other stitch of clothing I had. The gale was threatening to blow the tent apart. Oblivious to the tragedy unfolding outside and completely out of bottled oxygen, I drifted in and out of fitful sleep, delirious from exhaustion, dehydration, and the cumulative effects of oxygen depletion.

At some point, Hutchison shook me and asked if I would go outside with him to bang on pots and shine lights, in the hope of guiding any lost climbers in, but I was too weak and incoherent to respond. Hutchison, who had got back to camp at 2 P.M. and was less debilitated than those of us who'd gone to the summit, then tried to rouse clients and Sherpas in the other tents. Everybody was too cold, too exhausted. So Hutchison went out into the storm alone.

He left six times that night to look for the missing climbers, but the blizzard was so fierce that he never dared to venture more than a few yards from the tents. "The winds were ballistically strong," says Hutchison. "The blowing spindrift felt like a sandblaster or something."

Just before midnight, out among the climbers hunkered on the Col, Beidleman noticed a few stars overhead. The wind was still whipping up a furious ground blizzard, but far above, the sky began to clear, revealing the hulking silhouettes of Everest and Lhotse. From these reference points, Klev Schoening, a client of Fischer's, thought he'd figured out where the group was in relation to the tents. After a shouting match with Beidleman, Schoening convinced the guide that he knew the way.

Beidleman tried to coax everyone to their feet and get them moving in the direction indicated by Schoening, but Fox, Namba, Pittman, and Weathers were too feeble to walk. So Beidleman assembled those who were ambulatory, and together with Groom they stumbled off into the storm to get help, leaving behind the four incapacitated clients and Tim Madsen. Madsen, unwilling to abandon Fox, his girlfriend, volunteered to look after everybody until a rescue party arrived.

The tents lay about 350 yards to the west. When Beidleman,

Groom, and the clients got there, they were met by Boukreev. Beidleman told the Russian where to find the five clients who'd been left out in the elements, and then all four climbers collapsed in their tents.

Boukreev had returned to Camp Four at 4:30 P.M., before the brunt of the storm, having rushed down from the summit without waiting for clients — extremely questionable behavior for a guide. A number of Everest veterans have speculated that if Boukreev had been present to help Beidleman and Groom bring their clients down, the group might not have got lost on the Col in the first place. One of the clients from that group has nothing but contempt for Boukreev, insisting that when it mattered most, the guide "cut and ran."

Boukreev argues that he hurried down ahead of everybody else because "it is much better for me to be at South Col, ready to carry up oxygen if clients run out." This is a difficult rationale to understand. In fact, Boukreev's impatience on the descent more plausibly resulted from the fact that he wasn't using bottled oxygen and was relatively lightly dressed and therefore *had* to get down quickly: Without gas, he was much more susceptible to the dreadful cold. If this was indeed the case, Fischer was as much to blame as Boukreev, because he gave the Russian permission to climb without gas in the first place.

Whatever Boukreev's culpability, however, he redeemed himself that night after Beidleman staggered in. Plunging repeatedly into the maw of the hurricane, he single-handedly brought back Fox, Pittman, and Madsen. But Namba and Weathers, he reported, were dead. When Beidleman was informed that Namba hadn't made it, he broke down in his tent and wept for forty-five minutes.

Stuart Hutchison shook me awake at 6:00 A.M. on May 11. "Andy's not in his tent," he told me somberly, "and he doesn't seem to be in any of the other tents, either. I don't think he ever made it in."

"Andy's missing?" I asked. "No way. I saw him walk to the edge of camp with my own eyes." Shocked, horrified, I pulled on my boots and rushed out to look for Harris. The wind was still fierce, knocking me down several times, but it was a bright, clear dawn, and visibility was perfect. I searched the entire western half of the Col for more than an hour, peering behind boulders and poking under shredded, long-abandoned tents, but found no trace of Harris. A surge of adrenaline seared my brain. Tears welled up in my eyes, instantly freezing my eyelids shut. How could Andy be gone? It couldn't be so.

I went to the place where Harris had slid down the ice bulge and methodically retraced the route he'd taken toward camp, which followed a broad, almost flat ice gully. At the point where I last saw him when the clouds came down, a sharp left turn would have taken Harris forty or fifty feet up a rocky rise to the tents.

I saw, however, that if he hadn't turned left but instead had continued straight down the gully — which would have been easy to do in a whiteout, even if one wasn't exhausted and stupid with altitude sickness — he would have quickly come to the westernmost edge of the Col and a four-thousand-foot drop to the floor of the Western Cwm. Standing there, afraid to move any closer to the edge, I noticed a single set of faint crampon tracks leading past me toward the abyss. Those tracks, I feared, were Harris's.

After getting into camp the previous evening, I'd told Hutchison that I'd seen Harris arrive safely in camp. Hutchison had radioed this news to Base Camp, and from there it was passed along via satellite phone to the woman with whom Harris shared his life in New Zealand, Fiona McPherson. Now Hall's wife back in New Zealand, Jan Arnold, had to do the unthinkable: call McPherson back to inform her that there had been a horrible mistake, that Andy was in fact missing and presumed dead. Imagining this conversation and my role in the events leading up to it, I fell to my knees with dry heaves, retching as the icy wind blasted my back.

I returned to my tent just in time to overhear a radio call between Base Camp and Hall — who, I learned to my horror, was up on the summit ridge and calling for help. Beidleman then told me that Weathers and Namba were dead and that Fischer was missing somewhere on the peak above. An aura of unreality had descended over the mountain, casting the morning in a nightmarish hue.

Then our radio batteries died, cutting us off from the rest of the mountain. Alarmed that they had lost contact with us, climbers at Camp Two called the South African team, which had arrived on the South Col the previous day. When Ian Woodall was asked if he would loan his radio to us, he refused.

After reaching the summit around 3:30 P.M. on May 10, Scott Fischer had headed down with Lobsang, who had waited for Fischer on the summit while Beidleman and their clients descended. They got no farther than the South Summit before Fischer began to have difficulty standing and showed symptoms of severe hypothermia and cerebral edema. According to Lobsang, Fischer began "acting like crazy man. Scott is saying to me, 'I want to jump down to Camp Two.' He is saying many times." Pleading with him not to jump, Lobsang started short-roping Fischer, who outweighed him by some seventy pounds, down the Southeast Ridge. A few hours after dark, they got into some difficult mixed terrain 1,200 feet above the South Col, and Lobsang was unable to drag Fischer any farther.

Lobsang anchored Fischer to a snow-covered ledge and was preparing to leave him there when three tired Sherpas showed up. They were struggling to bring down Makalu Gau, who was as debilitated as Fischer. The Sherpas sat the Taiwanese leader beside the American leader, tied the two semiconscious men together, and around 10 P.M. descended into the night to get help.

Meanwhile, Hall and Hansen were still on the frightfully exposed summit ridge, engaged in a grim struggle of their own. The 46-year-old Hansen, whom Hall had turned back just below this spot exactly a year ago, had been determined to bag the summit this time around. "I want to get this thing done and out of my life," he'd told me a couple of days earlier. "I don't want to have to come back here."

Indeed, Hansen had reached the top this time, though not until after 3 P.M., well after Hall's predetermined turn-around time. Given Hall's conservative, systematic nature, many people wonder why he didn't turn Hansen around when it became obvious that he was running late. It's not far-fetched to speculate that because Hall had talked Hansen into coming back to Everest this year, it would have been especially hard for him to deny Hansen the summit a second time — especially when all of Fischer's clients were still marching blithely toward the top.

"It's very difficult to turn someone around high on the mountain," cautions Guy Cotter, a New Zealand guide who summited Everest with Hall in 1992 and was guiding the peak for him in 1995 when Hansen made his first attempt. "If a client sees that the summit is close and they're dead-set on getting there, they're going to laugh in your face and keep going up."

In any case, for whatever reason, Hall did not turn Hansen

around. Instead, after reaching the summit at 2:10 P.M., Hall waited
for more than an hour for Hansen to arrive and then headed down
with him. Soon after they began their descent, just below the top,
Hansen apparently ran out of oxygen and collapsed. "Pretty much
the same thing happened to Doug in '95," says Ed Viesturs, an
American who guided the peak for Hall that year. "He was fine
during the ascent, but as soon as he started down he lost it mentally
and physically. He turned into a real zombie, like he'd used everything up."

At 4:31 P.M., Hall radioed Base Camp to say that he and Hansen
were above the Hillary Step and urgently needed oxygen. Two full
bottles were waiting for them at the South Summit; if Hall had
known this he could have retrieved the gas fairly quickly and then
climbed back up to give Hansen a fresh tank. But Harris, in the
throes of his oxygen-starved dementia, overheard the 4:31 radio
call while descending the Southeast Ridge and broke in to tell Hall
— incorrectly, just as he'd told Groom and me — that all the bottles at the South Summit were empty. So Hall stayed with Hansen
and tried to bring the helpless client down without oxygen, but
could get him no farther than the top of the Hillary Step.

Cotter, a very close friend of both Hall and Harris, happened to
be a few miles from Everest Base Camp at the time, guiding an
expedition on Pumori. Overhearing the radio conversations between Hall and Base Camp, he called Hall at 5:36 and again at 5:57,
urging his mate to leave Hansen and come down alone. "I know I
sound like the bastard for telling Rob to abandon his client," confesses Cotter, "but by then it was obvious that leaving Doug was his
only choice." Hall, however, wouldn't consider going down without
Hansen.

There was no further word from Hall until the middle of the
night. At 2:46 A.M. on May 11, Cotter woke up to hear a long,
broken transmission, probably unintended: Hall was wearing a remote microphone clipped to the shoulder strap of his backpack,
which was occasionally keyed on by mistake. In this instance, says
Cotter, "I suspect Rob didn't even know he was transmitting. I could
hear someone yelling — it might have been Rob, but I couldn't be
sure because the wind was so loud in the background. He was
saying something like 'Keep moving! Keep going!' presumably to
Doug, urging him on."

If that was indeed the case, it meant that in the wee hours of the morning Hall and Hansen were still struggling from the Hillary Step toward the South Summit, taking more than twelve hours to traverse a stretch of ridge typically covered by descending climbers in half an hour.

Hall's next call to Base Camp was at 4:43 A.M. He'd finally reached the South Summit but was unable to descend farther, and in a series of transmissions over the next two hours he sounded confused and irrational. "Harold was with me last night," Hall insisted, when in fact Harris had reached the South Col at sunset. "But he doesn't seem to be with me now. He was very weak."

Mackenzie asked him how Hansen was doing. "Doug," Hall replied, "is gone." That was all he said, and it was the last mention he ever made of Hansen.

On May 23, when Breashears and Viesturs, of the IMAX team, reached the summit, they found no sign of Hansen's body but they did find an ice ax planted about fifty feet below the Hillary Step, along a highly exposed section of ridge where the fixed ropes came to an end. It is quite possible that Hall managed to get Hansen down the ropes to this point, only to have him lose his footing and fall 7,000 feet down the sheer Southwest Face, leaving his ice ax jammed into the ridge crest where he slipped.

During the radio calls to Base Camp early on May 11, Hall revealed that something was wrong with his legs, that he was no longer able to walk and was shaking uncontrollably. This was very disturbing news to the people down below, but it was amazing that Hall was even alive after spending a night without shelter or oxygen at 28,700 feet in hurricane-force wind and minus-100-degree windchill.

At 5 A.M., Base Camp patched through a call on the satellite telephone to Jan Arnold, Hall's wife, seven months pregnant with their first child in Christchurch, New Zealand. Arnold, a respected physician, had summited Everest with Hall in 1993 and entertained no illusions about the gravity of her husband's predicament. "My heart really sank when I heard his voice," she recalls. "He was slurring his words markedly. He sounded like Major Tom or something, like he was just floating away. I'd been up there; I knew what it could be like in bad weather. Rob and I had talked about the impossibility of being rescued from the summit ridge. As he himself had put it, 'You might as well be on the moon.'"

By that time, Hall had located two full oxygen bottles, and after struggling for four hours trying to deice his mask, around 8:30 A.M. he finally started breathing the life-sustaining gas. Several times he announced that he was preparing to descend, only to change his mind and remain at the South Summit. The day had started out sunny and clear, but the wind remained fierce, and by late morning the upper mountain was wrapped with thick clouds. Climbers at Camp Two reported that the wind over the summit sounded like a squadron of 747s, even from 8,000 feet below.

About 9:30 A.M., Ang Dorje and Lhakpa Chhiri ascended from Camp Four in a brave attempt to bring Hall down. At the same time, four other Sherpas went to rescue Fischer and Gau. When they reached Fischer, the Sherpas tried to give him oxygen and hot tea, but he was unresponsive. Though he was breathing — barely — his eyes were fixed and his teeth were clenched. Believing he was as good as dead, they left him tied to the ledge and started descending with Gau, who after receiving tea and oxygen, and with considerable assistance, was able to move to the South Col.

Higher on the peak, Ang Dorje and Lhakpa Chhiri climbed to 28,000 feet, but the murderous wind forced them to turn around there, still 700 feet below Hall.

Throughout that day, Hall's friends begged him to make an effort to descend from the South Summit under his own power. At 3:20 P.M., after one such transmission from Cotter, Hall began to sound annoyed. "Look," he said, "if I thought I could manage the knots on the fixed ropes with me frostbitten hands, I would have gone down six hours ago, pal. Just send a couple of the boys up with a big thermos of something hot — then I'll be fine."

At 6:20 P.M., Hall was patched through a second time to Arnold in Christchurch. "Hi, my sweetheart,' he said in a slow, painfully distorted voice. "I hope you're tucked up in a nice warm bed. How are you doing?"

"I can't tell you how much I'm thinking about you!" Arnold replied. "You sound so much better than I expected. . . . Are you warm, my darling?"

"In the context of the altitude, the setting, I'm reasonably comfortable," Hall answered, doing his best not to alarm her.

"How are your feet?"

"I haven't taken me boots off to check, but I think I may have a bit of frostbite."

"I'm looking forward to making you completely better when you come home," said Arnold. "I just know you're going to be rescued. Don't feel that you're alone. I'm sending all my positive energy your way!" Before signing off, Hall told his wife, "I love you. Sleep well, my sweetheart. Please don't worry too much."

These would be the last words anyone would hear him utter. Attempts to make radio contact with Hall later that night and the next day went unanswered. Twelve days later, when Breashears and Viesturs climbed over the South Summit on their way to the top, they found Hall lying on his right side in a shallow ice-hollow, his upper body buried beneath a drift of snow.

Early on the morning of May 11, when I returned to Camp Four after searching in vain for Harris, Hutchison, standing in for Groom, who was unconscious in his tent, organized a team of four Sherpas to locate the bodies of our teammates Weathers and Namba. The Sherpa search party, headed by Lhakpa Chhiri, departed ahead of Hutchison, who was so exhausted and befuddled that he forgot to put his boots on and left camp in his light, smooth-soled liners. Only when Lhakpa Chhiri pointed out the blunder did Hutchison return for his boots. Following Boukreev's directions, the Sherpas had no trouble locating the two bodies at the edge of the Kangshung Face.

The first body turned out to be Namba, but Hutchison couldn't tell who it was until he knelt in the howling wind and chipped a three-inch-thick carapace of ice from her face. To his shock, he discovered that she was still breathing. Both her gloves were gone, and her bare hands appeared to be frozen solid. Her eyes were dilated. The skin on her face was the color of porcelain. "It was terrible," Hutchison recalls. "I was overwhelmed. She was very near death. I didn't know what to do."

He turned his attention to Weathers, who lay 20 feet away. His face was also caked with a thick armor of frost. Balls of ice the size of grapes were matted to his hair and eyelids. After clearing the frozen detritus from his face, Hutchison discovered that he, too, was still alive: "Beck was mumbling something, I think, but I couldn't tell what he was trying to say. His right glove was missing and he had terrible frostbite. He was as close to death as a person can be and still be breathing."

Badly shaken, Hutchison went over to the Sherpas and asked Lhakpa Chhiri's advice. Lhakpa Chhiri, an Everest veteran respected by Sherpas and sahibs alike for his mountain savvy, urged Hutchison to leave Weathers and Namba where they lay. Even if they survived long enough to be dragged back to Camp Four, they would certainly die before they could be carried down to Base Camp, and attempting a rescue would needlessly jeopardize the lives of the other climbers on the Col, most of whom were going to have enough trouble getting themselves down safely.

Hutchison decided that Chhiri was right. There was only one choice, however difficult: Let nature take its inevitable course with Weathers and Namba, and save the group's resources for those who could actually be helped. It was a classic act of triage. When Hutchison returned to camp at 8:30 A.M. and told the rest of us of his decision, nobody doubted that it was the correct thing to do.

Later that day a rescue team headed by two of Everest's most experienced guides, Pete Athans and Todd Burleson, who were on the mountain with their own clients, arrived at Camp Four. Burleson was standing outside the tents about 4:30 P.M. when he noticed someone lurching slowly toward camp. The person's bare right hand, naked to the wind and horribly frostbitten, was outstretched in a weird, frozen salute. Whoever it was reminded Athans of a mummy in a low-budget horror film. The mummy turned out to be none other than Beck Weathers, somehow risen from the dead.

A couple of hours earlier, a light must have gone on in the reptilian core of Weathers's comatose brain, and he regained consciousness. "Initially I thought I was in a dream," he recalls. "Then I saw how badly frozen my right hand was, and that helped bring me around to reality. Finally I woke up enough to recognize that I was in deep shit and the cavalry wasn't coming so I better do something about it myself."

Although Weathers was blind in his right eye and able to focus his left eye within a radius of only three or four feet, he started walking into the teeth of the wind, deducing correctly that camp lay in that direction. If he'd been wrong he would have stumbled immediately down the Kangshung Face, the edge of which was a few yards in the opposite direction. Ninety minutes later he encountered "some unnaturally smooth, bluish-looking rocks," which turned out to be the tents of Camp Four.

The next morning, May 12, Athans, Burleson, and climbers from the IMAX team short-roped Weathers down to Camp Two. On the morning of May 13, in a hazardous helicopter rescue, Weathers and Gau were evacuated from the top of the icefall by Lieutenant Colonel Madan Kahtri Chhetri of the Nepalese army. A month later, a team of Dallas surgeons would amputate Weathers's dead right hand just below the wrist and use skin grafts to reconstruct his left hand.

After helping to load Weathers and Gau into the rescue chopper, I sat in the snow for a long while, staring at my boots, trying to get some grip, however tenuous, on what had happened over the preceding seventy-two hours. Then, nervous as a cat, I headed down into the Icefall for one last trip through the maze of decaying seracs.

I'd always known, in the abstract, that climbing mountains was a dangerous pursuit. But until I climbed in the Himalayas this spring, I'd never actually seen death at close range. And there was so much of it: Including three members of an Indo-Tibetan team who died on the north side just below the summit in the same May 10 storm and an Austrian killed some days later, 11 men and women lost their lives on Everest in May 1996, a tie with 1982 for the worst single-season death toll in the peak's history.

Of the six people on my team who reached the summit, four are now dead — people with whom I'd laughed and vomited and held long, intimate conversations. My actions — or failure to act — played a direct role in the death of Andy Harris. And while Yasuko Namba lay dying on the South Col, I was a mere 350 yards away, lying inside a tent, doing absolutely nothing. The stain this has left on my psyche is not the sort of thing that washes off after a month or two of grief and guilt-ridden self-reproach.

Five days after Namba died, three Japanese men approached me in the village of Syangboche and introduced themselves. One was an interpreter, the other was Namba's husband, the third was her brother. They had many questions, few of which I could answer adequately. I flew back to the States with Doug Hansen's belongings and was met at the Seattle airport by his two children, Angie and Jaime. I felt stupid and utterly impotent when confronted by their tears.

Stewing over my culpability, I put off calling Andy Harris's partner, Fiona McPherson, and Rob Hall's wife, Jan Arnold, so long that they finally phoned me from New Zealand. When Fiona called, I was able to say nothing to diminish her anger or bewilderment. During my conversation with Jan, she spent more time comforting me than vice versa.

With so many marginally qualified climbers flocking to Everest these days, a lot of people believe that a tragedy of this magnitude was overdue. But nobody imagined that an expedition led by Hall would be at the center of it. Hall ran the tightest, safest operation on the mountain, bar none. So what happened? How can it be explained, not only to the loved ones left behind, but to a censorious public?

Hubris surely had something to do with it. Hall had become so adept at running climbers of varying abilities up and down Everest that he may have become a little cocky. He'd bragged on more than one occasion that he could get almost any reasonably fit person to the summit, and his record seemed to support this. He'd also demonstrated a remarkable ability to manage adversity.

In 1995, for instance, Hall and his guides not only had to cope with Hansen's problems high on the peak, but they also had to deal with the complete collapse of another client, the celebrated French alpinist Chantal Mauduit, who was making her seventh stab at Everest without oxygen. Mauduit passed out stone cold at 28,700 feet and had to be dragged and carried all the way from the South Summit to the South Col "like a sack of spuds," as Guy Cotter put it. After everybody came out of that summit attempt alive, Hall may well have thought there was little he couldn't handle.

Before this year, however, Hall had had uncommonly good luck with the weather, and one wonders whether it might have skewed his judgment. "Season after season," says David Breashears, who has climbed Everest three times, "Rob had brilliant weather on summit day. He'd never been caught by a storm high on the mountain." In fact, the gale of May 10, though violent, was nothing extraordinary; it was a fairly typical Everest squall. If it had hit two hours later, it's likely that nobody would have died. Conversely, if it had arrived even one hour earlier, the storm could easily have killed 18 or 20 climbers — me among them.

Indeed, the clock had as much to do with the tragedy as the weather, and ignoring the clock can't be passed off as an act of God. Delays at the fixed lines could easily have been avoided. Predetermined turn-around times were egregiously and willfully ignored. The latter may have been influenced to some degree by the rivalry between Fischer and Hall. Fischer had a charismatic personality, and that charisma had been brilliantly marketed. Fischer was trying very hard to eat Hall's lunch, and Hall knew it. In a certain sense, they may have been playing chicken up there, each guide plowing ahead with one eye on the clock, waiting to see who was going to blink first and turn around.

Shocked by the death toll, people have been quick to suggest policies and procedures intended to ensure that the catastrophes of this season won't be repeated. But guiding Everest is a very loosely regulated business, administered by a byzantine Third World bureaucracy that is spectacularly ill-equipped to assess qualifications of guides or clients, in a nation that has a vested interest in issuing as many climbing permits as the market will support.

Truth be told, a little education is probably the most that can be hoped for. Everest would without question be safer if prospective clients truly understood the gravity of the risks they face — the thinness of the margin by which human life is sustained above 25,000 feet. Walter Mittys with Everest dreams need to keep in mind that when things go wrong up in the Death Zone — and sooner or later they always do — the strongest guides in the world may be powerless to save their clients' lives. Indeed, as the events of 1996 demonstrated, the strongest guides in the world are sometimes powerless to save even their own lives.

Climbing mountains will never be a safe, predictable, rule-bound enterprise. It is an activity that idealizes risk-taking; its most celebrated figures have always been those who stuck their necks out the farthest and managed to get away with it. Climbers, as a species, are simply not distinguished by an excess of common sense. And that holds especially true for Everest climbers: When presented with a chance to reach the planet's highest summit, people are surprisingly quick to abandon prudence altogether. "Eventually," warns Tom Hornbein, thirty-three years after his ascent of the West Ridge, "what happened on Everest this season is certain to happen again."

For evidence that few lessons were learned from the mistakes of May 10, one need look no farther than what happened on Everest two weeks later. On the night of May 24, by which date every other expedition had left Base Camp or was on its way down the mountain, the South Africans finally launched their summit bid. At 9:30 the following morning, Ian Woodall radioed that he was on the summit, that teammate Cathy O'Dowd would be on top in fifteen minutes, and that his close friend Bruce Herrod was some unknown distance below. Herrod, whom I'd met several times on the mountain, was an amiable 37-year-old with little climbing experience. A freelance photographer, he hoped that making the summit of Everest would give his career a badly needed boost.

As it turned out, Herrod was more than seven hours behind the others and didn't reach the summit until 5 P.M., by which time the upper mountain had clouded over. It had taken him 21 hours to climb from the South Col to the top. With darkness fast approaching, he was out of oxygen, physically drained, and completely alone on the roof of the world. "That he was up there that late, with nobody else around, was crazy," says his former teammate, Andy de Klerk. "It's absolutely boggling."

Herrod had been on the South Col from the evening of May 10 through May 12. He'd felt the ferocity of that storm, heard the desperate radio calls for help, seen Beck Weathers crippled with horrible frostbite. Early on his ascent of May 24–25, Herrod had climbed right past the frozen body of Scott Fischer. Yet none of that apparently made much of an impression on him. There was another radio transmission from Herrod at 7 P.M., but nothing was heard from him after that, and he never appeared at Camp Four. He is presumed to be dead — the eleventh casualty of the season.

As I write this, fifty-four days have passed since I stood on top of Everest, and there hasn't been more than an hour or two on any given day in which the loss of my companions hasn't monopolized my thoughts. Not even in sleep is there respite: Imagery from the climb and its sad aftermath permeates my dreams.

There is some comfort, I suppose, in knowing that I'm not the only survivor of Everest to be so affected. A teammate of mine from Hall's expedition tells me that since he returned, his marriage has gone bad, he can't concentrate at work, his life has been in turmoil. In another case, Neal Beidleman helped save the lives of five clients by guiding them down the mountain, yet he is haunted by a death he was unable to prevent, of a client who wasn't on his team and thus wasn't really his responsibility.

When I spoke to Beidleman recently, he recalled what it felt like to be out on the South Col, huddling with his group in the awful wind, trying desperately to keep everyone alive. He'd told and retold the story a hundred times, but it was still as vivid as the initial telling. "As soon as the sky cleared enough to give us an idea of where camp was," he recounted, "I remember shouting, 'Hey, this break in the storm may not last long, so let's *go!*' I was screaming at everyone to get moving, but it became clear that some of them didn't have enough strength to walk or even stand.

"People were crying. I heard someone yell, 'Don't let me die here!' It was obvious that it was now or never. I tried to get Yasuko on her feet. She grabbed my arm, but she was too weak to get up past her knees. I started walking and dragged her for a step or two. Then her grip loosened and she fell away. I had to keep going. Somebody had to make it to the tents and get help, or everybody was going to die."

Beidleman paused. "But I can't help thinking about Yasuko," he said when he resumed, his voice hushed. "She was so little. I can still feel her fingers sliding across my biceps and then letting go. I never even turned to look back."

PADGETT POWELL

Grappling with a Giant

FROM HARPER'S

AGAINST ITS REPUTATION as a pastime of drunks, against the notion that it is stupid, arm wrestling does most efficiently what sport is asked to do, which is translate the muddle of success and failure in life into the knowable: who wins and who doesn't and why. In these terms, arm wrestling looks consummately elegant, the lockjaw articulate and the grunting sublime. Your arm, your will, and victory or loss. There is precious little equipment, no brain damage, and you can walk away from it. It is a clear and possibly heroic moment in the smudged, fudged modern world. And if there can be an undisputed world champion in a sport as regionalized and unrecognized and marginalized and fractionated as arm wrestling, Cleve Dean of Pavo, Georgia, was once it and is vying to be it again.

Cleve Dean is a farmer and pulp wooder who disappeared from the sport of arm wrestling for nearly ten years after being on top of it for eight years. In his absence he ballooned to nearly seven hundred pounds and is thought by some arm wrestlers to have gotten so heavy that he died. He is going to Sweden in a week to try to be champion again, and I am going with him because I want to meet a world champion, of anything, but particularly a world champion who may weigh seven hundred pounds.

When I walk into his house in Georgia — which I have, because he has yelled, "Come on in!" — it is dark and there is something big on the floor that somehow commands my attention. It, like, moves. It's him — Cleve Dean. I judge him to be about five hundred pounds, but I can't tell or know yet how much he weighs. He hardly does himself. I have driven my truck instead of my wife's

Toyota to make a good impression (a man in hogs and logs who at
six seven might weigh seven hundred pounds might be a giant
redneck shitass), and now I have to try to shake hands with this pile
of man on the floor in order to keep making a good impression.
And I can tell that he is aware it is important for him to show his
manners too and that that ordinarily includes standing up when
you shake hands, but this is not ordinary. Five hundred pounds
getting up just to shake hands?

Cleve Dean's voice is deep and calm, southern FM quality. His
face is boyish under thinning hair. He looks gentle: partly tired and
partly ready to be amused. He moves his arm, the famous one,
slowly and widely to my approach, offering me the catcher's-mitt-
sized hand on the long end of a long arm that is one inch shy of
being two feet around, and it looks, this arm, like the leg of an
ordinary person down there attempting to legwhip me. It is not a
steroidy tacky veiny thing but a Michelangelo thing. It looks like
sandbags, or big stones under skin.

The hand that Cleve Dean is bringing me is fast and huge. He
can punch a digital stopwatch on and off in six hundredths of a
second. They told him at the World's Strongest Man Contest he
participated in a few years ago that he has the "largest natural bone
structure on earth." When you shake this hand, you don't shake *it*,
you shake, at best, a part of it — rather like grabbing a pommel on
a saddle when mounting a horse. The thumbhole in Cleve Dean's
custom-drilled bowling ball will accommodate a banana.

With two hands Cleve Dean can pick up a five-hundred-pound
hog by the ears and set it down gently on the other side of a fence.
With one hand he can pick up one end of a twelve-inch by twelve-
inch by sixty-foot heart-pine floor joist and with the other wrap a
chain around it and with either hand signal his brother to pull the
joist out of the pile of joists with the log truck while he surfs on the
joist.

Cleve Dean sits on the floor at the foot of his king-sized bed
and gets the phone, a Lucite model showing the internal parts and
held together with electrical tape. He is calling about his passport,
which he needs to go to Sweden. On one side of the bed is an arm-
wrestling trainer called a gripper, which looks like a squat rack for a
person about eighteen inches tall. A 12-gauge single-shot shotgun
leans on the night table. On the night table is a box of shells, two

PlenTPaks of Big Red Gum, two Big Gulp cups, and a pink ceramic pony.

The night table on the other side of the bed has on it an alarm clock with twin bells on top; a bowl with a fat turquoise candle in it and chewed gum stuck to the rim; a can of Glade Potpourri spray; a Bic pen; a Burger King fries box with cigarette butts in it; an empty Band-Aid wrapper; a used diaper; a book of blank personal checks; an orange Autolite solenoid wire; a coat hanger; a bottle of Nyquil; a pair of thong panties; a crucifix necklace on a gold chain; two arm-wrestling scrapbooks; a bottle of Ralph Lauren cologne on its side; a paperback volume of *Daddy's Girl: The Shocking True Story of a Child's Ordeal of Shame,* by Charlotte Vale Allen, with a lollipop stem in it serving as a bookmark; and, from National Financial Publications of Slidell, Louisiana, "The Complete Guide to Home-Based Employment."

Also on that side of the bed is an arm-wrestling trainer that is a regulation sit-down table fitted with a cable and pulleys for building what is called side pressure, the pressure that moves most directly to the pin pad you want to take your opponent's arm to; there are ninety pounds on the weight sled. The peg you grip with your non-pulling hand is wrapped with an empty Lay's potato-chip bag secured by a woman's elastic hair band. Cleve explains that the peg was hurting his hand. Of the machine itself he says, "That thing right there now, it'll bust your arm down quick."

In 1973, the man with the largest natural bone structure in the world (if you choose not to question the authority of whoever was backstage with the tape and calipers at the World's Strongest Man Contest, where Cleve Dean takes pride in having pulled a 17,500-pound Peterbilt tractor a hundred feet up a slight incline in twenty-nine seconds) secured a tryout with the Miami Dolphins without having played a down of organized football. Despite Don Shula's enthusiasm over Cleve Dean's running the forty faster than a 265-pound man was supposed to, which was as large a man as the NFL had performance profiles for at the time, and over his slinging things around in the weight room, the NFL's strict non-tampering policy with junior college students required a release from Pete Rozelle before the Dolphins could look seriously at him, and getting that took over a year, and by then he had ruptured a disk in his back. He did this joist surfing.

Unable to get into professional athletics, Cleve Dean entered a Columbus, Georgia, arm-wrestling tournament in December of 1977 and lost, but in July of 1978 in Atlanta he won a national title and went on to so dominate arm wrestling that for a while he made a living on its small purses. He would sometimes be unofficially conceded first place because people would forfeit against him, saving their arms for second-place pulling. Rules were created to thwart his hegemony. These rules Cleve Dean fought by becoming irritable, fighting with referees and competitors and promoters, and this, his being shitty, was not his style. He even once struck an official in the chest — "Hodhawmightyknows, they banned me from that association!" In 1986, he quit, eight years after his first appearance on arm wrestling's obscure stage.

He blew up to the life-threatening seven hundred pounds, was deemed 100 percent disabled ("Technically, I cannot walk. Any doctor will tell you, 'There's no way he can walk'"), and entered a depression proportional to his size. "I never did *quit* walking," he says, but you get the impression it was close.

From down where he was, he decided, as people do, to come out of retirement. He loaded a grocery cart with weights and started "pushing that joker" around his garage. "Then I joined the Y. Started riding the robicycle. Doin' water walking. Just kept going." So far he has dropped 250-plus pounds, and as mysteriously as he left the top of the world of arm wrestling in 1986, he is suddenly now back on it. Recently he won the Yukon Jack world title in San Francisco, and now is headed out to Stockholm for the World Armwrestling Federation Championships, his expenses paid for one week of publicity and one week of competition. It is known that his arm may be too sore to compete, the Yukon Jack affair having been "a real armbuster," which he won by beating the best super-heavyweight arm wrestlers in North America (John Brzenk and Gary Goodridge, by Cleve Dean's count, who will not be in Sweden). But in arm-wrestling terms having Cleve Dean on hand is not unlike having Jack Nicklaus or Babe Ruth or Muhammad Ali on hand.

What Cleve Dean did that revolutionized arm wrestling was develop what has come to be called the top roll. When he entered the sport the basic idea was to "hook and drag" — a clockwise hooking of the (right) hand and a motion down and sideways to the pad. The top roll involves not hooking and pressing down but prorating the arm (counterclockwise) and pulling up and toward yourself. This lays open the opponent's wrist and saps his power. In the top roll you pull toward yourself, called back pressure, and toward the pad, called side pressure, and the ideal effect is a 45-degree resultant up and across and then down the table your way, with your shoulder following and adding to the power. The shoulder is actually in it from the get-go and lines up outside the pulling arm, but we are already getting beyond the basics.

Cleve Dean credits an arm wrestler named Ricky Viars with starting to develop the top roll. "But that's all he had done was start it. . . . And I just took it and developed different *methods* of it, different ways of gripping."

He also brought in the notion of adaptability. Most arm wrestlers, he says, "stick with what works for them 75 percent of the time. They don't try new things. In the hand, and the positioning alone, there could be . . . twenty-five citable variables. Now, how many variables that are uncitable would be hard for me to even tell you. I could actually watch a guy pulling and see twenty-five different changes in his style in a matter of three seconds. That's just the way the hand can go: the way the fingers are setting, the way the hand is cocked, the way the thumb is presented in the grip, where the pressure's going to be coming to or from — *whoowee.*"

These variances of position and motion and countermotion are difficult to think of and talk of discretely. "It would be hard for me to tell another arm wrestler these things. It's one big blanket. It doesn't have an end to it, it's just a round blanket, and you got to draw from it whatever you need at the time. It cain't be, 'Well, I'm gon make *this* move,' because in the first place you're going against people, and people can change their mind in a — in a millisecond."

If you can adapt and wield this blanket of moves in three seconds against forces that can break your arm — most common are spiral fractures of the humerus (twist a piece of chalk until it snaps to get an idea) and avulsion fractures of the medial epicondyle (a bone-from-bone ripping off of the knob at the bottom inside of the humerus, to which all flexor muscles of the forearm attach) — you are a rare bird.

"Arm wrestling's got to be something you do instinctively; it can't

be something you got to think about. If you have to think about it,
it's done took too long, it's over with. It's like breathing, or opening
your eyes."

A week later in airy, clean, cool-blue Stockholm, not two hundred
feet from the train station, is a poster for the competition picturing
Ingemar Johannson, the former world heavyweight boxing champion, and, next to him, Cleve Dean. I round a corner, and before
me in a kind of plaza are about fifty blue-and-white athletic-suited
men and women. Before I can gather that these outfits suggest
rather clearly that the people in them are athletes, I am distracted
by a man nearby wearing lizard- or snake-skin boots and tight jeans
out of which mushrooms a tight barrel chest and, out of that, tight
worked-on arms — my first revelation that I have discovered arm
wrestlers; he has a pinch of Skoal in his cheek and small teeth and a
kind of peroxidey wide-trac mohawk hairdo — my first revelation
that I have discovered Americans.
      I go into the building facing this plaza thinking it a sports hall
and find it to be the hotel where most of the athletes in the event
(293 in all) are staying, most of them at that moment milling
around in the lobby, a boggling array of twenty-seven national team
uniforms, the most arresting of which are the fifty or so Japanese
(twenty athletes and, I learn, thirty support troops) wearing char-
treuse windbreakers with JAWA (the W in arm-wrestling logos con-
ventionally consists of two muscled arms arm-wrestling each other)
logged in red on the back and the rising sun on the left breast.
Placid in the din of weigh-in, in a chair from which he has removed
the seat cushions for a better fit, surrounded by a perpetual coterie
of arm wrestlers who know him and don't, is Cleve Dean, asleep. Jet
lag's got him. "This time's way yonder different," he says later,
"than at home."
      Asleep or awake, Cleve Dean will be in this lobby when he is not
arm wrestling, because his room is "so small you got to go outside to
change your mind!" and because sitting and talking, when they are
not arm wrestling, is what most arm wrestlers really like to do at
tournaments. In these gatherings, which can go into the wee hours,
Cleve Dean is godlike, if a god can be invariably agreeable. He is an
icon and an oracle people want to be near physically and histori-
cally he is Big Daddy.

He will be asked to sign everything in sight by everyone in sight for the next week. He will sign hats, shirts, scrap paper, programs, notebooks; have children sit in his lap for photos; arm-wrestle children for photos; have women sit in his lap for photos; arm-wrestle women for photos; have men sit in his lap for photos; arm-wrestle men for photos; he will sign a photograph of a man's wife and children the man has taken from his wallet. He will have black magic marker all over his hand one day, inexplicable until you see the outline of his hand traced around his signature "Cleve (Arm-breaker) Dean" on the backs of the shirts of the security guys working the event; and when his teammates suggest, "Hey, Cleve, you ought to do like the ballplayers — ten bucks a shot!" he will say, "I heard that!" and keep on signing; and when a German arm wrestler says, "Cleve Dean, you are an arm-wrestling legend! I am a fan to you!" he will say, "Thank you"; and when a fan yells, "Cleve Dean, good tournament!" he will yell back, "Good!"; and to the next hundred requests for anything he will say, "No problem"; and when an irritatingly hip British arm wrestler comes by and says in a false Southern accent, "How's it hangin', mayin'?" he will say, "Oh, about so"; and when a woman on the Swedish team sits on his lap and explains why she hasn't done so before ("I vas very shy") and says, "You can come to my place?" and tells him, "Smile to the camera!" he will; and when he nods off in the bleachers and his cane slips to the floor no one will be able to tell or remember whether it is the Israelis or the Germans who get there first to hand it to him, waking him up, to whom he says, "Thank you."

Contributing to this legendary aura is Cleve Dean's walk. It is a careful, slightly stooped, stately paced, fluid-filled placing of each step, like a camel's or elephant's stepping. Sometimes he uses a cane. Sometimes it looks as if he is being careful to avoid a fall; he is like a freighter in port in the pilot of small tugs.

As he approaches the arm-wrestling table he smiles at all around and shakes hands with the opponent and then most eerily seems to ignore him. He puts his elbow in the cup (sometimes it is an actual cup, sometimes a pad from which the elbow may not move), erects his arm, moves in close to the table, and waits — immobile. From the rear his back looks as tight and big as a hog, a particularly comfortable one you should not disturb. His face also is meaty and frighteningly placid. It is a boyish Zen blank of concentration that excludes, is beyond, the person of the opponent. The opponent is in for much worse than Cleve Dean's *thinking* about him. Cleve Dean is focusing on the round blanket of citable and uncitable variables running through his head. He is going to explode with the right variances on the arm that he gets a handful of and gets whatever early signals he can from. The opponent may not know about the blanket or about the hogs in Cleve Dean's past, or about my specious linking of him to those hogs in this moment, but he knows he is getting a handful of an arm that has the mass and heft of a fire hydrant and that knows what it's doing.

The competition begins in a bizarre Americanized atmosphere — Lynyrd Skynyrd's "Sweet Home Alabama" and Steppenwolf's "Born to Be Wild" seem to dominate the P.A. system. A Georgian arm wrestler — the *other* Georgia, which is present with a team of formidable-looking men managed by an unformidable-looking coach reminiscent of professional wrestling managers in the States — is wearing a Los Angeles Raiders cap. Cleve Dean enters the left-handed competition on the opening day, lamenting before entering that he has not trained for left-handed pulling. It is strategic, he says, entering the left-handed competition: anyone he beats should find unfathomable the prospect of his right hand, and anyone who beats him is going to develop a false sense of security with respect to his right hand. I ask if this psychology could perhaps work against him: "Naw."

He wins this competition, easily.

Two days later he is up for the real marbles. There is a little worry in the air, but it is mostly on my part, and I don't know what's going on, so it's dismissable. But a veteran puller on the American team, Jack Sanders, is worried that Cleve's arm is too sore from the Yukon Jack tournament for good back pressure, and the Georgians are all top rolling, which requires back pressure to counter. This makes me worried again.

Cleve has been invited to sit onstage between pulls, with the referees, a privilege that would probably draw protest were it extended to anyone else. He is so large that the numerous trips from the bleachers up onto the stage and back in the course of the dozen-plus pulls necessary in a competition this large would exhaust him. No one, not even the maniacal Georgian manager, who has bloodied his head banging it into a wall over some disappointment or other by this time, makes a peep.

Before the eliminations for a class begin, all the pullers in that class are called to the stage for a lineup and to bow to the crowd, and Cleve places himself for these affairs in the middle of the line, which seems to part for and expect him there, and shakes hands as far down each side of the line as he can. Shaking hands with the competition is number three on Cleve Dean's secrets to success in arm wrestling: 1. Know the top roll. 2. Start on command. 3. Learn to read your opponent. "And by read your opponent, learn to shake hands with him, and know where he's weak at. Whether he's weak in his hand, his wrist, his arm, or where. You know." He might merely wave to a puller who doesn't look like much.

The superheavyweight pulling begins, and, just as in boxing, interest picks up radically. People start standing up and sometimes going up to the stage and have to be called down. There have been hours of tooth-and-nail going at it: a woman has been sent to the hospital, another has collapsed in grief on losing, the Georgian manager has stormed the stage over a foulout and refused to leave it, drawing jeers and missiles. But no one has stood and crowded the stage as they do now. This is something. And it reaches its peak whenever Cleve Dean is up. The Germans and the Israelis, vying side by side to see him, have to be called down twice. The entire crowd has changed position a bit. And for the most part, in the beginning, there isn't much to see.

A pull generally lasts from half a second to half a minute, but Cleve's seem even quicker. His first opponent he drags halfway down, then he stands up a bit, pauses, and, as if doing something necessary but not particularly agreeable, presses the helpless arm down in a firm, definitive, but soft thump — or "carries him to the pad," in his gentle way of putting it. His second draw is a Hungarian, who looks to be wearing green surgical scrubs and is somehow reminiscent of Curly of the Three Stooges. A faster no-nonsense takedown, and Cleve shakes Curly's left hand while they are still in grip and raises Curly's defeated right hand. This is the courtesy extended someone who should not be at the table with him, I presume. Next it is the big Finn, whose size suggests problems, against the big other Georgian, who is the known contender. The Georgian has been beaten by John Brzenk, possibly twice, which is good news, sort of, and would be real good news if Cleve Dean's arm were not hurt. The Finn and the Georgian have their go and it is over so fast I have to ask an American arm wrestler what happened. "The Georgian top-roll him?" "I'd say he *flashed* him."

Cleve's up onstage with a guy from security rubbing onto his arm a liniment someone is hawking. His next draw is Kenny Hoban, of the wide-trac mohawk. He and Cleve have talked about their hopes that they not meet until the finals, but it hasn't worked out that way. Jack Sanders has asked Kenny what he plans to do, and Kenny has said, "Try to beat him. Have to." He goes up there to try to do that, and I, who don't know what's going on, say to Jack, "Jack, why not just concede and —"

"Really. Save his arm."

Kenny and Cleve face off at the table and we see Cleve ask him how he intends to act, and Kenny shrugs and smiles and we see his lips say "Have to" again. To this Cleve dips his face to one side almost imperceptibly and blinks his eyes slowly, respecting Kenny's doomed resolve. "Cleve's such a gentle man," Jack Sanders is saying. Cleve dumps Kenny.

Cleve comes off the stage with Kenny and says to him, "Nice fight. You hurt my arm."

Kenny says, "Thanks."

Then a huge Brazilian flashes Kenny, and Kenny pulls a Russian for fifth place and loses. Then the quarterfinals begin and Cleve flashes the big Brazilian that flashed Kenny.

Then the big Georgian flashes Cleve.

The huge hall is stunned into silence. The twenty-seven national teams, the Finns alone sounding like an entire high school basketball game; the Norwegians with their damned cowbell that someone has offered Cleve Dean money to go sit on; the ultrahip Brit, by this time drunk, going around saying "I'm going kill 'at fockin French cunt!" meaning someone (male) who has slurred him; the Georgian manager in whose path people are by this point putting crushed soda cans because he will invariably and apparently unconsciously crush them some more with his soft tennis shoes around which his slovenly pants are falling; all the people with all the Cleve Dean signature souvenirs and all the people planning to yet get theirs signed by Cleve Dean; all the Italians in their handsome blue *Braccio di Fèrro* (Arm of Iron) suits; all the drawn-faced Russians and

all the grim-faced Israelis; all the clear-faced Swedes, clean-faced
Americans, dark-faced Indians, and the one lone Turk — they all
freeze.

There is palpable woe in the hall.

The Georgians are moving, in celebration. Their new hero, Zauri
Tskadadze, at three-hundred-plus pounds and six something and "a
pretty big boy" according to Cleve Dean later, and rather gentle in
aspect himself, is getting off the stage before it is not true that he
just flashed Cleve (Armbreaker) Dean. The gymnasium has a say-it-
ain't-so-Joe pall in it, as if everyone but the Georgians has just now
briefly considered throwing up. But it is just briefly, because this is a
double-elimination setup and Cleve Dean and the Georgian will
pull again momentarily and things will right themselves then. This
odd non-music of the spheres will cease.

The security man with the hot new liniment for sale with snake
toxins in it goes into overdrive on Cleve's arm. He's got long hair
and for a moment looks the *ur* roadie working on a big fat rock star
if the rock star could play guitar with an arm like a Smithfield ham
after a roadie wobbled the meat off the bone.

Then Cleve Dean and Zauri Tskadadze are back at the table.
Cleve Dean shakes the Georgian out of grip a few times, a hard sign
to read. He may be deliberately tiring him or he may be honestly
bothered by his grip. The Georgian looks unspooked by any of
this. Someone has *trained* these sons of bitches, is the word going
around. They are reported to have films of John Brzenk. It can't get
much worse than this, this waiting and these not good signs, and
then at GO! it gets much worse than this.

The Georgian flashes Cleve Dean *again*. The Georgians, led by
their hysterical manager, explode, and beside himself and still in
grip the big Georgian slams Cleve Dean to the pad *again*, a kind of
jubilant replay. At this Cleve Dean grabs their two hands with his
left hand and slams all three to his pad, and then they scramble
around in grip as if they will arm-wrestle or try to again, and Jack
Sanders is intoning, like a chorus, softly, "Get out of there, Cleve.
Cleve, get out of there." The Georgian is smiling but Cleve Dean is
not. He turns without shaking hands and quits the stage. He looks
to have the cotton mouth.

The Georgians rather spill around Cleve Dean as he leaves the
stage, ignoring him. He looks really only a little disturbed, but you

do not want to see someone this large, with features this large, look even moderately disturbed. Everyone is quite disturbed enough. The day is rued.

I start bucking myself up already by trying to imagine all the country sayings Cleve Dean will be in possession of and will start trotting out to buck himself up with. I can't think of any, though, because for all those sayings' Bear Bryant gusto and all their invoking of our mommas and daddies and what they have told us, I don't believe in any of them, they don't work even if you can recite them, they don't work worth a damn. Cleve is hurt, I don't care what kind of there's-always-next-time-ain't-the-end-of-the-world poop is about to come out of him, if it does.

Cleve is standing behind Zauri Tskadadze and kind of whaps him in the back, shaking his head and saying as he does, "An American doesn't act that way," though Zauri can't hear him or understand him if he could, and Cleve Dean extends his hand and they shake.

Back in Pavo, Cleve Dean has butter beans and mashed potatoes and sliced tomatoes and hamburger steak and biscuits and cobbler and sweet tea at his mother's table, modest portions all. His parents have joined the Worldwide Church of God, which proscribes pork. "After all that pork," he says, agreeably shaking his head.

At the bank in Pavo, Cleve Dean pulls up to the drive-in window to deposit some logging money. "I'd like to deposit that please, ma'am."

"You win everywhere you went?"

"Yes, ma'am."

"What's your title?"

"World Champion again."

"Congratulations."

"Thank you, ma'am. I appreciate it."

"Have a good day."

"All right, you too."

Pulling away he says, "Why I didn't explain to 'em that I didn't win in Sweden, it won't make any difference to them. Only one they ever gon know about is the one in California they see on TV anyway." A moment later: "That was a pretty big boy. He was just solid built, he was just made. I'd love for my right arm to have been right, and him to have to try that all over again."

It's drizzly, and we pass swamps where Cleve Dean has hunted ducks, and it is reminiscent of duck-hunting weather, except it is not bone cold, and it's always bone cold for duck hunting. I mention new technology in waders. "We didn't use waders. We just went on in."

Apropos of nothing more than countryside sliding by, Cleve Dean says, "I may get involved in politics."

"What?"

"May run for office soon."

"What are you going to run for?"

"I'm not even sure about that but if I told you, if I told you what I'd really like to run for, probably shock you."

"Coroner? That'd shock me."

"Naw."

"Sheriff wouldn't shock me."

"I've thought about sheriff, believe me. Actually what I'd like to run for is governor."

This makes a kind of sudden, surprising sense. Jimmy Carter was a peanut farmer who got punched in the nose by another farmer as he canvassed a mall in his bid for governor of Georgia. No one is going to punch Cleve Dean in the nose, at least not while shaking his hand.

As politics more and more becomes iconography, what icon more becomes Georgia than Cleve Dean, who with his brother shoveled corn all day out of a two-and-a-half-ton truck faster than a six-inch augur could augur it out and then played tennis half the night; who excited Don Shula without credentials; whose elder grown daughter can say of a woman he likes: "There goes Daddy's dream!" and to the question what kind of dream: "A wet dream!"; who has tobacco buyers buying him steaks; who has worked thirty-six hours straight on a tractor, meals and all; who knows hogs but says, "There's a lot of mercilessness with hogs. I get on my brother and my daddy about it. I tell 'em they just sending their souls to hell. Now I been *rough* with hogs, but I don't pen 'em up and beat 'em just because they aggavating. I might hit 'em on the nose make 'em go where I want"; who, as south Georgia becomes the hottest retirement real estate in America in the next ten years, is sitting right smack dab in the middle of it, this fecund produce capital of the world, he says, with its peaches and pecans and peanuts and cotton and soybeans and corn and tobacco and tomatoes filling its fields; who is himself a large animal product of this produce; who can settle all political disputes in less than three seconds by arm wrestling; who can leave cellular phones on the seat of his open truck because people know whose truck it is while the mayor of nearby Moultrie has his car stolen and has to run down the street after it kicking it; who is the *biggest* redneck whether he is one or not (but who is by every sane measure a gentleman if anything at all is meant anymore by the term today) or whether you are allowed to call him a redneck or not, who as governor will probably not only allow you to but might *require* you to, and you will do what he wants you to do.

In 1998, if Cleve Dean is on the gubernatorial ticket, intercept him on the campaign trail and try to shake his hand.

TONY HENDRA

Man and Bull

FROM HARPER'S

IT'S THE THIRD DAY of the Feast of La Virgen del Mar on Spain's Costa del Sol, and the Hotel Torreluz has barred its glass doors against scores of squirming, giggling nymphets. Through the heavy etched panes, they are mouthing the names of their heroes: "Enrique!" "Emilio!" "Fran!" Those not dressed in Gap T-shirts and Reeboks are wearing bright doll-like flamenco dresses, little mountains of ruffles sweeping to the sidewalk; when they turn away, the deep V-cut backs reveal an iridescence of Andalusian tans — flan, olive, cognac, chestnut, cafe con leche. "Besos de Caramelo," by the rock-flamenco group Aurora, pours deafeningly from an overamplified sound system into the tiny plaza outside. Nearby, horsemen in traditional flat riding hats and elaborate chaps pick their way through a gridlock of diminutive cars.

Inside, the lobby is an island of apprehensive calm. Quiet, nervous men stand around smoking, chewing, murmuring: the advance guard of Spain's most ancient and enduring national pastime. Roadie types in jeans and sneakers mingle with banderilleros in their eye-popping costumes. By the door are a couple of archly phallic leather cases — long and cylindrical with bulbous bottoms — containing sets of razor-sharp swords. The matadors themselves are still dressing upstairs, but in one corner is a gaunt, haunted-looking torero who isn't fighting tonight: Emilio Munoz, the star of Madonna's "Something to Remember" video.

It's the August feria in Almeria, and the plaza beyond the excited tauro-groupies is stuffed with young Spaniards who wouldn't look out of place on spring break in Florida. They drink at booths sporting the Osborne Sherry logo — the silhouette of a black fighting bull — an image that rears sometimes unexpectedly, three stories high, from behind outcrops of rock beside the nation's arid highways; modern advertising tapping an archetype as old as the cult of the dead and resurrected moon god.

The animal-rights movement and modernist-reformist prejudices notwithstanding, the immemorial business of stabbing bulls is bigger than ever. After Franco died in 1975, bullfighting became unchic in left-wing circles, viscerally associated with the brutality of his regime. But the pendulum has now swung the other way, and bullfighting is enjoying a long boom with no end in sight. Last year, for the first time in history, eight hundred corridas were fought in Spain, up from fewer than five hundred a decade ago. Television — a relatively recent arrival in Spanish life — is one reason; it has raised the financial stakes and given toreros more instant celebrity than ever before. But the resurgence of bullfighting has another, deeper cause. Creeping Europeanization has brought on a wave of nationalism.

"Bullfighting is unique in the world," says Ignacio Alvarez Vara, a.k.a. "Barquerito," the bullfight editor of *Diario 16,* a large Madrid daily. "It makes Spain special." The Spanish are well aware of their low status in the European Union — "We are the tail of Europe" — but are determined not to give up their national identity. The homogenized middle-class benefits of Europeanization sit uneasily on a still wild, proud, and hierarchical land. The meritocracy Eurocrats promise must be as risk-free as possible to deliver its material rewards, but bullfighting is an embrace of risk, uncertainty, death — a slap in the face for comfy bourgeois values. Young toreros are rebels with a sword; hot-blooded Iberian cool, the spirit of grunge in spangled pants.

Last season, a new kid appeared on the burning sand beneath the ice-blue Spanish sky. His name is Francisco Rivera Ordonez. He is 22 years old. He is the grandson of Antonio Ordonez, whom Hemingway immortalized in his last book, *The Dangerous Summer,* and the great-grandson of Cayetano Ordonez, similarly immortalized, as Pedro Romero, in *The Sun Also Rises.* Of Romero's fighting Jake Barnes says that he "had the old thing . . . he kept the absolute purity of line in his movements and always quietly and calmly let the horns pass him close." For good measure, the new kid is also the son of an immensely popular matador, Francisco Rivera Paquirri, whose death in the ring remains one of Spain's most vivid national memories.

The product of these extraordinary bloodlines made his debut as a full matador in April of 1995 in Seville, during the Feria de Abril. La Maestranza, Seville's stately old bullring, exploded at his performances. "We were present at the birth of a new superstar," raved Jose Antonio del Moral, one of the country's most widely read Taurine critics. "Controlled power and brilliant aesthetics . . . a style . . . unlike anyone who has fought for thirty-five years or more," gushed the newsletter of Harlan Blake, a longtime American aficionado (and professor emeritus of law at Columbia University). On the Internet, Taurine Web sites buzzed with talk of "The Second Coming."

For the next six months, Fran, as the gossip sheets call him, crisscrossed Spain, stunning crowds with his precocious authority and heart-stopping courage. For aficionados of classical bullfighting, Fran's success confirmed the truth of *casta,* a word variously defined in English as "caste," "race," "generation," "pedigree," "kind," and "breed," although none of these really does the term justice. Casta is what ties Ordonez back through his immediate ancestors to the dead who have defied death before him, then to the age of El Cid, with its royal rituals of fighting bulls on horseback, and, further still, through the mountain passes of time, to who knows how primordial a form of combat. Bulls charge across the ceilings of Lascaux. On the walls of Paleolithic temple caves in Cantabria, bulls are slain by shamans of the sun. Indeed, casta is a term applied to bulls as often as it is to men.

The Spanish public may also feel some relief that the kid turned out so well. For Fran has been a tabloid celebrity for much of his life — an "*Hola* person." *Hola!* is the largest Spanish tabloid magazine, falling somewhere between the *National Enquirer* and *People.* The Spanish call such publications "la prensa de corazon," and Fran's passport to their pages was his mother, Carmen Ordonez, Antonio's daughter, a much-escorted beauty who is a staple of the haut monde in Marbella and other haute spots. (At the time of this interview she was engaged to a man only four years older than her son.) So Fran has grown up with not just the weight of casta on his shoulders but with the liabilities of its underside — the double-edged sword of being famous for being famous.

Upstairs in the suite at the Torreluz Hotel, the frenzy of the feria below seems remote. The life-and-death business at hand generates a heady hush of Catholicism and machismo. A side table has been transformed into an elaborate altar built around the ornately framed picture of a crowned and jeweled Virgin — La Esperanza de Triana — a patron of Fran's native Seville. Beside her is an anguished Iberian Christ; before her, rosaries and sodality medals.

Our brave torero is handsome and compact. He seems younger than his age — sixteen or seventeen at most. With his gentle, unmarked face, he looks as if he'd have trouble scolding a mutt, let alone sticking cold steel into warm animals. He discovers that I'm from New York. "I like the Hard Rock Cafe," he says. "That is cool." He's spent time in the States — a semester at Culver Military Academy in Indiana, where his mother sent him because "I'm a very bad student," and which he hated, and summers at a camp in Maine: "That was cool." His English is fluent, but his light tenor and heavy accent make him sound unnervingly like Manuel from Fawlty Towers. When a taurine critic calls him on his manager's cellular phone, he answers questions in monosyllables, rolling his eyes like a teenager talking to a parent. After he hangs up, I ask what the guy wanted. "He's retarded," says the man who may one day be Spain's greatest torero.

Half-dressed, Fran is wearing a skintight nylon undergarment — half pantyhose, half body stocking — that comes up to his armpits. He is very muscular, cut and buffed. His genitals are bunched and apparently taped, well below his crotch, to the inside of his left thigh. It looks painful. All toreros wear their units this way, unprotected and on the left side. I've never met anyone who knew why on the left. It doesn't seem like the right time to ask. He puts on rose-colored stockings, then a white shirt and ready-made black tie like a school uniform. Now he looks younger still. Next he pulls on his *taleguilla* — heavily embroidered, knee-length, chest-high pants. His dresser picks him up clear off the ground by the top of these, shaking him in midair like a piece of laundry, first to one side, then the other, to get each leg in. They couldn't be tighter if they were spray-painted on. He slips into black leather pumps. He fixes a tiny plastic pigtail to his hair — a vestige of the real one toreros once wore. He shrugs into his gorgeous, gold and sky blue, bauble-laden jacket. It's slathered with thick brocade, gold rosettes, tassels, satin balls, and spangles. He eases on his *montera*, the black, winged headgear that looks a little like a Mickey Mouse hat whose ears have slipped. He looks glorious and ludicrous: a human Christmas tree, an Inca sun god. Francisco Rivera Ordonez is ready for the ring.

A bullfight is a simple affair. A bull weighing at least 1,000 pounds (and sometimes well over 1,400) is killed in three formalized stages, then removed to be sold for meat. The bull is a thoroughbred, raised to enhance its fighting abilities, "as different from the agricultural variety," wrote critic Kenneth Tynan, "as an armoured car is from a hay-wain." A superb animal, often — but not always — jet black, its strength concentrated in its shoulders and a tossing muscle between them like the cockpit of an F-16, with dagger-sharp horns two or more feet long and as thick around at their roots as the business end of a baseball bat. The danger the bull conveys is atavistic, far greater than some modern, technically more lethal menace like a tank. The inverted triangle of its horns and head are as ancient as the Minotaur, but its threat is as immediate as a madman with a butcher knife. Most incomprehension of bullfighting, and perhaps some of the disgust many feel for it, derives from a failure to grasp just how dangerous the bull is. The notion that the bull is a harmless, docile creature goaded into action by its tormenters is a fantasy of the ignorant. "The bull came out of the *toril*," the American author Barnaby Conrad once wrote, "looking for something to kill." If it finds it, it can kill in a split second; as soon as bull meets man, you are mesmerized by that possibility. Time slows down. Movements that take only a second or two seem fluid and languorous, a dramatization before your eyes of the infinitesimal moment between life and death. This deceleration of mortal danger is at the heart of the intoxication of the bullfight — and of the bullfighter's art.

An hour or so after the investiture of the young sun king, I find myself crushed between the ample buttocks of feverishly happy Almerians. A measure of the popularity of bullfighting is the expense and discomfort people endure. Modestly scalped tickets can run over a hundred dollars for a few square inches of un-upholstered cement, but the plaza is packed to the flag, even on the cheaper "sol" side, where people deep-fry in full sun. Women in Day-Glo ruffle-laden flamenco dresses line the balconies; every railing is draped with long-fringed silk and satin mantas in shimmering

colors and dizzying designs. There are Peugots and Audis triple-
parked outside, but inside Goya would be quite at ease. The din is
immense — Andalusians must be the most relentlessly ebullient
people on the planet. Death in the afternoon means life in the
afternoon.

Nonetheless, something like a hush greets Ordonez as he steps
onto the sand to meet his 1,263-pound dancing partner. This is the
first time I've seen the kid live; his aura is palpable. Now he seems
much older than 22 — ageless, a star in the sense that your eye is
drawn to him, whatever he's doing, and that you have immediate
confidence in his smallest move. At five foot seven and 135 pounds,
he's perfectly proportioned for bullfighting. He has the springy,
slightly splayed gait of a ballet dancer and none of the poultry-
breasted bombast many toreros affect. For protection from the
mountain of mad black muscle that's hurtling toward him, he has a
piece of cloth called a capote. It's like an opera cloak except that
it's magenta on one side, sunflower yellow on the other. He takes
his stance in the line of the bull's charge. If he has miscalculated by
an inch or two he will either have to chicken out or let the left-hand
horn pierce his gold-encrusted heart. But the kid will not die, and
he'll never chicken out. He performs a perfect veronica — the
basic capote pass — so called because the matador offers the bull
the cape as St. Veronica offered her shroud to Christ. His body
arches round as the bull tears past him, the cape flaring across the
sand in a brilliant arc, his feet unyielding, his head down, every
nerve tuned to this one motion, apparently unaware of the half ton
of death he has cheated of its prize. He keeps absolute purity of line
in his movements, and quietly and calmly lets the horns pass him
close. The kid has the old thing. The kid is an Ordonez.

Several more veronicas and half-veronicas and the fractious, bois-
terous spectators are one. The picadors appear — medieval throw-
backs in Sancho Panza hats aboard heavily armored horses. Their
job is to "pic," or lance, the bull in that deadly tossing muscle.
Three banderilleros then place banderillas — several pairs of
brightly colored sticks with harpoon points — in the hide of its
back. They do this on foot, running toward the bull in an arc and
leaping up over the horns to shove them in. Now the central drama
begins: the faena. Ordonez faces the bull with a second cape, of
bright red felt and much smaller than the capote, called the mu-

leta, which he holds by a forty-centimeter rod inserted in it. The faena is the portion of the fight in which the most elaborate passes are used. The aim is to link a series of them in one fluid rhythm. When this happens the faena becomes a pas de deux between the slight, bright figure of the man and the dark mass of the beast that takes your breath away, at once exhilarating and melancholy.

Ordonez's first bull is a crabby beast. But great matadors set out to make bad bulls look good — to give the bull, as the Spanish say, his moment of glory. This takes guts, because a hesitant bull that slows or halts in mid-pass — right next to the matador — is even more dangerous than one that charges cleanly. Slowly Ordonez squeezes passes out of the reluctant beef, drawing the almost stationary bull around his body, gradually molding something out of nothing just as a jazz master takes a corny standard and builds it into a partita. The applause grows as his faena develops, graceful curves sewn together with ridiculous daring. But there is more, something I'd never experienced with another bullfighter: an intense sense that Ordonez has created a calm at the center of this vortex of danger, a bond with the bull that goes beyond an instinct for what it will do next, a sympathy for it at odds with what he is doing, a total identification with his victim.

Then, of course, he kills it. The bull's job is to die. Taurine apologists are fond of claiming that the bull may be pardoned or allowed to live out its days, but this happens very seldom. In 1994, of 4,673 bulls fought, only 8 were pardoned. Antibullfighting people often express outrage that the outcome is so predictable, as if a corrida ought to run more along the lines of the Golden Gloves. Such outrage is not confined to those the Spanish refer to as Anglo-Saxons. Jose Luis Barcelo is director of the Madrid chapter of ADDA (Asociacion para la Defensa de los Derechos de los Animales), which, nationwide, claims some 5,000 members and conducts ongoing campaigns against corridas, distributing literature and organizing street demonstrations and protest mailings to TV programs. A demonstration last year during the feria of San Ysidro in Madrid drew about 5,000 people, down from 15,000 at a similar demonstration three years earlier. Their catchiest slogan is "Tortura — ni arte ni cultura." Barcelo asserts, without citing a specific poll, that the public is about fifty-fifty on the corrida question. ADDA's long-term aim for bullfights is abolition, but, he admits, it's an uphill battle, "it's not credible for the government right now." The current policy is to take a gradual approach: for example, the ADDA is campaigning to ban the puntilla — a short dagger used to dispatch the bull at the end of the fight. ADDA feels it would be more humane if the bull were shot.

Some of the revulsion for bullfighting may arise from the misapprehension that it's a mere sport. (The term "bullfight" is an Anglo-Saxon coinage; the Spanish have no such term. What matadors do in the ring is *torear.*) Some of it, I believe, springs from the venerable British tradition of preferring animals to one another. But it certainly involves a double standard. All societies find ways to ritualize their fear of death — this is the method that has evolved on the Iberian peninsula. The matador faces death on our behalf; while he does, we experience the heightened feeling of mortality and immortality. You can go to the Indy 500 and see men die, but you will never feel that feeling, for it will have been an accident. You can go to what Hollywood calls entertainment and see hundreds die, but you will never feel that feeling, because it's only stunt people, pretending. The Spanish like their death ritual real, the blood glistening red in the sun. We prefer ours to reaffirm that death is either accidental or make-believe, a speed bump on the road to happy endings.

Fran had toreared excellently, although his kill was not perfect. Ideally, the sword should enter a small area between the bull's shoulder blades up to the hilt, which cuts its aorta, killing it within seconds. The matador must do this from the front, over the bull's horns — the most perilous moment of the fight. Still the crowd awarded him an ear, which it requests by bellowing even louder than during the rest of the fight and waving white handkerchiefs. The actual decision is made by the president of the corrida, who sits in a special box and is technically in charge of the whole affair. The president of the corrida can award a second ear or, for a truly stellar showing, both ears and the tail. The ear they awarded Fran that day was one of 106 he would win that season, along with 6 tails.

What remained most vivid from my first view of Ordonez was his intense oneness with the bull. That night, when I reviewed my notes of the moment, I'd wondered if it hadn't just been the mysticism induced by jet lag and drinking in the sun. But something very similar happened the next day. By then I was in Bilbao, on the other side of the country, a city as different from Almeria as Buffalo is from New Orleans — an industrial city in the far north where they take their bullfighting very seriously. Bilbao is considered one of the three "mountains" a bullfighter must scale to have truly arrived; the other two are Seville and Madrid. No botas, no mantas, no flamenco dresses here. The men are in suits, the women have hairdos like helmets. At crucial moments the place goes as quiet as a cathedral. A corrida in Bilbao is as close to a Protestant experience as you're likely to get in Spain.

This was Ordonez's debut in the northern mountains, and he more than rose to the occasion. With his second bull — a crazed 1,275-pound monster with enormous horns — he put together a beautiful faena, capped with an exemplary kill, for which he earned an ear. But it was the death of his first bull that stood out for me. His faena had been brief but skillful and the kill clean, the sword entering the beast up to the hilt. The bull began to die, first its hind legs and then its forelegs buckling underneath it. Ordonez waved away his crew. He was alone facing the bull, perhaps a foot or so from the horns. Matadors will sometimes point at the bull as it dies, then turn away for the crowd's applause — a gesture I always find cheap and disrespectful. Ordonez made something very different of the moment. The bull suddenly raised its head toward him. It was surely a vestigial reflex of attack, but in the theater of the sand it looked almost like an attempt to communicate. The plaza was so quiet that I could hear a woman's head scarf next to me whipping in the wind. For Ordonez, it seemed, there was no one present but him and the bull. He held out one hand, gently, as if to thank it and bid it farewell. At that instant it slumped down, dead. The sober citizens of Bilbao went nuts.

There is more to Ordonez's appeal than the classical severity of his style. Death hovers over this young man in a special way, charging everything he does in front of the horns with catastrophic possibility. More than ever, now that he has become a matador, he is a principal actor in a modern Spanish tragedy — the death of his father, Francisco Rivera Paquirri.

Paquirri's story was every poor Spanish boy's dream, a Spanish folktale, a real-life Juan Gallardo in a real-life *Blood and Sand*. He was born to a hardscrabble life in a little fishing village in Andalusia, where his father worked in the local slaughterhouse. He fought his way up with a little luck and a lot of courage to become a national hero, a wealthy man, and the darling of Seville. In 1972 he became a member of the royal family of bullfighting when he married Carmen Ordonez in a nationally televised ceremony. They had two sons, Fran and his younger brother, Cayetano. Paquirri was the very opposite of a classic torero — a flamboyant crowd pleaser given to mad feats of daring such as greeting the bull on his knees as it came into the ring, probably the single most dangerous thing a fighter can do. Throughout the 1970s, he rode the growing influence of television to become the number-one draw in Spain. He was a strikingly handsome man, athletic for a torero, with riveting green eyes.

Paquirri's death in the dusty little bullring of Pozoblanco, some fifty miles north of Cordoba, on September 26, 1984, is one of the best-remembered events in recent Spanish history. Jose Antonio del Moral puts it on a par with the attempted coup d'etat in 1978. Many toreros had perished in the ring before Paquirri, but none had ever died the slow and agonizing death of a *cornada* — horn wound — on television. For Spain, Paquirri's death was its Kennedy assassination, a moment burned forever into the national consciousness. To this day people can tell you where they were or what they were doing when they watched.

The bull's name was Avispado — every bull in every fight has a given name, and the ones that kill go down in history. It weighed 1,012 pounds and had been in the ring for only a few minutes. Paquirri had performed the first series of passes with the capote — something at which he particularly excelled. The last of these passes brought the bull face-to-face with the mounted picador. At this point in a fight there's almost always a momentary pause while the bull sizes up the picador and the public applauds the passes. For a second Paquirri took his eyes off the bull to mug for the appreciative crowd. In that instant, the bull attacked. Its right horn buried itself in Paquirri's right inner thigh, lifting him up like cotton wool into the air. For the next nine or ten seconds — long enough for the New York Knicks to lose a five-point lead — Avispado careened around the ring, spinning Paquirri on its horn, its massive tossing muscle ramming the point up along his thigh into his body. The horn severed his femoral artery and iliac vein, penetrated his abdomen, and caused two huge internal wounds, churn-

ing the inside of his groin into hamburger. Finally his *cuadrilla* —
ring crew — brought the bull to a halt, got the matador off the
horn, and rushed him to a primitive infirmary behind the bullring.

You can see what follows as often as you like. The videotape is
wrenching in its interminable confusion. Desperate hands cut away
Paquirri's blood-soaked *taleguilla* — those ornately spangled pants
— from a colossal wound. Others try to staunch the bleeding by the
traditional method of stuffing it with bandages. Intermittently we
see Paquirri, fully conscious, somehow controlling the pain. Like
most matadors, he'd suffered many cornadas in his long career,
and he tries angrily to instill order into the panic around him.
"There's one cornada high up, here," he snaps, "and another lower
down. Everyone shut up!"

The situation was dire. The infirmary had no operating theater and an inadequate supply of plasma. The decision was made
to rush the matador to a hospital in Cordoba, fifty-five miles away.
At dusk an ambulance set out with a police escort to make the
run. The road out of Pozoblanco is straight and flat across a plateau, and at first hopes must have been high that they could make
it. But the roads narrow as they descend to the plain, they're full of
potholes, riddled with 180-degree hairpin turns and unprotected
drops. Night fell and the pace slowed. Some forty-five minutes later,
out in the yellow-gray, olive- and pine-dotted scrubland of the Si-
erra Moreno, a few miles from help, the gilded life of Paquirri came
to an end. He was 37. It is said that his funeral in Seville drew more
people than Franco's.

"My father's death was an accident," says Fran smoothly. "Suppose he died in an airplane accident; what am I to do — never get
on an airplane again?" Two days after Bilbao, I'm back in Fran's
hotel room, this time in Linares, most of the way back to Almeria.
Our brave torero sits cross-legged on his bed, his eyes glued to
Baywatch. I ask if there's any element of revenge for his father's
death in his becoming a bullfighter. "No, if I wanted revenge, I
would be the bullfight Rambo. . . . I get my gun and go all over
the ranch killing bulls!" Has he seen the videotape of his father's
death? "Yeah, I don't like it." Is it disturbing that people can see it
over and over? "I never think about it. . . . People can think a lot of
things. I don't care." The responses are quite polished. He has an
occasional conspiratorial grin; he knows that I know he's given

them before. I've been warned that toreros are bad interviews, unused to the media, but Fran is a pro. He may have the old thing, but he has the new thing too — one foot in the mists of time, the other in MTV. His favorite singer is Bryan Adams. To me, Bryan Adams is a credit at the end of a VH-1 video, and anyway I can't get the name through Fran's Manuel accent. "Bryan Adams, man!" he yells, leaping off the bed and ripping through his travel bag. "You never hear of Bryan Adams?" He throws a CD at me. As well as Bryan Adams, he likes Simple Minds. Madonna's video is great. "She's a world star — it's good for bullfighting." He's unconcerned about animal-rights protesters: "Like rain beating on the roof." His fantasy is to meet Kim Basinger. This just about falls within my circle of acquaintance, and I allow as how it might be arranged. He starts bouncing off the walls. "Yeah? Really? That would be so cool!" I point out that in Hollywood — hotbed of animal rights — there are probably no two fiercer advocates than Kim and her husband, Alec Baldwin. "I don't care! Don't tell her anything! Tell her I'm a taxi driver!"

I tell him how fine I found the drama of the dying bull in Bilbao. Suddenly he's thoughtful — bulls are a subject that gets his attention. Does he have nightmares about bulls? "No, never. But I dream about them all the time. Every night. Three weeks ago I dream that I'm riding on the ranch and the bull starts talking to me." What did he say? "'Hey you! I am the bull!'" He laughs, then frowns, looking for words. "When the bull come out into the ring he start talking to you. Sometimes it's a good person. Sometimes it's a very bad person. He tells you what he likes. You have to give him what he likes. The bull is the best friend I have. The only one."

In Palencia on Labor Day weekend, the bulls were tough. One fighter, an inept kid named Ignacio Sanchez, had been badly tossed first eight or ten feet in the air, then some fifteen feet across the sand. Fran's second bull was a 1,210-pound roustabout that hooked viciously. There was ominous murmuring in the plaza as he struggled to dominate the animal, which almost caught him several times. Finally it did, under his left arm. He staggered back, clearly in great pain. I'd never seen him retreat an inch from a bull, and for a moment I thought the horn must have gone into his armpit. But it was a dislocation. He held out the arm to one of his *cuadrilla,* who yanked it hard. He strode back to the bull and did a series of four impeccable right-handed passes, which brought the crowd to their toes and left the bull staring at the sand. Then he threw away the muleta and sank to his knees in front of its horns.

Kenneth Tynan's book *Bull Fever* demonstrated with all the authority of his scholarship and critical expertise that bullfighting was dramatically legit, born of the same grand themes that drive the sap through the various branches of classic European theater. "A perfect faena imprints on the consciousness a pattern . . . of Senecan Stoicism as one finds it in the last act of a tragedy, when the hero stares death in the eyes and conquers it through indifference. . . ." But Tynan also understood that "the torero is the only artist who works in public, improvising every time with bizarre and unfamiliar material . . . to reduce to the language of art the multiple clangor, the loose ends and incoherencies of battle." True improvisation — as practiced by the original Second City and the Living Theater and the great jazz masters — is the key to understanding the theatricality of the bullring. A plunge into the unknown, solidly based on form, that takes artist and audience to places they've never been — a live, one-time-only, unrecreatable experience for everyone involved. The classical parallel goes only so far, for the torero's script, the bull, is not a fixed, canonical text to be interpreted anew by each actor. The bull is at best a rough. It can be relied upon — usually — to attack the picador's horse, and less often to charge in a straight line, but other than that, it is chaos on the hoof. Bullfighting is distilled improvisation, a story with a fixed beginning, middle, and end whose beauty depends on exquisite physical skills being adapted at lightning speed to mortal danger. Unlike any other kind of performance — theater, opera, rock — the art and the experience it celebrates are simultaneous. It's living theater in which the actors actually die, classical jazz with real horns.

Barquerito, *Diario 16*'s bullfight editor, expresses unreserved emotion about Ordonez. "I see 120 fights a year. I go to them with pleasure, but it's my duty. If I could, if I were a rich man, I would only follow Rivera Ordonez. He is the most moving thing I have seen in bullfighting since I became a professional." What moves him is Ordonez's solitude with the bull. "He is a very lonely man. He gives a sense of loneliness in front of the bull. Bullfighting is an expression of style. You fight the way you are. Rivera's style is the style of a lonely man."

Pozoblanco is a flat, bleak little town. Its bullring is small and, in a rough-hewn way, charming, an ancient stone structure held upright by countless coats of paint. It's ranked as a third-class ring, but when Fran fought there one day shy of the anniversary of his father's death there was more media in evidence than I'd seen at far larger ferias. In its next issue, *Hola!* would splash Fran across its cover and lead story, wallowing in the delicious drama of it all, the blue and gold suit of lights Fran wore just like his father's, breathlessly reporting his refusal to view the infirmary or change at the hotel where his father had, dutifully celebrating the absence of tragedy — "Gracias a Dios, nothing happened." Completing this journalistic tour de force was a full-page sidebar on Carmen — "daughter of a torero, ex-wife of a torero, mother of a torero — three kinds of fear in one body." Fran refused to play into such mawkishness: "Today is a normal day for me . . . but with much respect." Because of his restraint there was very real emotion in Pozoblanco. It swirled through the little plaza like a heavy, intoxicating gas. "Estamos Contigo Fran" ("We're with You Fran") blazed the T-shirts of one of his fan clubs. A stolid fortyish guy to my right, with a battered wedding ring, clenched his big mitts as Fran went out to fight his first bull. "Venga, nino," he muttered. The kid had set himself an ordeal, to face down history, torear with fate. Quietly and calmly he had to let the afternoon pass. And he did.

But at the very end of the fight there was another of those bull moments. Ordonez had composed an excellent faena beginning with several passes at the *barrera* — the wooden fence around the inside of the ring — considered extremely daring because the bull can pin a man to the wood like a butterfly in a display case. In an atmosphere thick with foreboding, it was a stomach-churning thing to do. When the kill came, he placed the sword well. But the bull would not die. He stood over it, willing it to go. Again he seemed utterly alone with the animal. It was dead on its legs, its head lowered, Ordonez inches from its horns. Still it wouldn't die. He took the bull's left horn, stroking it gently; then he ruffled the bristles between its horns as if it were an old friend.

Ordonez needed to know how much life was left in the bull, what it would take to finish it off. That's the prosaic explanation. But there's a prosaic explanation for why the reed in a clarinet makes a musical note; what you do with it is what counts. There was no explanation for his tenderness. In that place, on that day, the gesture was unforgettable.

Fran lives in the old quarter of Seville. He has a big BMW and a small apartment. It contains — when I visit three days after Pozoblanco — Fran; his kid brother, Cayetano; his 10-year-old stepbrother, Julian; Carmen; Carmen's 26-year-old fiancé, Eduardo; and a much-loved old housekeeper, Tata. It's crowded, friendly, noisy, Spanish. Fran, though, is more serious here. He behaves like the head of the family. And the strains of the week have left their mark. There are no pat answers this time. His words come in a rush of emotion or slowly as he searches his vocabulary for the right one. I ask about his bond with the bull.

"When the bull is good, you feel sorry that you have to kill the bull. You prefer that he go back to the ranch. But the bull is born to die. Sometimes the bull tells you that he wants to live. That is beautiful. He is telling you that he doesn't want to die. I can see it in his face. If the bull is difficult to beat and you beat him, you have to be a gentleman. I respect the bull. It is the thing I respect most in the world. The good ones you love."

I ask about his aloneness with them.

"Sometimes I leave out of my body, when I feel good. When I get a lot of concentration when I fight, I leave out of my body. I'm not even there. No people. No one. Just me and the bull. In that moment you take me and the bull and put us in another place, it would make no difference. You go outside of yourself — it's like a trip. When you kill him you come down. But all the time you're in another place."

I ask if the bull symbolizes anything for him. He frowns. I repeat what I said, and he says quite sharply: "I understand the question . . . but why are you asking me?" It seems to touch a nerve. "The bull is not symbolic. He's real. He is the center. The bull and the bullfighter has to be one. In life there are a lot of things that are not real. In bullfighting everything is real. The bull has strength and intelligence. You have only intelligence. You can die. Everything is real."

I ask about the death of his father.

"My father was very, very valiente. He got a strong cornada, but he was so calm. If you can see death right here in front of you, maybe you are nervous, maybe you cry. But he was so different, so calm: 'Don't worry, nothing's happened. . . . I have this and this' — it shocks people."

I ask him if he was close to his father. He is standing now. He is very intense. "Yes," he says quickly. His eyes have lost their youth; they're hard, ageless. I'm looking into the last thing the bull ever sees. He seems to be deciding whether to go on.

"To me my father was a god. I'm not the first kid that loses his father. But it was no good. It was no good. The life keeps going. Life don't stop. I do what I like — it is beautiful. If my father lived he would feel *orgulloso* . . . proud to see what I do and how I do it. Yes — he can see me. Sure. Of course. I give everything that I have every time that I fight. That's what he did. Everything that I do in life, like bullfighting like a man, is for my father. He is with me every day, every moment. I don't talk to him like I talk to you. But he is with me. I know."

RICHARD FORD

Hunting with My Wife

FROM SPORTS AFIELD

SOMETIMES WHEN I AM hunting with my wife — possibly we have just come to the edge of some vast sea-field of wheat stubble, or climbed hands-and-knees up out of a frozen river channel and stood on an open spot from where we can see off a long way through scattered trees toward mountains, gray and ivory at the pinnacles — sometimes at such moments of reconnoiter, Kristina will say to me, "Well, which way now? Where to?" and take a deep breath and smile toward where we're looking.

And I think to myself then — I think it every time — *Which way? There's a good question,* since farther on there seems to be more wheat, and pheasants will be there if it's early day, or late. Only, down the river the other way the banks are dense with rose briars and chokecherries, and back across there's alfalfa, which I hadn't seen till now. Birds can be there, too. Which way, indeed.

When I was a kid in Arkansas — this was in the fifties — I hunted with my grandfather. Quail only. Up in the direction of Clinton, or west in Yell County on a farm owned by Dizzy Dean's brother, Paul, or in a place he simply called "Bird Town," a spot I can never find now and that may not even exist. But on those cold December mornings, when we hunted, my grandfather always manifested a plan: "We'll go up this gravel road a quarter mile and cross a fence to the right side into the lespedeza field. Birds were there once, just beyond the fence." And later on, up the other side of a wooded limestone hill, to the margin of a disused cotton field: "Go up there, Dick, and see where the dog went, and if he's not on point, then come back down and meet me where that stone house was beside the road, and we'll cross over the river again and work up the other way. Once there was a big covey, right at the edge of the woods. It's birdy up there."

Of course I know now that he did not *know* which way. He went where he'd found birds before or he went toward what looked good at the moment he had to say where to go. The discovery of game was as much a shock to him as it was a mystery to me. He worked on faith and repetition and counted strongly on the dogs. And there were more birds then. Farming had not yet become so ruthless.

But ultimately, learning where to go next — learning where to hunt — must just have been distilled from the habit of hunting, and from his personality, and from our family's habit of not explaining things (we never knew the explanations for most things), nor asking for explanations, and also may have come from some devout connection between hunting and the wandering human condition — a faith that not knowing is sometimes the incitement to a pleasing act of imagination.

Even now, when I drive past some great stubble field, as I did last November near Havre, Montana, on my way to hunt pheasants, and I see geese in flight, lowering and lowering toward the ground, and can see the specks of men in their pits waiting for a flock to come in close, close enough to be shot, what I feel underneath my exhilaration is the small, scratchy anxiety from my young years now gone — the anxiety of not knowing: How do the hunters know to hunt this field, this day? How do they know where to sink their pits? Why do they think their decoys will work? Do they call the geese or simply wait? It is not such a bad thing to feel, this anxiety. It is a kind of longing, and I'm sure I'll have it all my life, even though I know now that the men drove out the night before in trucks and with their headlights spotted the geese feeding, guessed the birds would be back the next day, dug their pits, and simply came out and took their chances.

Sometime in the crystalline autumn of 1984, my wife decided she wanted to hunt with me — to carry a gun, to learn to find wild birds, to work hunting dogs, to shoot. And since then, in the falls and winters when I always hunt, I have tried to teach her what I know, as little as that might be. And especially, I have tried to teach her what I have just begun to describe: tolerance for the limbos and anxieties and ambiguities that seem to be near the heart of hunting.

It is, of course, hard for adults to learn anything new and complicated (retrained navy admirals and laid-off auto executives will bear this out). I have, for example, wanted and tried for years to learn to play the harmonica. I even had a friend who plays in a blues band in Mississippi try to teach me. But I've failed. I can never seem to make the hard leap from wanting to doing; can't get over the discouragement of entry-level complexity and frustration and proceed to the deeper, more profound gnarliness of the harmonican art. I can never bend a note, so that finally the nagging, silent repetition that "Life's too short" thrums in my ears and turns me balky.

But especially it is not easy, at any "advanced" age, to learn to rely on what are at best uncertain observations about where gamebirds might be — observations that may be the right ones but turn up no birds at all, or may be wrong (quite wrong) and turn up many, many birds. We modern adults have become addicted to life's proceeding only in the direction of surer certainties. Some manic-pathetic fury makes us want to do things only if we can do them well and precisely. Limbo, uncertainty, miscalculation, failure — these are all things we want strictly less of, whereas hunting requires us to think of them — failure, etc. — not merely as part of the whole but as part of its pleasure.

Likewise, it is hard for an adult to learn to walk through the woods or the open fields in a continual state of vivid readiness — to notice everything, to hear, to remember, to take care, possibly to shoot a gun — and to do it for hours and hours, and with your husband, wanting to please him and for him to please you, and for your union to ascend toward a newer realm of heaven, all the while knowing that if you were, say, 8 instead of 38 (when Kristina began), it would be so much easier. At that younger age, a "loving adult" could force it on you, as happened to me, and all your youthful miscues and wrongs and dead misses at slow-rising birds wouldn't matter, since at such a faultless age you would already do so many things inexpertly and without grace, no single one could matter, and eventually less grindingly, you'd learn.

Kristina is a woman of emphatic and unhidden talents. She has mastered difficult sciences, written useful books, attained an ad-

vanced degree and a high office of public trust. Without being a
cold-eyed and hard-hearted rationalist, she has never trusted the
spiritual and unproved in most things. She has compassion and
sympathy, and is no practicer of the deadliest sin — stubbornness.
But what I have tried to teach her in these years is fresh habits, to be
added by repetition to the already cut-and-fitted prism of her own
so as to change her behavior. They are my minor habits, practiced
by me essentially without plan and so nearly unconsciously as to
resemble instinct: to hunt up the wind whenever possible; to walk
in on a pointed bird with the confidence of having already calculated which way it might fly; to resist scouring the ground with my
eyes; to stay aware of changes in cover when trailing a pheasant; and
always to expect a wild flush. Beyond that, to watch flying birds out
of sight, always to *choose* my bird, not to shoot the dogs (or someone
else), not to shoot too fast, and not to get shot myself by standing in
front of someone when birds go up. Learning these things would
try anyone's patience.

Still, in another way, hunting is just working around out of doors,
doing what hunters insignificantly do: recounting prior flushes;
exhibiting bafflement that the birds "went out" the way they did;
detailing exactly where you stood and where he stood and where
the sun was; speculating why the birds flew toward the gravel pit
instead of to the woods or the edge of a beanfield or into the coulee
the way they usually do; opining over what the last bunch was doing
when found — going to roost, feeding ahead of a storm, getting
gravel, feeding behind a storm, "dusting"; on and on like that.
Kristina, I think, takes to this as much as to any of it, senses that in
such small talk there are small things to learn. Hunting is mostly a
thing that men do, but she likes men and their casual businesses.
She is inquiring and good company, likes to laugh, and she doesn't
take seriously what doesn't seem serious. And she does not think
that hunting is harvesting game. She seems to realize (and I did not
teach her this) that hunting is chiefly being there, taking that walk
toward that tree, crossing the river again, going into the swale,
seeing what there is to see at this time of day or year or life —
ordinary human goings-on that profit from being enacted more
meticulously, and then enacted over again. By her nature she seems
to know that if we could always come and find birds by some agate-
eyed calculation, if we could never not know, then finally we

wouldn't come at all, and that probably we register our humanness by coming when we aren't sure and by recording the changes in things and by recording change's opposite — dogged recurrence.

I am, as any of my friends can tell you, no encyclopedia of hunting lore and know-how, and no spiritualist, either. I have never intentionally gobbed ritual blood on my cheeks or "utilized" a trout. To me, all such hoodoo conveys is the idea that hunting's a thing out of reach of the ordinary soul and can be achieved only by a certain few with special magic. I believe, on the other hand, that if hunting birds were so hard to do, I of all people would never be able. So with that as my "theory," I haven't cared if Kristina becomes a great or a perfect hunter or does it better than I do. I have merely hoped to show her what I presumed she could do by herself if she chose. Mine is not a father's job, to replicate myself in a purer, more specialized and enlightened form, or a wizard's — instructing her in some sacred office — but a husband's: to give what I can give, to invite her to be herself, to show her my way and then let her figure out her own; to widen the limits of the institution of marriage so as to make them seem to disappear and make us be joined as friends who meet on some road and agree to go on together.

Learning to hunt is not the same as learning to shoot, even though learning one certainly seems to help the other, and it is hard to think now of a good hunter who is not also a pretty good shot. But long before I fell upon this significant distinction and encouraged Kristina off to an elaborate shooting school, bought her a gun of the right size and weight, and retired my old, hand-me-down L.C. Smith 16 that weighed eight pounds, I tried to teach her some things about shooting and the related skill of getting into position to shoot — both of these imagined as a prologue to a manual of hunting. From those early days, I still have a vivid picture in my mind. We are hunting, the two of us, in the wide, damp bottom of a place known as Timber Coulee, in central Montana — a pheasant heaven. My dog, Dixie, a little Brittany, is on point just at the edge of a long, reticulated rose thicket. Kristina is tentative but readying herself to shoot the big Smith should a rooster fly up and into her area. We are behind the dog, who's grown nervous because we aren't visible to her and are not moving up confidently to flush the bird, as she expects. Instead, I am furiously but silently waving my arm, trying to get Kristina to move up parallel with me and to push the hiding bird ahead of us toward the back of the thicket, where it will lose cover and probably fly. She is carrying her gun at port arms, trying to understand what my gestures mean, and by turns stealing glimpses at the dog, watching her footing, trying to find the safety on her gun though not yet clicking it off, wondering where the bird is in the dense briars, no doubt silently considering the possibility that she might soon shoot a live animal and dreading it — all that, when suddenly the bird launches itself wildly into the clean Montana air, cackling and flapping, only not out ahead of us but straight up into my face, startling my heart and thwarting any shot by me.

But not by Kristina. The shot's hers. The big bird flourishes higher to the air in an instant, and I reflexively fall to the ground to clear a shot alternately watching Kristina's alarmed face and the big rooster beating the empty molecules, heading up toward the coulee rim.

"Shoot!" I shout, flat on the ground. "Shoot it. Shoot it, Kristina!" She is looking at the bird, her gun correctly to her shoulder but pausing as if what she sees is what she can't believe. "Shoot!" I shout, agonized. "Jesus, shoot it! Shoot, shoot!"

But she doesn't. She has found the bird over the plain of her barrels, gone with it a ways, kept both eyes open, but not shot. Just stopped, watching. "Shoot!" I shout pleadingly, still wanting to have it happen. "Shoot the damn bird. Why don't you shoot?" And — bear in mind I am not proud that this is true — I pound the ground with the flat of my hand and press my forehead to the cold soil like a penitent and let some odd, awful fury rise, peak, and then drain out of me as the bird disappears forever.

She did not think she had a shot, she tells me on the spot. It seemed too far. Or maybe it's that she didn't get her safety off, or snagged the butt plate on her shirtsleeve. Or possibly she thought I would shoot the bird (from the ground). She is new to all this. I was yelling at her. The bird startled her. Her footing was wrong. It was all a chaos and she didn't care to shoot under such conditions.

Tears come then. She lays her gun, broken open, on the ground and sits beside it, staring at her boots, crying.

"Why are you such an asshole?" she asks. "Did you think I didn't want to do it right on purpose? Did you think that was why I came out here? To do it wrong?" She sobs. "I just don't know why you get so mad at me." She wipes her face with her sleeve and stares up at me where I lurk not far away.

"You can't hit a bird unless you shoot," I say. "You have to shoot."

"I *know* I have to shoot," she says, less miserable now than resentful. "I just don't know why *you* have to be *such* an asshole about it, you know? I really don't."

"I understand," I say. "I don't know, either. I'm sorry. I guess I just want you to like this too much."

"Well, you have a strange way of showing that," she says, and goes off to hunt by herself the rest of the morning.

This was early on, though only recently have I become certain that I hunt with Kristina at least somewhat for the satisfaction it gives her instead of just for what it brings to me — hunting being to an extent an insular, ruminant pleasure and hard to share, even unequally. I'm certain, now, that in those beginning days I wanted "a wife who hunted," a wife with bragging rights, a "finished" wife, as my pal Geoff Norman once said, borrowing a term used to describe a fine bird dog. Over these years, I have watched Kristina miss or not shoot or shoot badly at any number of birds, and each time felt a thick lump fall from one part of my insides to another. What I called "sharing," a willingness to teach Kristina what I loved, was, I suppose, just a wish in disguise to make myself happy with her success, and then to share that — an un-innocent generosity, I know.

Hunting requires avidity, a continual, alert responsiveness to the particulars of the changing situation you're in. Writers celebrate hunting so often partly because such exquisite, tuned readiness is not usual in life and can make one feel (though not write) like a Romantic poet, which some people seem to want to be. Most hunters know this avidity, though. Its evidence lies not in how well or fast you shoot, not how often you hit what you mean to, not even how quickly your gun comes to your shoulder, but how widely you see, how promptly you pick up a soft wingbeat and by its sound know it to be a hen's before you even see the colors. It is how quick you are to know that your young dog has lost a scent, and to find the bird yourself, then get your dog to refind it. It is concentration upon all the particulars of *one thing*, which is exhilarating and rare in life. Shooting — actually pulling the trigger, firing a shotshell — is the

last and in some ways least to be relished of these dedicated movements. And certainly one need not shoot to be rewarded. Though,
too, without the possibility of shooting, many argue that the rest,
the avidity itself, wouldn't matter, perhaps not even exist. Myself,
I'm simply not sure.

Kristina has been slow to acquire this brand of forwardness,
though. She has become a precise shot, but not routinely a fast one.
She does not always watch the dogs closely nor move to them with
sureness when they are near birds. She is often still startled by a
flushing bird, occasionally says "Oh!" when the bird appears where
she isn't expecting it. Sometimes she will walk too strictly by my lead
and close to me instead of hunting on her own. In a covey rise of
wild quail she is more likely to see the birds before she registers
hearing them. And I believe privately (now publicly) she sometimes
daydreams in the field, hikes the easy edges of the cover where her
mind can wander, instead of "busting briars" the way I think she
should and do myself. Her pleasures are, of course, her own.

I'm certain these reactions are not a "gender thing." The popular wisdom that women are more naturally nurturers and conflict
resolvers, and men better at kickboxing, shooting down enemy
MiGs, and staging public executions, has just never been interest-
ingly proved to me. Plenty of men are not good hunters — probably most of them. And women hunt as avidly and shoot as fast as
and sometimes much more accurately than men, if they've simply
hunted as long as the men they're compared to.

So it's probably only experience, or the lack of it, that makes
Kristina less avid. And it also may be just a personal trait, like a
quickness to laughter but not to anger, or a facility for staying up
longer on Rollerblades, or a sovereign dislike for the peremptory in
anything — qualities I wouldn't want her to trade for being a better
covey shot or, worse, for finding a way to be me. Ultimately, she
makes up for not having developed avidity before she knew what
avidity meant by being, in the useful spirit of comradeliness, not a
born competitor; by being hour after walking hour in rising spirits
about the whole enterprise of hunting, misses and all; by wishing
no one to make special concessions for her, which they don't; and
by determinedly getting better.

Still, if she had found after months of trying that she simply
couldn't do it, couldn't make progress, could please neither herself

nor me, I believe she'd have laughed it off, forgotten the whole thing, and gone on to other challenges. Hunting is worth no more than that nowadays — forget what those men with hushed voices say. In the modern era, hunting is just a choice you make over windsurfing.

I don't remember actually learning to shoot. I remember a few times my grandfather tossed up some No. 10 tomato cans out at the little farm lot he owned outside Little Rock, and I shot at them with an old side-lock Savage that belonged to his brother Buster. As I got better, he tossed up smaller cans. Later, my pal Danny Henley and I lied our way onto the skeet range at the Capitol Gun Club in Mississippi — saying we were the sons of men we were not the sons of — and there shot at clay pigeons part of one summer. No one instructed us. No one talked to us at all, and we weren't inclined to invite conversation on ourselves. We may simply have been afraid of being terrible shots in the presence of slightly threatening strangers and got better that way. We were young, too. Learning was easier.

I must have learned just by doing, as the poet advised, in those years when I had plenty of time and friends who were no better than I was — hiking out on cold January school afternoons to stalk but usually miss resident bluebills on Vickers Lake, or stealing into somebody's absent grandfather's cutover milo field to shoot roosting doves in the dusky tree lines. It was in the casualness of youth that these skills accrued.

Allied, of course, to the issue of learning to shoot is the issue of learning to miss, which ought to be spoken of at least briefly since from the beginning, as I've said, I have watched Kristina miss many, many birds in many, many situations, felt that thump in my chest many times, wished better luck for her, pummeled over why it didn't dawn, spoken encouragement, suppressed all comment, until over time her missing became a feature of *my* hunting life as well as her own.

Missing what you shoot at is a confounding aspect of learning to hunt, though not an inglorious one, since it means the bird gets away, somehow eludes you, which is no disgrace, and good for the bird. The goal is certainly, 100 percent, to hit everything. But hunting isn't a matter of succeeding by killing (hunting with someone you love makes this very clear). Men, the buckos I hunt with, men who have hunted all their lives, miss all the time. I miss, too, though God knows why. Maybe I'm distracted or hung over or too tired from hunting the day before. Maybe shooting's not as easy as it looks. Beyond that, all of us who have hunted all our lives have occasionally shot beside men and sometimes women who never missed, for whom missing simply wasn't a concept. And surprisingly enough, it isn't even dispiriting. Such aberrant precision's, in fact, a cause for speculation that the shooter is probably a bad person, a Mensa member, a person with odd habits, a man who's snide to his wife and too strict with his kids, and who does everything the same way: bitterly, mercilessly, well.

When you first go hunting, though, everything seems to be about shooting and missing. A novice — though Kristina never evidenced this in my presence — becomes possessed by the idea that people who don't know how to hunt almost always miss, and that people who know how almost always don't. Once, along the Smith River, below some chalky rimrock where there were clumps of still-green roses and wild sage scrub, an old rooster burst up in front of our dogs, and I cleanly missed it straight away, both barrels, not even feathers, after which Kristina just stood looking at me, her gun on her shoulder.

"Why didn't you shoot?" I asked, feeling once again the thunking sensation in my chest.

"Well," she said, in a way meant to encourage me, "*You* shot, and you always hit everything. So when the bird didn't fall, I was so surprised I just forgot to shoot. I didn't think you ever missed."

"So you know now," I said glumly.

"Well. Yes. I guess I do," she said. "I'll remember that."

In her case, in all those early hunting years with me in Montana and Tennessee and Mississippi and Arkansas, I don't know why she missed the birds she missed, though there are plenty of good possibilities: she shot behind the bird, shot under it, shot over it, shot through too-thick cover; she shot too fast, shot too slow, she lowered her cheek to the stock instead of raising her stock to the cheek, she didn't get her safety off smoothly; she closed one eye, closed both eyes, the bird was out of range. Or none of these. Moreover, for a beginner, as she was, missing is doubly, even triply, enigmatic, since you are never sure if you missed because you lack skill, or because you lack luck, or because of some other reason, some defect in your person you know nothing about and never will. Missing's a reproach, a disappointment, a mystery, a potential deal breaker.

Leading may also be a problem.

"Tell me how to lead them," Kristina asked me one warm February morning on the Cumberland Plateau, when I had persuaded her to stand in close on a covey rise, but without shooting, so she could hear the burst of wing sound, see the true size and shape of the quail, learn how much time she actually had to shoot. She'd missed some that morning.

"I *don't* lead them," I said, which seemed to puzzle her. The truth is I've never believed that I lead birds, not upland birds, anyway — grouse, quail, woodcock, partridge — birds that hide, flush fast and startlingly, and instinctively put obstacles between you and them. I have always been of the cover-the-bird-shoot-and-keep-on-swinging school, a protocol similar in spirit to a pitcher's habit of following through on his big fastball; this, rather than hanging a load of shot at a guessed-at distance in front of a flying, darting bird and expecting the two will collide.

Kristina's first hunting experience, long before I figured in things, was with her father, an air force flyjockey, and her younger sister, Lisa, on the dry sage flats of northern Utah, near where her father was stationed. Her pappy, a typical Kentucky boy, liked to shoot mourning doves in the late afternoons after work, and his pleasure was to find the birds in the trees near the water, take a position that offered cover but also clear shooting, then send his two little girls giggling and skipping across the open fields to worry the doves into flight, whereupon he would shoot as the birds passed over the water by habit, and the sisters would bring them back. Leading, I think, was *his* idea. "You have to lead them, Krissy," I'm sure he said to his breathless, slightly awed daughter, age 8, showing her the little duff-colored birds collected on the rough ground at his feet. And maybe he did lead them. Maybe, being a pilot, he knew how things flew. It's conceivable. But each time I have tried to lead a quail or a pheasant passing in front of me so that I thought the shot was sure, I have missed. Something seemed odd — something about not shooting straight at the bird (which seemed testing enough) but shooting instead at some supposed spot in the wide air you hoped the bird would occupy. Too much calculation seemed required in too little time. Though it's also a fact that many times I have stood under a flight of slow-winging Canadas, heard their sharp cries, raised my barrel to the nose of a bird and fired and missed, or, more unhappily, seen the one behind it — the wrong bird — fall. And I always say the same thing when this happens: "They fly faster than I think. Maybe I should lead them."

There is really no single rule that nicely applies to the problem of positioning yourself to shoot. In one way it just seems common sense to get as close as you can to a departing bird. Yet in another way the challenge of hitting a bird in flight is often met, not as a result of *common* sense, or doing everything right, but as a result of doing sometimes very few things right — often just pointing and pulling the trigger when a bird comes into view.

I'm sure I have been remiss in teaching Kristina how to position herself, an omission that resulted — at least at first — in her displaying a kind of tentative, wandering, atomistic behavior when the dog went on point. A basic, though not exclusive, premise of positioning is that the hunters (two is perfect, three stretches it, four is unwise) should walk toward where the dog seems to be pointing, staying in the dog's sight if possible and in view of the other hunters, expecting this movement to excite the bird or birds to flight. This scheme isn't always workable in dense cover or in trees, in which case one hunter moves to flush the birds by walking toward them, sometimes sacrificing a shot, while the other hunter positions herself so that, relative to the dog and the cover and her partner doing the flushing, and thoughtful of the wind and the sun and which direction the bird might fly, a shot becomes feasible. The presence of a body of water or some other close-by topographical oddity may also affect one's choice of position. Pheasants seem always to want to fly across a river where you can't go, so that positioning yourself to close off a river escape is always good. Pheasants will also often fly when they have run to the margins of thick cover, so that getting quickly up to where the cover thins is a wise idea. Hungarian partridge will often fly if they hear you or see you top a rise of land and become visible by silhouette, so that keeping to the low ground and downwind is useful. There are a lot of these things to think about, a lot more than I've said, and it all has to be done in a hurry, without much planning, or the birds will get up and fly far away, and you'll never see them again.

There seems to be a self-defeating human instinct in such situations as these — when birds are present and one is not sure where to stand — to stay back, to stay out of the immediate area of the dog, the birds, and the other hunters, as if what one really needs to shoot a flying partridge is not avid, prompt advancement toward a point of forced confrontation and flight but a wide panorama for the bird and oneself to occupy jointly, across which one will have available the fullest number of shooting strategies rather than simply the best one. Many times I have walked toward my dog, where she has locked in on I knew not what — a rooster, a flock of Huns, a skunk, a porcupine, a deer, a rattlesnake — only to look around to see Kristina poised, ready to shoot, but with her feet locked in cement like a hoodlum at the bottom of a river, twenty yards behind me, or farther. This is the occasion for more furious but silent arm-waving and stage whispers: "Get up here, get up here now!" (Actually shouting, "Get the goddamn hell up here and get ready to shoot!" would frighten most birds to flush, and also distract you from what you're doing — trying to flush the bird yourself so that *you* get a shot.) I can only suppose there must be something about this tableau — a poised dog in wild cover with precious, alerted birds ready to fly for their lives, and you yourself there with a gun in tense and expectant limbo — that has an element of danger in it and causes less-seasoned human beings not to want to make a mistake, or to risk shooting badly, or to be unsafe, or in any way to be less than the situation demands, and so keeps them at a distance.

I should do better. I should be more purely teacherly toward Kristina, and lately I have tried. I've stood back from the point, shouldered my gun, pledged not to shoot no matter what. I have calmly directed her forward, making soft-spoken, mindful mention of the cover and the topography and the footing and the wind and the impediments, and of what I guessed the dog to have found — a pheasant, a partridge. I have pointed out what was in range — those trees, those rocks, the edge of the plowed ground, that fence: "It's why you have a gun. You can reach things far away." Though I've told her, too, if you think a bird is not in range, then don't shoot at it. Crippled birds that you watch flutter and limp away leave a dry and bitter residue in memory, and is much, much worse for the bird.

Still, there is an urgency to these moments I can barely resist. This avidity in me, learned over such a long time, these nearly instinctual replies to the vital evidence of hunting, these will disappear out of me after a time — used up — and some jealous part doesn't like spending them in efforts to bestow them on someone else, even someone I love. Part of hunting's essentialness to those who do it involves loss of this peculiar, anticipated kind, and the attendant feeling that certain chances, certain moments, don't come twice, and you must be scrupulous to husband what you know and can do. Everything heads toward solitary extinction. And in a way that's affiliated, hunting is, in large part, an act you do for yourself alone.

When I began to hunt ruffed grouse, twelve years ago, with my friends Geoff Norman and Carl Navarre in southern Vermont, I was eager to prove myself a hunter, having put in all my years down South hunting quail and feeling I was up to whatever one hunted in the other latitudes. So that with them I was always eager to walk in to flush a pointed bird, no matter the weave of the cover, supposing I would get the best shot but also prove myself to be a selfless, stand-up guy by busting brush (a paradox all too standard in my nature). Yet my experience came to be that I would flush the bird and Norman would get the good shot, leaving me immobilized in a poplar thicket or a cedar clump or a dense orchard of fallen apples, where I would either miss or not even get to shoot, and could only listen, my heart tingling, as the bird rocketed through the branches, all but invisible.

Once we'd done this sort of hunting over a season, I heard Norman say to Navarre, quite definitely within my hearing, and even laughing, "Hunting with Ford's like hunting with two dogs, you know? One dog points [his dog, Molly], then the other dog, old Ford, goes in and flushes the bird out. I don't mind saying it: I really like to hunt with Ford."

I supposed even then that, in his indirect and jokey-derisive way, a way we white southerners adopt for coping with other white southerners we don't know too well but sort of like, Norman was trying to teach me something: that one can't codify what one knows and then do it that way time and time and time again — there are too many exceptions. Indeed, the allure of hunting is that there often seems to be nothing but exceptions, nothing by rote — and grouse in particular are different, anyway. Only he *would* hunt with

me, and what he wanted me to know — me, who had hunted then
for thirty years — was that I should pay attention and go along.
There was, he must've felt, no other way to learn.

So, then, myself: clearly, I have not so much taught Kristina how
to shoot, how not to miss, how to swing her gun, how to position
herself as much as I have given her the chance to go along, and to
learn in her own way, and then to relegate these skills to their
diminished place so that hunting itself can take up: imagining
where pheasants will be and won't, and going about finding them
(they will usually not be in trees or among large rocks or in ponds
or rivers, but often will be in damp or dry tule patches, in the rose
briars along riverbanks if food's nearby, or in standing wheat or
barley); finding Huns by their little gravelly chirps when they are
upwind of you; remembering that only rarely will you find one
woodcock or one sharptail, that grouse and pheasants often band
up after a snow, and that one or two quail will often "drop off" from
a flushed covey, so that you'll find them sooner than you think.
These are *data* I almost cannot think of, almost can't imagine outside the brief fascinating moments of their occurrence.

One could, I suppose, find most everything I know in books.
From books it's possible to account for a grouse's every whim,
wingbeat, and BM, to find him every place he strays and lights, to
be a detective seeking greater and greater degrees of effortlessness
and efficiency. Yet, and it may seem odd for a writer to admit as
much, I have never liked reading books about hunting, or reading
much of anything just for the purpose of learning to enjoy my
pleasures more. Not that I insist on a more primitive scheme of
knowing; I'm merely satisfied not to know everything, and to re-
serve most of my thinking about hunting and also my efforts to
impart it to Kristina for those notable moments when we are there
to do it.

Until I began to hunt with Kristina, I had never taught anyone to
hunt or, really, taught much of anything. I had once taught English
to some college students, a few of whom were actually grateful; and
before that, I'd taught the breast stroke to small children in Little
Rock. But it always seemed too much trouble to teach anyone to
hunt — too complicated, too much hunting time lost. My belief was
that if people wanted to hunt, they would already know how before
they got to me.

I did once and briefly instruct a friend about casting with a flyrod. This was twenty years ago, in Michigan. I took him out to the banks of the river near where we lived; I put a rod in his hand, let him waggle it, demonstrated it myself: talked about it and about fishing, then sat back in the grass and commented while he flailed and flapped it around. Later I discussed which rod he should buy for himself, and which line fitted his intention — which was, he decided, to fish in small streams in Michigan. We talked about flies, leaders, vests, waders, visited a few stores, traveled finally to a likely stream, and fished, side by side. And eventually I began not to like fishing as much.

What happened — and it's perfectly sensible — was that fishing almost immediately became a dense and feral obsession with him, as did many things in his life then, but so much so that he wanted to fish — and if not fish, then talk about it, plan to do it, analyze it and have it on his mind — all the time. He bought gear and books, took pictures, ordered catalogs. His jokes began to have fishing punch lines. I would see him working his wrist back and forth in a hammer motion, simulating a cast while he watched baseball on TV. Fishing became a disease and also a therapy, two things it never was for me, his friend and remorseful mentor. For me it was only a sweet diversion to be gone at mildly, then sweetly passed along (more casual than hunting), but which his "zeal," I'm sorry to have to say, altered for me in a small, regrettable way, so that I fish less now and cannot yet think about going with him again.

It's a risk to teach anyone anything, especially a skill we care for greatly, even though we do it to prove our faithfulness. It's a risk to codify what is second nature and possibly a source of inner happiness, since, in doing so, we not only bring to the level of thought what was once safely *not* there, but we require ourselves then to see what once was ours as *theirs*, risk seeing it differently, risk seeing how much our own investment animates it and makes it rich, risk seeing ourselves as being much like others in our loves, risk simply seeing ourselves. Seeing ourselves, period — always a dicey business.

The truth may be that I don't like teaching anything to anybody — especially adults — and have made an exception for Kristina for the same reason I married her: because she is a wonderful girl to do anything with. Most adults, frankly, aren't. Most adults don't want to learn anything; they only want to seem to want to learn, and be diverted a moment from their usual rounds — which seems no more than normal. People who do want to learn something entirely new, like my friend back in Michigan, seem suspicious to me now, malcontents, loose cannons. Why else would they want to quit what they've already freely chosen and been doing for years and start something new and difficult at a late date? How many true Renaissance people can there possibly be in the world?

Teaching someone to hunt means even more than the usual commitment. Among other things it means you would like, or at least be mildly willing, to go hunting with that person. And as anyone knows, you have to be careful whom you hunt with.

There's the death issue, first of all: the person you hunt with may not be as careful as you are, or as you want others to be around you, and may kill you — putting an end to everything. Two times I've come close to being shot while hunting with men I didn't know very well, and one time hunting with a man I've known and hunted beside all my life, causing both of us a lot of embarrassment. At the very least, hunting with a novice or a stranger means you have to be aware, if not actually scared, of her or him all the time; where she's walking, how she's holding her gun, whether she takes the safety off too soon, how close she shoots to the dog and you — all that and a lot more, just when what you want to be thinking about is hunting.

Then there's the etiquette issue: the new person may be a game hog and insist on shooting all the birds that fly; or he may claim your birds or talk all the time or yell at his dogs constantly, or yell at your dogs, driving you crazy, making your hunting day a nightmare, and further diminishing your own zeal. Talk that I don't like while hunting is what I think of as "consequential talk," talk about your divorce or your colonoscopy — subjects that might be very interesting in another setting. I once went quail hunting in Louisiana with two layabout rich guys who talked smirkingly and unceasingly about "Manny Hanny" and purchase agreements and "Big Blue" and the Fed, corporate takeovers and arbitrageurs (this was in the eighties, of course). It went on all day long. And I remember thinking, standing in the bottom of a dry and sandy streambed, watching my partners striding on ahead of me, still talking away: *if I ever get away from you two guys, I'll never hunt with you again.* And I haven't.

Talk that eventuates in distracting colloquy or arguments, or that requires a lot of to-and-fro and careful attention to your answers, can enter your mind like a taint just when you want to make certain your young dog is backing properly, or when birds are running along the ground and you need to keep up and pay attention to that. Such talk can make you shoot too fast, grip your gun too tightly, lose your footing, pull off on your shot — a dark bouquet of bad and unwanted results blossoming and making you sorry.

My experience with Kristina is that we tend to talk about novels (not mine) when we're hunting, about which ones she liked, which ones I did, which ones she thinks I should read. Or else it's TV or movies or poetry, all of it in the slightly emended spirit of Auden, who once wrote that poetry makes nothing happen — which, if not generally true, is true at least to the extent that anyone's opinion about a poem does not necessarily require an answer, and no money's involved.

There's also the physical issue. Hunting birds is chiefly a matter of walking, and your partner needs to keep up, not be reluctant to go into the brush or to cross the frozen river when the birds appear to be on the other side or be slow to keep up with a trailing dog that's run to the top of a coulee. My boyhood hunting memories are of that: of walking, miles and miles of it, and of wanting to quit walking and sit down, but of there being no offer. A house, some old car bodies scattered over a hillside, a tall pine top or a mountain — all of these revolved, changed position, returned, disappeared, as we walked and walked. When I would wake in the early mornings to go with my grandfather — only one lamp lit — I would lie in bed, half-dozing, watching him pull his "iron" pants up over his meaty, sinewy, pale legs, and I would think to myself, "Those legs walk. I'll never have those." But, in fact, I do.

Kristina, as it happens, can walk the legs off anybody. I don't know how, but she can. Maybe it's genes, or hours in the gym developing mind and muscle. Maybe her pappy taught her more than I thought, taught her to walk. But by whatever means, she does the thing that's required: she walks seemingly without thinking she's walking, covers ground as though she never tires, as though she were carried by means other than her own two legs. Without such reliance, I think, it's hard to be a delighted hunter.

And that is what she is, her delight being much the same as mine: the delight of sometimes finding what you seek and sometimes not; the delight of merely being there — the enlivening I have talked about. Sometimes, and I have watched her, she simply stops and looks around, leans her head back, takes a breath, takes it all in, says nothing.

Still, she is not a perfect partner. Maybe for me there is no perfect partner, since if one existed, surely she would be the one. I am hard on my partners, probably harder than on myself. I want them to be me in places I can't be, want them to hunt hard, not distract me, stay in the cover, persevere on a downed bird, shoot well (though not necessarily too well). Only last year did I begin to experience an even slightly smaller hollow feeling such that I could refrain from saying to Kristina, "You waited too long then," or "You didn't get your gun up," or "You stopped your swing," or "You positioned yourself behind that gum-tree trunk, so you'd have needed a rocket launcher to hit a bird in flight" — that is, such that I could begin to put myself in her boots, rather than over and over again putting her in mine.

My friend in Missoula, a linguistics professor I've hunted with for a decade, and who now often finds Kristina a more agreeable hunting companion than I can provide, has told me more than once that eventually I'll drive Kristina off from hunting with me and — he must've meant — drive him away, too. Could be I've already lost friends over it, people who have cut me loose without my knowing it, muttered behind my back. I haven't noticed. Though the truth may be that I prefer to hunt alone, that I shoot better alone, cover more ground, notice more, perform hunting's variable skills more satisfactorily by myself. If true, it's a loss, but not a damning fault.

As far as Kristina is concerned: sometimes I think she is too tenderhearted. I have a snapshot of her holding a pheasant she has moments before shot with a shotgun over our dog, Rosie. As usual, it's Montana. She is cradling the limp bird in her arms and smiling sweetly as though she were holding the dog, or a bird that *wasn't* killed — a pet. It is true that "locating" oneself in relation to the animals you've killed or are willing to kill is an unsimple matter and requires a series of emotional rachetings, enabling you to assume responsibility for their lives and their deaths (if that's possible), without it all driving you crazy and ruining your life. Maybe that's what the picture caught: the disjunctures of coming to terms.

Beyond that, she is not quick or especially adroit in dispatching birds that are down but not dead. She too vehemently dislikes hunting in the wind (always abundant in Montana). She told me once just as she turned and began walking to the car, hanging it up for the day, that the goddamned wind was so strong her shots were being blown off line, which was why she couldn't hit anything, and to hell with it.

There is also the matter of her clothes. Kristina is sensitive to the glamour angles of hunting and wants to took her best in the field at all times. She is a former fashion model and beauty-pageant queen, and wears tweed caps, occasionally a wide-brimmed felt hat for the sun, Hermès neckwear, expensive quilted shooting gloves, thick Scottish sweaters, thick Scottish socks. She likes her brush pants snug. To me, this makes her look like a rank amateur and lessens our chances of getting crucial access when we appear together in a muddy, cold and rainy, vehicle-strewn, dog-clamorous barnyard, wanting to ask some startled young farmer's permission to kick out his irrigation ditches for birds. I myself strive for a less memorable impression in my hunting clothes, and from time to time I've even asked Kristina to "dress down" — my wish being not to come on so strong, and for us to seem "authentic" — though authentic *what* I'm not entirely sure: authentic hunters, maybe, and not authentic jerks. Her view on all this has, however, been unchanging: in an encounter with a dazzling huntress, stepping off the pages of the Abercrombie's wish list, no farmer would say no for fear of ruining his private and well-earned fantasy. So far she's been right.

There is still the matter of deferring too much to me, and of not shooting promptly enough, and of not paying close attention to the dogs, and of not hunting the thick cover. For some reason having to do, I suppose, with her own Swedish background, she can't yet blow her whistle loudly enough — a liability when hunting in the wind with fast-moving dogs. And I do believe it's true she still daydreams when she should be concentrating.

I am not convinced there are things in the world too good to see alone, and as anyone knows, only so much is truly shareable. But for my hunting days from now on I have chosen the pleasure of Kristina to go with, and decided not to make solitude more severe by insisting on it so much. Over a long time in marriage you choose the other person again and again, marriage being not a teeth-grinding matter of finishing a course earnestly begun, but a preference that partakes of all contingencies and dodginess, overpowers them, and ardently turns them to good.

Am I proud, exactly, that Kristina has made a hunter of herself and with my help? Yes, more admiring than proud, and I do tell her so. Although, hunting being the solitary pursuit it is, I am, by her success, frequently and selfishly reminded of my own human failings — my undemonstrative, far too druidical willingness to say less than enough, to make less of her pleasures and even my own, for reasons I am not even sure of: for reasons of "proportion"? for reasons of jealousy? for reasons of simply wanting to get on with it? Maybe all of these things. These are qualities in myself that surprise me, qualities I wouldn't especially like in another man; that have, I'm sure, demanded much patience from my wife.

So if after I've "gone" she sells my guns, gives my sweet and faithful Brittany spaniels to a young Lutheran minister with small kids in eastern Oregon, donates my boots to an Episcopalian men's shelter (if such things exist), boxes away our snapshots in a mini-storage in Bogalusa, and marries a cardiologist with a time-share in Aruba, I wouldn't blame her. My view is: do what you want. If I've been successful, I've taught Kristina not to hunt with me, but to hunt alone; have shown her something to do again and again, a system for imagining her seasons more brightly, as I have imagined mine.

Eventually, it'll all dry up, anyway; scarce game, no access, hunting's opponents winning out, one's own embarrassment at hanging on too long. Best, while there's time remaining, to think of hunting the way Turgenev did, as an apt and vivid and unreplenishable circumstance for the more complicated and subtle and important of imaginative human events: being lovers, being friends, being both together.

RICK REILLY

Master Strokes

FROM SPORTS ILLUSTRATED

ON THE DRIVE to the golf course she saw a graveyard, and she secretly held her breath, closed her eyes and made a wish. When your dad is Greg Norman you stop trusting Sundays and you start working all the angles you can, six-shot lead or no six-shot lead.

But by the end of the day Morgan-Leigh Norman, 13, was just another mourner in a green-carpeted funeral procession, a red-eyed witness to the blackest golfing day of her father's life, the day he somehow spent all six of those shots and five more besides, stilled fifty thousand people and turned a glorious spring afternoon at the Masters into a four-and-a-half-hour cringe. "I been to several state fairs," an old Augusta native said, trudging home in the dying light, "and I ain't never seen nothin' like that."

It happened so quickly, it was hard to say what had been seen. A swing buried in a bunker at the start, three straight bogeys in the middle, a Maxfli in the water at the 12th and another at the 16th. Suddenly Norman's greatest rival, Nick Faldo, was walking past him straight into the green jacket that had been fashioned all week for Norman.

The last twenty minutes were unlike any seen in the previous fifty-nine Masters. Norman became a kind of dead man walking, four shots behind and all his dreams drowning in Augusta National ponds behind him. Spectators actually looked down, hoping not to make eye contact, as Norman passed among them on his way to the 18th tee. At the finish, as Faldo made a meaningless fifteen-foot birdie putt, the champion was unsure how to handle it. He barely raised his hands above his head, and he didn't yell or dance. He looked like a man in the back of church who had won a clandestine hand of gin. After he finally took the accomplice ball out of the cup, he turned to Norman, hugged him long and hard and said, "I don't know what to say. I just want to give you a hug. I feel horrible about what happened. I'm so sorry." Both men teared up.

Even for Norman, who has a master's in how to lose these things — from ahead to Tom Watson in '81, from behind to Jack Nicklaus in '86, from nowhere to Larry Mize in '87, from everywhere to Ben Crenshaw in '95 — this was gruesome. So the morning papers were right after all. They had predicted a runaway, and they had gotten it. Only the idea had been to hold an eighteen-hole parade in Norman's honor to make up for all the broken hearts and second-place crystal he had lugged home over the years. It would be his payback for having had to wait longer than any champion for his green jacket (sixteen years).

The green-jacket ceremony, however, was conducted as though Norman had been taken away by ambulance. "Our sincerest feelings go out to Greg," said Crenshaw, the presenter. "I do feel sorry for Greg," said Faldo, the recipient.

If you had been there the night before, you would not have believed what would transpire in less than twenty-four hours. In Saturday's third round Norman had stared down Faldo heroically, played him head-to-head and increased his lead from four to six shots. Afterward Norman relaxed in the dark of Augusta's first-floor locker room, the one reserved for nonchampions. He had been the last one off the course, and the attendant had turned out the lights and gone home. Norman didn't know how to turn them back on, so he just sat there in the dark, happily drained. "Your last night in this locker room," a friend had told him.

"Damn, I hope so," Norman had replied, laughing.

Then something eerie happened. A well-meaning British friend accosted Norman, held him by both shoulders, grinned wildly and said, "Greg, old boy, there's no way you can f— this up now!" Norman thanked him with a castor-oil smile and walked out into the Georgia night alone.

This *had* seemed like a happy ending that even Norman couldn't rewrite. Luck was supposed to have left him long ago and taken the car and the dog with it, but this week luck had been back with him, nuzzling his face. For instance, on Wednesday his back was hurting so badly that he left the course two hours early, unable to make much more than a half swing. "He was just so *frustrated*," said his wife, Laura. "It hadn't happened to him in forever. He kept saying, 'Why now, of all times?'"

So who calls up out of the blue? Fred Couples. He had heard the Shark was ailing, and he offered to send over his back therapist, Tom Boers, to fix him up. Boers is the miracle-thumbed genius who had fixed Couples up two weeks earlier, allowing him to win the Players Championship. He fixed Norman up too. On Thursday the Shark opened with a course-record-tying 63. Couples shot 78. "Well," said Couples's fiancée, Tawnya Dodds, half kidding, "you picked a helluva time to make Greg Norman feel like a million bucks."

On Friday, Norman had more Couples luck. At the par-3 12th, his eight-iron caught the wind, hit a bank and began rolling back toward Rae's Creek. Only it stopped inches from the water — a la Couples during his '92 win — and Norman saved par.

Through three rounds, Norman's 63-69-71–203 put him at a garish 13 under par, six shots ahead of Faldo, seven beyond Phil Mickelson, miles past everybody else. Faldo hadn't contended in a major in two years. He is in the middle of a $12 million divorce and a tabloid frenzy over his relationship with 21-year-old Brenna Cepelak, a former Arizona golfer. Faldo had tried to make his move on Saturday, but Norman had shut him down. Norman was more relaxed and playing more magnificently than he ever had among the humps and hollows and biosphere domes they call greens at the National. "I'd like to see ol' Norman win," another Augusta native said on Sunday morning. "He's just had this thing slud out from under him one too many times."

Still, there were some who went out of their way to note that where there is a Saturday-night Norman lead (seven times in majors), there are a whole lot of Sunday banana peels (only one win). "If he blows this," ESPN's Dan Patrick said on Sunday, "it will be the biggest collapse in modern golf history."

Faldo admitted that he did not expect to win. In fact, he was so nonchalant about what he assumed would be Norman's coronation walk that he got caught up watching auto racing on TV and showed up at the course a half hour behind schedule, unthinkable for someone as meticulous as he is.

But from the beginning on Sunday something in Norman's swing made you squirm. He hooked his drive at 1 into the trees and made a bogey. There was a nasty par save on 3, a bogey on 4, and a god-awful pull on 8.

Faldo, meanwhile, was as steady as rent, making 2-putt par after 2-putt par. (He 3-putted once all week.) He drilled a 4-footer on the 6th for a birdie and a 20-footer on 8 to cut the lead to 3. Then came the most catastrophic four golf holes in Norman's life.

His wedge came up six feet short of the pin on the rockface that is the 9th green and slid thirty yards back toward him, an ignominy from which he couldn't save par. Two-shot lead. Still, Norman had riddled the back nine all week: he had played those holes in 11 under going into Sunday. If ever a back nine could be a safety net, this was it.

It wasn't. On the 10th Norman put a butcherly stroke on a simple uphill chip, sending the ball eight feet past and missing the putt for a bogey. "That's when I knew," said Faldo, "things were going to be tight." One-shot lead.

Up on the hill Nick Price, Norman's best friend on the Tour, left the clubhouse looking pale. "I can't stand to watch," he said and headed to his car.

It got worse. At 11 Norman hit two perfect shots and a sweet ten-foot putt that lipped out. Then the three-foot tiddler coming back also stayed stubbornly out. No-shot lead.

Now there was an uneasiness among the dogwoods, a sickening feeling, as Norman came to the one hole you do not want to come to after blowing a six-shot lead. It is the 12th, the Drew Barrymore of par-3s: small, gorgeous, and sheer trouble. Norman had left that one ball on the bank on Friday and another in the water on Saturday, and the way he was swinging, the green must have looked like a TV tray.

"His routine is so different," said Faldo's coach, David Leadbetter. "He's standing over the ball an *incredible* amount of time. I'd say he's spending six, seven seconds longer per shot, fidgeting, moving around in ways I've never seen him do."

Behind Greg, Morgan-Leigh was praying and trying to calm Laura. "It's gonna be all right, Mom," she said. It might be, in time, but the shot definitely wasn't. Norman pushed it right of Faldo's ball, which sat happily on the green, and then watched as it slid back into the pond. Sorry, only one Couples Cling per Masters. Double bogey, Norman's fifth straight 5. For the first time all week he did not lead. Unfathomably, Faldo led by two shots. In five holes Norman had handed Faldo six shots.

The players traded birdies at the par-5 13th, Norman letting himself get talked out of going for it in two by his caddie, Tony Navarro, who argued that to hit a shot 213 yards off pine needles was asking too much of a man who had hit five greens all day. Norman and Faldo traded pars at 14 and birdies at 15, Norman missing an eagle by an inch with his chip on 15. As the ball crawled by the hole, Norman fell to his knees and then arched back on his haunches so that he looked like the vanquished Y. A. Tittle in that famous photograph. Then he toppled over, shot by an imaginary bullet. "*Really* thought that was in," he said.

So the world's No. 1–ranked player had three holes to make up two shots and avoid being the answer to the question, Who blew the biggest final-round lead in a major? "I needed to hit a hook in there," he said. "I sure hooked it." It was left. It was wet. Double bogey. Faldo by four.

Golf is the cruelest game, because eventually it will drag you out in front of the whole school, take your lunch money and slap you around. Golf can make a man look more helpless than any other sporting endeavor, except perhaps basketball when you air-ball a free throw in the clutch, and nobody we know has air-balled free throws for an afternoon on national TV. Norman shot 78. He had taken his glorious victory parade and driven it off a pier.

Afterward Faldo, whose 67 was the best score of the weekend, still couldn't believe what had transpired. Cepelak went back to their rented house to change for the traditional champion's dinner, and Faldo was left to wait outside Butler Cabin in the dusk, shoeless and almost wordless. "An amazing day," he said quietly, shaking his head. "Amazing. I don't know how it happened. He had played so great. It was the strangest turn of events I've ever seen. I *genuinely* feel for the guy. I feel so sad for him."

Cepelak is new at this business of escorting greatness to functions. When she came back, she kissed Faldo and said, quite seriously, "What are you going to wear?"

"What do I wear?" Faldo said with a grin. "Well, I've got a little something right here." He pulled on the cuffs of his Fashion Don't, the green jacket you cannot trade for with helicopters, Ferraris or money.

This day will wear on Norman forever, like it or not. This Masters will not be remembered as the third in Faldo's string of blazer thefts (he has come from three, five and six shots behind on the last day to win). Sunday will be remembered as the day Norman carved a little monument as the most tragic Masters figure since Roberto De Vicenzo, who signed an incorrect scorecard after tying for the lead after seventy-two holes in 1968 and penciled himself into infamy.

"I screwed up," Norman told the world's press, smiling. "It's all on me. I know that. But losing this Masters is not the end of the world. I let this one get away, but I still have a pretty good life. I'll wake up tomorrow, still breathing, I hope." He paused and then added, "All these hiccups I have, they must be for a reason. All this is just a test. I just don't know what the test is yet."

Later, as he was packing a red Suburban with Laura and Morgan-Leigh and his eighth second-place finish in a major and his third second in a Masters, he no longer looked like anything close to a million dollars. But whatever this day had done to him, it hadn't destroyed him. He is golf's black box, its unmeltable survivor. "I'll win here," he said. "I will. Something great is waiting for me down the line in golf. I don't know what it is, but I have to believe that. If I don't, hell, I might as well put my clubs away for good."

There were handshakes and keep-your-chin-ups all around, but something changed in Norman's face as he started the engine. Something in his eyes. Nobility and chins are easy enough to keep up in front of the crowds, but the more alone you get, the heavier they become.

And as her father wheeled slowly down Magnolia Lane, Morgan-Leigh probably didn't notice the Sunday newspaper in the back of the Suburban. She probably hadn't read in it what she will learn someday in school, that eighty-four years ago, on this same April 14, another unsinkable ship on its way to certain glory listed, gurgled and sank.

The *Titanic*.

ROGER ANGELL

Conic Projection

FROM THE NEW YORKER

LATE LAST WEEK, David Cone, the leader and prime starter on the Yankees' talented pitching staff, underwent surgery for the repair of a small aneurysm on the front of his right shoulder — on his pitching arm, that is. The operation was successful, but the news, which immediately darkens the Yankees' pennant outlook in the current campaign, came as a shock to his teammates and fans, for whom he has been a rock of certitude and accomplishment in the roiling seas of contemporary baseball. Cone has been exceptionally durable, never spending so much as a day on the disabled list over the past nine years, and if all goes well he might even be pitching again by late summer. Until that moment, there will be hovering doubts about the future of his career. It will also be a while before he knows whether the surgery will take care of the mysterious numbness that began to afflict the fingers of his right hand last month, altering his delivery. As it happened, I had spent many hours with Cone this spring, listening to him talk about his work, and, once I got past my initial flood of sympathy and outrage at this knockdown blow to a new friend, it occurred to me that the sudden sidelining of such a boringly reliable, high-octane performer might cause fans to notice Cone in more specific fashion, and perhaps better appreciate what he's been doing so well for so long.

Oddly enough, the presiding image of Cone before his hospitalization had also found him in deep trouble — bent double on the mound, with his head down by his knees, in despair and disbelief over the pitch he had just thrown. Battered with noise, burning with fatigue and combative desire, he had delivered a sinker into

the dirt that the batter exultingly accepted for ball four, moving up
three baserunners and tying the game. It was Cone's last pitch of
the 1995 season, and, for the instant, at least, it destroyed his year
and his peace of mind. Back home in New York, he went to bed
thinking about the moment, and found it waiting for him when he
woke up. For the next ten days, he stayed in his apartment, not
answering the telephone, slumping on his couch and then rest-
lessly arising, walking and staring, throwing the pitch over and over
again.

The pitch and the scene will be recognized, I think, by even the
most casual fans in New York and Seattle as the eighth-inning,
bases-loaded walk given up by Cone to the Seattle Mariners' Doug
Strange, a pinch hitter, in the fifth and final American League
divisional playoff game last October. The walked-in run tied the
score, as noted, and brought the surging Mariners even in a series
in which they had trailed from the outset; no one was entirely
surprised when they rallied for two runs in the eleventh inning to
win the thriller and eliminate the imperial Yanks. Never mind that
the Mariners went on to lose to the Cleveland Indians in the American League championship, or that the Indians themselves then fell
before the Atlanta Braves in the taut, stoutly pitched World Series.
The Mariners' brief glory in this, their first postseason effort after
nineteen years of relentless mediocrity, was a populist triumph that,
in effect, kept the Seattle baseball franchise in town. It was also a
huge boost for the new and widely disparaged extra tier of playoff
games (which had allowed the Mariners and the Yankees to meet in
the first place), and a television godsend for baseball itself at the
end of two unhappy, strike-shortened seasons. All this, one could
say, from a base on balls.

Game autopsies so often turn out this way that I sometimes think
of myself as a coroner of the pastime, with the motto *"Cherchez le
loser"* stitched on my bloody gown, and I was gratified to find that
Cone himself did not appear to find me ghoulish when I sought
him out in spring training this March in Tampa and asked him to
talk a little about the pitch. "There's been some second-guessing,"
he said. "A lot of critics think I should have thrown a fastball to
Doug Strange — they said, 'Who is he, anyway?' — but Junior Grif-
fey had hit a home run off a fastball of mine earlier in the inning,
and I didn't think I had much velocity left. I ended up throwing a

hundred and forty-seven pitches in that game, and I was running on empty. Thinking back, I was more concerned about my ability to finish my pitches than about the selection. I still believe that at any given point I can deliver any pitch in my repertoire. That was a three-and-two split-finger — I thought I could finesse my way through — but I didn't execute."

That Cone was the Yankee pitcher on the mound at this critical point is a vivid illustration of the fluid nature of modern big-time baseball. He had begun the year with the Kansas City Royals, where his 16–5 record in the strike-shortened 1994 season had earned him a Cy Young Award as the best pitcher in his league, but he was traded away to the Toronto Blue Jays just as the delayed spring training at last got under way. With both teams, it was Cone's second time around on the roster. Then, toward the end of July, he was traded to the Yankees, and his strong late-season performance — he went 4–1 in his last five starts — allowed them to squeeze into the playoffs as a wild-card entry. His combined 1995 pitching records placed him, as usual, among the league leaders in several categories — second in wins (he went 18–8 overall), fourth in strikeouts, sixth in earned run average, and first in innings pitched. Even before the season began, Cone had often been in the headlines or on the late news, as an American League representative of the Players Association. Indeed, his presence at the bitter labor negotiations and his suave postmeeting summaries of the latest deadlocked position before the cameras are surmised — by Cone and many others — as the probable cause of his swift dismissal from the Royals, once baseball resumed.

"Last year was the toughest year I've had, by far," Cone told me in the Yankees' spring clubhouse. "There was a stretch in the winter where we were living day after day in Washington hotel rooms, lobbying Congress, meeting with the president at the White House, on the phones with players and union reps, then going back to New York for more. It was impossible to stay in shape — I didn't pick up a ball — and, with the short spring training, I never did get back to even. I was traded twice, and that wild-card race with the Yankees took the last ounce of effort we had. By the time the playoffs came, I was physically and emotionally drained. The way I ended up in that game brought it all back in a rush."

Doc Gooden, who was sitting close to us at his adjoining locker, now brought his hands up in mock horror, and moaned "Oh, no! Oh, no! Too *much*, man!" and the two old Mets collapsed in laughter at the pity of it all.

Cone, who is 33, has an engagingly youthful air. His bright eyes and pale, faintly Fenian good looks (the name is Irish) have sometimes caused sportswriters to succumb to the "choirboy" epithet in describing him, but out on the mound he exudes a cold malevolence. As I wrote at the time, my wife, Carol, a long-term Mets fan, first noticed this after Cone was traded from the Mets to the Blue Jays, late in the season of 1992. "My God," she said, watching him on the tube in his strange new habiliments, "what's happened to David? He looks like an axe murderer out there."

That year, Cone's 261 strikeouts led all major league pitchers, and helped take him and Toronto all the way to the World Series; although he received no decisions, the Jays ended up winning both games he started against the Braves, and went on to a world championship. It was here, I think, that he first picked up the "hired gun" sobriquet that was heard so often again last fall, when his flexible loyalty and habitual courage and efficiency took still another team into the postseason battlegrounds. "He's like a Clint Eastwood character," a fan friend of mine said not long ago. "He comes in and saves the village, but you don't want him to stick around and marry your daughter." Cone became a free agent again at the end of 1995, and late last December, after extended negotiations with the Baltimore Orioles (and, more briefly, with the Mets), he signed a three-year, no-trade contract (with options for two subsequent seasons) with the Yankees, for nineteen and a half million dollars. The samurai was home.

So much about Cone fits the complaints and clichés aimed at modern-day ballplayers — they are overpaid, they have no loyalty, they care too much about their union — that the exceptional accomplishments of his eleven-year career must come to many as an irritating or infuriating paradox. Cone's obdurate work ethic — he is a strikeout pitcher but by no means an imperious one, and a typical inning for him requires a lot of pitches and high counts — also runs counter to the "spoiled babies" rap against today's stars. Nothing about him, in fact, is simple — least of all his pitching. Although his thousand and sixteen whiffs as of the end of last season put him second only to the Mariners' Randy Johnson in

major league strikeouts over the past five years, his fastball, which
tops out at 91 or 92 miles per hour, is distinctly secondary to the
subtle and intelligent combinations of pitches he shows the batters — the full range of slider, fastball, curve ball (he throws it as
a change of pace), and forkball sinker (the split-finger pitch) that
he delivers, in and out, to the corners of the plate, at slightly altered speeds and from higher or lower release points. (Sometimes
he drops down and goes sidearm to a right-handed hitter.) Cone
throws hard, make no mistake, and there has been as much speculation about the source of his heat — he is six feet one but looks
smaller out on the mound, perhaps because he is always a bit
hunched with concentration — as there has been (until just now)
about the amazing resiliency of his arm. Every Conean pitch goes
through the strike zone as if on a nefarious errand, and even the
fastball gnaws or bores disconcertingly, late in its journey. This
spring, Cone was mastering still another pitch — the sinking "two-
seam" fastball that the Braves' Greg Maddux used with such devas-
tating effect in the World Series last year. Who thinks the batters are
overpaid these days? Not me.

Beat writers have come to appreciate Cone's versatility as a talker
almost as much as his slider. Two hours before his first start with the
Yankees last summer, he held a clubhouse press conference to
discuss the state of his arm and his hopes for the team he had just
joined, thereby breaching a custom of mumbly reticence which the
club had inherited from its manager, Buck Showalter. Cone's responses and opinions come out in almost visible finished sentences.
When I asked him at one point why high player salaries were turning off the fans in such numbers, he said, "We'd be more popular if
we'd won a lottery, instead of being someone who's tried to perfect
his craft and put himself in a position to earn an exorbitant amount
of money."

He seemed happier when we got back to baseball. What about
the axe murderer, I said. Who was he?

"You gotta have an edge," Cone said. "You've got to have something that motivates you. You're taking this thing very seriously,
while at the same time you're trying to curtail your emotion, control yourself. There's a balance, and I think I've gotten better at
finding that. I used to pitch every game as if it was my last."

Yes. I quickly recalled a Mets game in Atlanta, early in 1990, when the umpire, Charlie Williams, blew the call on a close, second-baseman-to-pitcher (it was Cone) play at first base, and David hilariously lost it out there, screaming at length in the ump's face while two Braves baserunners came tiptoeing around, all unnoticed, to score.

More often, though, his high competitive fever brought a better result, as I noticed later that same summer, when I saw him fan the Pirates' Bobby Bonilla with a fastball for the last out in a critical inning, and then, after rushing in from the field, pound wildly and exuberantly on the dugout wall with his fists. "I was screaming and yelling," he told us later. "I was in the euphoric state of going berserk."

Cone's determination is also evident in his extreme reluctance to come out of games before they are finished. His new Yankee manager, Joe Torre, says, "David is a throwback. He starts a game and expects to finish it, and that's a vanishing American. He's a guy you can't ask to come out of a game. You've got to make that decision for him, and that can get a little scary late in the season."

Cone said that he had been brought up in the old school, with hard-bitten Royals veterans like Vida Blue and Dennis Leonard, and it was understood that when the manager came out for a late visit you always said, "I can get this guy out." He admitted that there was some speculation about the state of his arm this year. "Every time I've been traded or changed teams, I've told myself, 'Now I've got something else to drive me ahead.' This time, people are saying, 'He threw a lot of innings, a lot of pitches. Is his arm going to blow out?' There's also the size of my contract, and there's the age factor. Nothing is new. There've always been doubts about me, and I've always felt I had something to prove."

David was the youngest of four Cone kids, who grew up in the Northeast area of Kansas City; his father was a night-shift master mechanic in the Swift meatpacking plant. "Blue-collar all the way," Cone says. He describes himself as the runty kid hanging around the edges of his two brothers' crowd, hoping to get into the action. He got into Little League, but he couldn't play baseball at Rockhurst High School, because there was no diamond and no team; he made do with the Ban Johnson League, a summer circuit for high-

school and college-age kids. He showed up at a tryout camp staged
by the Royals, and was noticed. The spring after he turned 18, a
Royals scout signed him. It took Cone five years to make his way up
to the majors (a knee injury disabled him for an entire season), and
the next spring, in 1987, he was traded to the Mets.

Again and again in our talks, Cone referred to himself as an
"outsider" or an "orphan" in baseball, and the cast of eccentrics and
high-wire performers and big-salary egos he found waiting for him
in the clubhouse of those World Champion Mets — Lenny Dykstra,
Gary Carter, Roger McDowell, Keith Hernandez, Doc and Mookie,
Bobby O., Straw, and the rest — must have felt Dickensian, at the
least. Cone gave up ten runs in his first career start, and the next
day found a softball on his clubhouse chair, along with the note
"This is what your fastball looked like yesterday."

"I was devastated," Cone said. "Those were rough times, but
they taught me that you had to learn to take a shot. You had to
have some substance, develop some character in a hurry." Help, it
turned out, was no farther away than first base, where Keith Hernandez was giving his celebrated in-game seminars. "He was the guy
who taught me, early on," Cone went on. "I'd look over there, and
he'd be with me, pitch to pitch. That look in his eye, that intensity
— he was so far into the game, always a pitch or a batter ahead,
talking situations. He'd get right in your face, challenge you to get
the job done. Watching him, I felt, I want to play like that — that's
the style I want to emulate."

Those Mets of the late eighties and early nineties were a powerful
presence in the city, a celebrity force majeure, but they were always
a little short on the field. Heavily favored to sweep up another
world championship in 1988 (they won a hundred games, as Cone
was posting a 20–3 record), they fell before the Dodgers in the
league championships — a seismic shock from which they never
quite recovered. Cone had become a great strikeout pitcher (he
would fan nineteen batters one night down in Philadelphia), another star on a team of stars, but the high salaries and notoriety and
a penchant for second place had begun to replace some simpler
earlier hopes about the club. Drugs became the main clubhouse
news about the Mets for a time, while Cone, a dedicated nighthawk,
was named, along with others, in allegations of sexual improprie-
ties. (In the end, no charges were brought.)

"I was pretty wild," Cone says now. "There was some hard living there for a while. I had a girlfriend, Lynn DiGioia, and we had rocky times. We've been together ten years, and, thanks to her, we made it through." He and Lynn, a Connecticut real-estate agent, were married in the fall of 1994, and live in an apartment on the East Side. When David once told me that he had been "just a kid from Kansas City" at the time he and Lynn first met, and that she had taught him everything about New York, I was reminded again how much a child a professional athlete often remains, no matter how suave or experienced he appears within the arena. Kid Cone still lives somewhere inside the cold-eyed mound stopper, and sometimes jumps out. On Cone's very first road trip after rejoining the Royals, he unstrapped his seat belt when their airliner was about to touch down, threw his airline magazine (with its airline plastic cover) on the floor, and surfed the length of the aisle.

Poor performance more than poor image broke up the famous Mets, but management never stopped poking at the team — knocking pieces off, it seemed. Dykstra departed early (the Mets have yet to find his replacement in center field), then Gary Carter and, in 1990, manager Davey Johnson. Cone had already lost his closest friends on the club, Bobby Ojeda and Ron Darling, by the time he himself was traded to the Blue Jays in 1992, but the move still came as a shock. One of his last starts for the Mets had been a 1–0 complete-game shutout win over the Giants. The Mets were said to feel uneasy about Cone's price as a coming free agent, but there were off-the-record murmurings that he was too small to be throwing as many innings and strikeouts as he did, and that his arm could not be expected to stand up much longer. That was $748\frac{1}{3}$ innings and 519 strikeouts ago.

"We underachieved," Cone says of his old club, "but that team was broken up too soon. New York City belonged to the Mets then, and we were all proud of that. Part of me will always be a Met."

Early one morning in Tampa, Cone and I sat alone in the Yankee dugout while he talked pitching and showed me, with a ball, how he held each offering in his celebrated congeries — fastball, slider, his skulky back-door slider (it nips the outside corner to a left-handed batter), split-finger, and curve. Both varieties of slider depart from the norm, he said, because he throws them with his forefinger —

rather than his middle finger — pressing hard along a seam. Holding the ball across the seams in the standard fastball grip, he turned his hand over and pointed to his little finger, which was oddly gnarled, twisted away from the ball. "I shattered that pinkie when I was bunting once, years ago," he said. "It changes the way I grab the ball, and that gives me a natural cutting action on the fastball, so it bores away from right-handed batters. Three-Finger Cone. Listen — any advantage you can get."

I quickly realized that I would need morphing capability to make much of this stuff come clear on the page, but Cone's passion for his trade was eloquent. "I learned to throw the slider way back when I was playing Wiffle Ball with my brothers," he said at one point. "If you do it right, your fingers sort of pull across when you finish the pitch. It's like a painter finishing a brushstroke." He made a little de Kooning swash through the air.

Each pitch or pitching concept, I noticed, came with an attribution. Luis Tiant, the old Red Sox fandango artist — observed by 12-year-old David on television during the 1975 World Series — had first lured him toward the risks and glories of the mound. Playing winter ball in Puerto Rico while still in the minors, Cone picked up the split-finger from an ex-big-leaguer, Diego Segui — and then learned its refinement (a touch of thumb on the side of the ball, which causes the pitch to change its mind, diving back toward a right-handed batter's feet) from the grand theorist of the delivery, Roger Craig. "I've begun to develop a real feel for that pitch," Cone said. He sounded as if he were talking about a faithful hunting dog. He said that the value of changing speeds — "the philosophy of stretching the batters out" — often comes late in a pitcher's development, and here his guru had been Ron Darling. Whenever Cone changed clubs, it seemed, he had used the daunting shift of fortune as a means of consulting new pitching coaches — Bruce Kison, of the Royals; Galen Cisco, of the Blue Jays; Nardi Contreras with last year's Yankees — and new teammates as well. When he first came to the Jays, second baseman Robbie Alomar told him that he had been tipping off his split-finger pitch with a little movement of his glove. Cone thanked him and got rid of it.

The new two-seam fastball was coming slowly, Cone told me. "If you aim it at a left-handed batter's hip, it should be back over the plate at the last minute. If he tries to pull it, best he can do is foul it off, but most times he'll take it for a strike. But it's difficult to throw — you have to keep your hand on top and follow through, as if you were shooting a basket."

Was this a *fifth* pitch? I asked.

"Well, maybe," Cone said. "And then there are the different release points. That's the kicker. Don't let the batter be too sure where the pitch is coming from." He saw my expression and changed his tone. "Listen, the batters are working, too. Everybody tapes now — every pitcher is taped, every game, and the batters are looking. Tony Gwynn has a whole library of pitchers and situations. We can't tape back, because there are too many batters, but you have to do something — keep working, keep adding — just to stay even. It's tough out there, and it never ends."

Cone's new season started scarily, when he experienced increasing numbness in his pitching hand. His problems had begun with a victory on Opening Day, when he shut out the Indians over seven innings but lost feeling for the ball late on a wintry afternoon. After his fourth start, a losing effort against the Milwaukee Brewers, who racked him for nine hits in five innings, his right ring finger was blue and he felt twinges in his forearm. This was a new and distressing experience in his career. He won his next outing, against the Royals, but left the game after five innings, and soon underwent medical probing at Columbia-Presbyterian Medical Center. An angiogram excluded the possibility of a blood clot, and, once the doctors put him on an extended regimen of blood thinners, he began to feel better. No one — least of all David himself — knew what to expect when he walked out to face the White Sox, up at the Stadium, on the fifth Thursday of the season.

I was anxious for him at the outset, when he looked stiff and uncertain in his motion, and only a fortuitous double play took him out of difficulties. In the next stanza, he dropped down to strike out Danny Tartabull with a sudden sidearm delivery, ending the inning, and, just that quickly, the tension and foreboding seemed to drain out of the evening. Cone, set free, began to enjoy himself, unsettling the Chicago batters with first-pitch, off-speed curve balls for called strikes and slipping a cutting fastball under their fists. Before the game, he had said he would omit the split-finger, sparing his arm, but he threw an absolute Vermeer to Harold Baines in the fourth, and then fanned the next man, Robin Ventura, with another beauty. Good pitching, when the man out there is on a roll, always looks unfair. Cone went the full distance, striking out eight and giving up a lone unearned run, while his teammates, joining the party, banged four home runs and won by 5–1. This has been a terrible year for the pitchers, but cool-hand Dave had run his current record to 4–1, with an earned-run mark of 2.03, the best in the league.

Cone was relieved and upbeat in the clubhouse. "It's been a long time since I was that free and easy and effortless," he said. "I've had a lot of anxiety."

But his easy days were over. Later that week, the numbness and chilliness returned to his pitching hand, now afflicting the palm as well. Cone, in typical fashion, wanted to persist by pitching against the Tigers on his appointed day in the rotation, but he was at last persuaded to reenter the hospital for more extensive testing. The decision to operate was made two days later.

That news, and now the beginnings of Cone's anxious, closely watched period of recovery, have made me think back to that last triumphant start and to rerun it, so to speak, in the not-so-instant replay of my mind. Watching him that night from my seat in the press box, I had an intimate view of each slider, fastball, and spinning curve working inside or just outside the invisible seven-sided box of the strike zone, and at moments I sensed both the logic and the exulting pride that linked them together. Cone in mid-windup, staring through the dark slot formed by his cap brim and his upraised left shoulder, looked like a sniper. In talking to him at length, I had sometimes found a blandness, almost an absence of personality, in his affable manner and his ready answers to my questions. Out on the mound, on a hard night, no part of him was missing.

TOM BOSWELL

Controlling Force

FROM PLAYBOY

GREG MADDUX, the best pitcher since Sandy Koufax, is warming up in the Atlanta Braves' bullpen. Danny Bowden, 11, and Matt Korpi, 10, think they've gone to someplace better than heaven. They haven't died. But they do have front-row seats just ten feet behind the Braves' bullpen catcher. From behind a screen the boys can watch Maddux from a perch almost as good as the view an umpire gets.

The two children, decked out in baseball regalia from team caps to logo-laden shirts, are quiet as Maddux throws dozens of pitches.

"Looks like Greg Maddux, right?" says Matt finally, perplexed.

"Yeah," says Danny, pointing to the number 31 on the pitcher's back.

"I thought it was," says Matt.

"He's not even warming up yet," says Danny.

Maddux' motion is so compact and controlled it's hard to tell if he is making an effort. All his gestures — stretch, stride, leg kick — are so abbreviated they seem to be a preparation to make some real baseball motion. He's finished his delivery while you're still waiting for him to get up a head of steam. His pitches smack the catcher's glove with a small crack. Some arrive silently.

Maddux' pitches don't move much, either. A few feet in front of home plate, just as Danny and Matt are about to lose sight of the ball in front of the catcher, Maddux' pitches make quick but un-dramatic swerves. Some go down, some break in or out, others move a bit down and in or a tad down and away. It's hard to call these throws — which deviate only three to six inches off plumb — pitches at all. Playing catch, you can make a ball move as much.

Every Maddux pitch seems to travel about the same speed — but not exactly so. Each throw covers the last few feet a bit faster or a bit slower than the previous one. Occasionally, Maddux throws curve balls. They roll sharply. Good college quality. But to say they break would be generous.

On an adjacent mound, Steve Avery starts to throw. The sound is like cherry bombs blowing up soda cans. Danny and Matt arch their necks to see Avery. But those seats are taken. They are stuck with watching the 30-year-old who's won the past four National League Cy Young Awards.

"If Greg was throwing as fast as he could," says Danny, "we'd be ducking."

Later, Maddux is told about the two boys. He puts a pinch of snuff under his upper lip and adjusts his wire-rimmed glasses. He's not six feet tall, as the roster says, though he might live up to the 170 pounds. His eyebrows and forehead sometimes twitch involuntarily, like those of a tense nerd in school. His smile is shy, his voice so soft it's a strain to hear. "I hate to disappoint those kids, but I was throwing as hard as I can.

"That's all I've got."

If you want a series of interviews with a star athlete and you don't already have a personal history with him, this is what usually happens: You have to perform the goddamn twelve labors of Hercules.

You talk to his agent, his lawyer, his general manager, his team's public relations director. Your people talk to his people. You block out time. You do a courtship dance. The process can take weeks. Perhaps he blows you off. Finally, you go to a steakhouse or play golf or visit him in his home. But, underneath it all, here's the basic ground rule and the subtext: He's a star.

This is how it works with Greg Maddux. You walk up to him in the clubhouse and introduce yourself. He says, "*Playboy*, huh? Do I get to pose?"

You start chatting. John Smoltz walks past with a bagful of McDonald's cheeseburgers. Maddux mooches one. "Need grease," he says to appalled pitching coach Leo Mazzone, who hates antihealth food. "Gotta make that sinker drop."

Sitting hunched at his locker, Maddux munches his impromptu fast-food meal. He signs balls. He opens fan mail. And he talks — for an hour and a half, about any subject under the sun. He's shy, his voice quiet. It's obvious he loves to talk pitching theory. It's his passion. But he doesn't mind talking about himself either, though he finds the subject inherently less interesting. Finally, he says, "Gotta go do my running. Come back any time."

Greg Maddux has nothing to sell and little to hide. He has no image to cultivate or protect because he hasn't bothered to create one. He has no major commercial endorsements. He has no public persona whatsoever. He may be the most widely known athlete in American history who can walk down any street and go unrecognized. "Around the ballpark, they know who you are," he says, "but you go a couple of miles up the road, dude, they got no clue."

Once, when asked why he doesn't do commercials or promote himself, Maddux explained why a wife (Kathy), a 2-year-old daughter (Amanda), two dogs, one set of golf clubs with Mickey Mouse head covers, and a lot of movie rentals constitute his idea of a perfectly organized life. "I like my time off. I like golf. I like to be with my family. I just like to get up and do nothing."

To say that Maddux' candor is disarming would be an understatement. For example, his teammates insist the one aspect of his character that's unknown is his humor. "He's very funny," says Atlanta manager Bobby Cox. "But it's hard to think of anything in particular." Teammates can't produce illustrations either. "They're just covering for me," says Maddux, not bothering to cover himself. "They won't give examples because you can't print any of it. With my sense of humor, the more disgusting something is, the funnier it is to me.

"My brother probably started it," he adds, meaning 34-year-old Mike, now a Red Sox pitcher. "You know how you look up to your big brother. If you see him doing something vulgar and enjoying it, you learn to enjoy it and appreciate it, too. We had a lot of fun seeing how vulgar we could be in front of our sister."

There's something truly special about Maddux. No, not his mooning. Everybody in baseball senses his uniqueness. The realization that he's radically different starts as soon as you see him. His shoulders slope. He has no muscles to speak of. When he jogs, his stomach sticks out in front of him. An average-size man who can't run fast or jump high and who does not possess a single knee-buckling pitch should not have the best back-to-back earned run averages for the past two seasons since Walter Johnson in 1918 and 1919.

"I can't believe a regular-size guy with the stuff he has can do what he's done," says teammate David Justice. "It shouldn't be possible." Or as another teammate says, "I just saw Greg in the training room. He's working out with his four-ounce weights."

Even beyond his poise on the mound and his spooky control, there's more to Maddux. His very core — his temperament, his approach to everything — mystifies and attracts those around him. He has a secret, though he may not know it or lay claim to it. Without trying, he's a guru. In something as simple as wind sprints, the whole team takes its cue from Maddux. With two dozen players spread across the outfield, Maddux lines up out by the warning track. Gradually, you realize his teammates cut their eyes toward Maddux to see when he'll begin his next 50-yard run. When he breaks, they all follow a millisecond later. Maddux doesn't look at anybody.

"It's not his job to lead the sprints. But it wouldn't surprise me if they pick up his rhythm. They watch *everything* he does," says Braves general manager John Schuerholz. "Wouldn't you?"

The baseball subculture delightedly testifies to this "something" about Maddux and loves to speculate about it. "They say you have to have a big ego to be a great athlete. He must be the exception that proves the rule. He sure doesn't need much from a manager," says Cox. "He just loves to watch the game, learn the game, and then play the game."

"These days, athletes have the reputation of being rich, spoiled babies," says the Braves' Tom Glavine, who's the only pitcher in the past five seasons with more wins (91) than Maddux (90). "Greg is so far on the other end of the spectrum. If you found the most arrogant ballplayer there is, then his opposite would be Greg.

"He's the best pitcher of our era. But if people could see how he acts around us, they'd be mind-boggled. He never gives the impression he thinks he's anywhere near as good as he is. That's what's so refreshing about him," says Glavine.

Last season, two of the Braves' front-office personnel were leav-

ing the park. "Where you headed?" asked Maddux. "Burger King,"
they said. "Come with you?" asked Maddux. "He's got a $28 million
contract, but it felt perfectly natural for him to come to Burger
King with us," said the Braves employee.

"Off the field, he's like a kid in a man's body," says Rafael Pal-
meiro, a former Cubs teammate.

Maddux' pitching is simply the manifestation of something rare
and probably enviable within him. Let's not push this too hard. It's
a mean old world with lots buried deep. But he might be happy.

He actually says, without provisos, "I'm very happy with myself."
He's not bragging. He simply applies the Golden Rule to himself.
He treats himself as he would treat others. Since he's unfailingly
generous to others, he's also kind to himself. He allows himself to
be happy. Who would suspect that modernity's chimera — the uni-
fied sensibility — might be found inside a baseball pitcher?

If you try to make Maddux complex, you won't do justice to his
simplicity. He's a sort of accidental wise man. When you listen to
him talk, you'd swear he's doing a slacker's paraphrase of Ralph
Waldo Emerson, Michel de Montaigne, or Warren Buffett. Think of
all those sensible passages you've underlined and thought, If only I
could live like that. But, of course, I can't. I'm too screwed up.
Maddux hasn't read the books. He might not understand them if
he did. But, in some sense, he lives them.

Maddux has the guileless gifts of moderation and common sense
that sometimes lead an innocent through the world's maze as if he
were blessed. You want to grab him and say, "You've got something
the world craves. And you don't even know you have it. That's really
annoying." But you can't stay miffed at Greg Maddux. You just hope
some of it rubs off.

Maddux likes to watch. He's the ultimate baseball fan. Nothing is
more riveting to him than a three-hour ball game on a hot summer
night. Baseball's most addictive charm is the illusion that, if you
study the game and its people closely enough and long enough,
you can almost live a split second in the future. Love of detail gives
birth to a sixth sense.

Part of Maddux lore holds that, a couple of years ago, he warned
teammates that a foul ball would be hit into the dugout on the next
pitch. Four times that season he made his offhand prediction.

Three times, the foul ball arrived. Anybody can, occasionally, call a home run one pitch in advance. What Maddux did is like calling the row and seat number in the bleachers.

A knack for observation runs in the Maddux family. After retiring from the military, Maddux' father became a part-time poker dealer at the MGM Grand in Las Vegas. Life in the casinos is all about one thing: keeping your eyes open. If you don't, your wallet will be gone or you'll be dealt to off the bottom. If you don't, you won't know what cards are out or who blinks when he bluffs.

"I'll go and watch him deal or join the game and give him a hard time," says Greg. "I'll say, 'He's not a good dad. He never deals me a winning hand.'" Then, Maddux watches to see how people take his remark. What's the spin? What's the count? What's the tendency? What does every gesture mean?

Since childhood, Greg has been accused of having an obscene amount of luck. His family nickname: Nate Luck. Yet maybe it's not all mere good fortune. By the third grade, Greg was the Maddux who won at Concentration, the memory card game. As an adult, he's a successful system blackjack player in the casinos and a dangerously observant poker player. His agent, despite his advanced degree, is hopeless against Maddux at *Jeopardy!* "Shallow men believe in luck," said Emerson.

Maddux won't talk about current players. But ask him about anybody who's retired. Then you'll see the level of observation that makes him great.

"If you could get Dale Murphy to miss one fastball," says Maddux, "then you could throw him changeups."

Translated from the baseballese, this means Murphy was vain about his ability to hit the fastball. If he couldn't time the fastball, his confidence was under attack. If you snuck a fastball by him, he'd obsess on that one pitch until he proved to himself that he was back in sync.

"The only danger with Murphy was that one fastball. If you could get away with it — maybe up and in for a foul ball — then you could even throw a mistake changeup."

A mistake changeup is a mush ball that floats right down the center of the plate. Your grandmother could cream it. But if Maddux set up Murphy correctly, then he honestly felt he could throw the worst pitch on earth with impunity, with total confidence, and know that a man with 399 career home runs, two MVP awards, and a shot at the Hall of Fame would strike out.

"Mike Schmidt was the same way, but with the slider," says Maddux. "If you could make him swing and miss at the slider just off the outside corner, then he would give up on the fastball away."

So, here's the ideal Maddux sequence to Schmidt: start with a fastball on the low outside corner for strike one. Schmidt would probably take it because few sluggers chase the first pitch, especially if it's on the edge of the plate. That first pitch would logically set up the next: a hard slider. However, Maddux would aim it a few inches over the plate so it would resemble the previous fastball, but more tempting. Please swing: that would be Maddux' thought. Because if Schmidt did, then Maddux had him dead — not only on that pitch, but on the next one, too.

If Schmidt swung at that second-pitch slider, he couldn't hit it, because the pitch would end up out of the strike zone. And that would prey on Schmidt's mind. Early in Schmidt's career, he set humiliating strikeout records because he chased breaking balls low and away. That's why Schmidt would give up on the fastball after missing the slider. He wouldn't want to look bad twice in a row.

For the third strike, Maddux would throw a fastball that started out as though it would be an inch or two outside. But Maddux can make his fastball tail in or out a couple of inches in either direction. So, he would bend it back over the outside corner. And Schmidt, who hit 548 home runs, would take it for strike three.

"But I faced them only at the end of their careers, when their bats had slowed down," adds Maddux, not wanting to slight an opponent.

Last year in the playoffs, Maddux struck out Reggie Sanders, the Reds' best hitter, on a changeup with the bases loaded. However, it wasn't actually a changeup that fanned him. It wasn't even a pitch Sanders saw in that at-bat.

"Early in the game," says Maddux, "I had thrown him a very good down-and-in fastball that he fouled off. He wouldn't have hit it that hard unless he had been looking for it. He cheated to get to it. That meant he was really aware of the fastball running in on him." In other words, the pitch Sanders coldcocked early in the game was really the pitch he feared.

What do you do next time you face him? You throw the pitch

that, both in location and speed, is opposite to a fastball that runs into a righty's hands: a changeup on the outside corner. Maddux did. Sanders missed it by a foot.

Sometimes Maddux seems to be the only pitcher who's completely convinced of the difficulty — the near impossibility — of hitting a baseball consistently hard if it's thrown accurately and never twice in a row at the same speed.

"The hardest thing in the world, really, is to hit a baseball," says Maddux. "Even good hitters have to cut off half the plate. They look for the ball inside or outside. But they can't protect the whole plate. They can look for hard stuff or offspeed stuff. But they can't look for one and hit the other."

Perhaps Maddux' greatest insight into the suffering of hitters is that, for all practical baseball purposes, they're blind. The human eye is simply not good enough — either at judging speed or picking up spin — for a batter to hit a baseball consistently hard, unless it is thrown near the heart of the plate.

"You don't have to throw hard, because people can't judge speed, anyway," says Maddux. "We can go out on the freeway right now and we can't tell 80 miles per hour from 70 mph unless one car is passing the other. And if we stay there long enough, 70 mph starts to look like 40 mph. Your eye adjusts if it sees the same speed over and over. It's the same to a hitter. If he sees 95–95–95, it starts to look like 50 to him. Eventually, he can time it. You can be more effective throwing 90 to 80, and changing speeds with good location. In fact, you can be almost as effective working between 80 and 70."

Now Maddux is rolling. Nothing makes him happier than convincing himself of the most central truth in his job: He's the dealer, he's the house, he has the percentages on his side. All he has to do is use the cruel odds at the core of the game to torment the hitters into submission. He may be a little guy with glasses and no flashy pitches. But he knows something batters don't. He's found a method that renders them helpless. And he can do it over and over, year after year, just like his dad dealing stud. They'll never beat the casino. That Las Vegas confidence, his knowledge of the tricks of the game, gives him a chilly calm.

"You can pitch in and out, but you can also pitch back and forth," he says. By varying the speed on his fastball, he can make it arrive at the same spot a couple of feet sooner or a couple of feet later. "The hitter has only a three-inch sweet spot on the bat. If you can make the ball break just three inches, he can't see it if the break comes late. Nobody sees the ball hit the bat. They lose sight of it before that. It's late break, not amount of break, that matters. The closer you are to a moving object, the harder it is to see."

It's not just speed that stumps hitters. Few can pick up the rotation on the ball, either. Ted Williams said he could. Sometimes. "If hitters could recognize spin, everybody would hit .500," says Maddux.

But they can't. So they don't.

Maddux assumes, apparently correctly, that so long as his pitches break late, when they're less than ten feet from the plate, no living hitter has good enough eyesight to know what kind of pitch he's swinging at.

"Unless you help them, they don't know," Maddux says. "Don Sutton said to make sure all your pitches look the same when they're five feet out of your hand. Make everything come out of the same circle [i.e., the same release point] with the same arm speed. Make everything look the same. Then find ways to make the ball end up in different places and at different speeds. The more ways you can put it in more places at more speeds, the better. That's pitching."

No wonder those kids were bored watching Maddux. They were looking for big, breaking pitches — curves or split-finger fastballs that tumble. Maddux just wants that late, quick break. "If you want the pitch to break later, throw it harder. If you want it to break more, throw it easier," says Maddux. "It's just like bowling. If you want the ball to hook more, throw it easier. If you want a tighter line, throw it harder."

Maddux has the hallmark of the original thinker: He can simplify what others find complex. He sees the idea that runs through the welter of data.

For example, Maddux uses every part of the plate except the top of the strike zone. Even with his legendary control, he rarely tries to get a hitter to chase a high fastball, even if that's the batter's known weakness.

"Think about it," he says. "The only people who can pitch up successfully are the ones who, like Don Sutton or Nolan Ryan, have the big overhand curve ball." The hitter fears that the curve will drop in for a strike, even though it starts well above the zone. So, watching for the dastardly curve, he mistakes the fastball for the hook and chases it.

"To get a hitter to chase bad pitches, you have to have two pitches that look the same, but one of them ends up a strike and the other one doesn't," says Maddux. "That's why Nolan Ryan could pitch higher than high. When I pitch up, I don't get swings. But guys such as Tom Glavine, Billy Swift, and me, who have good sinkers and changeups, can do the same thing at the bottom of the strike zone. We can pitch lower than low."

If Maddux starts you off with a four-seam fastball at the knees for a strike, what do you do when the next pitch is apparently identical? Will it be another fastball for a strike? Will it be the two-seam sinker that ends up at your shins, seducing you into a weak, lunging ground ball? Or will it be the changeup that never seems to arrive, then finishes at your ankles as you strike out foolishly?

Of all the many theories concocted by veteran pitchers in the past twenty years, Maddux seems to have culled from the best, or else discovered on his own. For example, at the end of his career, 288-game winner Tommy John explained that he had always "subtracted one ball" from the count posted on the scoreboard. He trusted his control so much that he didn't fear walks. Far more important, he wanted a mental edge over the hitter. *They never knew the real count.* The count in John's head was the count that would inform the pitch selection. Even with the bases loaded and three balls on the hitter, John still pretended that he had only two balls on the batter. "But there's no base open," John was told. "Sure there is," he answered. "Home plate's open. It's only one run. A home run gives 'em four."

"I wouldn't be surprised if Greg does that, too. It feels that way," says Cox. "But sometimes it seems like he adds a ball to the count. On 0 and 2, he never wastes a pitch. He throws what other pitchers might throw on 1 and 2."

For decades, the Orioles have taught that the key to pitching is studying the hitter's reaction to the previous pitch. "If a hitter is late on a fastball on the outside corner and fouls it over the dugout, what do you throw on the next pitch? There's only one correct answer," says Baltimore pitching coach and Cy Young winner Mike

Flanagan. "He's waiting, looking for a curve or changeup. That's why he's swinging so late. Well, if he can't get around in time on an outside fastball, then he sure can't get around on one on the inside corner. It takes longer to get the bat over the plate on the inside pitch. You have to clear your hips and get your hands in front of the plate. If they're late on your outside fastball, then always pound 'em inside."

Many teams construct elaborate game plans for pitching to the opposing lineup; the football mentality takes control. Big thinking is nice. Maddux is for it. But it's the little stuff that's crucial. "What you remember from facing hitters in the past, or from scouting reports, is a starting point," he says. "But the last pitch is 90 percent of it. You react to what you just saw. What's he trying to do? If his back foot gets pigeon-toed, is he trying to pull the ball? If his back foot is open, is he looking to go the other way?

"If he's up on the plate, it usually means he likes the ball in. If he stands off the plate, he likes it away. Seems like it would be the other way around, but it's not. That's getting way too smart," says Maddux, shaking his head disgustedly at getting carried away with analysis. "There's such a fine line between doing what you do best and going after a hitter's weakness."

Yes, that's an eternal baseball dilemma. Pitch from strength or to weakness? There's no answer. Except Maddux has an answer. "It's an easy decision," he says. "You pitch to weakness — even if it's not your strength — when it can't hurt you. Like if you have a lead or nobody is on base. And you pitch from weakness where it can't hurt you. I'm not a breaking-ball pitcher. If I use my curve in a big spot, I'll throw it in the dirt to see if he'll chase it."

On any subject except pitching, you couldn't drag a pithy phrase out of Maddux with pliers. But as soon as he talks about his art, it's all brand-new stuff and boiled to the nub.

To look at him, you'd hardly spot Maddux for a contrarian. But he is, to the bone. When the Braves travel, the other players use expensive, identical, team-issued suitcases. Maddux uses a battered bag covered with stickers. Hence, no aggravation. Nobody takes his bag by mistake. In baseball, where century-old orthodoxy coats every concept, Maddux sees a world where everybody else has lots of big stuff backward.

In a jam a pitcher is supposed to "reach back" — throw harder and call up that extra adrenaline. It's a test of manhood, right? Maddux calls it a crock.

"I lost enough games trying to put more on. Finally, I said, 'Maybe I ought to try to take more off.'" That was Maddux' first career breakthrough. His first two seasons, he was battered (8–18), sent back to the minors, and considered a marginal prospect. "You get beat enough, eventually you change. I was pretty much forced to change," he says.

"Guys who are capable of putting more on, you can count on one hand — Dwight Gooden, Steve Avery. That's a special gift. I'm not physically capable of it. But everybody is capable of learning to take more off. Some do it better than others."

Maddux simply views his approach as an obvious response to raw necessity. Does the "take more off" philosophy require any special gift? "It takes a little more trust in yourself," says Maddux.

A little more trust? Yes, you could say that. Imagine you are Maddux. Let's see, the game and maybe the season are on the line. What should you do? You're tired. The bases are loaded. Barry Bonds is at bat. You've lost something off your fastball. Eureka, you've got it! You'll throw a fastball, but not a very fast one. Instead, you'll tail it away maybe another inch. And throw it in a great spot. Then come back with a changeup. But, remember, throw it even slower than normal to offer enough contrast to the fastball.

Maddux is sublimely indifferent to conventional wisdom. He rethinks every pitching proposition from scratch. "One man that has a mind and knows it can always beat ten men who haven't and don't," said George Bernard Shaw. Maddux certainly knows his mind, and he beats nine men at a time regularly. No pitcher throws as many fastball strikes on the inside corner as Maddux. It may be his greatest point of pride.

Maddux could always tail his fastball into righties, jamming them. But left-handed hitters drove him crazy. He could not attack the inside corner because he couldn't throw hard enough. He needed a pitch that would bear in to lefties, breaking their bat handles. The pitch is called a cutter, and when Maddux developed one four years ago, it transformed him.

"The biggest jump was when I learned to throw the cut fastball," he says. Since then, nobody else has won the National League Cy Young Award.

Pitching orthodoxy says that the outside corner belongs to the pitcher and the inside corner to the hitter. You should visit the inside corner, the saying goes, but nobody can live there. Well, the orthodoxy is wrong. Maddux knows it. "The game has changed," he says. "These days, you get more strikes on the inside and you get 'em out inside. Hitters used to concede the outside corner. But it was a different era back then. Pitchers still feel like they should stay away from the inside half."

They're wrong. The hitting theories of Charlie Lau and his disciples, such as Walt Hriniak, have permeated batting cages for fifteen years. Big, strong hitters now stand off the plate, charge toward the dish as they stride, then pummel the ball on the outside half of the plate just as though they were extending their arms to drive a golf ball off a tee. The day of the dead-pull hitter is long gone. But pitching coaches don't seem to know it. Now, home run champions are alley hitters who get their candy from one power alley to the other. To get them out, you have to tie them up inside.

Many pitchers don't have the guts for the work. Modern hitters know that the fastball on the fists is their weakness, so, if you come in their kitchen, they threaten to visit the mound and beat you to a pulp with those fists.

In last year's Series, Maddux threw underneath Eddie Murray's hat, clearing both benches. That's Maddux. Charge the plate on him and you take your life in your hands. Even as a rookie he challenged hitters, even the biggest. Once, he stood on the mound and screamed at six-foot-five, 250-pound Dave Parker. In a Cubs meeting, he interrupted to ask the sign for the knockdown pitch.

Lots of pitchers study film of hitters. Maddux, however, even watches ESPN highlights to test his pet inside-outside theory. "Watch when they show all the home runs hit that day," he says. "The majority are from the middle away, not the middle in. The little guys still hit home runs on the inside pitches, but the big sluggers hit the outside pitch."

So, virtually every other pitcher has it backward. The inside half is the safer half. As they say on Wall Street, you can't make the real big money unless you have a different opinion — and it turns out to be right.

Celebrity has replaced wealth as the great American aphrodisiac. That's why Maddux stumps us. If he despised fame, like a grouch, then we might dismiss him as a crank. He can't handle it, we'd say, or he fears it. He doesn't want to admit how high he has climbed because he'd be twice as scared about the eventual fall. But that's not Maddux. When it comes to the modern religion of fame, he's neither a believer nor an atheist, nor even an agnostic. He's as peculiar as a man to whom the existence of God has never seemed to be an interesting question.

"I've never liked arrogant people," says Maddux. "When I got to the majors with the Cubs in 1986, I saw enough of it. I thought, I don't want to be like that. You watch people. You see who you want to be like. In that clubhouse, I wanted to be like Ryne Sandberg, Scott Sanderson, and Rick Sutcliffe."

Not exactly three of a kind. Sandberg was classy but morosely silent, Sanderson a studious type, and Sutcliffe a six-foot-seven, red-bearded, hot-tempered, fiercely loyal good old boy. What they had in common was a realistic sense of themselves as normal people who happened to work an abnormal job.

"I grew up in a military culture where nobody is better than anybody else. Everybody lived in the same kind of house, just with a different number on the door," says Maddux. "We had discipline and all that. But we didn't go overboard about it. We were Air Force, not Marines or Army."

The incidents of his upbringing always seemed to help Maddux keep himself in perspective. He had a classic stage father. Dave Maddux was a fine fast-pitch softball pitcher for twenty-two years and vowed that if he ever had sons, he'd do what Mickey Mantle's father did: teach them baseball from the cradle. Every afternoon at 3:30, Dave would take Mike and Greg into the back yard for two or three hours of baseball before dinner.

Because Mike is nearly five years older, Greg had the dual advantages of adult instruction and a big brother who beat the hell out of him and forced him to develop fast just to survive. Mike was bigger. Mike was the extrovert. Mike was a star at every level, headed to the majors in the game their father adored.

Greg had a choice: He could become a fierce competitor. Or he could be an exile from the male side of the Maddux family. Greg insists that "my parents were real good about letting us make our own decisions. One year I didn't play baseball at all." Believe that if you want. Or you can look at the evidence. Maddux competes at everything. All the time. From golf to Game Gear. When he goes to minor league hockey games with Kathy, they even keep score of who wins the Name That Tune contest. Or, rather, Greg keeps a running score for the whole season.

"Greg is a playful perfectionist," says Braves coach Jimy Williams. That's a rare combination. Somehow, Maddux maintains a sense of relaxed fun while, simultaneously, being more focused and driven to succeed than almost anybody else.

"Sometimes he frustrates pitchers," says Glavine. "He'll throw a nine-inning, two-run game and talk about how bad he was and how lucky he was. We'll just look at him and say, 'We don't want to hear it.'"

The Dodgers once called Orel Hershiser "Bulldog" because the nickname matched his soul even though it contradicted his choir-boy face. Maddux' nickname is Mad Dog. It seems incongruous to those who don't really know him. Yet it's completely appropriate to those who watch him compete every fifth day.

Even other successful obsessives — such as John Schuerholz — hold Maddux in awe. "He's so reliant on information that he's almost paranoid. He keeps the data on opposing hitters going into his memory bank constantly.

"This season he's working on how to hold men on base better. So few of them get on, of course. But Greg doesn't like to have vulnerabilities. If he decided to make that something he does better than anybody else, he would do it."

Maddux' effectiveness can't be separated from his playfulness. He doesn't grind himself to dust. "My dad never makes a bad thing into the worst thing that's ever happened in his life. I'm like that," says Maddux. "Some people dwell on everything and drag it out. Blow it off. Same with the good stuff."

What does Maddux do during the off-season, when some players are in winter ball or doing head-to-toe makeovers of their physiques? "I stay in Vegas and have fun," says Maddux. "I work out four times a week for about an hour and a quarter. That's it. I'd say I'm a hard worker, but not a real hard worker. Not nearly as hard as people make it out."

If you're a huge success in America, then you must be a workaholic. It's a rule. But Maddux isn't. So there. Cope with it. The next time the boss says the competition is rising before dawn, tell him you and Maddux are sleeping in.

In everything, Maddux travels light. His idea of fashion is a new pair of sweatsocks. Lord knows what kind of clunker he'd drive if it weren't for Kathy. "That's why you get married," he says. "So there's somebody to say, 'Honey, let's go for a test-drive.'"

Like Brooks Robinson, and perhaps no other Hall of Famer of the preceding generation, Maddux has such a clean, sharp perception of himself as a dignified common man that his self-image is accepted as reality by everybody around him.

If you want to see his hackles rise just a bit, ask him why, if he's really what he seems to be, he lives in Las Vegas, the phoniest city on earth.

"It's my home. I grew up there. I have family and friends there. It's the people I know in the city that make the city for me," he says, as close as he gets to defiant. "People think Las Vegas is the Strip — a bunch of lights, a lot of gambling, drinking, and prostitutes. It's not like that. We got parks, Little League, churches, theaters, Denny's — all the things other cities have. The Strip is an extra bonus. We have the best entertainment in the world. If you want to go to the park and feed the ducks with your kids, you can do that. But if you have insomnia and want to knock out the grocery list at 3 A.M., they'll have a slot machine in the store."

No matter how much he accomplishes — and a pitcher with a 151–94 record on his 30th birthday has about a fifty-fifty shot at three hundred wins — it's doubtful that Maddux' profile will grow appreciably with the years. Virtue bores even those who have it.

"That's just the way it is," says Maddux of the human preference for chocolate ripple with walnuts over plain vanilla. "When I'm watching *Sports Center* and see linebacker Bryan Cox, I enjoy his interviews. They're different, controversial, emotional. Sometimes negative things are entertaining. If I were a producer and had an interview like that or a guy saying nice things about everybody, I'd run the one that was more entertaining, more of a story."

As the greatest players age or set records, they become central symbols of their sport, even if their performance has slipped a notch. They often pay the game back by becoming public icons at the expense of their personal privacy. Cal Ripken Jr. is already a public statue.

Would Maddux ever play the role that, in recent years, has been handled with such forbearance by Nolan Ryan and now by Ripken?

"Cal's in a different league. This guy was baseball for the last two or three months of last season. The only good coming out of the game was Cal. I know, as a player, I appreciated it," says Maddux. "If I had my choice, no, I really would not want that kind of fame. I'm not saying it would be that bad. But if I had a choice I would probably prefer that it not happen."

He's reached the point where the only way to avoid it is to stop going 19–2, the best season percentage in history, and winning the Cy Young every year.

Maddux probably isn't in the Hall of Fame yet. Four years of perfection is incredible. Make no mistake, in baseball terms a 75–29 record with an ERA of 1.93 is a working definition of perfection. But fans forget quickly. Jim Rice had three years in the seventies when he was to hitting what Maddux is now to pitching. His eyes went bad; he'll never get a sniff of Cooperstown. For six straight years in the eighties, Don Mattingly was as good as Stan Musial. But he got old fast. He's beloved. But he'll never merit a bronze plaque.

The distinction that Maddux can claim already is that, in his prime, he was the most effective right-handed pitcher — relative to his league and his era — since Walter Johnson. Maddux is the only pitcher since the Big Train (in 1912 to 1915) whose ERA (1.93) has been less than half of the league's ERA (3.96). In other words, Maddux has been twice as efficient as the league during the past four years.

Decency demands that Maddux not be compared to Koufax at his peak. From 1962 to 1966, Koufax went 111–34, compared with Maddux' strike-abbreviated 75–29 record. Also, Koufax won every ERA title and averaged 289 strikeouts a season.

Still, Maddux has reached a point where he wins most comparisons to any Tom Seaver, Jim Palmer, Bob Gibson, Bob Feller, or Steve Carlton you can name. True, Maddux strikes out only about 198 men per 162-game season. But no dominant starter since Christy Mathewson (pre–World War I) has matched Maddux' control. In 1994 and 1995 Maddux went 35–8 with just 54 walks in 53 starts.

We should appreciate Maddux now because, with the right injury, he could lose his almost mythical control within the strike zone. And that's the core of his craft. Game after game, he can pinpoint two different fastballs on both halves of the plate, and also throw changeups for knee-high strikes. Sometimes, he can even work his will over his curve and slider, too. Without that command, as it's now termed, he'd be Nolan Ryan without a fastball.

You can't find anybody in baseball who's ever seen a pitcher who had better control of more pitches in different parts of the strike zone than Maddux. Even as great a pitcher as Jim Palmer will tell you that the only pitch he was fairly sure he could locate within a couple of inches was a fastball on the outside half of the plate. He was never completely comfortable pitching in tight or throwing curves for strikes or putting a changeup in a specific quadrant of the plate. He approximated.

"I considered it an honor to face him. It was really a pleasure," says Bobby Bonilla, who, as a Pirate and a Met, faced Maddux for many years. "He has this ability to think like you're thinking. It's almost like he's playing a game with himself. You might not get one good pitch to hit in a whole game.

"He claims he pitches off the last pitch? There's something to that," says Bonilla. "But don't forget that first pitch: strike one. That's the one that makes him so good. Seems like he's always ahead of you. His first pitch could also be the last decent pitch you see. So don't wait too long up there."

For four seasons, Maddux has painted the black, lived on the long end of the count, and expanded the plate so mercilessly that hitters feel as if they're defending a manhole cover, not a 16-inch-wide dish. Six-time batting champion Tony Gwynn says Maddux has improved so radically that the terms of their confrontation have reversed. Once, Gwynn owned Maddux. Now, if a time at bat were played for life-and-death stakes, Gwynn admits he'd probably be dead.

Because Maddux has never missed a start, even in high school, and because he fields his position with such Gold Glove quickness that he seems an unlikely candidate to be maimed by a line drive, it's easy to assume that Maddux can stay in his blessed zone indefinitely. However, when other major leaguers watch a man on such a fantasy run, they tend to see a beautiful ice sculpture melting in the sun. They assume such a blend of youth, health, confidence, and luck can't last. Usually, it doesn't.

Maddux knows that the record book says that, pretty soon, he'll regress to the historic mean of his own career. From 1988 to 1991 he was 67–46 with a 3.24 ERA. Even if he stays healthy, Maddux will return to that form. But will it happen soon? Or in 2000? He says he doesn't care.

"I've gotten more out of this game than I ever dreamed. I'm on extra credit already," says Maddux. "I don't feel like I have the right to ask for more.

"I feel like I owe the game. It doesn't owe me. And I know I enjoy it more now than five years ago. I'll probably appreciate it more every season."

See, he pulls you in, this apotheosis of the average man, this decent, modest craftsman as athlete. He is all of us. Sort of. Yet he generates from his own experience, and lives out, the underlined passages that we just read. "There is always a best way of doing everything, if it be to boil an egg." "Not being able to rule events, I rule myself." Emerson, Montaigne, Maddux? You can't be sure. Maybe he's more than a pitcher.

"Sooner or later he's not going to win the Cy Young Award and people will say, 'What's wrong with Greg Maddux?' That's not fair," says Glavine. However, even Glavine senses that Maddux may be granted an uncommon kind of clemency in a culture that loves to raise up its celebrities and then dash them.

"His type of personality goes a long way," says Glavine. "Here's a guy who's so humble and so in tune with what he's doing that it's hard to find people who are waiting for him to fail. He's such an ordinary guy that everybody enjoys his success."

Greg Maddux, the ordinary guy, baseball's patron saint of moderation, is throwing between starts. His workout includes almost as many full-speed pitches as a complete game. He never changes expression, never says a word. Pitch after pitch nips a corner or dances just off the edge. Everything breaks late. Everything looks like everything else until the last split second. Lay the philosophy and the encomiums aside. Think of him as the dealer, the house, the sharp-eyed Vegas lifer who knows the trick of three-card monte. His confidence is absolute. The odds are with him. You need luck to beat him. He needs nothing. "Nate Luck" is a con. If he executes correctly, sooner or later you will go home in a barrel. Last year. Next year. Maybe for a long time.

In his entire workout, Maddux throws only two truly bad pitches in a hundred. Once, he holds on to a fastball too long. It bounces in the left-hand batter's box. Maddux breaks his silence. "Shit," he screams. Much later, he bounces a changeup in front of the plate. "Fuck," he bellows like a rifle shot.

Afterward he is asked if, perhaps, the playful perfectionist is a bit too hard on himself. Two bad pitches, two explosive curses? What hidden fires are these? After all, in hours of interviews he has barely said a swearword.

"There are a lot of shots in golf I can't hit, but I try to hit them anyway. The frustration is not there, because I'm still learning. But I really know how to do this. I'm not just hoping to get it where I want it," Maddux says, the playfulness receding, the commonsense, common-man philosopher completely absent and the Mad Dog poker-dealing competitor surfacing fast.

"Let the other guys do it half-assed."

DAVID REMNICK

Raging Bull:
Dennis Rodman and
the Sports Confessional

FROM THE NEW YORKER

CHILDREN YEARN TO READ about exemplary lives, and the children of the television age inevitably select the objects of their passion from the little screen. If the doings of Achilles had been televised when I was growing up, I might have memorized the Iliad and pursued a career in Hellenic studies, but, as it happened, Channel 9 broadcast the Knicks and Channel 11 the Yankees, leaving me in a state of addiction and with no choice but to read and reread the stories of such noble Athenians as DeBusschere and Reed, Mantle and Ford. Often my friends and I would read these books at the rate of two or three a day — consuming them like literary Cheez Doodles. Each tale had its thematic importance: Bob Gibson's *From Ghetto to Glory* was a Dickensian struggle against modern-day Grad-grinds; Ted Williams's *My Turn at Bat* was, like *Le Morte D'Arthur,* a primer in the art of noble battle; Gale Sayers's threnody for his teammate Brian Piccolo, *I Am Third,* was our version of *To an Athlete Dying Young;* Joe Namath was our Frank Harris, introducing us to sexual delicacies in the masterful *I Can't Wait Until Tomorrow, 'Cause I Get Better-Looking Every Day.*

And then there was the moral instruction of Sandy Koufax's autobiography, *Koufax,* written with the assistance of a greatly underestimated ghost, Ed Linn. (Linn is often overshadowed in literary studies by the suspiciously prolific Maury Allen and Phil Pepe.)

In my circle, *Koufax* was known simply as the Talmud. While I was a pupil of dubious standing at the Temple Emanuel Hebrew School, I successfully recycled on an annual basis my classic Linn-lifted dissertation, "Sandy Koufax: Great Pitcher, Greater Jew." By recounting with increasing fervor and commitment the story of Koufax's legendary refusal to pitch a World Series game on Yom Kippur, I sidestepped the need to work up to a new paper on the traditional twin towers of adolescent Jewish studies — Rabbi Akiba and Sammy Davis, Jr.

I pull this juvenilia down from the shelf not to riffle through its dusty pages but, rather, to understand the meaning of a current phenomenon. Dennis Rodman's *Bad As I Wanna Be* is No. 1 on the *Times* nonfiction bestseller list. How are we to account for this? Rodman is a certifiable star in a mainstream sport, and yet one is curious about how, as a matter of literary history, we got from the herculean tales of Mantle and Mays to the confessional style of an athlete who poses on the book jacket with his bare *tuchis* flush to the camera and who writes that "to put on a sequined halter top makes me feel like a total person and not just a one-dimensional man." This is not the first athlete confessional. (There are times, in fact, when it seems that the athlete memoir has picked up where *Life Studies* and *Ariel* left off.) So why is Rodman riding (literarily speaking) so high?

It is true that Rodman's team, the Chicago Bulls, is on its way to a National Basketball Association championship. Moreover, Rodman has famously unburdened himself of the details of his romance with Madonna Ciccone. ("She wasn't an acrobat, but she wasn't a dead fish either.") When Rodman first met Madonna, he told her that "I didn't like her music." But, he insists, "that was the one thing about this relationship — we were totally honest with each other. I told her that her house in Los Angeles sucked." In what must surely be the most selling passage in the book, Rodman describes his first night of intimacy with Madonna — more particularly, how he denied her a sexual favor that the lady had said would "get me loose."

"Believe me," our hero said. "I won't do that, darling." And, he duly reports, "I didn't do it. I think she was a little surprised that I said no to her, but I did: I said NO to Madonna." Admittedly, a scene as gallant as that is also in Rodman's commercial favor, but, still: No. 1?

*

Before the advent of television, the pivotal sports books were works of inspirational fiction, much like the homiletic prose inventions of Parson Weems. ("Father, I cannot tell a lie. I chopped down the cherry tree," etc.) John R. Tunis's *The Kid from Tomkinsville* and *World Series,* exemplars of the form, were sandlot tales of effort and sportsmanship. Many of the early ballplayers, including Ty Cobb and Babe Ruth, eventually found ghostwriters (Al Stump for Cobb; Bob Considine for Ruth), but only after their playing days were long over. Autobiography existed, but not as the dominant form. I think I know the reason. As Roger Angell has pointed out in these pages, when baseball was the preeminent American sport, before the Second World War, it was a game known mainly through radio, sports columns, and box scores. In order to see a player, one had to actually go to the park, and even at the stadium there was a sense of enormous distance. One was never close enough to begin wondering about a player's wife, his history, his halter top.

The books of my childhood, however, derived from our intimate access to the game through television. We knew the players with the help first of the zoom lens ("Look, there's a fly on Boog Powell's ear!") and then of the biographies. The books themselves followed strict narrative patterns: triumph over tragedy, victory through work, etc. As a result, a thoroughly unpleasant man like Mantle could be portrayed as an archetype. We learned of Mutt, Mantle's doomed and devoted father, and of the way Hodgkin's disease haunted the entire clan, generation after generation. But we were spared the details of ol' No. 7 being hung over in the dugout on game day and of his womanizing on the road.

It's not as if no one knew any better. Ty Cobb, Hemingway once said, was "the greatest of all ballplayers — and an absolute shit." Cobb's ghost, Al Stump, suffered every indignity possible in a literary venture. Old, psychotic, and sick, Cobb hurled empty booze bottles at Stump, and even threatened him with a pistol. Needless to say, none of this unpleasantness was recorded in *My Life in Baseball: The True Record,* published in 1961. The contractual agreement among star, ghost, and publisher was that the publisher would hire the ghost to delineate and glorify the deeds of the star as a noble man: ghosts were meant, as Plutarch wrote of his own approach to the lives of Alexander and Caesar, "to epitomize the most celebrated parts of their story, rather than to insist at large on every particular circumstance of it." The athlete in question was then meant to live up to the chronicle; he was not required to read it. The great Houston Rockets forward Charles Barkley was once asked about a particular remark he had made in his autobiography, *Outrageous*. Barkley didn't even fake it. "I was misquoted," he said.

Times have changed, of course. Stump eventually did write an independent account of Cobb's life, portraying him in all his ugly brilliance. But that came in 1994, thirty-three years after Cobb died. Wilt Chamberlain, for his part, wrote a book in which he claimed to have slept with twenty thousand women (a scoring record that will stand even after his hundred-point-game mark has been broken). But Chamberlain's confessional was late: he retired from basketball eighteen years before its publication.

The book that changed everything in the commercial sports-literature field was Jim Bouton's baseball memoir, *Ball Four,* which came out in 1970. Although Bouton had known some winning moments as a pitcher, next to teammates like Mantle he was a pipsqueak. As a writer, however, he was fresh, funny, and irreverent, informing an astonished public that some players cheated on their wives, popped pills, and, during the national anthem, looked up the dresses of women in the stands — a practice known among the Yanks as "beaver-shooting." The book was, at once, elevated to the bestseller list and denounced by everyone from Bowie Kuhn, the baseball commissioner, to Dick Young, the reactionary *Daily News* columnist, who wrote, "I feel sorry for Jim Bouton. He is a social leper. He didn't catch it, he developed it." Trying to imagine the commotion around *Ball Four* now is a bit like wondering what all the fuss was over *Les Demoiselles d'Avignon*. Bouton's younger readers tended to appreciate him; the older ones thought he had "torn down" heroes and betrayed what was inevitably called "the sanctity of the game."

As it turned out, of course, one might as well have tried to resist free verse. Publishers would continue to put out reverent books about sports heroes — the shelves are filled with hagiographies of everyone from Michael Jordan to Joe Montana — but Bouton had changed the form.

The history of the sports autobiography most closely parallels that of the other form of literary junk food, the Hollywood life story. But, since the sports-trash form tends to do its work on a younger and more impressionable audience, it is more important. I don't know of many kids who are terribly interested in the life of Tom Cruise, or are under any misapprehension that what Tom Cruise does is as difficult as hitting a major league curve ball.

I can still remember with a weird clarity hundreds of details from books I read before I was twelve. And whether I like it or not, I can already see signs of this fascination in my elder son, Alex, who is almost six. Five seems to be the genetically encoded starting point. I made the mistake of once taking Alex to a Mets game when he was not quite four: after he made his way through a hot dog, a pint of Coke, popcorn, another Coke, and a miniature batting helmet filled with chocolate ice cream, he declared his desire to get back on the subway and go home. It was the top of the second. And yet the next year he started drawing pictures of Patrick Ewing and wearing a Knicks road jersey as pajamas.

So far, Alex's loyalties are imitative. He has declared himself a Knicks fan and a registered Democrat. But he has also taken a disturbing interest in the opposition: he has, for example, told me that Michael Jordan is "real awesome" and Scottie Pippin is "also real awesome." He doesn't quite know what to make of Dennis Rodman. Kids are not often scared or offended by the bizarre, but they are deeply curious — they notice everything. Certainly Alex has noticed what there is to notice about Dennis Rodman. "Why is his hair red?" he has asked. Or yellow. Or green. And "Why can't I tattoo my shoulders?" One day, to help him understand, I'll give him *Bad As I Wanna Be*. Like when he's thirty-two.

Rodman is not the only player-literateur who is selling himself as an anti-hero, but most of his competitors do nothing to risk shocking the consumer of fast foods and sneakers. Barkley's *Outrageous* is full of "controversial" chat, but he still manages to rake it in with McDonald's ads. *Bad As I Wanna Be* ("with Tim Keown") goes well beyond Bouton's *Ball Four*, getting in our collective face with an absolute, and desperate, authenticity. There is no whimsy. Here we are on the edge of a new sports form: autopathography.

The book opens with the scene of Rodman, at the height of his talents, sitting in his pickup truck with a rifle and "deciding whether to kill myself." His championship team, the Detroit Pistons, is being dismantled; his coach and father figure, Chuck Daly, is gone; his marriage is a ruin; he is a tortured mess. Mostly, Rodman was haunted by the undeniable truth — that if he were not six feet eight and a master of the art of grabbing a basketball as it bounces off the rim, he would more than likely be dead or back in the hole he came from.

Rodman grew up in Oak Cliff, a dismal housing project in Dallas. His father was the aptly named Philander Rodman. He ran out on the family when Dennis was three years old. As Rodman tells the story, his sisters were successful students, while he himself was slow, homely, and, in general, a disappointment to his mother. He felt rejected by everything and everyone around him. "There have been many times, none of them recent, when I sat back and wished I was white," he writes. "I grew up in the projects, where everyone was black. But I feel I was abused within that culture. I wasn't accepted there. I was too skinny, too ugly, too something."

At nineteen, when so many of Rodman's eventual peers in the game were already assured of multimillion-dollar contracts, Rodman was adrift: homeless at times, working odd jobs at others. He had barely played any organized basketball. "I was a nobody, just bumming around with some hoodlum buddies." He worked the graveyard shift as a janitor at the Dallas–Fort Worth airport but was fired for stealing fifty watches from the gift shop. Having flunked out after a semester of junior college, he ran across a coach from a tiny school in Oklahoma who thought he had some promise. Rodman became a twenty-one-year-old freshman. (At twenty one, Shaquille O'Neal was already a bazillionaire and had published an autobiography, *Shaq Attaq!* — a book with all the spontaneity of a Pepsi ad.)

At Southeastern Oklahoma University, Rodman proved himself an eerily tireless player, notable as much for his effort as for his skills. Suddenly, he was accepted in a community; he knew, though, that it all depended on his ability to play ball. "When I was twenty, those people would have crossed the street to get away from me."

Rodman was drafted by the Detroit Pistons as a "project" player; that is, the coaches wanted to see if a twenty-five-year-old rookie could play with men who had been stars since they were in the sixth grade. Rodman more than acquitted himself on the basketball court. What was really difficult was learning to deal with the impossible strangeness (no matter how delicious) of being a poor, lonely kid one day and an impossibly rich object of desire the next.

"Fifty percent of the NBA is sex," he writes. "The other 50 percent is money." Rodman is exaggerating only slightly. As a newspaper reporter, I covered the NBA for a season, and wherever the players stayed the hotel lobby resembled the waiting room at a modeling agency. The women fairly auditioned for them. One reporter told me that a player he covered — one of the greatest in the history of the game — used to have a friend roam the arena for him searching out the best-looking women; the friend would line up the women he had selected, and as the player headed for the bench he would nod his approval or disapproval of the gathered chattel. "This is the ultimate turnaround," Rodman writes. "When I was a kid, the girls made fun of me and didn't find me attractive at all. I was skinny and small and they thought I was funny-looking. Now, they all want me. Too many of them want me." (For the record, Rodman does not believe Chamberlain's boast of having slept with twenty thousand women. "That's three or four women a day for fifteen or twenty years. I dare anybody to keep up that kind of pace.") But while Rodman, like so many of his colleagues, availed himself of his sexual privileges, he did it, he tells us, with a darkness in his soul: "Once you've had a total stranger ask you to fuck his wife while he watches, you're not going to be easily shocked. There's only one thing that shocks me: I'm still here."

Rodman is hyper-aware of his mortality, both as a man and as a commodity. Because he's not much of a shooter (the skill that attracts the most attention in the NBA, and thus the biggest salaries), he must do the dirty work of basketball: defense, setting screens, and, especially, retrieving the missed shots of others.

About basketball itself, Rodman is a cultural conservative. He despises the "fifty-year-old white men," the executives who crowd every second with bogus entertainment: "You've got guys flying off a trampoline to dunk a ball, you've got dancing gorillas and highlight shows during time-outs." This is the sort of grouchy rant that Michael Jordan, with his awareness of his place on the corporate marquee, would never indulge in.

Rodman not only resists the NBA's blandishments to be a "role model" (a dubious concept plucked out of the social-science jargon of the fifties) but insists on his own confusions. "Sometimes I don't even know who I am, and these people are calling me their hero?" The sports-addicted American public now has a player willing to descibe his sexual anxieties (he fantasizes about making it with another man); a black man who admits that his alienation from black culture is so deep that his favorite band is that icon of Seattle grunge Pearl Jam; a star who shows up late at the opening of a new arena in San Antonio because he wanted to go blond and "the damned bleach job took too long." I am not sure we have ever known a star athlete so eager to tell us that he paints his fingernails and that his pickup truck is pink and white. Whereas Michael Jackson denies up and down his ambiguities in a music world that would be more likely to accept them, Rodman celebrates his in a realm of conspicuous machismo:

> I don't think painting my fingernails is a big deal. It's not like I'm sitting at home by myself, trying on lingerie. That's not my style. I don't do lingerie. . . .
> When I cross-dress now, it's just another way I can show all the sides of Dennis Rodman. I'm giving you the whole package, I'm becoming the all-purpose person. . . .
> I'm not gay. I would tell you if I was. If I go to a gay bar, that doesn't mean that I want another man to put his tongue down my throat — no. It means I want to be a whole individual.

Rodman is right to complain that he is making only two and a half million dollars a year when inferior, lazy players like Derrick Coleman make three times that. But sometimes his insistent honesty is just too much. His insults directed against other players are unappealing and so are his attempts to portray himself as unawed and superior to nearly everyone he encounters. ("I said, 'I'm Dennis,' and she said, 'I'm Madonna,' and we both said, 'Great.'")

At least one teammate, John Salley, claims that Rodman gives himself an easy ride in the book, but I think our man comes across with some real truth. Jordan's sponsors demand of us that we "Be Like Mike." Rodman wants to be a different kind of hero, a frontiersman of the soul. He is an embodiment of the times: a gender-bender filled with racial anxiety. As Rousseau puts it in his own confessions, Rodman can claim to have "shown myself as I was; contemptible and vile when I was so; good, generous, sublime when I was so." In the end, we like him — or, at least, we don't mind him. Besides, it's hard not to look forward to the future performances of someone who says, "I want to play my last game in the NBA in the nude." He gives us a reason to go on living.

DAVID HALBERSTAM

Anatomy of a Champion

FROM VANITY FAIR

THE AMERICAN FENCERS spent three days living the comparative
high life in Madrid after competing in La Coruña, on the western
coast of Spain. They practiced during the day at a Madrid fencing
club, and they lodged in two rooms at the Hotel Lisboa, which cost
them $20 each a night. On tour they sometimes stayed in one room
— breaking down hotel beds to put their mattresses on the floor
was a necessary skill for American fencers. But at the Hotel Lisboa
they had their own bathrooms, as well as telephones and television
sets, so it was a considerable bargain. With a World Cup event
coming up in Venice, they had to decide whether to stay on in
Madrid or go to Rome.

It was not an easy call. On the side of Madrid was the relative luxury of the Hotel Lisboa and the fact that Madrid was significantly
cheaper than Rome. In Rome's favor was the fact that Nick Bravin,
at 24 the senior member of the team as well as its de facto travel
agent, translator, and general mentor, spoke better Italian than
Spanish. Also, Bravin believed that the younger members of the
team, who did not know Rome well, would benefit by wandering
through the streets of one of the great cities of the world.

Rome it would be. The next morning Bravin went to a local travel
agency, where he found that it would cost them some $700 each to
fly to Rome, but less than $200 each to get there by train (second
class) — a grim, cramped, exhausting twenty-three-hour trip. The
airfare represented a good deal of money for the team; their dilemma was of the kind shared by many amateur athletes from
America who, while representing one of the richest countries in the
world, play sports that do not televise well or about which the

American public cares little. Bravin was certainly used to these kinds of problems and was skillful at getting around them; he soon found just what he was looking for — a leg of a Thai Airways flight that would take them from Madrid to Rome for about $100 a person.

At the Rome airport Bravin consulted his tattered notebook containing a list of the cheapest hotels in the world's capitals and started calling around. At the first seven places, he struck out, but at the eighth, the Hotel Contilia, he found one room still available, at $120, or $30 a head. On this trip there were only four of them, rather than the usual five, since teammate Peter Devine was sick with the flu and had gone ahead to Venice to rest for the World Cup event there. They played hearts to see who got the worst bed — the one they jokingly called "the crippler."

Fencers are marvelous athletes, smart and surprisingly strong, with great footwork and great hand-to-eye coordination. The three events (and their weapons) in fencing are the foil, the épée, and the saber. Foil fencing, which uses a thin, rectangular-shaped blade, is athletically and intellectually demanding because it has the smallest target area — the torso, back, and groin. Bravin, in addition to being a world-class poor person's travel agent, was also a star of the individual foil in America, a three-time NCAA champion as a Stanford student, and a three-time national champion. He had been the first American in years to show that he might be able to compete at fencing's highest level — against the mighty Europeans, who dominate the sport and who subsidize it handsomely. According to Carl Borack, a former Olympic fencer who now serves as the captain of the American team, the annual American budget is roughly $400,000, while the Italian government gives its team more than $6 million.

Nevertheless, Nick Bravin had come to believe that adversity had its own rewards, that by dint of being forced to economize he knew not only Europe's castles and museums but also its working-class bars. He had made friends as he might not have had he been protected by wealth and celebrity status. Best of all, he and the other American fencers had learned to make sacrifices and to take care of one another; they had learned to be teammates and good friends, even as they had to be fierce competitors.

This current group of Americans in the foil — Bravin, 24, Cliff

Bayer, 18, Peter Devine, 19, Sean McClain, 20, and Zaddick Longenbach, 24 — were surprisingly closely matched in skills and the
most talented team this country had produced in years, thought
Bravin's old college coach, Zoran Tulum. Tulum, originally from
Yugoslavia, had come to America ten years before and developed a
grudging admiration for the toughness of American fencers, whose
rewards had to be completely internalized.

Among the teammates that Nick Bravin was steering to the Hotel
Contilia was a young man named Cliff Bayer. As a high school
senior, he had burst onto the national scene to become the wun-
derkind of American fencing, stunning Bravin in particular by coming from behind in the 1995 national championship finals and
beating him. When Bravin looked at Bayer he saw nothing less than
the image of his younger self. "Cliff is extremely hungry — just like
I used to be," he said. "He has a lot of physical gifts, but above all he
has the gift of attitude. He wants to beat you on every point, and he
is afraid of no one, afraid of no reputation."

Bravin himself had won the first of his three national championships in 1991 at age 20. In the words of Zoran Tulum, he was as
hungry as a wolf then, as audacious as he was fearless, and he had
taken particular pleasure in knocking off better-known fencers. By
1994 he had begun to beat some of the best fencers in the world,
Elvis Gregory of Cuba and Dimitri Chevtchenko of Russia among
them. There was talk that he might become one of the giants of the
sport.

Then, to Tulum's dismay, Bravin entered Columbia Law School
and lavished the singular intensity he had previously given to fencing on his studies. By March of this Olympic year his ranking had
fallen to No. 4, just behind Bayer, Devine, and McClain. Since only
the top three will make the Olympic team, decided in June after the
national championships, Bravin found himself in a tight spot. He
was certain that technically he was a better fencer than ever, but he
had begun to wonder whether he still had the hunger that Tulum
talked about so often. The wolf, according to Tulum, was always the
hunter. It sized up its prey and thought of nothing else. Hunting
was a matter of life and death to the wolf; so should fencing be to
the true champion. Bravin was still fast — Rápido, his Cuban competitors had nicknamed him — but fast was not enough. The ante-

lope is fast, but you cannot fence if you are an antelope, Tulum would say. The wolf triumphs because it thinks of nothing else, it is always the hunter.

As a fencer, Bravin knew that Tulum was right, but at this point there were other things in his life. He found, as had other athletes before him, that the ascent was the easy part. On the way up you had no title to lose.

He had been drawn to the sport almost by chance while growing up in Los Angeles. His older brother, Jess, had tried fencing, and Nick, who was then about 12, tagged along. He immediately decided that he too wanted to take fencing lessons. Shawn Bravin, his mother, was skeptical. She knew her youngest child was bright and gifted at many things, but he was also easily bored. She had seen many of his fads, including Bravin piano and Bravin violin lessons, evaporate overnight. Yet eventually she gave in and bought him all the requisite gear.

At first he had not particularly liked fencing, but he stayed with it, in no small part, he decided later, to prove his mother wrong. He had always been quick, no matter what sport he played, and almost from the start his coaches saw great potential. Soon, with their encouragement, he began going more than once a week.

It was not the dashing, swashbuckling swordplay he imagined from the movies, the glorious pleasure of sticking his opponent with a sword. Rather, it was technical drudgery, footwork drills, using muscles in his arms and legs in ways he had rarely used them before. But after six months or so, his coaches finally let him compete, and he loved it.

He won his first four tournaments. At the start, perhaps, he loved competitions too much. He was brash and impatient, hotheaded and unwilling to listen to his coaches. He loved the individual nature of the competition, and he found out something about himself: he hated to lose. His coaches homed in on that instinct. "How many fencers in the final eight actually want to win a tournament?" Ed Richards, one of his first coaches, asked him. "All eight," Bravin answered. "No," said Richards, "four of them are happy just to be there, two want to do well, and *two* want to win. Remember that and be one of the two."

Jess Bravin, who was six years older than Nick, went off to Harvard and fenced on the Harvard team. Coming home from college for a holiday break, he was stunned to find the change in his little brother. Not only had he become a superior fencer, but all his exceptional qualities, intellectual and physical, had been fused together through this demanding sport. It was also who Nick Bravin had become as a person — skillful, strong, confident, audacious.

He fenced at increasingly higher levels, while still playing football at Alexander Hamilton High School in Los Angeles — he was one of the smallest men on the team. His schedule was brutal: up at 6:00 A.M., school starting at 7:00, football practice from 2:00 to 5:00 in the afternoon, fencing practice at 6:00. His biggest decision in those days was whether to go home briefly for a bite to eat after football practice or go directly to fencing.

He was 16 years old, still growing, and perpetually exhausted. But his friend Al Carter would not let him sleep through his fencing lessons. They were about the same age and the two best fencers in the area. Carter would call up, listen to his friend's complaints that he was tired and in pain, and then tell Bravin he would pick him up in fifteen minutes. The two thought of little else but college and future Olympic glory; the vanity license plate on Carter's car in those days read: 92 GOALD. They would attend the same college and lead it to a national championship. Many schools courted them and the University of Pennsylvania, a traditional fencing power, seemed likely to get them.

But Bravin visited Stanford and was overwhelmed by the beauty of the campus if not the quality of the fencing. Stanford was hardly known as a powerhouse in the sport. That meant the level of competition in daily practice was not nearly as good as it was at Penn or Columbia. Also, Tulum, the new coach, was unknown to Bravin, and in fencing the personal relationship of the coach to his fencers is considered critical. Tulum was wary of the ways of American college recruiting. When Bravin asked Tulum for a trial lesson, Tulum said no, he did not do auditions. What do you mean, no? thought Bravin. I'm twice as good as any fencer you have, and I may be the best fencer you ever get, and you're saying no to me? "No," Tulum repeated as Bravin stood there dumbstruck. "I'm not going to give you a practice lesson. You're not going to try me out." Zoran Tulum had his rules, and he had his suspicion that altogether too many middle-class American kids were spoiled. "We'd like to have you, but if you want to take your talent elsewhere, that's fine with me."

Bravin was stunned. Every other college in the country with a fencing team wanted him; his choice meant committing four years of his life to a school and a coach, risking his chances of becoming a national champion. Yet this man would not even give him a trial lesson. "All I can offer you," Tulum added, "is hard work and good weather. Period."

In a way their meeting was like a fencing bout, Bravin later figured out. Tulum was pitting his ego against Bravin's. There was something about that and something about Tulum's sheer bluntness that Bravin liked. In the end it was a hard decision, so he called his older brother and asked his opinion. Jess told him that fencing was important but that competitive fencing was not forever — he might break a leg on any given day and end his career. Jess told him to make his decision based on the school, not the fencing team or coach. So, while his friend Al Carter went to Penn, Nick Bravin decided to go to Stanford.

Bravin and Tulum were both driven and willful, and at first the two constantly battled. Bravin did not consider the competition among his teammates good enough, so he would go off to practice at a club in San Francisco. This meant missing practice, which irritated Tulum and his teammates. Tulum threatened to kick him off the team. "We're better off without you," Tulum would say.

Yet Tulum was a very good coach. He was shrewd at knowing how to challenge his young star. One of the first things he did was print up a sign for Bravin: SECOND SUCKS, it said. Not only did Bravin become a better fencer, he became more passionate about fencing. His objective was not merely athletic but in time spiritual as well. He wanted the peace of mind that came with reaching the highest level of his abilities. He wanted to try to be the best at one thing even if he did his best and failed. He was aware of the danger implicit in so singular an ambition, that it demanded an overwhelming amount of sacrifice — exams taken on airplanes to tournaments, fitting in homework while his classmates were having fun. He knew he was giving up part of his youth. But the alternative was worse: to stop just short of true excellence. There were, he thought, altogether too many people who did that, who were haunted for the rest of their lives by the question of how good they might have been had they tried just a little harder. Whatever else, he vowed, that question would not go unanswered in his life.

Tulum preached that fencing was 50 percent athletic and 50 percent psychological and intellectual, that in addition to the physical talent of a Michael Jordan you needed the strategic ability and the psychological acumen of a Gary Kasparov because you had to stay several moves ahead of your opponent. Attitude was crucial. In fencing, if you think someone is better, he'll end up being better. For years a kind of national inferiority complex had plagued American fencers. At international meets they saw foreign teams that were so well subsidized they even came with their own cooks. Such wealth and power engendered a certain amount of swagger. The Americans felt like the poor stepchildren of the sport and were beaten all too readily. To draw an American in an international tournament, Bravin noted, was virtually regarded as drawing a bye. He himself had done poorly in the 1992 Olympics. But then he had been only 21, and since fencers reach their peaks in their late 20s and early 30s, he still had a bright future.

Two years later he was coming into his own and just beginning to beat some of the best fencers in the world. It was at this point that he entered law school, and he found it was hard to be a wolf both at fencing and at his studies. Tulum, of course, had not been happy with the idea of law school — it was a terrible distraction, he thought. "Every day you don't practice all out," he said, "is like losing three days: the day you lose by slipping just a little, the day you lose by not getting just a little better, and the day you lose because your opponent gets better." Bravin had tried to stay in shape, but it was difficult. In 1995 when he arrived in Louisville for the nationals he thought he was fencing well and was confident he would win his fourth national championship. But Tulum thought he had been coasting on his name for a while.

Now, as Bravin negotiated Rome for his younger colleagues, Cliff Bayer was No. 1. When Bravin was winning his first national championship, Bayer had been only 13, still collecting baseball cards. True, he collected them feverishly, determined to have a better set than any of his friends. The son of a New York City doctor, he walked a neighbor's dog for $20 a week so he could buy more cards. He also became so skillful at trading cards, his brother, Greg, later remembered, he picked up the nickname Rip-off Cliff. There were complaints from neighboring parents to the senior Bayers that Cliff had snookered their kids.

Bayer, like Bravin, took up fencing because his older brother had done it. He had become impatient with baseball — he thought his teammates did not play as hard as he did. In fencing he found a sport where there was no one to blame but himself when things went wrong. His first coach, Miklos Bartha, a Hungarian émigré now in his 70s, was a distinguished figure in New York fencing circles. Bayer's father, Dr. Michael Bayer, remembers when Bartha told him his son would make a champion. "I looked out and saw nothing, but Miklos had a practiced eye and he knew what made a great athlete — the willpower and the instinct. He could look at a little boy of nine and see it all: the character, the inner toughness, and the drive." Like Bravin, Bayer did not enjoy the drudgery of the early training — the repetitious drills of advance and retreat, the dancing classes with swords. But he rose to competition, often beating older and seemingly more talented boys with the intensity of his will.

The first time he saw Bayer at a tournament, when Bayer was only 15, Tulum was struck by the boy's courage and instinct for combat. "That child has a heart the size of his chest," thought Tulum, "the heart of a champion." Bayer himself did not think he was a natural for the sport, but he knew his desire was so strong that he could turn his weaknesses into strengths. "Some people know instinctively why it is important for them to be the best," says Dave Micahnik, the University of Pennsylvania coach who successfully recruited Bayer for next fall. "Cliff is that way — it is vital that he be the best."

On occasion the pressure of school and fencing was almost too much for someone so young. Once, he fenced at the Junior World Cup in Giengen, Germany, with melancholy results. To get there he had to take an international flight to Stuttgart, a train to Heidenheim, and then a bus to Giengen. He was tired upon arrival, which affected his concentration, and he fenced poorly, not even making the top 32. Then he had to retrace his steps, lugging all his gear, trying to do his homework on the train, in order to rush back to school in New York. Unable to get a decent night's sleep on the plane, he wondered whether it was all worth it and thought about quitting.

But he knew he was getting better. In 1994, while still a high school junior at Riverdale Country Day School in New York City, he came in third at the U.S. national championships. It was a stunning achievement. He was amused by the response of the older fencers to his success: "Who's this upstart kid who's doing so well, they were thinking, and I was thinking, Third, *that's not good enough, I can do better. I can win this whole thing.*"

By the time of his high school graduation, at age 17, he was already ranked No. 3 in the country. He defeated Zaddick Longenbach, an Olympian in 1992, at a senior-circuit tournament in New Jersey. Both Longenbach and Bayer had worked out at Salle Santelli and the Metropolis Fencing Club in New York City, and Longenbach had been beating Bayer since Bayer was nine. Bayer's older brother, Greg, a former captain of the Princeton fencing team, had watched the match and was startled by what he saw. For the first time, he realized, his brother's physical abilities had caught up with his competitive instincts. Bayer himself felt he was ready to take on Bravin in Louisville.

In the first round of the 1995 nationals, Bayer was nervous. Yefim Litvan, his coach, sensed it immediately. "Relax," he said. "Just have fun here." That helped and as he relaxed he began to see his opponents' moves more clearly. He made the semifinals and thus qualified for the Senior World Championships and the World University Games.

The semifinal match with Longenbach was intense. For a while it was touch for touch. Bayer had never seen Longenbach so focused in a bout. But Bayer won, 15–13. That meant he would face Bravin in the final.

In 1994, Bravin had beaten Bayer, 15–11, at the nationals, but Bayer was not intimidated. His hero was the great Italian fencer Stefano Cerioni, the 1988 Olympic gold medalist, who was known as the most aggressive of fencers, a man who approached every match as if it were a street fight. Bayer wanted no part of a silver medal. He and his friend Sean McClain had their own saying: "Silver sucks." Now Bayer was sure that he could beat Bravin — after all, Bravin had not been much older when he had won his first national.

As the two prepared to fence, the air was electric. Bravin knew that he was now the hunted and that it was much harder than being the hunter. He knew also that the physical gap with Bayer had narrowed. He sized up the younger man and found he was altogether too much like he himself used to be, with little respect for existing hierarchies. Bravin remembered his second NCAA championship, in 1992. He had been ranked 24th, which annoyed him greatly, because in his own mind he deserved to be the favorite that year. He had responded by winning.

They both were fencing well. Bravin took an 11–8 lead. He was pleased and felt certain he would get a fourth national title. He began to think that Bayer too believed that the old order would hold, that Bravin was the champion and would continue to be so. Here he made his mistake. He relaxed and became overconfident. Certain he had established his superiority, he became less focused, less aggressive. Watching the match, Dave Micahnik saw Bayer go to the end of the strip after Bravin won a point, slap himself on the leg in anger, and let out a roar, as if he were waking up from some long hibernation. Then he came back and stormed past Bravin to win the bout, 15–12.

Yefim Litvan now believed that Bayer would become an Olympic medalist, but perhaps in 2000 — this year, 1996, would be one in which to gain international experience. But Bayer, with the fearlessness of the young, thought otherwise, that there was no reason to enter a match thinking of it only as experience for the future.

In defeat Bravin realized he had probably lost something of his edge and certainly something of his mystique. He decided to take a year off from law school to work on his fencing and get ready for the Olympics. He needed to find out whether he still had the hunger, whether he could still be the hunter.

LINDA ROBERTSON

Platform Pitfalls

FROM THE MIAMI HERALD

RUSS BERTRAM was three stories high, clutching his shins in a triple somersault dive, when one wet hand slipped. He spun out of control and hit the water at 35 miles per hour, ripping his shoulder out of its socket.

Scott Donie's wrists were sliced open to remove scar tissue so thick from years of platform diving that it was strangling two tendons.

Li Kongzheng crash-landed and detached a retina.

Kent Ferguson belly-flopped and blacked out underwater. When he came to, he coughed up blood.

Herniated discs, ruptured testicles, collapsed lungs, dislocated shoulders — these are not just football injuries, but the price platform divers pay for their defiance of gravity. Divers are rewarded and applauded for their effortless grace, yet no one sees their grimaces under the surface.

The water may look soft, but divers say it feels like a sheet of glass when they land palms-first and the impact slams from wrists to elbows to shoulders to neck to back in a bone-jarring chain reaction.

"When you hit the water correctly, you feel like you're shooting through it like a missile," said Patty Armstrong, who will dive at the U.S. Olympic trials Wednesday in Indianapolis despite degenerated vertebrae in her neck. "When you don't, you feel like you're smacking into concrete."

Three-time national platform champion Patrick Jeffrey compares diving off the thirty-three-foot tower to being in a car crash.

"We say it's ten meters up and a hundred meters down," said

Wendy Williams, platform bronze medalist at the 1988 Olympics. "It is a contact sport. It looks so easy, but when you get up there you're like, 'Oh, no, I'm going to throw up.'"

Platform divers say nothing compares to the exhilaration of nailing a dive — or the terror of "getting lost" — becoming disoriented in midair.

Veronica Ribot-Canales was petrified when she first tried platform diving, then she learned to love the feeling of skydiving without a parachute. She reluctantly gave it up when doctors discovered two bulging discs in her neck.

"You're diving off a three-story building and landing in a handstand," she said. "You come up out of the water smiling and everybody's clapping, and you feel like you left your neck at the bottom of the pool."

The trauma to the body causes so much soreness that divers usually limit their practice off the platform to three or four days a week.

"The difficulty doesn't come through on TV," Donie said. "You have to go up there and just jump off. It will hurt your feet. It will hurt your crotch."

On the days when they make the long climb to the top, divers often wear braces on their wrists, tape around their thumbs and sponges on the backs of their hands. Divers enter the water with hands clasped, heels of the hands turned outward, palms punching a hole in the water, which, when they are perfectly vertical, sucks in the rest of the body for a nearly splashless, high-scoring "rip" entry. If a diver's triceps can't hold the arms straight upon impact, the back of the hands smack into the head.

The sponges protect the hands, but no one has come up with a way to protect the parts of the male and female anatomy that protrude, although former Ohio State coach Mike Peppe experimented with a padded "tower suit" for men.

"The speed that the water cuts up your body can be quite painful," Bertram said. "You get racked. I've heard women say they felt like they had a breast sheared off."

Diving off the three-meter springboard causes less wear and tear because the speed on impact is only 20 miles per hour. Many divers

have abandoned platform diving and concentrate solely on springboard.

"I had a great career up there. I'm glad it's over," said Donie, who
shifted to springboard after he won a silver medal at the 1992
Olympics.

Bertram will dive off the platform at the trials in what could be
his last attempt to make the Olympic team. If anything should have
brought him down, it was the painful dive of last March. He landed
just five degrees from vertical, but it was enough to destroy his
shoulder.

Close to fainting underwater, he glanced at where his shoulder
used to be and saw concave skin. He saw an alien arm, hanging
limply from his chest, four inches lower than it should have been.

He underwent surgery to repair six separate muscle and joint
injuries. Six months later, Bertram was back on the tower.

"You can break bones, tear flesh, wrench joints. It sounds like a
horror movie," said Bertram, a member of the Fort Lauderdale
Diving Team. "I'm a thrill seeker. There's an element of maso-
chism. You're flirting with disaster. But my fear doesn't outweigh
my goals. I've won two national titles up there and I want to make it
to the Olympics."

Fort Lauderdale's Mary Ellen Clark returned to the tower after a
yearlong struggle to overcome vertigo that was likely caused by
trauma to her inner ear. Eileen Richetelli will compete for one of
the two women's Olympic team tower diving spots despite vivid
memories of a bad landing that bruised her spinal cord and caused
numbness and tingling in her limbs and back for two months.

Miami Diving Team member Kent Ferguson was a platform diver
for ten years, until chronic back pain and a dislocated shoulder
caused when he "missed his hands" — the divers' term for losing
their grip — at a meet in Australia.

Fort Lauderdale's Jenny Keim was scared off platform by a bad
landing and is focusing on springboard for now. Only 17, she's had
torn thumb ligaments, shoulder surgery, and a stress fracture in her
back that required a body cast for five months.

"I hate platform because I'm scared to death of heights, but it's
something I forced myself to do," said Ferguson, who gets weekly
acupuncture treatments on his lower back, where he has two herniated discs.

*

Ribot-Canales, a Miami Diving Team member, was the only diver at the 1992 Olympics to advance to the finals of both springboard and tower. Less than two years later, she was shown MRIs of her cervical discs, which are like jelly doughnuts cushioning the vertebrae of the spine. Two of Ribot-Canales's discs were squishing out into the spinal canal. She was advised to reduce the pounding on her vertebrae. Quit tower diving, her doctors said.

She had experienced the usual litany of minor tower diving injuries: jammed thumbs, wrenched back, "scalp stingers," "neck crunchers," "eyeball washers."

"You think it's part of the business," she said. "Everybody tweaks his or her neck. People come out of the water with their head sideways and work it out. Be tough, ice it, take Advil — the panaceas of diving."

She thought of her neck as an accordion that could get squeezed one too many times. At 34, she was told she had the neck of a 50-year-old.

"I didn't want to risk taking one bad hit and winding up in a wheelchair," Ribot-Canales said. "The back two-and-a-half pike with a blind entry — that was my bread and butter. Platform was my best event. When I gave it up, I went through a grieving period."

Ribot-Canales was diagnosed because she participated in a cervical spine study sponsored by U.S. Diving. Former diver Beth McFarland, a St. Louis radiologist, Steven Anderson, a Seattle orthopedist, and Michael Zlatkin, a Hollywood radiologist, evaluated the chronic wear and tear on fourteen elite platform divers. Although all the divers reported having symptoms of neck pain and stiffness, only two had disc injuries. Minimal degeneration of the spine — bony spurs, signs of arthritis, loss of range of motion — were found in some athletes.

But overall, the doctors concluded that serious injuries are infrequent among divers. Only two divers — a Russian and an Australian — are known to have died while diving, both from hitting their heads on the platform.

"I was quite relieved [by those findings]," McFarland said. "In my own career, my neck became my Achilles' heel. I want to watch our sport. We need to follow this cohort as we go faster, higher and stronger at younger ages to make sure it's a safe sport."

The study was similar to one done thirty years ago on cliff divers, who plunge from 130 feet. Although the platform divers' necks didn't look as bad as those of the cliff divers, Anderson said the damage may not show for twenty years. "Maybe we didn't see the worst of what's out there because our numbers were not big enough," he said.

Divers today are doing dives with a much higher degree of difficulty than they were ten years ago, when an inward three-and-a-half somersault in the pike position was unheard of. That increases the risk of missing a dive. The divers of the 1990s also train harder and compete more often.

Anderson found that the stress on the neck was similar to that felt by a football player making a spear tackle. The divers also had lower back and wrist, elbow, and shoulder injuries common to those of gymnasts.

Preventive measures can reduce injuries. Young divers should not be rushed up to the tower. U.S. Diving restricts divers under 14 to the 5- and 7½-meter platforms at meets. In Australia it's under 17.

Li Kongzheng, former Chinese Olympic bronze medalist now coaching in Orlando, began diving before he could swim. He said the cumulative effects of platform diving and spinning in dry-land workouts led to his eye problems, which were corrected by laser surgery. Platform divers can do much of their technical work on the lower platforms. Upper-body exercises must be performed diligently. Strengthening the triceps is essential.

"I have mixed feelings about young divers doing platform," Williams said. "Like the Chinese kids. What are their lives going to be like when they get older? Will they all have arthritis? There's so much we don't know yet."

Williams was 8 years old when she witnessed her older sister's last dive, one on which she missed her hands and dislocated a shoulder.

"From that day on, I said I would never dive platform," Williams said.

Coaches tried to coax her up, but when she got to the top, she could only whimper and climb back down.

She was a University of Miami diver when she finally took the plunge. "On my lunch breaks, I started hanging out up there, getting a tan, enjoying the view," she said. "One day I did a backflip. I got more comfortable."

So comfortable that she won a bronze medal at the 1988 Olympics. But by 1990, she had a bulging disc and sprained ligaments in her lower back. As she was training for the 1992 Olympic trials, she was diagnosed with a bulging disc in her neck.

"I had a bad landing in February and another in March, where I couldn't move my head sideways or even shake the water out of my ears," she said. "Each time, I'd take a few days off. The pain was like having a knife stuck between your shoulder blades. I took anti-inflammatories. I was getting pretty high on painkillers, but I always came back."

While warming up at the U.S. national meet in April, Williams heard a click in her neck and her left arm went numb. The disc in her neck had ruptured.

"My coach said to hop in the hot tub and work it out, but I knew right then I was done," Williams said. On the drive to the hospital, every bump in the road drew a scream from Williams.

She opted not to have surgery, which would involve making an incision through the front of the neck and moving the trachea aside. Over time, the two vertebrae may fuse together and she may lose some range of motion.

"At the time, it felt tragic to miss the Olympics," she said. "But my body was saying enough is enough."

Williams will attend the Olympic trials as a spectator this week. She expects to feel a fleeting temptation to climb back up those three stories.

"When you do a reverse layout, with your chest and face rising up," she said, "there's a moment at the top, before you start to fall, when you're looking at the sky. It's magical."

THOMAS McGUANE

The Way Home

FROM SPORTS AFIELD

I HAD A SETBACK in my hunting. I used to hunt everything —
big game, waterfowl and upland birds. In a ten-year period it had
shrunk to upland birds, which is the only kind of hunting I'd done
from the beginning. I'd had a number of dogs, all pointers: one
heartthrob of middling achievement (trained by me) named Molly;
a great dog named Babe, bought trained in Arkansas, who once
pointed a crack in the ground, causing me to wonder about her
good sense until a fifteen-bird covey poured out of the crack; a
couple of brilliant dogs who would get on the wrong side of a hill
and give you a horizon job; and Sadie, a "gentleman's shooting
dog" I bought at age 2 from Jarrett Thompson in Texas. She is a
great dog, always in birds, smart about her objectives from Alberta
to Alabama, and she has made me friends in strange places because
of her phenomenal usefulness in the field. She has so little self-
hunt in her that she has never needed to be kenneled. Now 14,
she's had hip surgery, has cataracts, and is stone deaf, but for about
an hour at a time can keep me in game as well as any dog.

Her physical limitations began to descend upon her around 10,
and with them a kind of gloom befell me. At about that time, my
youngest daughter, Annie, then 11, sat down next to me and said,
"Poppy, you really love to hunt birds, don't you?" "Yes, Annie, I do."
"Well, then" she said, "I think you should hunt birds. But I have to
tell you: I think it is the saddest thing I ever heard of"

Then I read a Chekhov story in which two young gentlemen
go hunting and one shoots a woodcock. His companion picks it

up and looks at it outstretched in his palm. He says, "Aren't we a couple of great fellows."

Finally, one day I stopped at a ranch with a friend to ask permission to hunt birds, and a weather-beaten old cowboy — a hired man, about six-five with iron-black-and-gray hair, a man who must not have had the say of this particular piece of land — addressed us from a reddened face and in tones of unconcealed bitterness. "Sure, fellas, go ahead. Kill every one. I been watching them all summer from the tractor. You boys just go out there with your guns and kill all the little birds."

And it didn't help when, that winter in Georgia, I met a man who managed hunting "plantations" (the only thing they plant is quail feed) and who continuously called our pursuit "hunting entertainment" and referred to quail as "the product."

Recently I was in communication with a breeder of French Brittany spaniels who offered an unconditional money-back guarantee. The breeder pointed out that you simply returned the dog, the money would be sent by return mail, and the dog would be immediately "euthanized."

Several years ago, I heard a cavalcade of rifle fire as a famous Mississippi field-trial trainer and former national champion "euthanized" the less-talented half of his string of pointers before heading back to Mississippi. The grove of trees from whence the sounds emanated shall forever be an image of American play gone septic, the standards of war applied to leisure.

In short, the result was that my crippled bird dog and I spent two falls afield with only one of us putting any heart into it. I began to try to understand the pull I had to hunt, to consider whether it even existed anymore.

I thought back to the early 50s when my father would take me out just at sunup, before he went to work. We would take our Brittany, Jenny, and slip over to a sprawling commercial nursery whose roughlands ranged close to our house. I was a shooting nut at the time and when the pheasants got in front of Jenny, I rained them down with my 20-gauge Model 12, my father craning around guiltily while darting to pick up the birds as they fell. Days later, loafing at the hardware store, we joined in the speculation as to who the poachers could be. There is no question that that outlaw glow persists for some in hunting. A friend of mine who flies a small plane and has learned to drop whisky by parachute into dried-out elk camps reminds me that the Hell's Angels might be a step up from the stream of hot-orange nitwits that ply the logging roads during elk season.

When I was in the ninth grade my father acquired, one boozy night, a pointer named Dot, for free. She was demented beyond imagining. My brother and I took white canes and deck glasses, and went around the local department store pretending we were blind: Dot was our Seeing Eye dog, whirling at the end of a chain leash like a white tornado. That was the only fun we ever got out of her. Any bird she found, she killed and ate. Eventually my father found a new home for her; the theory then as now was that if a dog ran too big, move the dog to bigger country. Or to a younger owner, someone who, in effect, ran too big himself. There were just enough rumors going around of some pathological liver-and-white land jet that ended up winning Ames Plantation, that people flung onto these lunatics till no shred of dignity was left. Then they moved them to bigger country.

I have always been a solitary hunter and my bird-hunting friends are a chattering, happy lot who bolster one another, fanning the tradition when times are thin. But when I began to sink from sight as a hunter I just kept sinking, hunting only enough to keep aging Sadie happy, and rarely shooting. And of course, Annie's words rang in my ears. But buried away somewhere was the pressure to be afield again hunting, without which I was someone else.

Last fall, imagining it might be Sadie's last season, I decided I owed it to her to take this thing a bit more seriously. There wasn't enough time left in her life for me to try, at my glacial rate, to understand the deep things that drew me. With the first hunt, I was back where I started from, trying to think how to do it better. Hunting will always lie beyond my capacity to explain it yet remain the sort of trembling mystery to which we are drawn. Life in our time has become extremely thin on ceremony, religious ceremony, family ceremony. College students often skip their own graduations. The funerals of parents are either a long plane ride or too far to go. People rarely dine but feed as opportunistically as coyotes. The indoctrination of one generation by another is at best a paltry matter; at worst, it is farmed out with the rest of our acculturation to television. Our popular culture is wholly trained on the lives of celebrities, that tiny minority. Perhaps they have ceremonies. We would like them to. They are our royal family and we want their lives to be either perfect so that we may love them or imperfect so that we may hate them. We have strong feelings about our celebrities. We assume that lives are full of ceremonies, like the Academy Awards.

But some of us want our own ceremonies. I love my little ranch for, among other things, the regularity of its cycles, of irrigation, of haying, of feeding, calving, weaning, and shipping. They come at more or less the same time each year and are as unavoidable as weather. To avoid them, you have to get rid of the ranch. After all those years in school, I'm still on the semester system. I like that rhythm too, which is my secret; no one can tell that I am on "spring vacation" wandering uselessly around the property and perhaps recalling the beer and poontang expeditions to Florida in my cherished yesteryears.

But highest on that chain of values are the seasons of hunting and fishing. If you grew up hunting, crisp fall days can mean only one thing, not to be supplanted by tailgate parties at football games or anything else. And that one thing will not go away, even if you quit hunting. I found that out. I would have to go on. I would have a few new rules to freshen things up, but I would go on. It was too late to change. In the words of Popeye, "I yam what I yam."

Since there is no catch-and-release hunting that I know of, a self-imposed limit would be in order. Mine is the capacity of my wife, Laurie, and I to eat gamebirds as we eat from our garden, taking it that the land is bountiful. No freezing allowed and no banquets. That could be pretty constraining. But if you start with an untrained pup and never shoot except over a solid point, a good whack comes off the top.

I also decided that I wasn't going to make trips to exotic birdfields, unless to hunt with a friend. I live in a tough, canyon-creased country without a terrific concentration of birds. You have to hunt hard to get anything at all. Fourteen inches of rain, that's how it is. But it's country you can have to yourself. No one is going to drive that far for so few opportunities or such a struggle. You can get turned around or caught in sudden weather changes that will give you deep pause. If you hunt in it for long enough, you can conjure up a pretty good picture of your undiscovered bones whitening in a ravine that sees forty-two minutes of sun a day. Old Shep kind of a deal with the dog watching ice vapor from the airliners.

Hunters and fishermen are always sort of picturing themselves. That is why they are such a boon to the clothing industry. But they also wonder whether or not they look better with a 12-gauge or a 20-gauge. Some feel shooting a 16-gauge ties them to a more authentic past and separates them from the gaudy newcomers with grotesque things like ventilated ribs. Of late, the hills are alive with side-by-sides and waxed cotton as our heroes go on picturing themselves. The fashion-conscious may set up a countercurrent and appear in cast-off army camo and Remington automatics. Some hunters feel their legend is best served by associating themselves with only one bird. "I'm a Hun' man." "Bobwhite is all I'm about." "Timberdoodle!" and so on. I myself am quite conscious of being a mishmash: side-by-side, baseball hat, jeans, hiking boots, Red Hot Chili Peppers T-shirt. I catch a glimpse of myself in a stock tank while my dog drinks and feel I am viewing the unresolved self.

Sadie could no longer make it through a day. She was enjoying her retirement on the couch. We went out as much as she could and the hunts were oddly absorbing. She couldn't hear or see very well, but her nose worked as well as ever. So, as I couldn't call her or signal to her in any way, I followed the inflexible cones of scent, getting so caught up in her world that I began to imagine myself to be a great nose, as in the Gogol story, this time following a dog through the sagebrush.

I would have to train the next dog myself. That was one of the new rules. Robert Wehle, the breeder of the great Elhew line of pointers, once told me: "If you don't train it, it's not your dog." While I don't entirely agree, there is some truth to the remark. I knew that I was too old and corrupt to train a pointer again, to run over the heather, heart pounding through my wheezer bones preaching religion at the top of my lungs to a canine land hog: *follow the bouncing white dot, there go the deer, maybe we can wait for her at the truck, leave your coat and we'll come back tomorrow.* In the words of Weird Al Yankovic, I'd rather have a thousand paper cuts on my face.

I decided to get a Gordon setter. I honestly don't know why; I'd never seen one hunting. I knew that the field strain had been safeguarded from the bench ninnies and I had it in my mind that they had found favor in years past with solitary hunters like me. There are some very good ones here in Montana. Their decline was associated with their being hard to see in the woods, but I don't hunt in the woods very much and if that was the criterion, why not hunt with a pink angora bunny, for crying out loud? I did a lot of phoning around America to owners and breeders. I got the impression that not only were Gordons responsive to being trained by reasonably experienced owners but that they didn't do particularly well at the hands of professional trainers and often bloomed when liberated from their kennels and returned to their homes. Having once been sent away to school, I identified with this trait, though I hardly bloomed at home either, where a craving for rich food, showgirls and bourbon seemed, to my parents, grotesque in a 15-year-old.

I spoke to a Gordon breeder in Missouri, Roger Casey. I talked to all of them about available litters. He had two on hand. One bitch, Miss Liberty, had a single ovary and bore only two pups in a litter. He didn't think I'd want one. They weren't "stylish." I asked Casey if by stylish he meant a twelve-o'clock tail. He said that he did. I said let's go on to the other traits. I talked to some of the owners and concluded Miss Liberty's pups were the kind you'd want if you had to make a living with a shotgun. I bought one.

Gracie arrived at the Billings airport in the fall of 1994, age 49 days. I had all the anxiety associated with an arriving puppy, though her breeder was fastidiously cautious about how and when he shipped dogs. You wait at baggage claim and the dog doesn't appear at baggage claim. You go to the special side door where skis and bicycles are delivered. No dog. You go to the counter. The weary man at the counter says, "She's back here," and you are delivered the pup around whom you have imagined your future in the manner of a young husband.

I carried the small kennel outside and when I found a bit of grass, my wife and I let her out. She walked straight from the kennel with what can only be described as nonchalance. *So this is Montana.* There is a curious aloofness associated with Gordons and this was a glimpse. They are detached almost and their affection is displayed in subtle ways, the most striking of which is their uncanny knowledge of what you are up to every minute of the day. None of the whorish demonstrations of man's best friend. A kind of privacy. But at that moment, my only real thought was, "If this pup's no good, my hunting days are over."

I worked with her every day that fall and winter. *Here, heel, whoa* and *no*. That was it, but we got those down. I also took her to the field very early on and, as I had been taught by a dog trainer in Georgia, kept her to the front on our little expeditions by refusing to take a single step unless she moved out ahead of me. If she got too far away, I hid in the brush and adjusted her range by exploiting her natural fear of being left alone. When she seamed too short, I followed noiselessly and accepted everything she did. I changed directions on the tap of a whistle or, when she was close, on her name. Since she is too independent to cold track another dog, I dared to brace her with Sadie so that she could gain a little instruction in the mystery and logic of scent.

At the end of each session, we had a wild wrestling match, and for several months I was covered with scratches from her sharp little teeth. When she was tired of the battle, she would suddenly sit back, drop her long patrician nose, and give me a "look" that meant enough was enough. She was young and beautiful and extremely serious. When Guy de la Valdéne and I hunted her — and I was anxious because I had praised her on several occasions when we'd talked and I feared a bad day when we finally hunted — he said she reminded him of one of those happy models one saw in the discos twenty years ago, joyous bouncing emphasized by the flying curly ears. She covered ground at moderate range with high energy, stopping or changing directions with real electricity. It was hard to keep your eye off her, the kind of dog that, with or without game, produces continuous pleasure. She hunted for me, and if she couldn't see me she went airborne, vertically scouting the land around her.

On mild winter days, I took Gracie afield across the saddle of my horse. Upon reaching promising ground, I put her down and followed her slowly with the horse. The first time she found a covey, I didn't believe her. Thereafter, I got off the horse, threw the reins down, steadied her, and flushed the birds. A horse trainer once told me, "It takes a real hand to train a mediocre horse. A good horse can be trained by damn near anyone." I think some of this was the case with this pup. She came together very quickly indeed. In my favor, I kept it ridiculously simple and worked at it every day, even when it meant going in insulated coveralls and working her behind a snowfence. No electric collar, no planted pigeons. Sydney Lea, who wrote a wonderful book, *Hunting All the Way Home*, and who, unlike most sporting writers, is the Real McCoy, said, "Throw that check-cord away." I left it on the nail it has occupied since my last dog with a twelve-o'clock tail. When you watch an open field trail and see four men on lathered horses trying to bring the champion dog in from his home on the horizon so that he may contribute to the hunting dog gene pool, you will know why the check-cord has become *de rigueur*. It ought to be one thousand feet of aircraft cable through-bolted to a five-by-five concrete dead-man to really bring the job to a finish. Sadly, it is just a common device for rope-burning the owner and adding to his list of grievances.

Gracie's first hunting season had just opened, a test for us both. There was a storm coming in, the first of this hot autumn. It was approaching from the north but sucking up warmer air from Wyoming. The sunny sky that had burned my skin yesterday was closing in overhead and the air was full of palpable, blowing moisture. It was a relief.

The clouds were coming down around me. The air seemed to have faint lines angling through it. I felt cool moisture settling on my skin as I walked through the buffalo grass hollows and coulees. I remembered fishing a small peat stream in western Ireland, through the endless summer twilight that faded insinuatingly into night. It was country like this. I was alone and at last light I looked up the miles of sloping land that was full of something unspoken. It was nightfall where numberless generations had come and gone, where pagan ring forts moldered in pastures, and where lost populations of the famine had left their farm fences high on now-uninhabited mountainsides. As I looked, two greyhounds swept down toward me at such alarming speed I began to feel like their quarry. They stopped at the edge of my vision and I stared at them so fixedly that I barely realized it when they were joined by two children, a boy and a girl of 10 or 11, barefoot and in appearance wilder than any humans I have ever seen. I spoke to them out of sheer nervousness and they, with their two greyhounds, vanished into the darkness without a reply. Today, with Gracie, I felt I was back in the same country.

But this was fog and I was hunting a ten-month-old Gordon setter bitch. She cracked back and forth on the damp ground that felt new and strange now that we could no longer see the Absaroka

Mountains that were always our backdrop. I remembered other days and a pageant of hunting fields. I had put a bell on her and a red, reflective collar. She can sometimes be hard to see, even in bright sunlight when she vanishes into the shadow of heavy sagebrush. When I can't find her with my eye, I can pick up that bucolic little tinkling. But as the fog thickened, it was the reflective collar that helped the most, sometimes floating disembodied through the fog with the mysterious bell punctuating its bounces.

We couldn't really see where we were going. The wind was swelling up out of the south, and the coulees we were hunting ran at right angles to it. The pup was at a little disadvantage. At the limit of my vision, racing downhill, she overran a covey of sharptails. Half a dozen got up and disappeared into the thick air. I hollered "whoa" and she stopped in her tracks. Well, things were looking up. Gracie was on point. I felt there were birds around her. Now when I sent her forward with an "all right" she just got stauncher. Yes, more birds.

We were at the beginning of the new beginning and I knew that it was important that the big chief show Gracie that his 16 gauge was indeed big medicine and that there had been real merit in accepting me as a hunting partner. I walked up behind her and the rest of the flock took flight. I shouldered my gun but the birds were arcing downhill beyond her and I was afraid to shoot. Well, hell. Nothing to do but offer her praise for that stop-to-flush or stop-to-whoa, which I did. And so we went on. I directed her around in a big arc to get us downwind of the disappearing birds. It was all just a guess because we couldn't see where they went and could see only about twenty-five yards of gray-green wet prairie in front of us, anyway. But it had been a quiet day and we knew there were birds around us. So we pressed on. Gracie's flat back-and-forth casts eventually crossed some scent; there was suddenly forward motion in her race and just like that, she locked up. She gave just a slight movement of the end of her tail and a glance to the rear. Yes, dear, big chief is once again coming with his medicine stick. Now you will see why I am necessary. Suddenly, I felt the pressure. When the bird got up, a nice going-away at moderate range, a no-brainer, I missed with the right barrel and, upon reflection, missed with the left barrel. Gracie was steady through the shooting, perfect. There was no question about it: I was the feckless fool.

I couldn't let my disappointment show. My ten-month-old had

just been steady to wing and shot. A miracle! I praised her, held her, regarded her, murmured her name. Forget the quality of the shooting and keep the glass half full.

And we went on. Now we really couldn't see and the heavy mist drifted in veils before us. My thought was: opportunity gone; dog feeling doubt. I no longer commanded the wilderness. I was the chump with the chow and the noisy toy.

Gracie handled so well that I was able to turn our hunt in the direction in which I believed my truck lay. In a little while I knew that I had lost my truck entirely, no easy trick with a three-quarter-ton Ford parked on a knoll. The brush and timothy began to thicken. I didn't remember this brush. But Gracie liked it; the reflective collar looked like a bouncing ball to sing to. I did sing to it — "you got a lot a nerve to say you are my friend" — in my best Bob Dylan snarl when — was this possible? — I made note that dream dog was on point again.

Thought: Maybe I put down the gun; I steady her with one hand on her chest, whisper sweet nothings in one curly black ear while the birds float up and away into the pea soup. But no. I was going to take it like a man. I was going to shoot the unforgiving 16-gauge British smoke pole and let the chips fall. As Gracie had not entirely distinguished grasshoppers and songbirds from wild chickens, I was relieved by a small doubt while I advanced upon the point: maybe I wouldn't have to take the shooting test again.

In an instant, a crowd of chickens was in the foggy air. The light was so dim that I saw fire from the barrels, and birds fell, that special tumble. I released Gracie and called upon her to hunt dead as she is not yet a retriever, except of tennis balls. She pointed the dead birds on the ground and was astonished when I reached down and held up a grouse. Where did I get that?

Yes, people, I was restored in her eyes and Gracie was treated to the sight which must become the *omnium desideratum* of every broke gundog: the chief putting dinner in the back of his coat. And what I hope will not appear pompous to the sensible reader, I was somewhat restored in my own eyes, not as a gunner, nor as a dog trainer, but as someone who has stepped back into the river of things which matter most to him and which allow him to glimpse a few truths that preceded him and will be here when he is gone. He imagines that they are once again among his belongings.

Heaven Help Marge Schott

FROM SPORTS ILLUSTRATED

ALONE IN HER BEDROOM, alone in a forty-room mansion, alone on a seventy-acre estate, Marge Schott finishes off a vodka-and-water (no lime, no lemon), stubs out another Carlton 120, takes to her two aching knees, and prays to the Men. To Charlie, the husband who made her life and then ruined it. He taught her never to trust. To Daddy, the unsmiling father who turned her into his only son. He taught her never to be soft. To Dad Schott, the calculating father-in-law, whom she may have loved most of all. He taught her never to let herself be cheated.

"I pray to them every night, honey," she says. "How many owners do that, huh? Hit their knees every night?"

Hard to say. For that matter, how many baseball owners keep in their kitchen drawer plastic bags containing hair from a dog that died five years ago? Or are worth millions but haven't shopped for clothes in nine years? Schott just wears the stuff people send her. "If it fits, honey," she says in her No. 4 sandpaper voice, "I wear it."

Honey is what Schott calls everybody, unless you're *baby* or *sweetheart*. It's what she does instead of remembering your name. "This guy is from SportsChannel, honey. He's here doing a big story on me."

"Sports Illustrated, Mrs. Schott."

"Right, honey."

Schott does not really have to remember anyone's name, because she's 67 years old, as rich as Oman, and she answers to nobody. She owns 43 percent of the Cincinnati Reds, but she hasn't had time to actually learn the game yet. After all, it has only been twelve years since that Christmas when she "saved the team for Cincinnati," as she has said over the years. (Why ruin the story by mentioning that the previous owners insisted that they never would have sold the Reds to anyone but a Cincinnatian, and there were no offers on the table from any other city. None of the men in Cincinnati were stepping up to buy the team, she says now.)

It is not unusual, for instance, for Schott not to know the names of her players. Oh, she knows a few — Eric Davis, Barry Larkin, Chris Sabo — but the rest are just uniforms that she steers her current Saint Bernard, Schottzie 02, around before games, hoping to spy a familiar face.

"Who's that, honey?"

"George Grande, Mrs. Schott."

"Oh."

Grande has been the Reds' TV broadcaster for four years.

Marge sees Sabo. "Hi, honey."

"Hi, Mrs. Schott."

"Tell Schottzie you're going to win for her tonight."

Sabo looks around uncomfortably, then mutters at the ground, "Uh, we're going to win for you tonight . . . Schottzie."

In a recent game against the Philadelphia Phillies, there was a hot smash to Reds first baseman Hal Morris, who shouldn't have meant anything to Schott except that he has played on her team since 1990 and was leading the club in hitting at the time. Morris bobbled the ball. "Oh, you stupid guy!" Schott screamed.

Morris recovered and flipped the ball to the pitcher, who covered first.

"Who was that, honey?"

"Who was who?"

"Who ran over?"

"The pitcher?"

"Oh, good."

Schott is not big on baseball history, either. There is not a single banner commemorating the Big Red Machine years in Riverfront Stadium, not a single retired number on display to honor Pete Rose, Johnny Bench, Joe Morgan, or Tony Perez. Not a single reminder of Rose's record 4,192 hits. That kind of thing sounds expensive, and Schott is much bigger on saving money than memories. Besides, who can remember all that stuff? During a rain delay in the game against Philadelphia, the Jumbotron was showing high-lights of the classic 1970 World Series between the Reds and the Baltimore Orioles, in which Orioles third baseman Brooks Robin-son was merely Superman.

"Who's that, baby?"

"Brooks Robinson."

"Brooks Robinson? I thought he was one of the first black players."

"That was Jackie Robinson."

"No. . . ."

Of course, having Aunt Bee as your team's owner has its advan-tages. For instance, Schott doesn't raise her ticket prices every season, as a lot of other owners do. You don't do that to family members, which is what Reds fans are to her. Riverfront's most expensive seat is $11.50, cheapest in the majors. Schott still charges only $1 for a hot dog. (A jumbo frank costs three times as much at Shea Stadium in New York.) She does not often meddle in player deals, mostly because she has no real interest in baseball. Night after night she sits alone in her vast luxury box with just her tele-phone and Schottzie, not paying much attention to the game, wait-ing for some high-ranking employee to show up at the door and take Schottzie for a walk. Afterward there's always a report.

"Tinkle or poo?" she will ask.

"Just tinkle," the director of marketing or some other front-office-type will answer sheepishly.

In the sixth inning Schott moves down to her box seats behind the Reds' dugout to chain-sign autographs, hardly looking up ex-cept after loud cracks of the bat. She hates it when the bats break, but she does not lose money on them. She has an employee take them to the gift shop at a downtown Cincinnati hotel and sell them. (To show their undying love for her, some Cincinnati players smash their cracked bats into two pieces so they're in no condition to be sold.)

After the game Schott drives the twenty minutes to her man-sion in suburban Indian Hill, where she is even more alone: no husband, no kids, no grandchildren, no live-in help, precious few friends, a tiny television sitting cold in the kitchen, the newspaper lying unread, books untouched. She doesn't sleep much at night, despite all the Unisom she takes, not to mention the vodkas (Kamchatka, the cheap stuff). She sits in bed making picture frames to match her furniture and falls asleep, only to wake up in half an hour to smoke another cigarette. Finally she rises, fresh from a good night's nicotining, ready to seize the day.

Because she's set apart from the world like that, it's no wonder Schott's political and social views have not really changed since the Edsel. Over the years she has insulted homosexuals ("Only fruits wear earrings"), blacks ("Dave is my million-dollar nigger," she said of Dave Parker, a Reds outfielder from 1984 to '87) and Jews ("He's a beady-eyed Jew," she said of Cincinnati marketing director Cal Levy, according to *Unleashed,* the exhaustive biography of Schott written by Mike Bass in 1993). As for Adolf Hitler, she takes a compassionate view. "He was O.K. at the beginning," she says. "He rebuilt all the roads, honey. You know that, right? He just went too far." Two weeks ago she repeated that opinion in an interview with ESPN, setting off a storm of protest, including outrage from the Anti-Defamation League and other Jewish organizations, and casting baseball in an embarrassing light yet again. Two days later she issued a written apology, which was accepted by the Jewish Community Relations Council of Cincinnati.

Schott is a proud third-generation German-American. Her mother's sister had five sons who fought for Germany in World War II. "She used to send us little Nazi soldier dolls with the swastikas and everything, honey. We used to play with them," says Schott. She even has a Nazi armband she keeps in a bureau drawer in the hallway leading to her living room. She forgot about the armband until a Christmas party in 1987, when Levy happened to find it and asked her about it. "Figures a Jewish guy would find it, huh, honey?" Schott whispers, which she does when a matter under discussion is a little sticky. "What's a Jewish guy looking through my drawers for anyway? Right, honey?" (Levy, who is no longer with the club, says Schott had sent him in search of a dinner bell.)

She says she's not really a Nazi sympathizer, although she once told ABC's Diane Sawyer that the armband "is not a symbol of evil to me." Mostly it's a case of Schott not throwing anything away. If a bag lady had a trust fund, her house might look like Schott's: crammed with junk. There's a room full of stuff she received on two baseball goodwill visits to Japan. There are closets full of mementos and stuffed Saint Bernards and clocks with miniature baseball bats for hands, most of which were given to her. Charlie's suits still hang in his closet, right where he left them, and he has been dead, what, twenty-eight years?

MargeVision is set on the 1950s, and she sees it clear as a bell. She often feels like speaking out for what she believes, and it hasn't hurt her much. While Al Campanis, Jimmy the Greek, and Ben Wright lost their jobs for saying one fiftieth of what Schott has said, she got only a one-year suspension from baseball in 1993 for making racial and ethnic slurs. A sensitivity-training course was thrown in for good measure. The course didn't really take. Sending Schott to sensitivity training is like sending a pickpocket to a Rolex convention.

Take a recent night, when Schott was leaving the Montgomery Inn restaurant in suburban Cincinnati after actually tearing up over the all-American vitality and clean-cut looks of a girl who had asked her for an autograph. As Schott was piling into her junk-strewn Riviera, she saw a group of high school–aged Asian-Americans walking down the street, laughing and talking.

"Look at that," she said.

"What?"

"That's not right, honey."

"What isn't?"

"Those Asian kids."

"It's not?"

(Whisper) "Well, I don't like when they come here, honey, and stay so long and then outdo our kids. That's not right."

If you were her public relations adviser, you would have her followed by six men in flame-retardant suits with a fire hose. In 1989 at Riverfront Stadium, as *60 Minutes* cameras rolled on her and Bart Giamatti, who was then the baseball commissioner, Schott saw something she didn't like.

Schott: "Is this a girl batboy or a boy that needs a goddamn haircut?"

Giamatti: "Well, Marge, that's a question you ought to take up with the young person after the game."

Schott: "Is that a boy or a girl?"

Giamatti: "It's a young man with a modern haircut."

Schott: "Well, he'll never be out here again with long hair like that. . . ."

Giamatti: "Marge, you're killing me here!"

Even in trying to say something nice about someone, Schott gets it all wrong. In boasting recently of her meeting with Japanese prime minister Kiichi Miyazawa on one of her baseball goodwill visits, in 1991, she recalled what he had said to her, using a cartoonish Japanese accent: "He says to me, honey, he says, 'No want Cadirrac, no want Rincoln, want Mosh Shott Boo-ick.'"

In the first six weeks of the 1996 season, Schott rewrote the book on loafer-in-mouth disease.

Chapter 1: When umpire John McSherry died of a heart attack after collapsing at home plate on Opening Day at Riverfront, Schott objected to the cancellation of the game and complained about how McSherry's death put *her* out: "I don't believe it. First it snows, and now *this!*"

Chapter 2: The next day Schott took flowers somebody else had sent her, ripped off the card, wrote a new one with heartfelt condolences, and sent the flowers to the umpires' room at Riverfront.

Chapter 3: At the start of the season the Reds weren't providing fans with scores from other games on the Riverfront scoreboard. "Why do they care about one game when they're watching another?" argued Schott, who had stopped paying her bill for the service (it costs $350 a month) during last season.

Chapter 4: Following the sixth home game, after being raked over the coals by the media for her stinginess, she reversed her scoreboard decision and blamed it on her employees, saying in front of a roomful of reporters, "I've got to have the worst public relations staff in America!" Now those employees have to track the scores by calling to other ballparks and listening to the radio.

Chapter 5: On April 14 she tried to apologize for her McSherry gaffe minutes before the first pitch against the Houston Astros by approaching the umpires working the game — none of whom were at Riverfront on Opening Day and all of whom resented her publicity-minded opportunism. One, Harry Wendelstedt, turned his back on her.

Not that sheer Jell-O-headedness is always behind Schott's troubles. Many of her idiocies are clearly thought out in advance. For years she has made it known that she would prefer that the Reds not hire women of childbearing age. Women in the workplace is not a cause Schott champions, despite the fact that she is one herself. (Besides the Reds, she owns two car dealerships, at least three vehicle-leasing firms, a concrete company, and several other businesses in various states, not to mention a large chunk of General Motors stock, most of it under the control of her Cincinnati-based holding company, Schottco.) "I'll tell you something, honey," she says. "Some of the biggest problems in this city come from women wanting to leave the home to work." And: "Why do these girl reporters have to come into the locker room? Why can't they wait outside?" And: "I don't really think baseball is a woman's place, honey. I really don't. I think it should be left to the boys."

She despises the city ordinance that prohibits smoking at Riverfront, the one that keeps her sitting alone in her twenty-chair luxury box instead of behind the dugout with the fans, whom she loves. Besides, MargeVision doesn't see cigarettes as being all that bad. "I'll tell you something, honey," she says in her smoker's rasp. "They had a jazz festival here awhile ago, and we walked around, and they were doing nothing but crack!"

Schott detests facial hair, too, and forbids it on any player or employee. The close, comfortable shave, she feels, is her lasting contribution to the game, even though it was a long-standing club policy that Cincinnati players not grow facial hair when she bought the team. "If nothing else, the thing I'm most proud of [about the Reds] is the no–facial hair and earrings," she said recently to Chip Baker, her one-man marketing department (by comparison, the Atlanta Braves' marketing department has ten employees), even as she looked at a photo of the 1896 Reds, all of them bewhiskered.

"Don't you think, Chip?"

"Yes, ma'am."

"Did Jesus have a beard, Chip?"

"I think so, Mrs. Schott."

"Oh." Pause. "Have you met our friend from Sports America here, honey?"

"Sports Illustrated, Mrs. Schott."

"Right, honey."

It is not just baseball Schott is a little behind on. She seems to have been on Neptune for much of the twentieth century. Once, she showed up very early for a meeting in a Chicago hotel and then was overheard growling into a pay phone, "Hey, why didn't you tell me there was an hour difference between Cincinnati and Chicago?"

Schott and computers don't see eye to eye, either. At her car dealerships and other local businesses, which she usually visits in the mornings before going to the ballpark, some employees have taped signs to their computers begging her not to turn them off. She does that to save electricity, even though, she admits, it makes a computer "lose all those thingies on the screen."

Schott doesn't read much anymore, either. "I don't like the words so much, honey. I like the pictures. Pictures mean so much more to me than words, honey."

She is always ready with her stack of photos. Here's a shot of Marge as a baby, one of five daughters of Edward Unnewehr, who made a fortune in the lumber business (mostly from plywood and veneer). Five daughters, and all Daddy ever wanted was a boy.

"Well, what'd you have, Ed?" people would ask him.

"A baby," he would snarl.

Daddy was strict. "Very *achtung!*" as Schott says. When Daddy wanted Mother, he would ring a bell. Daddy did not eat meals with his children until they were over the messy age — about four. And you had better be tough. "You didn't get sick in Daddy's family, honey," Schott says. "We coughed into our pillows."

Since Daddy couldn't have a boy, he treated Marge like one. He called her Butch. She grew up the wisecracking girl Daddy took to work whenever he could, the circle-skirted jokester who would bring cigars to slumber parties and smoke them. She was less comfortable around women than men, whom she was learning to love and hate all at once.

And here's a photo of Butch marrying Charles Schott, son of a wealthy society family in Cincinnati. Here's Daddy, sulking throughout the wedding. "He wanted me to run his business, honey," she says, "and now he was losing me." Here's Marge with Charlie's father, Walter, who took her on the road with him, took her to make the boys in the board meetings laugh at all her one-liners. Once the meeting started, though, she had better stay quiet.

Still Marge learned a lot at the feet of Dad Schott, who in 1938 had become the largest auto dealer in Ohio. Today she knows where every penny goes, how every tax shelter works, how wide every loophole can be made. Schott may come off as having sniffed too much epoxy, but she knows her way around a financial statement and the county courthouse. "I hate lawyers, honey," she often says, "but I keep 'em busy."

The Men ran her life, enriched it, and, ultimately, ruined it. According to *Unleashed,* Charles was a hopeless alcoholic, who left her alone on their wedding night to play cards and left her alone hundreds of nights after that.

Yeah, she learned lots about men. Like when she found out years after the fact that it had been two male members of her family who, shortly after she was married in 1952, had sneaked one of her Saint Bernards out and had it killed because they didn't like it. You don't think that hurt? Men, honey.

Here's one last picture of her with the chubby, grinning Charlie. When he died in 1968 of a heart attack, he was rumored to have been found in the bathtub of his mistress, Lois Kenning. It is a subject Schott does not like to discuss but has not quite figured a way to lie about.

"Where did your husband die, Mrs. Schott?"

"I don't know, honey."

Since then she has waged a one-woman war for fidelity. Her goal is to rid baseball of "cutesy-poos," as she calls them: the groupies who end up in ballplayers' hotel rooms. She says she has hired private investigators to videotape her players getting on and off buses and going in and out of hotels, to make sure there is no cutesy-pooing going on. Reds general manager Jim Bowden confirms only a little of this. "A couple of years ago we videotaped our players getting off a couple of charter flights, just to make sure our rules and regulations were being followed," he says. "At no time were rules being violated."

The last two seasons Reds players have complained that their mail has been opened and taped shut again. "Ray [Knight, the team's rookie manager] thought some of the boxes that came in the mail looked like they'd been opened," says Bowden. "He told Mrs. Schott, and she said she would look into it." Some of the players suspect Schott did the opening. Schott says she doesn't know a thing about it.

Then there are the phone calls. "I tape every call in and out of the clubhouse," Schott boasts. "These players are not going to pull any cutesy-poo stuff on me."

"But isn't that illegal, Mrs. Schott?"

"Oh. Oh, no. Not tape, honey. I just mean I have the operator log every call to the clubhouse. That's all, honey."

Schott is tighter than shrink-wrap, but whatever price she has to pay to protect the Great American Family, she will pay it. This is because she never had children herself. It is her single greatest sorrow. "I just don't think I did my job," she lamented recently in her Riverfront office. "In my day girls were raised to raise kids, and I didn't do it. My life would've been completely different with kids. I wouldn't be here, honey, I can tell you that."

It did not help that her sister Lottie had ten kids, the way Marge thinks good Catholic girls should. And it was not because Marge didn't try. She hired the best doctors, up to and including one who she says had treated the Shah of Iran. "And he about killed me, honey, giving me all these drugs," she says. "About killed me." She says she tried to adopt twins once, "but the nuns wouldn't let us, honey. Wouldn't let us." She whispers: "'They're interbreds,' they told us. 'They'd only be a frustration to you.' I told 'em, 'No, we'll educate 'em,' but they wouldn't let us have 'em." In *Unleashed*, Bass reported that Charlie's mother attempted to arrange adoptions, but Marge and Charlie refused to follow through because they didn't know the children's backgrounds.

When Charlie died, Marge was only 39. She could have tried for kids again, but all the men who seemed attracted to her were already married. "I never knew so many guys' wives didn't understand them, honey," she cracks. She was going to marry Harold Schott, Charlie's uncle. She says he called her six times one day to tell her he was flying back from Florida to ask for her hand, but he died that same day. "First the family said it was a heart attack," Marge explains. "Then they said he drowned. The best swimmer in the family. Something funny going on there."

And so she was left alone to raise other things: twenty-two Saint Bernards, a baseball team, and even cattle, though she refused to let anybody slaughter the calves. She let them live. She looks out on the calves in the distance from her yard and grabs your elbow and says, "Look at them. Isn't it beautiful seeing the families out in the field?"

Adults, especially ballplayers and newspaper people, she's not so big on, but she is nuts for animals and children. Once a week or so she will get to the ballpark early, gather up twenty or so small kids, and let them run out to the right-field wall and back before a game. Once she went to the opening day of a little league for disabled children and spent most of an hour crying like a baby.

On April 3, Reds second baseman Bret Boone flew to Birming-

ham to have elbow surgery just hours after his wife, Suzi, gave birth
in Cincinnati to their first child, Savannah. Immediately after the
operation he flew home to be with her and their hours-old baby.
Schott went to the hospital that night to check on them. She took
gifts and stayed with Suzi for a couple of hours while Bret, still
groggy from his surgery, slept on a couch. "It was weird," says one
former marketing employee. "She was great to our families. Absolutely terrific. But she treated us like s—."

Whatever generous spirit there is inside Schott flickers out when
she sits behind that owner's desk. "I think she is the single worst
person I've ever known," says one longtime Reds employee. "Spite-
ful, mean-spirited, and evil."

Says a former top-level employee, "She's the most cold, calculating person I've ever known. To feel sorry for her is ridiculous."

Schott believes she must be bottom-line tough, like the Men,
coughing into her pillow all the way. Drink hard, work hard, feel
hard. And this is how you get the dimly lit discount hell that is the
Reds today. There is not a drop of sweetness left in the organization, possibly because Schott watches even the candy. In a stadium
storeroom there are boxes and boxes of leftover donations from a
Leaf candy promotion tied to the Celebrity Bat Girl and Bat Boy
nights at Riverfront. But Schott did not hand it out. She did not
give it away to charities. She hoarded it for special occasions. One
was last January, when she indicated to her shrinking, pitifully paid
front-office staff (Exhibit A: former public relations assistant Joe
Kelley more than doubled his salary by taking a similar job with
the city's minor league hockey franchise) that there would be no
holiday bonus again by throwing some Leaf candy on each person's desk. How old was it? On the outside of some of the wrappers
was an ad for a contest. It said, "Win a trip to the 1991 Grammy
Awards!"

Schott has a front-office staff of only 41 people, fewest in the
league. Almost every other team has twice as many employees.
The New York Mets have 120, the Colorado Rockies 111, the San
Diego Padres 104. This does not include scouts, on whom Schott
has never been big. "All they do is sit around and watch ball games,"
she once said. The Reds have 25 scouts. The Los Angeles Dodgers
have 57.

Schott is paranoid about being cheated. Reds policy is that she must sign any check over $50, and any purchase over that amount requires three bids before she'll agree to it. "That means even if you're reordering paper clips," says a former publicity employee, "you have to call around and get two more bids, even though you know exactly what you want already."

During the 1994–95 baseball strike Schott stopped having the Reds office bathrooms professionally cleaned, so some employees did the job themselves. She has been known to rummage through the trash barrels to make sure scrap paper is written on both sides. She eliminated free tissues for employees. She keeps the lights off whenever possible, extinguishing them when you leave your office just to walk down the hall. The hallway carpeting is so old and tattered that the seams are held together with duct tape. Schott wants the heat turned down to 55 [degrees] at five o'clock, so some employees have been known to bring in their own space heaters. She does all of this at every place she owns.

No wonder, according to Bass, that male employees of Schott's occasionally ask her to sign a publicity shot for a "niece," then take it into the men's room, place it in the urinal, and fire away.

Schott has eliminated the Reds' customer-service and community relations departments. Her private secretary became fed up with Schott and quit last spring, and for a year Schott answered her own calls rather than hire a replacement. The *New York Post* called last season to request head shots of the Reds' players, and after the playoffs Schott had a member of her staff call the newspaper and ask for them back.

"It's so crazy," she says. "You're spending millions and millions out on the field for these players, honey, and you find yourself arguing about envelopes and paper clips in the office. You try to cut on silly stuff. It's like Disneyland on the field and the real world in here."

"No," says one employee. "It's like Disneyland on the field and Bosnia in here."

Schott does have one of the major leagues' highest player payrolls — "They [Bowden and her other baseball advisers] con me into spending money on the players, honey," she says — though she has cut back this year and plans to make serious cuts next year. But just because she has had to purchase a Rolls-Royce doesn't mean she won't use the drive-thru window. Schott won't pop for video equipment to let players check past performances against certain pitchers and hitters. She won't pop for Cybex machines. She won't even pop for extra hats or sweatshirts. "Anything extra," says outfielder Davis, "we pay for ourselves."

Even when the glory comes, Schott does not seem to be able to pry open her pocketbook. When the Reds won the World Series in 1990, she didn't throw a party for them. Some of the players finally went out and brought back hamburgers.

To Schott, most of the players are just empty uniforms into which she pours money, and it sticks in her craw. One game in April, Cincinnati pitcher Mark Portugal gave up a line drive base hit. Watching from her front-row seat in the stands, Schott shook her head. "Three million dollars," she grumbled, apparently unaware that Portugal is earning $4.33 million this year, "and he's just not worth a damn."

Then there was this exchange during the same home stand in April, as she sat looking at the program in her luxury box, waiting for the coat-and-tied security director to come back from his walk with Schottzie.

"There's what's-his-name, honey."

"Who?"

"The guy I'm paying $3 million a year to sit on his butt."

"Jose Rijo?"

"Yeah. Three million, sweetheart. For crying out loud."

Rijo, the 1990 World Series MVP, who actually is making $6.15 million this season, hasn't pitched for the Reds since July 18, 1995, because of a serious elbow injury.

"It's kind of a circus atmosphere, but you do your job," says Larkin, the 1995 National League MVP. "The only thing I don't like is when the dog takes a crap at shortstop, because I might have to dive into that s— ."

Even though Cincinnati won the 1990 World Series and was the NL Central champion last year, anybody in baseball will tell you privately that the Reds are leaking oil three lanes wide. They routinely lose their best scouts to better-paying clubs. Attendance is down for the second straight year. In the playoffs last year there were more than 12,000 unsold seats for one game at Riverfront and more than 8,000 for another. For some reason, aside from Bowden, who is considered one of the best young executives in the game,

top-notch baseball minds aren't inclined to come to work in an
office chilled to 55 degrees for substantially less than what other
teams are paying, bringing their own tissues to the office and wondering who else is listening to their phone messages.

The Reds don't often bid for high-priced free agents, which is
fine with Schott, who prefers to bring in players from her farm
teams. But Cincinnati's minor league system is unraveling. *Baseball
America* recently listed the top 100 teenage prospects, and no one
in the Reds' organization was listed in the top 50. No problem. One
day recently Schott returned from seeing a thrilling trapeze act and
had a great idea. "We need to start checking that circus for ballplayers," she reportedly told a member of her staff. "There are some
real athletes there."

Another of her ideas is to have a woman playing on her team.
"I've got my scouts looking for a great girl," Schott says. "Wouldn't
that be something? Her coming in and striking all these boys out,
honey?"

Incredibly, the county plans to build new stadiums for both the
Reds and the NFL Bengals, and town leaders are petrified about
the influence Schott might have over the new ballpark. Pay toi-
lets? Bugging devices in every showerhead? A dog run in left center? "I just wish she'd get out," says one source high in the Reds'
ownership structure. "We all wish she'd get out. She's a despicable
person."

Baseball would not miss her, to say the least. She is on none of the
owners' committees and has shown no interest in helping to resolve
the issues that plague the game. Wouldn't baseball be better off
without her? "There is no appropriate answer to that question,"
says Bud Selig, acting baseball commissioner and owner of the
Milwaukee Brewers. But one owner did say that Schott is "truly
embarrassing. Worse than embarrassing."

Wait your turn. People want Schott out of more than baseball.
General Motors has tried twice over the last eight years to take her
Chevrolet dealership from her. The reason, says Chevrolet, is the
franchise's poor sales performance. Schott twice hauled Chevrolet
before the Ohio Motor Vehicle Dealers Board, which regulates auto
manufacturers and dealers throughout the state, and on both occasions she managed to retain her franchise. But there may be questions still. According to documents obtained by *SI*, a former Reds

employee has received ownership notices and a service reminder for a 1996 vehicle he does not own and says he has never seen. In fact, last weekend the car the former employee supposedly bought was on one of Schott's lots. Schott says that if these facts are correct, they are the result of an innocent mix-up, and she denies that her dealership is falsifying records to inflate sales figures in order to meet quotas set by Chevrolet. Chevrolet says it will look into the matter.

So, you've got to ask, why doesn't Schott just take the $30 million profit she stands to make if she cashes in her stake in the Reds, go ahead with her plans to build a new elephant wing for the Cincinnati Zoo ("Elephants never ask you for any raises, honey," she says), sell the car dealerships, the concrete company and the holding company and just find a good canasta game somewhere?

"I don't know, honey," she says, sitting all alone in that luxury box, the lights off, the thick windows keeping her from the cheers and the sun and the joy of the baseball game that is being mimed below. "As long as the little guy out there still thinks I'm doing a good job, that's all that matters. I don't give a damn what the stupid press thinks."

Actually, the little guy may have had it up to here. Schott has fallen drastically in popularity polls in Cincinnati. Last summer a *Cincinnati Post*–WCPO-TV poll found that approximately 47 percent of the public had a positive impression of Schott, compared to only 34 percent for Cincinnati Bengals owner Mike Brown. The most recent poll, though, gave Brown a 49 percent favorable rating, compared to only 37 percent for Schott. But she has an explanation: "I think somebody's trying to get me out, honey, somebody that wants to buy the team. It's a kind of vendetta against me, honey. It's kind of like a woman thing." She asks herself all the time, would the Men have given up?

"Nah," she says, "I don't wanna cave, baby. I've been through bad times before. Besides, I'm always best when I'm battling."

Right about then, an employee in a full-length dress and pearls comes back from walking Schottzie.

"Poo or tinkle?"

"Tinkle."

"Hey, have you met this guy from Sports Thingy?"

KEN FUSON

Guts and Glory

FROM ESQUIRE

GRAB YOUR JOCK, KID, they've come to play. First question, right out of the chute — they want it all: *Were you scared?*

This is it, one chance to ask Brett Favre about his addiction to prescription pain pills, then everyone will return to what matters most: bringing a Super Bowl championship to Green Bay for the first time in twenty-nine years. ESPN and three local stations are carrying this mega press conference live — and they're panting. They want tears! They want contrition! They want Oprah! Face it, kid, they want your sorry Cajun ass down on the floor, begging America for *ab-so-lution!*

They'll forgive, too, in a heartbeat they will. Forget the Packer fans. You own them. You throw thirty-eight touchdown passes in a season, the cheeseheads won't care if you sniff glue in the huddle. But you're national now, kid. You're the Most Valuable Player in the National Football League. You're the star quarterback on the last hometown team in America. You're the hero who will slay the Dallas/Nike/Pepsi/Pizza Hut Cowboys and bring the Lombardi Trophy home to its rightful case on Lombardi Avenue in the town Vince Lombardi made famous.

See them standing outside? Those sweaty guys with the dreamy doofus grins, the ones wearing the authentic $149.95 green jerseys with the number 4 on the front and FAVRE on the back? (A top-ten seller for NFL Properties!) They couldn't even pronounce your name four years ago (Brett *Favor*? No, *Favre*, rhymes with *carve*), but they need you now. Baseball's dead, you can't really bet on hockey, and basketball saves its best seats for Jack and Woody and

JFK Jr. Players and franchises move around more than military wives. Owned Cleveland Browns season tickets? Tough, pal. Bought a Shaq Orlando Magic jersey? Sorry, loser. The only thing you can count on is that the Packers will play football in Green Bay, just as they have since 1919. The fans own this team. Nobody's moving them unless they haul the whole runt town, too.

So let's go, kid. *Confess!* Tell them about the pills you popped until it got, well, out of hand, and how you had a seizure that scared your daughter, and how you went to a treatment center in the middle of Kansas, and how the NFL took away your alcohol — *your Miller Lites!* — for two years. *Get real,* as the therapists say. Bawl until the snot pours. You know what's next. Fox will put you in the studio, under that soft halo light. Maybe you and Summerall can trade recovery stories. ("Step Five was a bitch, Pat.") They'll call it "MVP: My Vicodin Problem" and hire John Tesh to write the score.

"I wasn't scared at all.

"To everyone else, what happened to me was a big deal," he told me two days after that press conference. "To me, it wasn't. I'm no different. I still act the same way. Still curse. Still want to drink beer. Still want to wear my flip-flops and not shave. Nothing's changed."

But the counselors . . .

"I fought with them every day. I mean, I put a hole in the wall because I was ready to leave. I told them, 'Look, I'm tired of listening to your shit. You don't know me.'"

Grab your jocks. The kid's come to play.

"You buzzin', kid?"

"I'm buzzin', kid."

Nothing like a pinch of Skoal to get the juices flowing. Brett Favre spits and clutches a golf club. This is the first week in May, the heart of the NFL off-season, and Favre and Mark Chmura, the Packers' All-Pro tight end, squeeze in some golf following their morning workout in Green Bay.

At the first tee, Chmura — "Chewy" — rests an index finger against his nose, bends over, and blows a snot rocket.

"That's nice, kid," Favre says.

Just cutting loose, what's wrong with that? Earlier, Favre tried to depants Chewy in the clubhouse — it's one of his favorite pranks — but Chewy was ready. You've got to watch Favre. He'll wait until you're in the stall, perched on the toilet, then dump a bucket of ice water on your head.

How can you get mad? His laughter is too innocent. Look at him — tan, six two, the brown hair finger-combed, like Timothy Hutton's in *Ordinary People;* the face covered with an Arafatesque stubble, not for effect but because he'd rather not shave; sideburns more Sha Na Na than Luke Perry; the wardrobe all J. Crew khakis, T-shirts, and flip-flops; the voice deep with a Mississippi Gulf Coast drawl that could talk Becky Thatcher into whitewashing a fence. He's having *fun.*

It's the same way when he fires a touchdown pass. He's no Cool Hand Luke like Montana, no Robo QB like Aikman, no Golden Arches Boy like Bledsoe. Favre's a jazz artist, all improv, impossible not to watch, because one way or another — five TDs or five INTs — he's going to blow the house down. He dives into the end zone for a touchdown with the clock running out and a playoff berth on the line. He scampers to his left and heaves the ball across his body to the right for a forty-yard winning touchdown. He goes back to pass, trips, gets up, and in one motion fires a completion. He plays football the way fans like to think *they* would play football.

He's fearless. In the final regular-season game last year, on a frozen field (what else?) in Green Bay, two Pittsburgh Steelers created a Favre po'boy. He broke a blood vessel in his esophagus and staggered to the sidelines.

"Favre's bleeding," a trainer told Packer head coach Mike Holmgren.

"O.K., how *much* is he bleeding?"

Favre returned for the next play and threw a touchdown to Chewy. Chewy now sinks a putt.

"You own that hole, kid," Favre says.

This is the life. This is what you do when you're 27 years old, make $3.8 million a year, and can throw 70 yards on a line. People will pay $300 for a helmet with your autograph on it. Doctors invite you to mingle with them. Women send amazing things. Remember the photograph of that lady wearing only a cowboy hat and boots, sitting spread-eagled in a chair? Life is just golfin' and goofin' and . . . whatever the hell you want!

They were in Phoenix a couple of years ago, Favre and Chewy. Didn't have a game, wanted to play some golf, so they just went.

Golfin' and goofin' . . . saw a tattoo parlor. What the hell. Favre drew the design — the Superman logo. Now he and Chewy have matching Superman tattoos.

Too bad Porky wasn't there. Porky is center Frank Winters, Favre's roommate during training camp and road games. "My hands are under Frank's butt a hundred times a day," Favre says. "I have a unique job and so does he."

The Three Amigos — Porky, Chewy, and Kid. They're give-a-shit guys, as in, "We just don't give a shit," Favre says. They work hard, play every game — Favre has started sixty-one straight, the longest active streak among NFL quarterbacks. "The way we've always looked at it," Chewy says, "take your three best guys, and we'll take us three, and we'll whip your ass in a fight."

What a life — dormies on spring break, Animal House in shoulder pads, just golfin' and goofin', foolin' and fartin' . . . oh, yes, Favre can turn the quarterback film room into a Porta Potti at the Texas State Fair. He had so much gas at the drug-treatment center that a staff member took him aside. "Brett, there's stuff we can give you for that."

He's raw, ribald, raunchy. Tell him a joke, he'll reciprocate by asking if you've heard of the new book *Yellow Stains on the Wall* by I. P. Freely. Seventh-grade material! But there's such a purity about him that you laugh right along.

Like that Packers-Raiders game in Green Bay. Cold enough to freeze lava. Favre calls a time-out to consult with Holmgren. He jogs to the sidelines and bursts out laughing.

"What?" Holmgren says. *"What?"*

"Mike, you've got a frozen shield of snot all over your damn mustache."

Back on the nine-hole course, Favre sinks a putt on the last hole to beat Chewy by a stroke. "Next time, kid," Favre says. During the next round, the jocular jock is gone. Favre is antsy, increasingly agitated with the group in front of him — why are they so damn slow? After four holes, he has had enough.

This personality change is surprisingly abrupt, but others have seen it before — his wife, Deanna; their daughter, Brittany, seven; his parents; even Porky and Chewy. They were worried about him, especially Deanna.

"I was cleaning out the closet," she says at their home in Green

Bay. "I found a bunch of little packs kind of rolled up in there. A week later, they'd all be gone. I'd think, Jeez, that's a lot of pain pills. So I started asking him, and he got real defensive. I just kept finding stuff like that."

Superman had found his kryptonite: Vicodin, a narcotic pain-killer that packs more punch than codeine. Housewives' heroin, doctors call it, but it's also a favorite of NFL players. You get the hell beat out of you week after week, you need *something* to keep playing.

Brett Favre kept playing, whatever it took despite a first-degree separated shoulder (vs. Philadelphia, 1992), a deep thigh bruise (vs. Tampa Bay, 1993), a hernia (entire 1994 season), a concussion (vs. Pittsburgh, 1995 preseason), and a sprained ankle that swelled to the size of a grapefruit (vs. Minnesota, 1995). Each time, he either led the Packers to a win or came back and played great the next week.

"Last year, he was always stressed out," Deanna says. "He wanted to make sure he didn't lose what he had. He always worried — 'I got to do it, I got to do it.' It's constant."

The pills changed him. He stayed up all night, fidgety, anxious, couldn't seem to sit still. Deanna remembers the fights. "He was very mean — 'Don't talk to me, don't look at me.' I couldn't say anything. We didn't communicate at all."

Every time she discovered a new stash, Deanna threw some away, hoping Brett wouldn't notice, but it didn't seem to matter. She kept finding more. Where were they coming from? Other players, certainly. "They try to take care of each other," she says. That's essentially what former Packer John Jurkovic told the authors of the book *Return to Glory:* "If my quarterback comes to me and says, 'Hey, tighten me up,' it's a no-brainer. You give him the Vike."

Deanna couldn't live like that. She told Brett he had to stop. If he didn't, she would move — away from Green Bay, away from Brett and the pills — and she would take Brittany.

"Everybody thinks Brett's so tough, but they haven't met me yet."

In February, as he was recovering from ankle surgery at a hospital in Green Bay, Favre suffered a seizure. Deanna yelled at the nurse to make sure he didn't swallow his tongue.

"Gosh, I mean, we were in shock. Brittany just kept saying, 'Is my daddy going to die? Is my daddy going to die?' It was really scary for both of us."

Three months later, Brett was on television, reading a statement:

"Throughout the last couple of years, in playing with pain and injuries and suffering numerous surgeries, I possibly became dependent on medication."

The next day, at 5:00 A.M., he was on a private plane, headed to the Menninger Clinic, a psychiatric hospital in Topeka, Kansas, that helps addicts. He looked scared.

He looked like he gave a shit.

His life had become unmanageable.

He had been at the Menninger Clinic, what, a month? . . . and the bastards wouldn't let him leave. They refused to let him go to the Packers' June minicamp. He told them what he thought, all right. Punched a hole in the wall just in case they missed the point.

But they put the hammer down. They wouldn't even let him go home for the very first Brett Favre Celebrity Golf Tournament. You're not Mr. MVP here, they told him.

Yeah, well, the very first day, somebody behind the lunch counter at the clinic asked for his autograph. He went out to a movie once. Mob scene.

The counselors kept talking about denial. He wasn't denying anything. He had a problem, sure, but hadn't he quit taking the Vicodin on his own, in February, after the seizure? Hadn't he agreed to enter the NFL substance-abuse program? To do what the NFL-approved doctors told him so he wouldn't be suspended for three games?

So that's how he got to Menninger. He didn't know what to expect, but he had his own room, a television, and access to a kitchen. The other patients were nice, not the gutter bums he had expected. "Fortunately, my problem never got as bad as everyone there. A couple of the therapists I met with there were not even sure that it was a problem yet."

He never used pills on game day. He thought people should know that. He used them during the week, when his body hurt so much he could barely walk. Yes, he asked other players for pills, but it wasn't as if he was roaming the locker room, begging like a junkie. This wasn't the Cowboys' Michael Irvin getting caught in a hotel room with cocaine.

The therapists disagreed: An addiction is an addiction. Recovery requires constant vigilance. Addicts have a disease. "Some of it stuck," Favre says, "but most of what they said went in one ear and out the other."

There *were* good points. He needed a vacation. It gave him time to think about the people he had hurt. He wanted to be better to Deanna and Brittany. That Brittany. Such a smart kid. Look at the card she sent him: "Daddy, I love you very much and loved how you played football. But most of all, I love how your heart is kind, gentle, and loving."

Once they let him out of here, that would be it. If he gets hurt this season, he'll take pain medication less addictive than Vicodin. They can talk about hitting rock bottom, but he never did. He'd show them.

Brett Favre spent forty-five days at the Menninger Clinic before he was released. The average patient stays twenty. "If we can all forget about this, that would be terrific," he said upon leaving. "Because I have."

It was time to head home, to "the Kiln."

He was born stubborn. When Brett was little, he wouldn't drink water from anyone's cup or eat from anyone's plate or share a bedroom with his brothers.

Big Irv was stubborn, too. Irvin Favre — Big Irv, Brett calls his father — coached football for twenty-four seasons at Hancock North Central High School, near the Mississippi Gulf Coast. Squat and solid, with a flattop, Big Irv looks as if he could crack walnuts on his forehead.

"Stubborn can get you into trouble," Big Irv says. "Stubborn can get you out of trouble, too."

They knew something was wrong, all of them. "You know your kid," Bonita Favre says. They had heard enough from Deanna to know Brett was taking a lot of pain pills. He told them he could handle it.

He always had. You never saw a kid with such willpower. Every night, before bed, he'd do pushups. Every day, he'd run the half mile from the Favre house to the nearest road. He had plans. He had dreams.

That a kid could grow up outside Kiln, Mississippi, and aspire to a career grander than auto salvage is remarkable. Locals call it the Kill, presumably because "the Dead and Decomposed" has too many syllables. The Kill is, essentially, a caution light surrounded by a few businesses. There is no town park, no grid of streets, nothing that would suggest a community — just red-clay roads that snake off into the vegetation. If there were a welcome sign, it would say, COME ON IN. WE DARE YOU.

Big Irv and Bonita live so close to Rotten Bayou that you can fish for bass from their deck; Brett's seventy-eight-year-old grandmother, Mee-Maw, lives in the trailer next to them; Brett's aunt, Kay-Kay, lives in the house next to her. It's a nonstop family reunion, a twenty-four-hour open house, always somebody ready to boil shrimp and ice some beer.

When Brett met Deanna, she was in tenth grade, he in ninth. He asked her what her favorite football team was. The Cowboys, of course. His, too. Cool. They talked on the telephone all night, Brett describing how he would play for the Cowboys someday. She believed every word of it. She was a good athlete, too. If Brett needed someone to play catch, she was there.

"Don't throw it so dang hard," Big Irv yelled one time as Brett was firing fastballs.

"Why?" he shouted back. "She's catchin' 'em."

When Brett went to Southern Mississippi University, Deanna followed. When she got pregnant and had Brittany, she agreed that they were too young to get married. When he started as quarterback in the third game of his freshman year, she cheered for him. When he nearly died in a car wreck before the start of his senior year, she was there.

That was July 1990. Favre was a mile from home when he hit some loose gravel, lost control of his car, and flipped three times, higher than in a NASCAR highlight video. His brother Scott, following behind, smashed the car's windshield with a golf club and pulled him out. Brett was a mess — a fractured vertebra, a severe concussion, cuts, and bruises. He was barely conscious in his hospital room when he heard a TV announcer: *Will Brett Favre ever play football again?* He answered to himself: You're damn right I will.

A month later, doctors removed thirty inches of dead intestines from him. A month after that — *four weeks!* — Favre ran onto Legion Field in Birmingham. He was thirty-five pounds lighter, his uniform sagged, and even the eighty thousand Alabama fans cheered his courage.

"I had chill bumps ready to break out of my skin. That's the greatest feeling. I went out there and I told the guys, 'Look, we're getting ready to whip Alabama's ass.' They're looking at me. Shit's falling off me. My uniform doesn't fit me. My teammates were crying. It was unbelievable."

Southern Miss won, 27–24. Sometimes Brett's mother wonders if that's when it started, the pain and her son's willingness to do whatever it took to feel those chill bumps again.

Nothing came easy. He got the last football scholarship Southern Mississippi had to offer only because another player returned one. In a big game his sophomore year, his first pass was picked off by Deion Sanders — Prime Time was at Florida State then — and returned for a touchdown. That Alabama game? "First play, I drop back to throw, and I get hit right in the balls," Favre says.

He was Brett Favre, the sloshbuckling QB. He liked the image. Party all night, play ball all day. It's a football archetype that dates back to Bobby Layne. Look at the Packers. Didn't Max McGee catch two touchdown passes in Super Bowl I despite a hangover?

Favre was drafted in the second round by the Atlanta Falcons. Prime Time was there and gave him the nickname Country Time, but it could just as easily have been Miller Time. Favre compiled more bar tabs than practice snaps in Atlanta. When he was fined $1,500 for missing a team photo, he told head coach Jerry Glanville he had been delayed by a car wreck. "You are a car wreck," Glanville replied.

Who gave a shit? He wasn't going to play anyway.

So the Packer cheeseheads howled in 1992 when the Green Bay general manager traded a first-round draft pick for Favre, this good-time Charlie, who had thrown exactly five passes in the NFL, with a completion percentage of .000.

Favre was smart enough to know he wasn't going to play in Green Bay, either. The starting quarterback was fan favorite Don Majkowski, the "Majic Man." Favre would hold a clipboard. That lasted until the third game, when Majkowski was injured. With thirteen seconds left, Favre threw a 35-yard touchdown pass and the Packers won by a point. Poof! The Majic Man was gone. Favre has started every game since.

There would be no more anonymous tomfoolery for the Three Amigos, no more road trips for a little cutting loose. Not when you lead the Packers to four straight winning seasons and three consecutive playoffs, not when you come within a quarter of beating the Dallas Cowboys and playing in the Super Bowl, not when you return glory to a team that had gone 147–203–9 since Lombardi left.

Now every time you go to Lambeau Field, an autograph clot has formed, their arms outstretched, their mouths open like baby birds awaiting supper, cawing, "Brett! *Buh-rett!* Please, *Buh-rett!*" Now if you ever appear in public, there is always somebody waiting to "suck you off."

That's what the Three Amigos call it, the constant *Ohmigod, it's you, you're the greatest football player who ever lived!* Don't get them wrong — they love Green Bay, think the fans are the best in the world, but it's tough to stay current in the Give-a-Shit Club when somebody's slobbering on you.

"That's why I love to go back home," Favre says. "It's all people who don't give a shit. It keeps me sane. I can go back and no one could care less. It's like, hey, you're just one of us. I get called a slack click just like they call everyone else."

Just another slack click who cared so little he occasionally hyperventilated during college games. Who got so pumped during the NFC championship game last year he threw a couple of early passes ten feet over the receiver's head. Who is bugged that the Packers haven't renegotiated his contract to that $6-mil-a-year range the other top QBs get. Who wonders why he doesn't get the endorsement contracts other NFL stars do. Who took pain pills rather than risk sitting out a game and letting some other kid steal his job.

Favre has a childlike faith in his own ability and a childlike fear that it can all be taken away. "Nobody knows how hard it is to get to the top and how hard it is to stay on top. Now that I'm here, it doesn't make it any easier."

As a matter of fact, it can get damn *complicated.* The Miller Time reputation was always exaggerated — well, mostly exaggerated — but the NFL doctors told Favre he couldn't drink alcohol for two years as part of his treatment plan. Porky and Chewy say they'll drink Cokes with their postgame pizza, which Favre calls a nice but unnecessary gesture. He'll keep alcohol in his house.

"We're still going to have good times," Favre says. "As long as I'm in this program, I can't drink. That could be two weeks, it could be two years, I don't know. I'll tell you what — us three had some pretty good times. They're not over with, I can promise you that."

There's one good time in particular that Favre dreams of now. He wants another date with Prime Time. Someday, he says, the Packers are finally going to beat the Cowboys — they've lost seven straight — and go to the Super Bowl.

"We know we'll win a Super Bowl, we really do," Favre says. "I think it's going to be this year. It's close."

Titletown, July 1996.

I saw a man with a Packer logo stitched into his yarmulke. I heard a woman implore her sons, "Be aggressive" before dispatching them for autographs. I saw a nun leafing through Lindy's football magazine. I saw a woman grab Reggie White's hand and shout, "Thank you so much for being a Christian in Wisconsin!" ("You're welcome," the Minister of Defense said.) I found forty-two businesses in the Green Bay yellow pages with the word *Packer* in their name. I saw four thousand people wedged against the practice gate for the opening of training camp at 8:30 on a Saturday morning. I heard them cheer wildly when Favre completed his first training-camp pass — to a receiver who was not being covered.

Favre didn't even notice them; he was distracted. Deanna had called that morning with terrible news — Brett's brother Scott was in a car wreck. He would be fine, but Mark Haverty, one of Brett's best friends, was killed. "I didn't need to hear that," Favre says. An early lesson in how to play with pain.

He was still looking forward to training camp. Put the summer behind him, prove everyone wrong. "I think this year is going to be excellent," Deanna says. "I've got my old Brett back."

The Favres have moved into a bigger, more remote home in Green Bay. She says Brett is so much calmer now. He has a foundation to help charities. He spends more time with his family and would like three more kids. He's married. Back in May, when everyone was wondering how best to disclose Favre's drug treatment, Brittany interrupted with a question: "When are you going to ask Mommy to marry you?"

On July 14, sixteen days after he left the Menninger Clinic, six days before training camp opened, Brett Favre married Deanna Tynes at St. Agnes Catholic Church in Green Bay. They had been dating for twelve years.

"She has been there every single time I needed her," Favre says.

"Somebody wondered why I didn't sign a prenuptial. You know what, after all the shit Deanna's had to go through with me, she's entitled to half of everything."

He's still dreaming. He still sees himself leading the last home-town team in America on the field for Super Bowl XXXI. It will be held on January 26 in the Louisiana Superdome in New Orleans, less than an hour from Rotten Bayou. Everyone will be watching the quarterback with his hands parked under Porky's ass, the one with the Superman tattoo under his shoulder pad, the one who acts as if serenity can be found one play at a time.

But if he hasn't grown up, he has at least *wised* up. Brett Favre knows he can look in the stands and find the striking woman with black hair and green eyes, the one who fell asleep on the phone while listening to him spin his dreams when he was a boy. He knows he can find the smart little girl who likes *I Love Lucy*, Goosebumps books, and sitting on her dad's back when he does his nightly pushups. When the game is over, when he takes off that helmet, when the fans have stopped cheering, Deanna and Brittany will be there.

They give a shit, kid.

JEFF COPLON

The Man Who Loves Basketball Too Much: The Exquisite Torment of Jerry West

FROM MEN'S JOURNAL

IT'S TIP-OFF TIME at the Great Western Forum. The Los Angeles Lakers are hosting the Dallas Mavericks, two young teams in a young season. The national anthem has been tortured. The Laker Girls have swiveled their way into your wistful libido. It's time to sit down.

Jerry Buss is settled in his owner's box. Jack Nicholson has eased into his padded chair on Celebrity Row. Even Del Harris, the silver-haired ordained former lay minister who serves as the Lakers' coach, is seated for the moment.

But the heart and soul and hot-wired brain of the Lakers is not sitting down. Jerry West hasn't sat through a game for five years now, ever since the great Lakers "Showtime" team — the group he pieced together into a ten-year dynasty, an eon in basketball years — began to deteriorate. "The games started getting closer, and I just couldn't take it," he says. "It was like being in an electric chair."

So the Lakers' executive vice-president — the man who picks the players and calls the shots — stands. Stands fifteen rows up, in the mouth of a concourse tunnel, next to an usher checking tickets. It's been thirty-six years since West arrived in Los Angeles as a

high-strung All-American out of West Virgínia, just one generation
from the mines, all knobby limbs and fast-twitch muscle. His face is
rounder now, and his torso thickened, yet West, at age 57, remains
an angular man. His improbably long arms (at six-foot-four, he
takes a 38-inch sleeve) are swathed in a proper navy suit — but
where can he put them? He tries folding them, then dangles one
over the sloped concrete wall. He's never still for long.

West is somewhat subdued this evening, still grappling with his
annual autumn flu. He has a narrow, pursed mouth and a searching gaze; he takes in more than he lets out. But make no mistake,
West is up for this game. One large, tanned hand eventually grips a
guardrail on the other side of the wall; his hawk's eyes sweep the
burnished court before him. As Hubie Brown, the former NBA
coach and no slouch himself in the bleeding-ulcer department,
once remarked, "He looks like he's going to bust right out of his
skin sometimes."

Then L.A. center Vlade Divac blows a lay-up. In the next possession, Divac shambles into a travel. A Maverick hits a short jump
shot. The Lakers are losing. We are just forty-three seconds in, the
scab referees have barely botched their first call, but West's shoulders are sagging. "It should be a 4–2 game," he mutters with the
trace of a twang that never quite homogenized, even in California's
social Cuisinart.

If the game doesn't get better, West won't stay in the tunnel long.
He may retreat down the corridor and into a private lounge to
watch it on television. When it gets *really* excruciating, when the
Lakers are bricking free throws and blowing three-on-one fast
breaks, West may up and leave the building to pace the parking lot.
He'll catch up on videotape the next day, fast-forwarding through
the rough spots.

"When you've been around long enough," he explains, "you
know what players are going to do. You can see a mistake coming,
and you know the same players are going to make the same ones
over again. . . ."

The crowds arrive fashionably and late in L.A., and abide by the
house rule: Wait for a break in the action to take your seat. Which
means West is continually besieged by chubby preteens and shuffling octogenarians — not to mention his 7-year-old son, Jonathan,
the second child of his second marriage, who is hanging out with

Dad. West is shyly gracious, signing pictures over a sea of suede and denim, of bleached blondes and peanut vendors, to keep his laser pupils tracked on the action.

"I have some crazy things that I do," West admits. He's always been superstitious, dating back to his playing days. Before each home game, he'd stop at the same joint at the same time and wolf down the same dinner: a cup of soup and a turkey sandwich. Always first in the locker room, he'd lodge half a stick of Juicy Fruit in his mouth, then put on his socks and jersey . . . and just sit, silent and smoldering, mulling defensive tactics for the game ahead. His teammates knew better than to speak to him; they left West alone with his demon nerves. "I could sit there and sweat would just be dripping off my hands. I'd always have a towel," he says.

At the very last moment, when West felt he was primed, he'd don those tight gold and purple shorts and trot out, always third in the lay-up line. "I felt if I didn't follow the pattern, I was cheating," he says.

He still honors his taboos. West hasn't attended a Lakers playoff road game since 1983, when his team was swept by Philadelphia in the finals. He rarely travels with the club, even avoiding the Sports Arena across town for bouts with the Clippers. He's embarrassed by the fuss made over him, and fears he'd put "undue pressure" on his coach and players with his "intrusion."

Then, too, it might be fair to note that even the better professional basketball teams lose roughly half their games on the road. Would you dive from a plane if the odds were fifty-fifty that your chute would fail? "If you care, games are hard on you," West says softly, earnestly. "The games mean a lot. They mean a *lot*."

The truth about Jerry West is that he mastered every skill on the basketball court, save one. He could glide like the breeze and jump to the moon. He could score at will while wrapping up the enemy's top gun; those simian arms were hell to get around. He could do everything better than most anyone else, except for this:

Jerry West never learned how to lose.

By any sane standard, it should be the best of times for West, the master builder. "The Laker Show," precocious son of "Showtime," proved a smash hit in 1995. While other NBA powers of the '80s — Boston, Philadelphia, Detroit — floundered, Los Angeles reloaded after but a single year in purgatory, a.k.a. the draft lottery, the consolation prize for teams barred from the playoff party.

With no starter older than 27, the Lakers went 48–34 last season. They upset a deep and gifted Seattle team in the first round of the playoffs, then took David Robinson's Spurs to six hammer-and-tongs slugfests before bowing out. When Laker Nick Van Exel buried a wrong-legged, off-balance, hold-the-phone three-pointer to win game five in overtime, he lit up the whole sport.

"Those guys played so hard, they played with a purpose," West says admiringly. "They thought they could win a game anywhere they played, against any team. . . . Last year was probably more gratifying than all the championships we won. It makes you feel like you can make a difference."

It was a coup for all involved, but for West most of all. His old friend Harris, scorned by some NBA observers as an out-of-touch retread, won over his hip-hop crew en route to being voted the league's Coach of the Year. Cedric Ceballos, the relentless scorer whom West plucked from Phoenix, blossomed into an All-Star. The propulsive Van Exel, an assumed attitude problem whom West had selected with a thirty-seventh draft pick, crashed the top tier of NBA point guards. Swooping swing man Eddie Jones, West's first lottery pick in 1994, looked like Michael Cooper reincarnated, with more offense.

All of these players are cast in West's image. They are competitive, fearless, passionate, and born to run — the style of play that West believes is simplest and most natural, and therefore most beautiful to watch.

And last year, in his thirteenth season as chief steward of the Lakers, West was finally honored as the NBA Executive of the Year. Which merely confirmed what insiders had known all along: that West has *the feel*. A 24-karat legend — on the short list of all-around greats, West stands beside Oscar, Magic, Jordan, and Bird — he has reinvented himself as the game's top architect. More than a simple eye for talent, West owns a sublime sixth sense of which talents will best mesh together. He hangs aloof from the herd mentality and shuns the collective secondhand insights about a 22-year-old's character that pass for fact if repeated often enough. (At the predraft camps in Phoenix and Chicago, West books his staff at a hotel apart from the NBA hoardes, in part to avoid undue "outside influences.") West talks to everyone, but keeps his own counsel. For all the hard losses he's suffered, he knows *winning* better than anyone.

"I don't think we should insult Jerry West by giving him Executive of the Year," declared Scott Layden, West's counterpart with the Utah Jazz. "We should name the award after him."

Yet West is not known as the Most Negative Man in the World for nothing. He relaxes when discussing his setbacks and gets flustered when recounting his triumphs: "It's so difficult for me to talk about myself, it's almost painful." He is indifferent to fame, allergic to celebrity. ("You don't know me," he once told the writers who cover his business. "You think you do, but you don't.") He treats each new season as a precipice; the higher you've climbed, the gaudier the expectations, the steeper the plunge ahead. He made this note to himself in training camp last fall: "This could be a real exciting year, but it could be real painful for a lot of us that work here."

His foreboding was on the wing as we spoke, the day before the Dallas game, in his smallish office with the rose-colored, Marriott-surplus furniture. Jones, a ligament torn in his thumb, had yet to suit up. Divac wasn't doing enough, and Van Exel was pressing to do *too* much. The Lakers had lost four of their first six games, "and all of those positive things that were going around here don't look very positive today," West said. "We have some nice young pieces, but we're real fragile."

Draped in a plain black zippered jacket, he waved a hand at a sticker on his wall, a quote from Jefferson: "I like the dreams of the future better than the history of the past." It is a motto for a lifetime, the fuel for West's white-phosphorus furnace; but it doesn't keep him warm at night. Because there are loads of bad dreams out there.

What with expansion, parity, and funny money in the flesh mart of free agency, rough weather lay ahead. Just nine days before, Alonzo Mourning, one of the top five centers in the league, had forced a trade from Charlotte to Miami by rejecting an offer of $11 million a year. In one stroke a franchise was gutted; these days the center will not hold, or even stick around. Instability and decay lurk at every turn. In the Nike Basketball Association, the old-time religion — respect for one's coach, commitment to craft, five men playing together as if with one brain — often seems in eclipse.

"We look like baseball right now," said West in melancholy analogy. He'd long held that his game was the greatest of them all, "but sometimes I have my doubts."

West still treks out to see seventy college games each year, still starts awake at two in the morning with brainstorms to better his team. But sometimes it is not enough; sometimes there is nothing he can do. Everyone knows that the Lakers are thin up front, in need of a physical post-scoring threat. Last summer, West had New York Knicks free agent Anthony Mason in his sights, only to be thwarted by an eleventh-hour change in the league's salary-cap rules. "That was unbelievably frustrating," West said. The failure ate away at him, soiled his summer.

West is not one to sit on pat hands. Even when the Lakers were reeling off five titles in nine years — when they had, in his words, "an almost perfect team" — he kept molding and shaping, like a potter at an ever-spinning wheel. In a context where one sour role player might have ruined the mix, West gambled and won by adding a widely trashed Bob McAdoo ("a model player, one of the most competitive people we had"), then the underachieving Mychal Thompson ("probably the reason we beat Boston, because he could defend Kevin McHale"). He drafted James Worthy over the flashier Dominique Wilkins. And he traded the popular Norm Nixon, a charter member of "Showtime," for an untried rookie named Byron Scott, knowing full well the risk and repercussions.

"That was probably the hardest thing I ever had to do," West said. "I really, *really* liked Norm Nixon, but we had two point guards trying to play one position. And for the team to be as successful as it could be, Magic Johnson had to have the basketball."

Soon Nixon had faltered with age and injury, while Scott thrived as the essential shooter to complement Magic and Kareem. Like all of West's maneuvers, the move came out of "things that you sense and you feel," from a man who'd learned to trust his instincts, and damn the hate mail.

But for now West is locked in. He has few options till the next off-season, when Shaquille O'Neal, to name one, may go on the free-agent market. The stakes are high, for West senses that this Lakers team — without Kareem or Magic, the dynasty's power and glory — is the one he will ultimately be judged by.

And so many things might go wrong.

"I just don't feel good about it when we lose, because you'd like to do more, and many times your hands are tied," he said. "You *can't* do more, regardless of how much time you spend on the phone, talking to people about trades.

"I put so much more pressure on myself than I should, my job sometimes seems more critical than life or death. I've always been that way — if we lost a game, it was my fault. I think the one thing that's driven me in life is fear of failure."

As a manager, West said, "every time you do something you hold your breath." He carried the same fear as a player, with one critical difference: the release he found on the floor. "It's a helpless feeling, not to be able to play. Playing is wonderful. You're not strapped in. You're free. And that's why I don't sit in my seat — I'm free.

"When you do something well as an athlete, you know you can influence a game. That's a powerful feeling, a real powerful feeling."

The *ultimate* freedom?

West loosed a low whistle. "Absolutely," he said.

Of course, it didn't always feel so wonderful at the time.

As a child, West said, "the only thing I had was my dreams." Dreams were free, a big plus when you were born next to last in a family of six children and your father was a mining electrician often idled by strikes, poor even by the standards of Chelyan, West Virginia. "When people are not working," West noted, "I don't think anyone feels very good about anything. When you have a large family, kids sometimes can't be nourished — and I'm not talking about eating."

West was much younger than his two brothers, small for his age, and generally ignored. "Here was a different child in the house than the others," he related. "Quiet, more sensitive, not a lot of self-confidence. And who had a lot broader dreams than they probably had."

One dream was to own a car, which West's father could never afford, to catch a movie or go fishing anytime he felt like it: "I felt so confined at times." But the dream that drove him most was bigger than that. To get what he wanted, West understood, he'd have to "do something better than someone else." To be stronger and tougher than the rest. To excel.

Early on, it didn't look like basketball would prove to be his escape hatch. In Chelyan (pop. 1,616) there were few potential playmates, and West found himself the odd man out. The skinny, bashful boy wouldn't be picked last; he wouldn't be picked at all. He can still remember the boys' chorus: "You're too little." He couldn't even dress for his tiny school's team till he reached the seventh grade.

"It's terrible to be told you can't do something," West said. "When you're told no, those are the things that compel you. That's all I need to hear — because when people tell me no, it's not no with me." He stared daggers, still angered by the slight.

"When they're telling you that you're not good enough to play, it's hard to conjure up the energy to continue. But even though I would get discouraged, I didn't have anything else to do. And so I started to look for positive things, and the positive things were in my mind. That was my best friend — my mind."

Basketball may be the most intimately social of team sports, but West learned it by his lonesome. He spent every odd moment heaving a ball, shaved smooth from use, at a naked rim nailed to the side of a neighbor's storage shed. The dirt court was a dust bowl in summer, a bog in winter. But West didn't care. He was engrossed, obsessed. He was an 8-year-old perfectionist — "a horrible burden," he said. "You're not ever satisfied with anything."

In ninth grade he suddenly gained inches and grace, and by his junior year West had arrived. He eagerly awaited the announcement of the All-State team — and was crushed to make only honorable mention, "the greatest single disappointment I ever had in my life." It didn't help that West, a superior student, had yet to receive even one scholarship offer for college.

That summer he attended a West Virginia scholar-athlete training camp and joined the daily pickup games that featured three All-Staters. "The first day they were picking these guys that I'd heard of. I was one of the last ones left," West recalled. But after four or five days, he added, "things changed." West savored the memory. "All of a sudden I knew who the best player in the state was: me." That revelation thrilled him, but it also killed forever his joy in individual honors and awards. West would never again trust the judgment of outsiders. He would strive to satisfy himself, first and last. He would measure his progress by the one objective gauge that mattered: his team's success.

From that point on, as he led his high school team to a state championship in his senior year, each contest he waged took on a terrible urgency. When West lost a game, he lost his sense of self, his battered ego's touchstone. He won, therefore he was.

Eventually a two-time All-American at West Virginia University, West was shocked nonetheless when the Lakers picked him second, after Oscar Robertson, in the 1960 NBA draft. With the insecurity of the self-taught, the self-proclaimed "country bumpkin" felt unworthy.

"'There were so many holes in my game,'" West told Charles Salzberg in *From Set Shot to Slam Dunk*, a history of basketball.

"'I had no idea I'd be good enough to play successfully in the pros. . . . I was never an accomplished ball handler.'" He fretted about his weak left hand, which meant that he always went right — not that anyone could stop him. And he picked up a nickname he loathed, a tribute to his country accent and the neighboring town where his family got its mail: Zeke from Cabin Creek.

But by his second year in the pros, West was an All-Star, tallying up thirty points a game and (with a little help from Elgin Baylor) leading his team to the finals. One of the seminal modern jump shooters, he'd plant his outside foot, pound his last dribble extra hard, and rise in a blink, the ball released with no trajectory to speak of, a breathtaking line drive that rang the back rim and vanished into the hoop. West did all this so quickly that a typical photo in the next day's sports pages would feature him in the air, his right hand extended in perfect form — and his defender still rooted to the floor. It was as if he were playing on a different plane, in a game of his own.

"No one could stop me one-on-one when I was in my prime," West allowed to me, too matter-of-factly to be bragging. At his best in the endgame, more than once he would pull up at the buzzer, flick the pivotal shot, and sprint into the locker room, *knowing* it was true. "A deadly, deadly gun," recalls Walt Hazzard, once a teammate and now a Lakers aide. "If he's open, he's not missing. If the game's on the line, count it — just count it." Soon West had won a new nickname: Mr. Clutch.

But he did so much more than score. West was a perennial all-league defender, driving for loose balls like a starved hound, sticking his nose in till it was broken — nine times. When his team needed him to play the point, West did it so well that he even led the NBA in assists one year, ahead of maestros like Lenny Wilkens and Nate Archibald. There was no glitz to his game; he preferred lay-ins to dunks. He excelled with composure and efficiency and an understated brilliance that eschewed punctuation.

And he even learned how to go left. The next time you see an NBA team jersey or jacket, look closely at the league's tricolor logo, a silhouette of a man driving with the basketball. It is a silhouette of Jerry West — dribbling with his left hand.

The league's choice, made in 1969, was apt — no one was more popular among teammates or opponents. "Oscar Robertson was probably a better player fundamentally," says "Hot Rod" Hundley, a more flamboyent fellow West Virginian who welcomed West to the Lakers, "but his biggest weakness was his mouth. He'd bitch at his teammates, cry all the time at the referees. West just played the game. He could make a perfect play, and you'd mess it up, and he wouldn't say a word other than 'My fault.'"

And therein lay the rub. For when a man is so much better than the rest and his team *still* falls short, who else can he blame? During West's fourteen-year playing career, the Lakers made it to the NBA finals nine times — and lost in eight. West averaged 29 points in the postseason, a figure since surpassed only by Michael Jordan, but it never seemed to be quite enough. His most famous shot, in the 1970 finals, was a 60-foot, buzzer-beating heave to tie the Knicks in regulation.

As usual, however, there was a bitter postscript: Los Angeles dropped that game in overtime, then succumbed in the series, four games to three.

But the losses that hurt West the most came in a blur of Celtics green. Six times the Lakers squared off against Boston, and six times they came up empty. West played Sisyphus, rolling his boulder up a mountain named Bill Russell, only to tumble down and crash at the end. Worst of all was 1969, after the Lakers had imported Wilt Chamberlain. West played through the finals with a torn hamstring, the shrieking muscle dulled by shots of Novocain.

"He could hardly run," Hundley recalls. "When the shot wore off, he couldn't even walk up the steps from the dressing room — he had to take them one at a time." In the seventh and deciding game,

unable to drive off his bum leg, West backed in and limped his way
to a performance for the ages: 42 points, 13 rebounds, 12 assists.

And the Celtics won by two, after a fluke jump shot by Don
Nelson struck the rim, bounced four feet in the air, and fell dead
through the net.

Russell ended his playing career that day. After the game, he
strode straight to West's locker, to the exhausted man who'd just
been named the finals' Most Valuable Player — the only time the
award has gone to a member of the losing team. The great Celtic
took West's hand and squeezed it for a long moment, beyond
words. It was almost, thought Hundley, by then a broadcaster, as if
Russell were apologizing.

"I have no idea how many points I scored in my career," West told
me, leaning forward in his office chair. "But the one thing I remember is all the losses we had against the Celtics. It changed my life
forever. There's a lot of pain from that." Three decades later, his eyes
moistened at the memory.

"There were times when I wanted to say, 'The hell with this —
I don't want any more of this pain,'" he continued. "Because it
seemed like the more I gave, the worse result I got. That was a
special time of year for me — the playoffs, that was my time to
shine. And I usually did, with no result."

Then came the magical year of 1972, when Los Angeles won a
record 69 games, including 33 in a row, and finally broke through
against the Knicks to win a title, thanks in large part to Chamberlain's MVP performance. But that one championship, West insisted, could not erase the heartbreak of all his near-misses. As
Chick Hearn, the venerable Voice of the Lakers, said, "I've *never*
seen a player take defeats like he did." Even at West's peak moments, the old hurts gnawed at him.

Two years after winning the title, before a preseason exhibition
game, West began his locker-room rituals, then stopped cold.

For the first time, his hands weren't sweating. His nerves were
still.

Something was dreadfully wrong.

"It's terrible to go into the locker room and just feel completely
dead," West said. "There was nothing left, nothing left to give. I
wasn't even nervous. . . . I thought it was cheating the people who
pay to see you play."

West performed that night, but he never played in the NBA again. At the age of 36, still an All-Star, he retired.

Casting for a new challenge, he turned to a smaller ball and a smaller hole. He joined the Bel-Air Country Club and practiced golf shots every morning, playing 18 each afternoon. His marriage was cracking and his future was in limbo, but on the fairways West could lose himself in a solitary hunt for perfection, just as he had as a boy on a dusty dirt court. An outstanding putter, impervious to pressure, West whittled his handicap to plus-two — touring-pro territory.

"I just couldn't *wait* to hit balls," West said. "I had an incredible passion for it. I had a golf-abuse problem — the gratification you can get as a golfer is second to none." Finally West found what he needed to be happy: total control of his competitive destiny. With a club in his hand, he could get out exactly what he put into the game, no more and no less.

In his most memorable outing, West destroyed Bel-Air's treacherous back nine with a 28, six under par, a record that still stands. It was an "unbelievable" feeling, better than the day his Lakers won their title, he insisted, "because it was personal, inside me." West was aiming at a round in the 50s — and then his old devil came calling. "Patience," observed Eddie Merrins, the Bel-Air club professional, "was not one of his great virtues." On the front nine, where West finished the round, he took to rushing. He wound up with ten birdies, a bogey, and two double bogeys. "The worst 65 in the history of golf," he called it.

But while West had run from basketball, he couldn't hide. In 1976, he was coaxed back to coach his old team, a decision he regrets to this day. The Lakers were in disarray, coming off a 40–42 season, but West somehow guided the motley bunch to the best record in the league before losing in the second round of the playoffs.

The next year was less successful, and West couldn't stand it. At its highest level, basketball is a high-risk game played at terrific speed, and mental errors are brutally exposed. West saw selfishness and laziness all around, and it killed him that he couldn't race out on the floor and show how simple the game was — unless you made it hard. There were nights when he "felt like jumping out a hotel window," he recalled. He'd always been more patient with others than with himself, but now he had patience for no one. According to *Winnin' Times,* a book by Scott Ostler and Steve Springer, he once called Abdul-Jabbar "a dog." After forward Lou Hudson played poorly, the coach declared: "If Hudson were a horse, we'd have to take him out and shoot him."

But West was hardest on himself. He felt powerless to do anything but shoulder the blame, and he did that with a vengeance. "Emotionally it got worse and worse," he said. "It wasn't the players, it was me. I was going through a divorce that was incredibly painful, because it was my own doing. I was angry at the world."

After three years on the sidelines, West moved into the Lakers' front office. For a long time, he considered himself a coaching failure: "I thought I was terrible in what I did, absolutely terrible." Then one day he looked at the record book, and weighed the numbers with a cooler eye: 145 wins, 101 losses.

"What I did," West concluded, in a rare stroke of self-charity, "was pretty darn good."

"I am a much better person today than I was yesterday," West will tell you. "Every year I've gotten to be a better person. And I think I see a bigger picture than I did as a player."

Which is not quite to say that he has mellowed. "He's able to take things better on the outside now," says Karen West, his wife of seventeen years. "But I think inside it still really hurts if things aren't going right. In the morning he still looks at the paper and the stats, and it becomes fresh again in his mind. . . . He's still the perfectionist, and he still takes every loss very hard."

The morning of the Dallas game, the slumping Van Exel stopped by West's office for a talk. "He wants to put the weight of the world on his shoulders, and it doesn't work," West reported, knowing well of which he spoke. "I encouraged him."

Van Exel later elaborated. "He tells me how competitive he used to be, how he didn't want to hear anything from anybody, and that's pretty much the way I am. Anytime he tells me something, I listen, 'cause I know he's telling me for my own good. And he told me not to worry, I'll play my way out of it."

That advice seems prophetic this evening against the Mavericks, as Van Exel hits two three-pointers early and directs the offense with crisp assurance. Ceballos runs riot, guard Anthony Peeler gets hot, and forward "Easy" Elden Campbell, a twenty-seventh pick in the 1990 draft, dominates inside. But the man in the tunnel dies a little with every mistake. West kneels and winces when Ceballos double-clutches an air ball: "He should have shot the first one." He mutters, "No, no!" after a confused double-team leaves a Maverick free.

When the first-quarter horn sounds, with Los Angeles up by 17, West allows a nervous laugh and says, "Three more quarters like that and I can leave." Feeling restless, he paces back to the lounge, where he sees his team push its margin to 20 at the half. West knows they are not safe; the rhythm of basketball lends itself to big swings. In the third quarter, the Mavericks' Jamal Mashburn showers in 15 points in 5 minutes, and the Lakers' lead abruptly shrinks to 10.

West flees down a corridor and into his office to switch on his Zenith and writhe in private. "We have no energy at all in this half," he moans. He props a polished shoe on his desk and fiddles with his lower lip. His fourth finger is girded by a heavy gold ring. It isn't the '72 ring he won as a player, but the '85 edition, from the year the Lakers finally exorcised those damn Celtics — in Boston Garden, no less — and West heard the great news from three thousand miles away.

"C'mon, guys," West roots. "We need this game bad, we really do." Campbell clangs a turnaround. "Boy, oh boy," West breathes. "It's a ball game now — this'll be five or six points at the end of the quarter." Dallas guard Jason Kidd drives for a lay-up, and the lead is nine. "No defense . . . oh, boy." It is a world-weary exhalation.

His suit jacket discarded, West's voice rises half an octave when Peeler misses a rushed jumper: "You can't keep *doing* this, guy!" Mashburn hits another, and the lead is five. Harris calls time-out.

West anticipates every mismatch and blown assignment, just as he did as a player. But where his gift once translated into the prescient steal or the knifing drive to the basket, it now serves up anxiety and dread. At this moment he looks like a man who sees doctors emerging from his best friend's hospital room, faces grim.

"Miss one!" West calls out as play resumes and Dallas' Jimmy Jackson strikes from twenty-three feet. "Get back — you've got to get back!" he growls when the Lakers are slow in transition off a free throw.

"What are you doing?" he yells at Van Exel, who is dribbling aimlessly. "No, no, get it inside to Cedric!" Van Exel does just that, and Ceballos drives the baseline for a three-point play.

The Dallas bombs finally begin missing, and the Lakers briskly put the visitors away. But late in the fourth quarter, well after Chick Hearn proclaims the game to be "in the icebox," West is still haranguing the glowing screen, still fearing to fail at the game that he loves too much.

Ali in Havana

FROM ESQUIRE

IT IS A WARM, breezy, palm-flapping winter evening in Havana, and the leading restaurants are crowded with tourists from Europe, Asia, and South America being serenaded by guitarists relentlessly singing *"Guan-tan-a-mera . . . guajira . . . Guan-tan-a-mera"*; and at the Café Cantante there are clamorous salsa dancers, mambo kings, grunting, bare-chested male performers lifting tables with their teeth, and turbaned women swathed in hip-hugging skirts, blowing whistles while gyrating their glistening bodies into an erotic frenzy. In the café's audience as well as in the restaurants, hotels, and other public places throughout the island, cigarettes and cigars are smoked without restraint or restriction. Two prostitutes are smoking and talking privately on the corner of a dimly lit street bordering the manicured lawns of Havana's five-star Hotel Nacional. They are copper-colored women in their early twenties wearing faded miniskirts and halters, and as they chat, they are watching attentively while two men — one white, the other black — huddle over the raised trunk of a parked red Toyota, arguing about the prices of the boxes of black-market Havana cigars that are stacked within.

The white man is a square-jawed Hungarian in his mid-30s, wearing a beige tropical suit and a wide yellow tie, and he is one of Havana's leading entrepreneurs in the thriving illegal business of selling top-quality hand-rolled Cuban cigars below the local and international market price. The black man behind the car is a well-built, baldish, gray-bearded individual in his mid-50s from Los Angeles named Howard Bingham; and no matter what price the

Hungarian quotes, Bingham shakes his head and says, "No, no —
that's too much!"

"You're crazy!" cries the Hungarian in slightly accented English,
taking one of the boxes from the trunk and waving it in Howard
Bingham's face. "These are Cohiba Esplendidos! The best in the
world! You will pay $1,000 for a box like this in the States."

"Not me," says Bingham, who wears a Hawaiian shirt with a camera strapped around his neck. He is a professional photographer,
and he is staying at the Hotel Nacional with his friend Muhammad
Ali. "I wouldn't give you more than fifty dollars."

"You really are crazy," says the Hungarian, slicing through the
box's paper seal with his fingernail, opening the lid to reveal a
gleaming row of labeled Esplendidos.

"Fifty dollars," says Bingham.

"A hundred dollars," insists the Hungarian. "And hurry! The
police could be driving around." The Hungarian straightens up
and stares over the car toward the palm-lined lawn and stanchioned
lights that glow in the distance along the road leading to the hotel's
ornate portico, which is now jammed with people and vehicles;
then he turns and flings a glance back toward the nearby public
street, where he notices that the prostitutes are now blowing smoke
in his direction. He frowns.

"Quick, quick," he says to Bingham, handing him the box. "One
hundred dollars."

Howard Bingham does not smoke. He and Muhammad Ali and
their traveling companions are leaving Havana tomorrow, after
participating in a five-day American humanitarian-aid mission that
brought a planeload of medical supplies to hospitals and clinics
depleted by the United States' embargo, and Bingham would like
to return home with some fine contraband cigars for his friends.
But, on the other hand, one hundred is still too much.

"Fifty dollars," says Bingham determinedly, looking at his watch.
He begins to walk away.

"O.K., O.K.," the Hungarian says petulantly. "Fifty."

Bingham reaches into his pocket for the money, and the Hungarian grabs it and gives him the Esplendidos before driving off in the
Toyota. One of the prostitutes takes a few steps toward Bingham,
but the photographer hurries on to the hotel. Fidel Castro is having
a reception tonight for Muhammad Ali, and Bingham has only a

half hour to change and be at the portico to catch the chartered bus that will take them to the government's headquarters. He will be bringing one of his photographs to the Cuban leader — an enlarged, framed portrait showing Muhammad Ali and Malcolm X walking together along a Harlem sidewalk in 1963. Malcolm X was 37 at the time, two years away from an assassin's bullet; the 21-year-old Ali was about to win the heavyweight title in a remarkable upset over Sonny Liston in Miami. Bingham's photograph is inscribed, TO PRESIDENT FIDEL CASTRO, FROM MUHAMMAD ALI. Under his signature, the former champion has sketched a little heart.

Although Muhammad Ali is now 54 and has been retired from boxing for more than fifteen years, he is still one of the most famous men in the world, being identifiable throughout five continents; and as he walks through the lobby of the Hotel Nacional toward the bus, wearing a gray sharkskin suit and a white cotton shirt buttoned at the neck without a tie, several guests approach him and request his autograph. It takes him about thirty seconds to write "Muhammad Ali," so shaky are his hands from the effects of Parkinson's syndrome; and though he walks without support, his movements are quite slow, and Howard Bingham and Ali's fourth wife, Yolanda, are following nearby.

Bingham met Ali thirty-five years ago in Los Angeles, shortly after the fighter had turned professional and before he discarded his "slave name" (Cassius Marcellus Clay) and joined the Black Muslims. Bingham subsequently became his closest male friend and has photographed every aspect of Ali's life: his rise and fall three times as the heavyweight champion; his three-year expulsion from boxing, beginning in 1967, for refusing to serve in the American military during the Vietnam War ("I ain't got no quarrel with them Vietcong"); his four marriages; his fatherhood of nine children (one adopted, two out of wedlock); his endless public appearances in all parts of the world — Germany, England, Egypt (sailing on the Nile with a son of Elijah Muhammad's), Sweden, Libya, Pakistan (hugging refugees from Afghanistan), Japan, Indonesia, Ghana (wearing a dashiki and posing with President Kwame Nkrumah), Zaire (beating George Foreman), Manila (beating Joe Frazier) . . . and now, on the final night of his 1996 visit to Cuba, he is en route to a social encounter with an aging contender he has long admired — one who has survived at the top for nearly forty years despite the ill will of nine American presidents, the CIA, the Mafia, and various militant Cuban Americans.

Bingham waits for Ali near the open door of the charter bus that is blocking the hotel's entrance; but Ali lingers within the crowd in the lobby, and Yolanda steps aside to let some people get closer to her husband.

She is a large and pretty woman of thirty-eight, with a radiant smile and a freckled, fair complexion that reflects her interracial ancestry. A scarf is loosely draped over her head and shoulders, her arms are covered by long sleeves, and her well-designed dress in vivid hues hangs below her knees. She converted to Islam from Catholicism when she married Ali, a man sixteen years her senior but one with whom she shared a familial bond dating back to her girlhood in their native Louisville, where her mother and Ali's mother were sisterly soul mates who traveled together to attend his fights. Yolanda had occasionally joined Ali's entourage, becoming acquainted with not only the boxing element but with Ali's female contemporaries who were his lovers, his wives, the mothers of his children; and she remained in touch with Ali throughout the 1970s, while she majored in psychology at Vanderbilt and later earned her master's degree in business at UCLA. Then — with the end of Ali's boxing career, his third marriage, and his vibrant health — Yolanda intimately entered his life as casually and naturally as she now stands waiting to reclaim her place at his side.

She knows that he is enjoying himself. There is a slight twinkle in his eyes, not much expression on his face, and no words forthcoming from this once most talkative of champions. But the mind behind his Parkinson's mask is functioning normally, and he is characteristically committed to what he is doing: He is spelling out his full name on whatever cards or scraps of paper his admirers are handing him. "Muhammad Ali." He does not settle for a time-saving "Ali" or his mere initials. He has never shortchanged his audience.

And in this audience tonight are people from Latin America, Canada, Africa, Russia, China, Germany, France. There are two hundred French travel agents staying at the hotel in conjunction with the Cuban government's campaign to increase its growing tourist trade (which last year saw about 745,000 visitors spending an estimated $1 billion on the island). There is also on hand an

Italian movie producer and his lady friend from Rome and a one-time Japanese wrestler, Antonio Inoki, who injured Ali's legs during a 1976 exhibition in Tokyo (but who warmly embraced him two nights ago in the hotel's lounge as they sat listening to Cuban pianist Chucho Valdes playing jazz on a Russian-made Moskva baby grand); and there is also in the crowd, standing taller than the rest, the 43-year-old, six-foot five-inch Cuban heavyweight hero Teófilo Stevenson, who was a three-time Olympic gold medalist, in 1972, 1976, and 1980, and who, on this island at least, is every bit as renowned as Ali or Castro.

Though part of Stevenson's reputation derives from his erstwhile power and skill in the ring (although he never fought Ali), it is also attributable to his not having succumbed to the offers of professional boxing promoters, stubbornly resisting the Yankee dollar — although Stevenson hardly seems deprived. He dwells among his countrymen like a towering Cuban peacock, occupying high positions within the government's athletic programs and gaining sufficient attention from the island's women to have garnered four wives so far, who are testimony to his eclectic taste.

His first wife was a dance instructor. His second was an industrial engineer. His third was a medical doctor. His fourth and present wife is a criminal attorney. Her name is Fraymari, and she is a girlishly petite olive-skinned woman of twenty-three who, standing next to her husband in the lobby, rises barely higher than the midsection of his embroidered guayabera — a tightly tailored, short-sleeved shirt that accentuates his tapered torso, his broad shoulders, and the length of his dark, muscular arms, which once prevented his opponents from doing any injustice to his winning Latin looks.

Stevenson always fought from an upright position, and he maintains that posture today. When people talk to him, his eyes look downward, but his head remains high. The firm jaw of his oval-shaped head seems to be locked at a right angle to his straight-spined back. He is a proud man who exhibits all of his height. But he does listen, especially when the words being directed up at him are coming from the perky little attorney who is his wife. Fraymari is now reminding him that it is getting late — everyone should be on the bus; Fidel may be waiting.

Stevenson lowers his eyes toward her and winks. He has gotten the message. He has been Ali's principal escort throughout this visit. He was also Ali's guest in the United States during the fall of 1995; and though he knows only a few words of English, and Ali no Spanish, they are brotherly in their body language.

Stevenson edges himself into the crowd and gently places his right arm around the shoulders of his fellow champion. And then, slowly but firmly, he guides Ali toward the bus.

The road to Fidel Castro's palace of the Revolution leads through a memory lane of old American automobiles chugging along at about twenty-five miles an hour — springless, preembargo Ford coupes and Plymouth sedans, DeSotos and LaSalles, Nashes and Studebakers, and various vehicular collages created out of Cadillac grilles and Oldsmobile axles and Buick fenders patched with pieces of oil-drum metal and powered by engines interlinked with kitchen utensils and pre-Batista lawn mowers and other gadgets that have elevated the craft of tinkering in Cuba to the status of high art.

The relatively newer forms of transportation seen on the road are, of course, non-American products — Polish Fiats, Russian Ladas, German motor scooters, Chinese bicycles, and the glistening, newly imported, air-conditioned Japanese bus from which Muhammad Ali is now gazing through a closed window out toward the street. At times, he raises a hand in response to one of the waving pedestrians or cyclists or motorists who recognize the bus, which has been shown repeatedly on the local TV news conveying Ali and his companions to the medical centers and tourist sites that have been part of the busy itinerary.

On the bus, as always, Ali is sitting alone, spread out across the two front seats in the left aisle directly behind the Cuban driver. Yolanda sits a few feet ahead of him to the right; she is adjacent to the driver and within inches of the windshield. The seats behind her are occupied by Teófilo Stevenson, Fraymari, and the photographer Bingham. Seated behind Ali, and also occupying two seats, is an American screenwriter named Greg Howard who weighs more than three hundred pounds. Although he has traveled with Ali for only a few months while researching a film on the fighter's life, Greg Howard has firmly established himself as an intimate sidekick and as such is among the very few on this trip who have heard Ali's voice. Ali speaks so softly that it is impossible to hear him in a crowd, and as a result whatever public comments or sentiments he is expected to, or chooses to, express are verbalized by Yolanda, or Bingham, or Teófilo Stevenson, or even at times by this stout young screenwriter.

"Ali is in his Zen period," Greg Howard has said more than once in reference to Ali's quiescence. Like Ali, he admires what he has seen so far in Cuba — "There's no racism here" — and as a black man he has long identified with many of Ali's frustrations and confrontations. His student thesis at Princeton analyzed the Newark race riots of 1967, and the Hollywood script he most recently completed focuses on the Negro baseball leagues of the pre–World War II years. He envisions his new work on Ali in the genre of *Gandhi*.

The two dozen bus seats behind those tacitly reserved for Ali's inner circle are occupied by the secretary-general of the Cuban Red Cross and the American humanitarian personnel who have entrusted him with $500,000 worth of donated medical supplies; and there are also the two Cuban interpreters and a dozen members of the American media, including the CBS-TV commentator Ed Bradley and his producers and camera crew from *60 Minutes*.

Ed Bradley is a gracious but reserved individualist who has appeared on television for a decade with his left earlobe pierced by a small circular ring — which, after some unfavorable comment initially expressed by his colleagues Mike Wallace and Andy Rooney, prompted Bradley's explanation: "It's *my* ear." Bradley also indulges in his identity as a cigar smoker; and as he sits in the midsection of the bus next to his Haitian lady friend, he is taking full advantage of the Communist regime's laissez-faire attitude toward tobacco, puffing away on a Cohiba Robusto, for which he paid full price at the Nacional's tobacco shop — and which now exudes a costly cloud of fragrance that appeals to his friend (who occasionally also smokes cigars) but is not appreciated by the two California women who are seated two rows back and are affiliated with a humanitarian-aid agency.

Indeed, the women have been commenting about the smoking habits of countless people they have encountered in Havana, being especially disappointed to discover earlier this very day that the pediatric hospital they visited (and to which they committed donations) is under the supervision of three tobacco-loving family physicians. When one of the American women, a blonde from Santa Barbara, reproached one of the cigarette-smoking doctors indirectly for setting such a poor example, she was told in effect that the island's health statistics regarding longevity, infant mortality, and general fitness compared favorably with those in the United States and were probably better than those of Americans residing in the capital city of Washington. On the other hand, the doctor made it clear that he did not believe that smoking was good for one's health — after all, Fidel himself had given it up; but unfortunately, the doctor added, in a classic understatement, "some people have not followed him."

Nothing the doctor said appeased the woman from Santa Barbara. She did not, however, wish to appear confrontational at the hospital's news conference, which was covered by the press; nor during her many bus rides with Ed Bradley did she ever request that he discard his cigar. "Mr. Bradley intimidates me," she confided to her California coworker. But he was of course living within the law on this island that the doctor had called "the cradle of the best tobacco in the world." In Cuba, the most available American periodical on the newsstands is *Cigar Aficionado*.

The bus passes through the Plaza de la Revolución and comes to a halt at a security checkpoint near the large glass doors that open onto the marble-floored foyer of a 1950s modern building that is the center of communism's only stronghold in the Western Hemisphere.

As the bus door swings open, Greg Howard moves forward in his seat and grabs the 235-pound Muhammad Ali by the arms and shoulders and helps him to his feet; and after Ali has made his way down to the metal step, he turns and stretches back into the bus to take hold of the extended hands and forearms of the 300-pound screenwriter and pulls him to a standing position. This routine, repeated at each and every bus stop throughout the week, is never accompanied by either man's acknowledging that he has received any assistance, although Ali is aware that some passengers find the pas de deux quite amusing, and he is not reluctant to use his friend to further comic effect. After the bus had made an earlier stop in front of the sixteenth-century Morro Castle — where Ali had followed Teófilo Stevenson up a 117-step spiral staircase for a rooftop

view of Havana Harbor — he spotted the solitary figure of Greg
Howard standing below in the courtyard. Knowing that there was
no way the narrow staircase could accommodate Howard's wide
body, Ali suddenly began to wave his arms, summoning Howard to
come up and join him.

Castro's security guards, who know in advance the names of all the
bus passengers, guide Ali and the others through the glass doors
and then into a pair of waiting elevators for a brief ride that is
followed by a short walk through a corridor and finally into a large
white-walled reception room, where it is announced that Fidel Castro will soon join them. The room has high ceilings and potted
palms in every corner and is sparsely furnished with modern tan
leather furniture. Next to a sofa is a table with two telephones, one
gray and the other red. Overlooking the sofa is an oil painting of
the Viñales valley, which lies west of Havana; and among the primitive art displayed on a circular table in front of the sofa is a grotesque tribal figure similar to the one Ali had examined earlier in
the week at a trinket stand while touring with the group in Havana's
Old Square. Ali had then whispered into the ear of Howard Bingham, and Bingham had repeated aloud what Ali had said: "Joe
Frazier."
    Ali now stands in the middle of the room, next to Bingham, who
carries under his arm the framed photograph he plans to give
Castro. Teófilo Stevenson and Fraymari stand facing them. The
diminutive and delicate-boned Fraymari has painted her lips scarlet
and has pulled back her black hair in a matronly manner, hoping
no doubt to appear more mature than her twenty-three years suggest, but standing next to the three much older and heavier and
taller men transforms her image closer to that of an anorexic teenager. Ali's wife and Greg Howard are wandering about within the
group that is exchanging comments in muted tones, either in English or Spanish, sometimes assisted by the interpreters. Ali's hands
are shaking uncontrollably at his sides; but since his companions
have witnessed this all week, the only people who are now paying
attention are the security guards posted near the door.
    Also waiting near the door for Castro is the four-man CBS camera
team, and chatting with them and his two producers is Ed Bradley,
without his cigar. There are no ashtrays in this room! This is a most

uncommon sight in Cuba. Its implications might be political. Perhaps the sensibilities of the blond woman from Santa Barbara were taken into account by the doctors at the hospital and communicated to Castro's underlings, who are now making a conciliatory gesture toward their American benefactress.

Since the security guards have not invited the guests to be seated, everybody remains standing — for ten minutes, for twenty minutes, and then for a full half hour. Teófilo Stevenson shifts his weight from foot to foot and gazes over the heads of the crowd toward the upper level of the portal through which Castro is expected to enter — if he shows up. Stevenson knows from experience that Castro's schedule is unpredictable. There is always a crisis of some sort in Cuba, and it has long been rumored on the island that Castro constantly changes the location of where he sleeps. The identity of his bed partners is, of course, a state secret. Two nights ago, Stevenson and Ali and the rest were kept waiting until midnight for an expected meeting with Castro at the Hotel Biocaribe (to which Bingham had brought his gift photograph). But Castro never appeared. And no explanation was offered.

Now in this reception room, it is already 9:00 P.M. Ali continues to shake. No one has had dinner. The small talk is getting smaller. A few people would like to smoke. The regime is not assuaging anyone in this crowd with a bartender. It is a cocktail party without cocktails. There are not even canapés or soft drinks. Everyone is becoming increasingly restless — and then suddenly there is a collective sigh. The very familiar man with the beard strides into the room, dressed for guerrilla combat; and in a cheerful, high-pitched voice that soars beyond his whiskers, he announces, *"Buenas noches!"*

In an even higher tone, he repeats, *"Buenas noches,"* this time with a few waves to the group while hastening toward the guest of honor; and then, with his arms extended, the 70-year-old Fidel Castro immediately obscures the lower half of Ali's expressionless face with a gentle embrace and his flowing gray beard.

"I am glad to see you," Castro says to Ali, via the interpreter who followed him into the room, a comely, fair-skinned woman with a refined English accent. "I am very, very glad to see you," Castro continues, backing up to look into Ali's eyes while holding on to his trembling arms, "and I am thankful for your visit." Castro then releases his grip and awaits a possible reply. Ali says nothing. His expression remains characteristically fixed and benign, and his eyes do not blink despite the flashbulbs of several surrounding photographers. As the silence persists, Castro turns toward his old friend Teófilo Stevenson, feigning a jab. The Cuban boxing champion lowers his eyes and, with widened lips and cheeks, registers a smile. Castro then notices the tiny brunette standing beside Stevenson.

"Stevenson, who is this young woman?" Castro asks aloud in a tone of obvious approval. But before Stevenson can reply, Fraymari steps forward with a hint of lawyerly indignation: "You mean you don't remember me?"

Castro seems stunned. He smiles feebly, trying to conceal his confusion. He turns inquiringly toward his boxing hero, but Stevenson's eyes only roll upward. Stevenson knows that Castro has met Fraymari socially on earlier occasions, but unfortunately the Cuban leader has forgotten, and it is equally unfortunate that Fraymari is now behaving like a prosecutor.

"You held my son in your arms before he was one year old!" she reminds him while Castro continues to ponder. The crowd is attentive; the television cameras are rolling.

"At a volleyball game?" Castro asks tentatively.

"No, no," Stevenson interrupts, before Fraymari can say anything more, "that was my former wife. The doctor."

Castro slowly shakes his head in mock disapproval. Then he abruptly turns away from the couple, but not before reminding Stevenson, "You should get name tags."

Castro redirects his attention to Muhammad Ali. He studies Ali's face.

"Where is your wife?" he asks softly. Ali says nothing. There is more silence and turning of heads in the group until Howard Bingham spots Yolanda standing near the back and waves her to Castro's side.

Before she arrives, Bingham steps forward and presents Castro with the photograph of Ali and Malcolm X in Harlem in 1963. Castro holds it up level with his eyes and studies it silently for several seconds. When this picture was taken, Castro had been in control of Cuba for nearly four years. He was then 37. In 1959, he defeated the U.S.A.–backed dictator, Fulgencio Batista, overcoming odds greater than Ali's subsequent victory over the supposedly unbeatable Sonny Liston. Batista had actually announced Castro's death back in 1956. Castro, then hiding in a secret outpost, thirty years old and beardless, was a disgruntled Jesuit-trained lawyer who was born into a land-owning family and who craved Batista's job. At 32, he had it. Batista was forced to flee to the Dominican Republic.

During this period, Muhammad Ali was only an amateur. His greatest achievement would come in 1960, when he received a gold medal in Rome as a member of the United States Olympic boxing team. But later in the sixties, he and Castro would share the world stage as figures moving against the American establishment — and now, in the twilight of their lives, on this winter's night in Havana, they meet for the first time: Ali silent and Castro isolated on his island.

"Que bien!" Castro says to Howard Bingham before showing the photograph to his interpreter. Then Castro is introduced by Bingham to Ali's wife. After they exchange greetings through the interpreter, he asks her, as if surprised, "You don't speak Spanish?"

"No," she says softly. She begins to caress her husband's left wrist, on which he wears a $250 silver Swiss Army watch she bought him. It is the only jewelry Ali wears.

"But I thought I saw you speaking Spanish on the TV news this week," Castro continues wonderingly before acknowledging that her voice had obviously been dubbed.

"Do you live in New York?"

"No, we live in Michigan."

"Cold," says Castro.

"Very cold," she repeats.

"In Michigan, don't you find many people that speak Spanish?"

"No, not many," she says. "Mostly in California, New York . . ." and, after a pause, "Florida."

Castro nods. It takes him a few seconds to think up another question. Small talk has never been the forte of this man who specializes in nonstop haranguing monologues that can last for hours; and yet here he is, in a room crowded with camera crews and news photographers — a talk-show host with a guest of honor who is speechless. But Fidel Castro plods on, asking Ali's wife if she has a favorite sport.

"I play a little tennis," Yolanda says, and then asks him, "Do you play tennis?"

"Ping-Pong," he replies, quickly adding that during his youth he had been active in the ring. "I spent hours boxing . . ." he begins to reminisce, but before he finishes his sentence, he sees the slowly rising right fist of Muhammad Ali moving toward his chin! Exuberant cheering and handclapping resound through the room, and Castro jumps sideways toward Stevenson, shouting, *"Asesorame!"* — "Help me!"

Stevenson's long arms land upon Ali's shoulders from behind, squeezing him gently; and then, after he releases him, the two ex-champions face each other and begin to act out in slow motion the postures of competing prizefighters — bobbing, weaving, swinging, ducking — all of it done without touching and all of it accompanied by three minutes of ongoing applause and the clicking of cameras, and also some feelings of relief from Ali's friends because, in his own way, he has decided to join them. Ali still says nothing, his face still inscrutable, but he is less remote, less alone, and he does not pull away from Stevenson's embrace as the latter eagerly tells Castro about a boxing exhibition that he and Ali had staged earlier in the week at the Balado gym, in front of hundreds of fans and some of the island's up-and-coming contenders.

Stevenson did not actually explain that it had been merely another photo opportunity, one in which they sparred openhanded in the ring, wearing their street clothes and barely touching each other's bodies and faces; but then Stevenson had climbed out of the ring, leaving Ali to the more taxing test of withstanding two abbreviated rounds against one and then another young bully of grade-school age who clearly had not come to participate in a kiddie show. They had come to floor the champ. Their bellicose little bodies and hot-gloved hands and helmeted hell-bent heads were consumed with fury and ambition; and as they charged ahead, swinging wildly and swaggering to the roars of their teenage friends and relatives at ringside, one could imagine their future boastings to their grandchildren: on one fine day back in the winter of '96, I whacked Muhammad Ali! Except, in truth, on this particular day, Ali was still too fast for them. He backpedaled and shifted and swayed, stood on the toes of his black woven-leather pointed shoes, and showed that his body was made for motion — his Parkinson's problems were lost in his shuffle, in the thrusts of his butterfly sting that whistled two feet above the heads of his aspiring assailants, in

the dazzling dips of his rope-a-dope that had confounded George
Foreman in Zaire, in his ever-memorable style, which in this Cuban
gym moistened the eyes of his ever-observant photographer friend
and provoked the overweight screenwriter to cry out in a voice that
few in this noisy Spanish crowd could understand, "Ali's on a high!
Ali's on a high!"

Teófilo Stevenson raises Ali's right arm above the head of Castro,
and the news photographers spend several minutes posing the
three of them together in flashing light. Castro then sees Fraymari watching alone at some distance. She is not smiling. Castro
nods toward her. He summons a photographer to take a picture
of Fraymari and himself. But she relaxes only after her husband
comes over to join her in the conversation, which Castro immediately directs to the health and growth of their son, who is not yet 2
years old.

"Will he be as tall as his father?" Castro asks.

"I assume so," Fraymari says, glancing up toward her husband.
She also has to look up when talking to Fidel Castro, for the Cuban leader is taller than six feet and his posture is nearly as erect as
her husband's. Only the six-foot three-inch Muhammad Ali, who
is standing with Bingham on the far side of her husband — and
whose skin coloring, oval-shaped head, and burr-style haircut are
very similar to her husband's — betrays his height with the slope
shouldered forward slouch he has developed since his illness.

"How much does your son weigh?" Castro continues.

"When he was one year old, he was already twenty-six pounds,"
Fraymari says. "This is three above normal. He was walking at nine
months."

"She still breast-feeds him," Teófilo Stevenson says, seeming
pleased.

"Oh, that's very nourishing," agrees Castro.

"Sometimes the kid becomes confused and thinks my chest is his
mother's breast," Stevenson says, and he could have added that his
son is also confused by Ali's sunglasses. The little boy engraved
teeth marks all over the plastic frames while chewing on them
during the days he accompanied his parents on Ali's bus tour.

As a CBS boom pole swoops down closer to catch the conversation, Castro reaches out to touch Stevenson's belly and asks, "How
much do you weigh?"

"Two hundred thirty-eight pounds, more or less."

"That's thirty-eight more than me," Castro says, but he complains, "I eat very little. Very little. The diet advice I get is never accurate. I eat around fifteen hundred calories — less than thirty grams of protein, less than that."

Castro slaps a hand against his own midsection, which is relatively flat. If he does have a potbelly, it is concealed within his well-tailored uniform. Indeed, for a man of seventy, he seems in fine health. His facial skin is florid and unsagging, his dark eyes dart around the room with ever-alert intensity, and he has a full head of lustrous gray hair not thinning at the crown. The attention he pays to himself might be measured from his manicured fingernails down to his square-toed boots, which are unscuffed and smoothly buffed without the burnish of a lackey's spit shine. But his beard seems to belong to another man and another time. It is excessively long and scraggly. Wispy white hairs mix with the faded black and dangle down the front of his uniform like an old shroud, weather-worn and drying out. It is the beard from the hills. Castro strokes it constantly, as if trying to revive the vitality of its fiber.

Castro now looks at Ali.

"How's your appetite?" he asks, forgetting that Ali is not speaking.

"Where's your wife?" he then asks aloud, and Howard Bingham calls out to her. Yolanda has once more drifted back into the group. When she arrives, Castro hesitates before speaking to her. It is as if he is not absolutely sure who she is. He has met so many people since arriving, and with the group rotating constantly due to the jostling of the photographers, Castro cannot be certain whether the woman at his side is Muhammad Ali's wife or Ed Bradley's friend or some other woman he has met moments ago who has left him with an unlasting impression. Having already committed a faux pas regarding one of the wives of the two multimarried ex-champions standing nearby, Castro waits for some hint from his interpreter. None is offered. Fortunately, he does not have to worry in this country about the women's vote — or any vote, for that matter — but he does sigh in mild relief when Yolanda reintroduces herself as Ali's wife and does so by name.

"Ah, Yolanda," Castro repeats, "what a beautiful name. That's the name of a queen somewhere."

"In our household," she says.

"And how is your husband's appetite?"

"Good, but he likes sweets."

"We can send you some of our ice cream to Michigan," Castro says. Without waiting for her to comment, he asks, "Michigan is very cold?"

"Oh, yes," she replies, not indicating that they had already discussed Michigan's winter weather.

"How much snow?"

"We didn't get hit with the blizzard," Yolanda says, referring to a storm in January, "but it can get three, four feet —"

Teófilo Stevenson interrupts to say that he had been in Michigan during the previous October.

"Oh," Castro says, raising an eyebrow. He mentions that during the same month he had also been in the United States (attending the United Nations' fiftieth-anniversary tribute). He asks Stevenson the length of his American visit.

"I was there for nineteen days," says Stevenson.

"Nineteen days!" Castro repeats. "Longer than I was."

Castro complains that he was limited to five days and prohibited from traveling beyond New York.

"Well, *comandante*," Stevenson responds offhandedly, in a slightly superior tone, "if you like, I will sometime show you my video."

Stevenson appears to be very comfortable in the presence of the Cuban leader, and perhaps the latter has habitually encouraged this; but at this moment, Castro may well be finding his boxing hero a bit condescending and worthy of a retaliatory jab. He knows how to deliver it.

"When you visited the United States," Castro asks pointedly, "did you bring your wife, the lawyer?"

Stevenson stiffens. He directs his eyes toward his wife. She turns away.

"No," Stevenson answers quietly. "I went alone."

Castro abruptly shifts his attention to the other side of the room, where the CBS camera crew is positioned, and he asks Ed Bradley, "What do you do?"

"We're making a documentary on Ali," Bradley explains, "and we followed him to Cuba to see what he was doing in Cuba and . . ."

Bradley's voice is suddenly overwhelmed by the sounds of laughter and handclapping. Bradley and Castro turn to discover that Muhammad Ali is now reclaiming everyone's attention. He is holding his shaky left fist in the air; but instead of assuming a boxer's pose, as he had done earlier, he is beginning to pull out from the top of his upraised fist, slowly and with dramatic delicacy, the tip of a red silk handkerchief that is pinched between his right index finger and thumb.

After he has pulled out the entire handkerchief, he dangles it in the air for a few seconds, waving it closer and closer to the forehead of the wide-eyed Fidel Castro. Ali seems bewitched. He continues to stare stagnantly at Castro and the others, surrounded by applause that he gives no indication he hears. Then he proceeds to place the handkerchief back into the top of his cupped left hand — pecking with the pinched fingers of his right — and then quickly opens his palms toward his audience and reveals that the handkerchief has disappeared.

"Where is it?" cries Castro, who seems to be genuinely surprised and delighted. He approaches Ali and examines his hands, repeating, "Where is it? Where have you put it?"

Everyone who has traveled on Ali's bus during the week knows where he has hidden it. They have seen him perform the trick repeatedly in front of some of the patients and doctors at the hospitals and clinics as well as before countless tourists who have recognized him in his hotel lobby or during his strolls through the town square. They have also seen him follow up each performance with a demonstration that exposes his method. He keeps hidden in his fist a flesh-colored rubber thumb that contains the handkerchief that he will eventually pull out with the fingers of his other hand; and when he is reinserting the handkerchief, he is actually shoving the material back into the concealed rubber thumb, into which he then inserts his own right thumb. When he opens his hands, the uninformed among his onlookers are seeing his empty palms and missing the fact that the handkerchief is tucked within the rubber thumb that is covering his outstretched right thumb. Sharing with his audience the mystery of his magic always earns him additional applause.

After Ali has performed and explained the trick to Castro, he gives Castro the rubber thumb to examine — and, with more zest than he has shown all evening, Castro says, "Oh, let me try it, I want to try — it's the first time I have seen such a wonderful thing!" And after a few minutes of coaching from Howard Bingham, who long ago learned how to do it from Ali, the Cuban leader performs with sufficient dexterity and panache to satisfy his magical ambitions and to arouse another round of applause from the guests.

Meanwhile, more than ten minutes have passed since Ali began his comic routine. It is already after 9:30 P.M., and the commentator Ed Bradley, whose conversation with Castro had been interrupted, is concerned that the Cuban leader might leave the room without responding to the questions Bradley has prepared for his show. Bradley edges close to Castro's interpreter, saying in a voice that is sure to be heard, "Would you ask him if he followed . . . was able to follow Ali when he was boxing professionally?"

The question is relayed and repeated until Castro, facing the CBS cameras, replies, "Yes, I recall the days when they were discussing the possibilities of a match between the two of them" — he nods toward Stevenson and Ali — "and I remember when he went to Africa."

"In Zaire," Bradley clarifies, referring to Ali's victory in 1974 over George Foreman. And he follows up: "What kind of impact did he have in this country, because he was a revolutionary as well as . . . ?"

"It was great," Castro says. "He was very much admired as a sportsman, as a boxer, as a person. There was always a high opinion of him. But I never guessed one day we would meet here, with this kind gesture of bringing medicine, seeing our children, visiting our polyclinics. I am very glad, I am thrilled, to have the opportunity to meet him personally, to appreciate his kindness. I see he is strong. I see he has a very kind face."

Castro is speaking as if Ali were not in the room, standing a few feet away. Ali maintains his fixed facade even as Stevenson whispers into his ear, asking in English, "Muhammad, Muhammad, why you no speak?" Stevenson then turns to tell the journalist who stands behind him, "Muhammad does speak. He speaks to me." Stevenson says nothing more because Castro is now looking at him while continuing to tell Bradley, "I am very glad that he and Stevenson have met." After a pause, Castro adds, "And I am glad that they never fought."

"He's not so sure," Bradley interjects, smiling in the direction of Stevenson.

"I find in that friendship something beautiful," Castro insists softly.

"There is a tie between the two of them," Bradley says.

"Yes," says Castro. "It is true." He again looks at Ali, then at Stevenson, as if searching for something more profound to say.

"And how's the documentary?" he finally asks Bradley.

"It'll be on *60 Minutes.*"

"When?"

"Maybe one month," Bradley says, reminding Castro's interpreter, "This is the program on which the *comandante* has been interviewed by Dan Rather a number of times in the past, when Dan Rather was on *60 Minutes.*"

"And who's there now?" Castro wants to know.

"I am," Bradley answers.

"You," Castro repeats, with a quick glance at Bradley's earring. "So you are there — the boss now?"

Bradley responds as a media star without illusions: "I'm a worker."

Trays containing coffee, tea, and orange juice finally arrive, but only in amounts sufficient for Ali and Yolanda, Howard Bingham, Greg Howard, the Stevensons, and Castro — although Castro tells the waiters he wants nothing.

Castro motions for Ali and the others to join him across the room, around the circular table. The camera crews and the rest of the guests follow, standing as near to the principals as they can. But throughout the group, there is a discernible restlessness. They have been standing for more than an hour and a half. It is now approaching 10:00 P.M. There has been no food. And for the vast majority, it is clear that there will also be nothing to drink. Even among the special guests, seated and sipping from chilled glasses or hot cups, there is a waning level of fascination with the evening. Indeed, Muhammad Ali's eyes are closed. He is sleeping.

Yolanda sits next to him on the sofa, pretending not to notice. Castro also ignores it, although he sits directly across the table, with the interpreter and the Stevensons.

"How large is Michigan?" Castro begins a new round of questioning with Yolanda, returning for the third time to a subject they had explored beyond the interest of anyone in the room except Castro himself.

"I don't know how big the state is as far as demographics," Yolanda says. "We live in a very small village [Barrien Springs] with about two thousand people."

"Are you going back to Michigan tomorrow?"

"Yes."

"What time?"

"Two-thirty."

"Via Miami?" Castro asks.

"Yes."

"From Miami, where do you fly?"

"We're flying to Michigan."

"How many hours' flight?"

"We have to change at Cincinnati — about two and a half hours."

"Flying time?" asks Castro.

Muhammad Ali opens his eyes, then closes them.

"Flying time," Yolanda repeats.

"From Miami to Michigan?" Castro continues.

"No," she again explains, but still with patience, "we have to go to Cincinnati. There are no direct flights."

"So you have to take two planes?" Castro asks.

"Yes," she says, adding for clarification, "Miami to Cincinnati — and then Cincinnati to South Bend, Indiana."

"From Cincinnati . . . ?"

"To South Bend," she says. "That's the closest airport."

"So," Fidel goes on, "it is on the outskirts of the city?"

"Yes."

"You have a farm?"

"No," Yolanda says, "just land. We let someone else do the growing."

She mentions that Teófilo Stevenson has traveled through this part of the Midwest. The mention of his name gains Stevenson's attention.

"I was in Chicago," Stevenson tells Castro.

"You were at their home?" Castro asks.

"No," Yolanda corrects Stevenson, "you were in Michigan."

"I was in the countryside," Stevenson says. Unable to resist, he adds, "I have a video of that visit. I'll show it to you sometime."

Castro seems not to hear him. He directs his attention back to

Yolanda, asking her where she was born, where she was educated, when she became married, and how many years separate her age from that of her husband, Muhammad Ali.

After Yolanda acknowledges being sixteen years younger than Ali, Castro turns toward Fraymari and with affected sympathy says that she married a man who is twenty years her senior.

"Comandante!" Stevenson intercedes, "I am in shape. Sports keep you healthy. Sports add years to your life and life to your years!"

"Oh, what conflict she has," Castro goes on, ignoring Stevenson and catering to Fraymari — and to the CBS cameraman who steps forward for a closer view of Castro's face. "She is a lawyer, and she does not put this husband in jail." Castro is enjoying much more than Fraymari the attention this topic is now getting from the group. Castro had lost his audience and now has it back and seemingly wants to retain it, no matter at what cost to Stevenson's harmony with Fraymari. Yes, Castro continues, Fraymari had the misfortune to select a husband "who can never settle down. . . . Jail would be an appropriate place for him."

"Comandante," Stevenson interrupts in a jocular manner that seems intended to placate both the lawyer who is his spouse and the lawyer who rules the country, "I might as well be locked up!" He implies that should he deviate from marital fidelity, his lawyer wife "will surely put me in a place where she is the only woman who can visit me!"

Everyone around the table and within the circling group laughs. Ali is now awake. The banter between Castro and Stevenson resumes until Yolanda, all but rising in her chair, tells Castro, "We have to pack."

"You're going to have dinner now?" he asks.

"Yes, sir," she says. Ali stands, along with Howard Bingham. Yolanda thanks Castro's interpreter directly, saying, "Be sure to tell him, 'You're always welcome in our home.'" The interpreter quotes Castro as again complaining that when he visits America, he is usually restricted to New York, but he adds, "Things change."

The group watches as Yolanda and Ali pass through, and Castro follows them into the hallway. The elevator arrives, and its door is held open by a security guard. Castro extends his final farewell with handshakes — and only then does he discover that he holds Ali's rubber thumb in his hand. Apologizing, he tries to hand it back to Ali, but Bingham politely protests. "No, no," Bingham says, "Ali wants you to have it."

Castro's interpreter at first fails to understand what Bingham is saying.

"He wants you to keep it," Bingham repeats.

Bingham enters the elevator with Ali and Yolanda. Before the door closes, Castro smiles, waves goodbye, and stares with curiosity at the rubber thumb. Then he puts it in his pocket.

The Tiger King

FROM ESQUIRE

MIKE TYSON IS LISTENING to a grain of exotic information about
the king-cobra catchers of Burma; he likes this kind of chat. "Say
again?" he asks. "I'm going deaf. Maybe it's all those years of listening to loud music. God's own truth, I don't hear too good." He
narrows his mail-slot eyes, leans in as if he were slipping a left hand.
The cobra, so the story goes, rises to such a height that it often
strikes the catcher's head, where a tourniquet cannot be applied.
When that happens, it is said, go find the shade of a tree, sit back,
and die like a man. It's a metaphor, he is told, for his insidious
punch, the power of his return to the ring after three years in
prison. "Oh," he says.

His eyes fade, and he slumps back on his white battleship sofa.
Hey, sorry, so the cobra story isn't Tolstoy. Maybe he doesn't like
snakes, or the idea of sudden expiration, say, in his fight against
Frank Bruno. "I won't miss him as much as I did Buster Mathis," he
says softly, with a smile. The words suggest an interior expedition.
He is aware that thick layers of ring rust will have to be scraped off
with industrial energy. He is aware, too, that he must lower his ring
rhetoric to bass; no more "knockin' motherfuckers out is what I do"
or "rammin' his nose up into his brain."

"Talking isn't my game," he says in the living room of his Las
Vegas mansion. "It pains me to think of what I used to say. A
fighter's power isn't his words. It's fake."

"You have more power and are bigger than before prison."

"Power doesn't interest me," he says. "I don't want power. It's a
drag. Power corrupts the soul."

"A soul? That's going to surprise so many who think you don't have one."

"Yeah. All those who expect me to be what they want. The Beast."

For someone who says he disowns the idea of power, Tyson is forced to look at his own every day in Las Vegas. When he goes into town, he has only to look up to see a forty-eight-foot rotating cube high above the MGM Grand Hotel with his sullen eyes peering down the Strip. When he returns to his home, a fountain plumes silvery over ornamental lions, and Mercedes limousines are parked like jets for takeoff. There is more security around him than in a precinct station; it looks like a mob base camp, with people standing around outside, waiting for his smallest wish. Inside, others hover in wait for his next belch or sigh.

After ordering a big pitcher of ice water, Tyson circles back to the king cobra. He says, "I would've cut his fuckin' head off before I looked for the shade. Excuse me, the language. I like the dyin' like a man. It's my kind of thing." He has a lot of "things" these days. He has a thing for tigers and lions. He has a thing for words like serious, stable, dignity, and pride. He has a thing for Islam. A thing for ancient Greece, a thing about legendary gangsters like Meyer Lansky and Bugsy Siegel, who began in the same Brownsville neighborhood he once worked as a pickpocket. He has a thing about Wayne Newton, who lives next door, and his main thing is about being a man. He even has a thing about being a thing.

"I don't want to be perceived as a fighter anymore, just a violent thing," he says. "I want to be seen as a man who is ferocious in life, will not be stopped."

Oh, my, is this going to be like talking to George Burns, waiting for the jokes, only to hear for hours about a reform in Mexico? Where have you seen this tack from a fighter before? Right, Muhammad Ali: ask him about his craft and you'd get an hour on movie westerns or broken-backed renditions of world politics. So many fighters have desperately wanted to flee what they do; even a grim tradesman like Joe Frazier would emphasize his side career as a dissonant singer. Tyson can be extremely articulate, though, about his work, better than anyone before. Right now, however, he's obdurate, clumsily evasive. When he doesn't fancy an inquiry, his voice breaks up like a cloud into a mumble.

"Are you bored?" he is asked.

"I'm bored some with training." He pauses. "I hate interviews, really hate them. I don't want to be here." He frowns.

"Consider it a conversation. People want to know what's on your mind. With all these millions, this comfort, they want to know if the passion is still there.

"Don't you know?" he says. "I'm not supposed to have a mind. I'm a monster." He thinks. "Look," he adds, "fighting to me is what theory was to Einstein or words were to Hemingway. Fighting is aggression. Aggression is my nature." His eyes look away. "I don't wanna talk about boxing. Do you like Hemingway? I like his writing, but I don't like him personally. Too much ego."

The cloud starts to become a wisp. So to pack it full of fleece again, you tell him a little story about ancient Greece. He likes the subject. He has a doorstop of a book on the Greeks in front of him. The Greeks, he is told, valued courage in a fighter. This one fighter, Eurydemus, had a heart full of it. He took a terrible blow to his mouth, uprooting his front teeth, but instead of spitting them out, he swallowed them, rather than show the other guy he was badly hurt. "Is that right?" says Tyson. "That's not in my book. That's courage. Wow! Like Wayne Newton."

Wayne Newton? How did we go from the Golden Age of Greece to a Vegas singer? "He lives right next to me," Tyson says. "I wandered over, and we talked. I'm not impressed by many people, but he impressed me. Ronald Reagan came to see him, was waiting for him in front of his house. The pope wrote him. Here's a guy who started on the road when he was fifteen, had nothing, nearly starved, and became so big. He says, 'Mike, I've seen money and fame come and go, come back again and go again. Everybody falls. Just don't stay down. And be very careful about people you trust.' He's supposed to be bankrupt now. You'd never know it. The man is serious. You're talking to a strong, very stable man. I see big courage there. Dignity."

Tyson seems hungry for life lessons. He picks through examples as if he were strolling through a societal flea market. In antiquity, he finds and likes the realization that he is just a dust mite in the wind blowing across thousands of years. In reading about the old hoods, he finds that, compared with them, he wasn't such a wretch in his more primeval days; he was just a punk kid who couldn't stand being who he was and sought the drunk in the alley, or the wallet, deftly pulled, of the guy on the bus to express himself. He is essentially a romantic, eternally dissatisfied with who he is, even now, in his cocoon of materialism, forever hacking through the thicket to some good and right evolution he can live with.

His conversion to Islam is just one more hack. "Look," he says, "I'm not going to split the Red Sea. I'm a very private Muslim. I feel at peace with it. I'd like to go to the mosque, but I don't. Muslims are human beings first, and knowing that, I know what they'll be thinking. The signals will go off in their heads: Here comes the rapist, the thug, to defile their holy place. I can't allow exposure to that kind of thinking. But I go to the prayer rug every day. And now it's Ramadan, a time for fasting for thirty days. I've been doing it for four years. No food from sunup to sundown, then just enough for dinner, no pigging out. I love it. Look forward to it. I feel like a different man. It's a high, makes you feel a little light-headed."

He found Islam in prison. Some think he sought out Muslims, a lethal, protective faction in many prisons, for personal security. "How ridiculous," he says. "When I first went in, my hair started to turn white. The psychiatrist told me I was spoiled, used to control. Well, screw him. It's a hell, with people being robbed, assaulted, and raped and everybody applauding. It turned my stomach. People tried to attach themselves to me because I was Mike Tyson. They soon learned that I'm a very unpleasant person to live with."

Tyson seems to like talking about the time he did in the Indiana Youth Center. He approached prison like a warrior, as if one of the Greek gods had assigned him a test of will. "I rebelled," he says, "every chance I got. Guards harassed me, called me names. But I still rebelled. Never stopped, talked back. I did this for a reason. If the rest of the inmates saw me this way, they'd rebel. If they saw me kneel, they would kneel, broken. Even people who didn't like me watched to see how I'd deal with that kind of pressure." He was even put in the Hole, he says, for smacking a guard who'd shoved him, the light on day and night, almost a complete deprivation chamber, which showed him that silence is the purest of sanities if you are strong.

"I was going to make those guards respect me no matter what," he adds.

"You could've been in there forever."

"I didn't care. I had no one to go back to. I thought I was a worthless human being. Sounds incredible. I could have done a lifetime there. I just didn't care."

"What about the Hole?"

"If you want me to say it broke me, forget it. I was cool, just my head and me. I like being alone. I could've done the whole trick there. It was the best time I did."

"Did you get a bad deal?"

"I didn't rape anyone, and she knows it. I was the one raped. I got fucked over, sorry, by everybody. They all got a piece of Mike. The prosecutor, Greg Garrison, was a shameless opportunist. He's famous now, all over television. The judge, Patricia Gifford, well, I was her big moment. Twenty years from now, all she'll be able to claim is that she put this famous nigger away. If I was guilty to twelve jurors, why didn't she give me the maximum, sixty years? I hated everybody when I left prison. I was bitter. I wanted to blow up the world. No more. Hate wastes you away, man."

"What about your own lawyer, Vincent Fuller, when he said that everybody knows you're an animal?"

"I was shocked," he says. "I was devastated, absolutely devastated. It was worse than prison. The whole world heard that. Later, I just walked over to him and said, 'Never come to see me again. I —'"

His head suddenly turns to a huge wall totally covered by TVs, like electronic wallpaper. Then the images combine into one massive picture. It is of O. J. Simpson conducting his defense, or offense, against public opinion. "I don't wanna hear him," Tyson shouts. The sound is immediately cut off. "This is an incredible individual right here." You prepare for a declaration of confederacy here, a fusillade of deep sympathy. He scowls, then jerks his head away from the screen. The disgust is palpable. If he had popcorn, he'd hurl it at the screen. Tyson cannot tolerate being witness to what he senses to be weakness or an abdication of pride.

"Cus [D'Amato, Tyson's founder and creator] used to tell me about the Great Depression," he says. "He told me about rich men jumping off buildings they owned because of pride. About rich men, now broke, who refused to get in soup lines because of pride." He mimics Cus: "'Ya hear, Mike! They starved to death, some of them! That's pride! I want you to have that kind of pride!'" He continues: "What O.J.'s doing is sickening. The man has no dignity. The way he's trying to win public opinion. That's making him look very unstable. People like a vicious fighter in life. I'm not saying O.J.'s a bad guy. Look at this! He's laughing. He's not dealing with a situation that calls for that. I believe the more he keeps his mouth shut, the more it'll go away. But he keeps bringing it up. God's allowing this to happen. God's planning to screw him. Go on. Keep talking."

He snaps his fingers, and the image of O.J. disappears, fades back into the checkerboard of televisions. He jumps up and says, "Let's go play with my white tiger. His name is Kenya. Only seven months old. The lion, Omar, isn't here. He's getting his nails clipped."

"What's the appeal of tigers?" "They're solitary. They don't need anyone." "Lions?" "They're great family men." "Do you see these things in yourself?" "Maybe." "Can they ever be joined?" "Maybe never," he says emptily.

Mike Tyson is enthralled by boxing history; he got that from Cus, too. He says that he admires the old fighters in the smaller weights, like Stanley Ketchel, the unruly cowboy who was shot in the back over a woman problem during breakfast. Secretly, though, he measures himself against the heavyweights of the past; he wants the iconic futurity of Joe Louis, Rocky Marciano, and Muhammad Ali, the king of kings. As his old trainer Kevin Rooney says, "Cus, from the start, had Mike in with history. He was to be the greatest champion. The plan was to fight five times a year, smash Marciano's perfect record, and go 55–0."

Louis was the template for the great heavyweight for those who saw him: a face of cathedral stone, short punches struck like unexpected rings from a bell tower, then stillness. He was a treasure to his people and among many whites, even while blacks were hanged from dusty trees. He spoke for the dispossessed, who listened to him on small radios in dark southern shacks, for the dignity of his race and the racial harmony that must one day come. Marciano — mute, a gluttonous eater of punches until he could detonate his own savagery. By his every word, he was the exemplar of the fifties: the tract house with the plot of grass, the new appliance.

Ali shattered the matrix of the old champion. Boxing became verbal for the first time and visual like never before. "Be loud, be pretty," he used to say, "and keep their black-hatin' asses in their chairs." The television camera lingered greedily on the lines of Ali's style and attitude. Though Ali was the memorable real thing, the most gifted big man in ring history, and a model of a generation's racial rectitude, he was also the father of the contemporary ring, where the show, the microwavable event, is the intense focus, where mediocrity is made to look like quality by undiscerning media for an audience with a connoisseurship an inch deep. The unexamined part of Ali's legacy is that he generated a whole line of babbling mimics and created a sport that has now become dangerously close to pro wrestling.

There is a tendency to forge a narrative link between Ali and Tyson because of their exiles and religion. Ali in the first half of his career was detested, then immortalized; the reverse is true of Tyson. And both men played with the fire of sex. The difference was the media reaction, when they looked at all. With Ali, it was considered cute; with Tyson, it became menace. The most striking part of Ali as a fighter was his sense of ring geometry. His whole game was built on time and space; he was a light show of improvisation, and in his early days that was not what big men were supposed to be about.

With the coming of Tyson, the ring returned to the dark heath. When you looked at him, you didn't see neon; you saw the way the ring used to be decades earlier: the single light over the rubbing table, the backed-up toilet, and the cold shower. Tyson put you near small black-night fires where rocks and bones were being shaped into killing points, and thwacked the reptilian brain in all of us. He brought back the primal rush — men seizing the maleness of other men.

As a presence, Tyson can be more closely linked to two other strange heavyweights: Sonny Liston and Floyd Patterson, another Cus D'Amato production. He has the same grave aura, the same introspection as Patterson, except that Tyson has a winning, disarming castrato voice. To speak with Patterson was to be led through a psychic wood of mist, over topics like fear and courage. Often, you felt as if you were sitting in a Chekhovian summer dacha, with the smell of bitter tea and souls looking for clarity in a suffusion of grayness. Liston presented an image of imminent danger and defiance. He went through life like a big rat in a familiar granary. He and Tyson share the same early jail pedigree, but they divide in the matter of conscience: Liston had none; Tyson seems to have found one.

What hurls Tyson forward is more than other great heavyweights. It's the old idea of the title, as pounded into him by Cus D'Amato. The tide was mythic, tribal, an "office" like that of president. Indeed, when JFK had Patterson to the White House, he wasn't looking for a photo op; he was schmoozing with the constituency of the heavyweight tide.

"To be a champ then," says Tyson, "meant something. That kind of respect isn't out there now." Does he have a constituency? "I just have myself," he says. "And the memory of Cus. As long as I rule the crown, he will rule with me." Tyson, it's clear, has a ghost for a manager.

You can see a lot of D'Amato in Tyson; the old man's paranoia and bitterness can leak into Tyson's head in a second. He was a spooky mystic and spoke once of how he would "put the look" on people on a bus, and they would feel it and turn toward him. "Cus is in my head," Tyson says. "He knows. Others think they know; they don't."

Others would like to know what's left in Tyson's head for the ring. What does he have left, if anything? Kevin Rooney doesn't think there's much, though he qualifies his own feelings of betrayal. "When he came up and was knockin' everybody over," says Rooney, "he had 50 percent of the capability we wanted. In '87 and part of '88, he was on the road to greatness." What does he have left? "He's an ordinary fighter. He's rusty. Everything is wrong with him. Doesn't jab at all now; he's not slipping punches. He still has hand speed and power but nothing in the head."

Teddy Atlas, a trainer who worked under Cus with Tyson, says, "He's not the same fighter he was before. In his first return, there was a moment against [Peter] McNeeley. He could have dropped him. Instead, he grabbed him. Tyson likes to call himself a blood man. I didn't see any blood man. A blood man obliterates. Grabbing for guys — that's a crock. But I don't know if there's enough guys to exploit it." Atlas has no love left for Tyson, adding, "He's never had any character or discipline, and he's manipulative." Has he mellowed? Atlas says, "Forget it. He's a very incomplete man brought up by Cus, who was another emotionally incomplete man."

For a down-the-middle view of Tyson, it's best to go to Eddie Futch, the finest trainer the ring has produced, with nineteen champions, six of them heavies. Says Futch, who now trains Riddick Bowe, "I want him still here for Bowe. I hope he has it back. But you just don't know about his reflexes. When they leave, it's subtle. A fighter knows what to do but can't do it. Tyson's the kind of fighter who won't have much longevity. He expends so much energy exploding that not much is left after six rounds. It doesn't make for a long career; there's too much waste of energy for a little man. Tyson can't relax in the ring. He's always tight."

What kind of fighter can beat him? "Tall men — they make him go more than six rounds. A puncher who can back him up. He's never been backed up. We'll see now."

Futch, now in his eighties, is asked, "Do you put Tyson in your top five all-time?"

"No," he says. "Louis had too much in either hand for Mike — short, deadly combinations that shake you to your shoes. With Ali, Mike wouldn't hit him with a hand grenade. Jersey Joe Walcott would've been too smart for him. Liston was too big and powerful and had a jarring jab. Rocky would be hit, that's for sure, but Mike would see violence in spades."

Which brings us to the hole in Tyson's young legend. Tyson says he hates fame, "all those people screamin' and starin' at you," but he cherishes glory. Real glory comes from serious and gallant inquisition, when a champion is taken to hell and back by an opponent of certain merit who allows the champion to express his greatness. Louis had Max Schmeling and Walcott. Marciano had Walcott and Ezzard Charles. Ali had the full wagon of Joe Frazier two times (don't count the middle one), the most dramatic fights in history, and a young, destructive George Foreman had even Ali's fans fearing for his well-being. Where is the glorious, defining series, Mike, the kinds of fights that exact your true worth and mettle, that leave people gasping with each shot, their hands clenched, their palms wet? Has it hurt his psyche not to have this hombre a hombre?

"Can we talk about literature?" he asks curtly.

"Sure."

"You like Tolstoy? He had me all screwed up in jail, made me want to give everything away. Tolstoy was a square. Dickens wasn't. He knew villains and celebrities. [His father] did time in jail, and I believe, as he wrote: 'I shall not forget. I will not forget. I cannot forget.'" He pauses.

"You like Fitzgerald?"

"Very much. *The Great Gatsby*. Especially the part about Tom and Daisy. How 'they were careless people. . . . They smashed up things . . . and then retreated back into their money or their vast carelessness . . . and let other people clean up the mess they had made.'"

Tyson eyes you closely, then says, "I cleaned up my own mess. And the only wreckage I left behind was me."

"What do you think about women?" He has been reported ready to marry Monica Turner, a pediatrician who is expecting his baby.

"I love women," he says. "I'd be insane not to. I just won't love as deeply again. It's dangerous for me. I'm attracted to independent women, not the ones who try to devour you."

"Have you ever been a fool?"

"I've been a fool, felt like a fool, and acted like a fool. I've been through a lot of shit. I've been humiliated in my first marriage. I've been humiliated by girls who said I grabbed their butts. I've been humiliated about being in prison. I've lost my belief in humanity, at times my humanity as well."

Tyson jumps off the sofa and bounds up the stairs. He is weary of talking, or maybe he's suspicious of the excavation going on, the effort to get at what the master biographer Leon Edel called "the figure under the carpet." The figure here is safe; Tyson defies concreteness over a sprint. As he said earlier: "I have a serious thing going on between me and my head; it's just me and my head." How this wicked duel will leave him is anyone's guess. He could end up as a rare book collector, a prophet with a long beard in the back of a limousine, or rolling on the grass with his children while the steaks sizzle, his violence long at bay and his inherent humanity in full restoration. Or . . . well, let's say there's hope in a dream he's always had, a dream in which he steps into the ring to fight Mike Tyson. He used to lose the bout, giving the signal that the real Tyson was "not meant to be beaten."

How does the dream end now? "I beat him every time," he says.

IAN FRAZIER

Big Fish, Little Fish

FROM SPORTS AFIELD

MOST ANGLING STORIES involve big fish. For a fish to be literary, it must be immense, moss-backed, storied; for it to attain the level of the classics, it had better be a whale. But in fact, mostly that's not what we catch. Especially when first learning the sport, we catch little ones, and we continue to catch them even when we gain more skill and know how to find and fish for big ones. In the retelling, the little ones are enlarged, or passed over as if mildly shameful. There's just something not flattering about the contrast between over-equipped us and a trophy that would fit with five others in a King Oscar of Norway Sardines can. You rarely read a story in which the author catches a fish of five inches — it's as if a fisherman's numbers don't go much below twelve. A recent euphemism is "fish of about a pound." When I hear of a slow day on the river where the angler is catching fish of about a pound, my mind corrects that estimate to "nine inches, tops."

I've told my personal big-fish stories so often to myself and others that now I may remember the stories better than the events they describe. The little fish I've caught remain unglazed by myth, and if I do happen to remember them they are perhaps in some ways more real than the big ones in my mind. Once on the Yellowstone River a pocket-sized rainbow trout startled me by coming clear out of a patch of riffle water to take a dry fly before it landed, when it was still about a foot in the air. Little rainbows are more vivid in color; this had a line like a streak of lipstick on its side. In a rivulet next to a campsite in northern Michigan, a friend and I heard small splashes one night as we sat around the fire. When we investigated with a flashlight, we saw a spring peeper frog swimming on the surface with one leg gone, and fingerling brown trout slashing at him from below. Near the campsite ran the Pigeon River, a brushy stream full of browns. During a hendrickson hatch, I waded with great care toward a little sipping rise in place almost impossible to cast to under tag-alder branches — just the sort of place you'd find an eighteen-inch fish. I hung up a fly or two, and broke them off rather than disturb the water. Finally, miraculously, I laid the fly in the exact spot; a four-inch brown hit so hard that his impetus carried him well up into the alder branches, where he remained, flipping and flapping and complicatedly entangling the line. Once in a river in Siberia reputed to hold *farel,* a troutlike gamefish, I found instead millions of no-name silvery fish about the size of laundry marking pens. They were too small to net, but would take a fly; I caught fifteen or more, and a Russian friend wrapped each one whole in wet pages from her sketchbook and baked them, paper and all, in the campfire coals. We took them out and unwrapped them and ate them steaming hot, with river-temperature Chinese beer.

Little fish make my mouth water, like the mouths of the hungry cave-guys in the movie *Quest for Fire* when they see a herd of antelope across the plain. A seine net full of smelt looks delicious, almost as good as a dozen golden deep-fried smelt with lemon wedges on a plate. In Ohio we used to eat little fish by the mess — as in, a mess of bluegill or a mess of perch. My cousin and I used to catch white bass by the dozens in Lake Erie in the Painesville harbor, right by the docks of the Diamond Shamrock Chemical Company, and then take them back to his house for fish fries, which no doubt left certain trace elements that we carry with us to this day. Once I was fishing for shad in the Delaware River with a friend and somehow snagged a minnow only slightly bigger than the fly itself. I showed it to my friend, examined it, and popped it in my mouth. His face did that special deep wince people do when they watch you eat something gross. But the taste wasn't bad — sushi, basically, only grittier.

When I went to Florida on a family vacation as a boy, I was disappointed to find that no tackle shop carried hooks small enough for the quarry I had in mind. Like everyone else I went out on the bottom-fishing boats in the deep water over the wrecks and the reefs. I cranked up a cobia longer than my leg, and a man from Cleveland in a scissor-bill cap caught a shark which the captain finally had to shoot with a handgun. On later trips I remembered to bring small hooks, and a spinning rod light enough to cast morsels of shrimp with no sinkers. In the quiet shade beneath the new overpass at the Key West charterboat basin I fished for triggerfish, Frisbee-shaped fish with sharp dorsal spines and pursed, tiny mouths. They fought hard, turning sideways to the line and soaring among the riprap and the mossy bases of the pilings. From the boardwalks of docks and next to highway bridges I fished for mangrove snappers, grunts, porgies, and unidentified fish with colors luminous as an expansion team's. At a boat canal near our motel I spent hours casting to needlefish, little bolts of quicksilver on the surface that struck the bait viciously again and again without ever getting themselves hooked. If I happened to be near deeper water, sometimes the dark shape of a barracuda would materialize, approaching a little fish I'd hooked and then palming it like a giant hand. The moment the rod folded with his weight, the ease with which the line parted, the speed with which the rod snapped back, were as much of the monster as I wanted to know.

At times, catching even a single little fish has been far preferable to catching no fish at all. Often I have landed my first with relief, knowing that at least now I can say I caught something. One afternoon four friends and I rented boats to fish a Michigan pond supposedly full of bluegills and largemouth bass. In twenty man-hours of determined fishing, between us we did not catch or see a fish. One of us, however, drifting bait on the bottom, did catch a clam. About the size of a fifty-cent piece, the bivalve had closed over the hook so tightly that it required needle-nosed pliers to dislodge. Of course it was of no use to us other than as a curiosity, and did not dispel the gloom with which we rowed back to the jeering locals at the boat-rental dock. But it did reveal its usefulness later when we reported to friends and family about the day. They asked how we did, and we said, "Well, we caught a clam." Such a statement will always set non-fishermen back on their heels (*You caught a clam? Is that good?*) and defangs the scorn that awaits the fishless angler's return.

I look for fish in any likely water I see — harbors, rivers, irrigation ditches, hotel-lobby fountains. Every decade, maybe, I spot a long snook lurking in the shadow of a docked sailboat somebody's trying to sell, or a tail among the reeds at the edge of a pond that connects itself to a body that connects itself to a head improbably far away, or a leviathan back and dorsal fin breaching just once in the Mississippi that even today I can't believe I saw. More often, I see nothing, or little fish. The two are not so different; if a big fish is like the heart of a watershed, little fish are like the water itself. I've taken just-caught little fish and put them in the hands of children watching me from the bank, and the fish gyrate and writhe and flop their way instantly from the hands back to the water, not so much a living thing as the force that makes things live. I've spotted little fish in trickles I could step across, in basin-sized pools beneath culverts in dusty Wyoming pastures, in puddles in the woods connected to no inlet or outlet I could see — fish originally planted, I'm told, in the form of fish eggs on the feet of visiting ducks. One of the commonplaces of modern life is the body of water by the gravel pit or warehouse district where you know for a fact not even a minnow lives. The sight of just one healthy little brook trout, say, testifies for the character of the water all around, redeems it, raises it far up in our estimation.

Near where I used to live in Montana was a brush-filled creek that ran brown with snowmelt every spring, then dwindled in the summer until it resembled a bucket of water poured on a woodpile. I never thought to look in it, or even could, until one winter when I noticed a wide part, not quite a pool, by a culvert under an old logging road. Thick ice as clear and flawed as frontier window glass covered the pool, and through the ice I saw movement. I go down on my knees in the snow and looked more closely; above the dregs of dark leaves and bark fragments on the creek bottom, two small brook trout were holding in the current. Perhaps because of the ice between us, they did not flinch when I came so near I could see the black-and-olive vermiculate markings on their backs, the pink of their gills when they breathed, the tiny red spots with blue halos on their sides. They were doing nothing but holding there; once in a while they would minutely adjust their position with a movement like a gentle furling down their lengths. Self-possessed as any storied lunker, they waited out the winter in their shallow lie, ennobling this humble flow to a trout stream.

STEVE RUSHIN

Dog Days

FROM SPORTS ILLUSTRATED

THIS IS A MAN-BITES-DOG story. Americans eat 20 billion hot dogs a year, which works out to sixty sausages per citizen. Or so says the National Hot Dog and Sausage Council, a wiener advocacy group whose raw data (which also come grilled) project that 26 million franks will be consumed this season in the twenty-eight major league baseball parks alone. Laid end to end, those dogs would stretch from Baltimore to Los Angeles, a sausage superhighway. Come follow its yellow center line: a trail of ballpark mustard dispensed from a flatulent squeeze bottle.

The road winds past Cooper Stadium in Columbus, Ohio, where the Triple A Clippers host gluttonous Dime-a-Dog nights. On April 15, 3,395 paying customers at Cooper ate 21,365 Oscar Mayer wieners, a frank-to-fan ratio of more than 6 to 1. Given that some spectators abstained, one has to wonder. . . .

"I've had people say they ate fifteen to twenty dogs," says the Clippers' general manager, whose name is Ken Schnacke. (Of course it is.) He quickly adds, "We've never had anybody get ridiculously sick and be taken to the hospital to have his stomach pumped." But as baseball fans everywhere know, there's always next year!

The point is, Americans certainly ken schnacke, and in few places do they snack more heavily than at baseball parks. The reasons for this are manifold and, in the view of some experts, quite complex. "Sports are a primitive ritual of aggression and release — the id hangs out," *Psychology Today* editor Hara Estroff Marano once told *New York Times* food writer Molly O'Neill, whose brother Paul plays right field for the New York Yankees. "In such a situation, the primitive part of the brain, 'Me want hot dog,' overrides the restraints of the more rational part of the brain, which would say, 'Am I hungry?' or 'Would I like a hot dog?'"

Tell Boog Powell that his id hangs out, and he's apt to check his fly. The former first baseman for the Baltimore Orioles knows only that food tastes better at the ballpark and that every time the O's played in Milwaukee, his brain said, "Me want bratwurst." So between at-bats, he would dispatch a clubhouse attendant to the stands to procure a pair of sausages slathered in red sauce, later to be immortalized as Secret Stadium Sauce. Standing in the tunnel behind the dugout, Boog would down those brats in a violent trice, as if feeding timber to a wood chipper. "Then I'd walk to the plate with red sauce all down the front of my uniform," he recalls. "I'd tell the manager, 'I'm bleeding like a stuck pig!'"

A giant man who bleeds condiments, Powell embodies the bond between baseball and food, an association "as strong as the movies and popcorn," according to sports sociologist Bob Brustad of the University of Northern Colorado. In fact the sports-food bond is stronger. When an ad man tried to encapsulate America for his automaker client, he wrote, "Baseball, hot dogs, apple pie, and Chevrolet," front-loading the jingle with the two most surefire evocations of American culture.

And you thought American culture was an oxymoron. "Of course there is American culture," says Allen Guttmann, a professor of American studies at Amherst College. "It includes symphonies as well as jazz, literature as well as comic books." And at its apex are what Bob Dole calls "America's greatest diversions: sports and food."

If that description rings with American decadence — you can bet Bangladeshi leaders don't call food a diversion — it happens to be accurate. What is more diverting than eating a chocolate sundae from an inverted miniature batting helmet while watching other people work? What, for that matter, is more decadent?

Of all sports, baseball most vigorously stirs the appetite. Because of the game's unhurried pace and frequent lulls, baseball fans tend to make more trips to the concessions stands than football, basketball, or hockey crowds. In those last three sports, "food sales are driven by intermissions," notes Michael F. Thompson, president of Sportservice, which supplies seven major league ballparks. "Baseball games are a constant, leisurely grazing period."

In that spirit we invite you to graze.

Just as baseball's birthplace is disputed, sausage, too, comes encased in controversy. Who conjoined the ballpark and the frank? Was it St. Louis saloonkeeper Chris von der Ahe, who owned the Browns baseball club and brought sausages to Sportsman's Park near the turn of the century to serve as sop for his popular beer? Or was it Harry M. Stevens, a former bookseller who in 1901 began to sell ten-cent "dachshund" sausages at the Polo Grounds in New York City? This much is clear: when cartoonist Tad Dorgan captured the Polo Grounds scene for the *New York Evening Journal* that year, his caption shortened the vendors' pitch — "Get your red hot dachshunds!" — to the snappier "Hot dogs!"

Still, one hopes the von der Ahe–Stevens matter is adjudicated at the next meeting of the National Hot Dog and Sausage Council, whose members rule on the world's wiener-related controversies and are responsible, one suspects, for the diabolical fact that hot dogs are sold in packs of ten, while hot dog buns come in packs of eight.

In the hypercompetitive world of ballpark concessionaires, it really is the size of the dog in the fight, and not the size of the fight in the dog, that matters. "Ten to one" is food-service shorthand that means ten hot dogs will be produced from every pound of beef, pork, or poultry. A 10-to-1 frank is common in the industry, though baseball's dogs tend to skew bigger. Volume Services sells a zeppelinesque 2-to-1, or half-pound, hot dog in Kansas City and Minneapolis. In Kansas City it is called the King Colossal (in Minneapolis, the Jumbo Dog), and it's the biggest dog in the majors now that Vince Coleman is in the minors. In short, the lower the ratio, the larger the sausage, which means these numbers also serve handily as odds that a given hot dog will kill you.

"One pig-out is not significant," says Patricia Hausman, author of seven books on diet and nutrition, refusing to rain-delay our parade. "But I think people have to ask themselves, Is what I eat at the ball game representative of what I eat all the time? If so, then they've got a real issue on their hands." With that in mind, many stadiums now serve kosher franks, whose ingredients have been blessed by a rabbi. San Francisco's 3Com Park even offers something called a tofu dog. Tofu apparently derives from toenail fungus, but the product's very inedibility ensures against ill effects on one's health.

Kosher and tofu franks are but two of the myriad new offerings from Major League Baseball's four principal concessionaires: Aramark, Ogden, Sportservice, and Volume Services. Big league teams gross tens of millions of dollars a year from food sales, so a popular new item, such as nachos, the surprise hit of the last fifteen years at major league parks, can be more valuable to a franchise than a good left-handed reliever.

Like baseball itself, concessions companies keep sophisticated statistics. "White Sox fans tend to buy more apparel," says Aramark's Bernhard Kloppenburg, who runs the food and merchandise business at Camden Yards in Baltimore. "Yankee fans tend to drink more beer." Kloppenburg proudly points out that the Orioles' Cal Ripken Jr. wasn't the only record breaker at Camden Yards last September 6, the night he surpassed Lou Gehrig's total of consecutive games played. Aramark did an absurd $40 per fan in sales that evening, to the delight of Fancy Clancy and the Terminator, local beer hawkers whose sales totals can earn them a chance to work the All-Star Game and other big events.

Vendors and other ballpark food workers occupy their own subculture. Some seem born for the job — the wearer of beer-vendor badge number 0003 at Coors Field in Denver is named Eric Beerman — and all use a *lingua franca* that is unintelligible to outsiders. Say the words mother Merco, for instance, and they'll know that you're talking about the most essential of concessions-stand appliances. It is the plastic-front wiener grill that allows patrons filing past to view rows of hot dogs in repose, much as citizens of the former Soviet Union once filed past the embalmed body of Lenin in Moscow's Red Square. The difference, of course, is that mother Merco's pilgrims come to stuff themselves.

Los Angeles has baseball's best-known dog-and-kraut combo, if you no longer count Schottzie and Marge. "Nothing is as famous as the Dodger Dog," notes Lon Rosenberg, Aramark's general manager at Dodger Stadium, and this is as it should be, for L.A. gave the world the hot-dog-shaped building (see Tail 'O' the Pup on San Vicente Boulevard) and frankophile movie stars: Marlene Dietrich's favorite meal was hot dogs and champagne, while Humphrey Bogart once said, "A hot dog at the game beats roast beef at the Ritz." You can just hear him, can't you?

The Dodger Dog's nearest rival is three thousand miles away in

Boston, where the Fenway Frank generally cuts the mustard with the most discerning of critics. "The dog was very good," says TV gourmand Julia Child, recalling a Fenway Frank she recently digested. "But the bun was wet and soggy."

In an unrelated bun-related incident, two former concessions-stand workers at the Kingdome told the *Seattle Times* in March that they had been instructed to pick the mold off hot dog rolls before serving them to the public. The story is credible because the Kingdome's concessions stands, run by Ogden, have been cited 158 times in the last three years by the Seattle–King County Department of Public Health for ominous-sounding "red critical" food-safety violations.

Yet hot dogs continue to dominate ballpark food sales. King Colossal indeed. "You'll find there are still six major food groups," says Thompson of Sportservice. "There's a sausage product — tube steak, as it's called in some places; popcorn; soda or beer; nachos; peanuts; and malts and frozen things."

In this last category is the Dove Bar, which is giving some stiff competition to the frosty malt as the frozen thing of choice in many ballparks. The frosty malt, you might recall, is a cup of chocolate-malt-flavored ice cream that comes with a flimsy three-inch tongue depressor that its manufacturers quaintly call a spoon. If the Dove Bar should displace the frosty malt, it would be the death knell for yet another baseball tradition. As Thompson concedes, "You can't throw the lid of a Dove Bar," Frisbee-like, from the second deck of a stadium.

What price progress?

For the better part of this century, ballpark cuisine comprised the few, unwavering, aforementioned staples. That all changed with the advent of nachos: tortilla chips submerged in something called "cheez," an orange substance with the viscosity and thermal breakdown of forty-weight Pennzoil. People lapped it up, often literally.

Nonexistent in ballparks circa 1980, nachos now account for 8 percent of all food sales in stadiums served by Sportservice. "Nachos were introduced in the theme restaurants, like Friday's," says Aramark's Kloppenburg. "Then they came to the ballparks."

Things would never be the same. Before the decade was out, the door was thrown open to other arrivistes, including Dove Bars, Dunkin' Donuts, and Pizza Hut. Buy me some peanuts and Cracker Jack? "With Cracker Jack, you find young kids don't enjoy it much," says Thompson. "They have gone to the Crunch 'n Munch." In what may be a final act of desperation, some Cracker Jack boxes carry a banner that says "fat free," the '90s equivalent of "a prize in every package."

According to Sportservice, the number of women attending major league games has tripled, to more than 35 percent, in the past ten years, expediting an explosion of light ballpark food, such as salads, pasta, and Fat Free Cracker Jack. The age and affluence of baseball fans — most customers at Camden Yards are between 31 and 40 years old, with an annual income of at least $50,000 — have also pushed the trend toward yuppier fare, such as boutique beers. 3Com Park serves twenty bottled brands at one stand alone, including Oregon Berry Brew, which tastes like cherry Robitussin but doesn't provide the pleasant buzz you get from the cough syrup.

In addition, most stadiums serve some sort of regional cuisine: Cuban sandwiches in Miami, cheese coneys in Cincinnati, clam chowder in Boston, barbecued brisket in Texas, indigenous seafood in Denver, and Maryland crab cakes in Baltimore.

Crab cakes were on the menu in Orioles owner Peter Angelos's luxury box at Camden Yards on April 2 when President Clinton threw out the first pitch to open the season. So were fresh fruits, crudites, and other foods so extraordinary at a ballpark that the collective spread impressed even the president's jaded entourage. "They were saying they'd never seen anything like it," recalls Michelle Milani, the luxury box attendant that afternoon.

"Uh, Michelle?" asked the president, surveying the spread as the game got under way. "Can I just have . . . nachos?" A platter was summoned, and Clinton inhaled it as if he were a Hoover upright. "And he had some shelled peanuts," says Milani.

Adds Zachary Henderson, the stadium's executive sous-chef, "I believe he also had a shrimp cocktail . . ."

Says Milani, "And hot dogs . . ."

Well, you get the idea.

Baltimore is the city that gave us Babe Ruth, who once ate a dozen hot dogs between games of a doubleheader. In terms of local legend, Babe begat Boog, whose favorite ballpark food is barbecue. Hang around him long enough and you learn barbecue is not just a verb. Barbecue is not just a noun. "Barbecue," says Boog, "is an attitude."

Back when the Minnesota Twins played their home games at

Metropolitan Stadium in Bloomington, Boog often didn't get out of the parking lot. "I used to leave that park after a weekend day game and never make it to the hotel," he says. "Those people could tailgate. You'd sit down, have a couple of beers, the grill is going, and the next thing you know, they're saying, 'Hey, it's late, you might as well stay here.'" And Boog would crash in his newfound friends' Winnebago, a mobile home away from home.

Boog's has always been a barbecue state of mind. In Baltimore he couldn't wait to return home after Sunday afternoon games and "fire up the barbecue." This was easy to do because he lived in a row house behind Memorial Stadium, where the Orioles played in those days. "Hell, I'd grill after night games," he says. "Fire it up at eleven o'clock, smoke is pouring in the neighbors' windows, their heads are popping out, and they're yelling, 'We know you don't have to work in the morning, but the rest of us do.'"

Boog replied, "Hell, if I had to work in the morning, I wouldn't be out here."

Freed of the burdens of ballplaying after seventeen years in the big leagues, Boog now practices the full barbecue lifestyle, drinking beer professionally as a pitchman for Miller and overseeing Boog's barbecue stand beyond the right-field bleachers at Camden Yards. The stand grosses $2 million a year, and so popular is its proprietor that Orioles manager Davey Johnson once told him, "You could sell these people a dog s— sandwich, and they'd buy it."

But Boog knows better than that. What draws the crowds to his stand is the barbecue attitude. "It's a smile," he says. "It's the smell." It's the secret sauce, and the sun, and a story or a signature from Boog himself. It's the sound of baseball beyond the bleacher wall behind Boog, who has one hundred beer-buzzed patrons in his line and three Weber grills cooking up 1,500 pounds of beef, pork, and turkey a night and sending smoke to the blue heavens.

Fans call his name with an easy familiarity. They're not booing, they're Booging. At this moment he looks more than enormous. He looks enormously content. Boog Powell and all those around him are feeling very barbecue indeed.

DAVID FOSTER WALLACE

The String Theory

FROM ESQUIRE

WHAT HAPPENS WHEN ALL of a man's intelligence and athleticism is focused on placing a fuzzy yellow ball where his opponent is not? An obsessive inquiry into the physics and metaphysics of tennis.

When Michael T. Joyce of Los Angeles serves, when he tosses the ball and his face rises to track it, it looks like he's smiling, but he's not really smiling — his face's circumoral muscles are straining with the rest of his body to reach the ball at the top of the toss's rise. He wants to hit it fully extended and slightly out in front of him — he wants to be able to hit emphatically down on the ball, to generate enough pace to avoid an ambitious return from his opponent. Right now, it's 1:00, Saturday, July 22, 1995, on the Stadium Court of the Stade Jarry tennis complex in Montreal. It's the first of the qualifying rounds for the Canadian Open, one of the major stops on the ATP's "hard-court circuit,"[1] which starts right after Wimbledon and climaxes at N.Y.C.'s U.S. Open.

The tossed ball rises and seems for a second to hang, waiting, cooperating, as balls always seem to do for great players. The opponent, a Canadian college star named Dan Brakus, is a very good tennis player. Michael Joyce, on the other hand, is a world-class tennis player. In 1991, he was the top-ranked junior in the United States and a finalist at Junior Wimbledon,[2] is now in his fourth year on the ATP Tour, and is as of this day the seventy-ninth-best tennis player on planet earth.

A tacit rhetorical assumption here is that you have very probably never heard of Michael Joyce of Brentwood, California. Nor of Tommy Ho of Florida. Nor of Vince Spadea nor Jonathan Stark nor

Robbie Weiss nor Steve Bryan — all American men in their twenties, all ranked in the world's top one hundred at one point in 1995. Nor of Jeff Tarango, sixty-eighth in the world, unless you remember his unfortunate psychotic breakdown in full public view during last year's Wimbledon.[3]

You are invited to try to imagine what it would be like to be among the hundred best in the world at something. At anything. I have tried to imagine; it's hard.

Stade Jarry's Center Court, known as the Stadium Court, can hold slightly more than ten thousand souls. Right now, for Michael Joyce's qualifying match, there are ninety-three people in the crowd, ninety-one of whom appear to be friends and relatives of Dan Brakus's. Michael Joyce doesn't seem to notice whether there's a crowd or not. He has a way of staring intently at the air in front of his face between points. During points, he looks only at the ball.

The acoustics in the near-empty stadium are amazing — you can hear every breath, every sneaker's squeak, the authoritative *pang* of the ball against very tight strings.

Professional tennis tournaments, like professional sports teams, have distinctive traditional colors. Wimbledon's is green, the Volvo International's is light blue. The Canadian Open's is — emphatically — red. The tournament's "title sponsor," du Maurier cigarettes, has ads and logos all over the place in red and black. The Stadium Court is surrounded by a red tarp festooned with corporate names in black capital letters, and the tarp composes the base of a grandstand that is itself decked out in red-and-black bunting, so that from any kind of distance, the place looks like either a Kremlin funeral or a really elaborate brothel. The match's umpire and linesmen and ball boys all wear black shorts and red shirts emblazoned with the name of a Quebec clothier.[4]

Stade Jarry's Stadium Court is adjoined on the north by Court One, or the Grandstand Court, a slightly smaller venue with seats on only one side and a capacity of forty-eight hundred. A five-story scoreboard lies just west of the Grandstand, and by late afternoon both courts are rectangularly shadowed. There are also eight nonstadium courts in canvas-fenced enclosures scattered across the grounds. There are very few paying customers on the grounds on Saturday, but there are close to a hundred world-class players:

big spidery French guys with gelled hair, American kids with peeling noses and Pac-10 sweats, lugubrious Germans, bored-looking Italians. There are blank-eyed Swedes and pockmarked Colombians and cyberpunkish Brits. Malevolent Slavs with scary haircuts. Mexican players who spend their spare time playing two-on-two soccer in the gravel outside the players' tent. With few exceptions, all the players have similar builds — big muscular legs, shallow chests, skinny necks, and one normal-size arm and one monstrously huge and hypertrophic arm. Many of these players in the qualies, or qualifying rounds, have girlfriends in tow, sloppily beautiful European girls with sandals and patched jeans and leather backpacks, girlfriends who set up cloth lawn chairs and sun themselves next to their players' practice courts.[5] At the Radisson des Gouverneurs, the players tend to congregate in the lobby, where there's a drawsheet for the qualifying tournament up on a cork bulletin board and a multilingual tournament official behind a long desk, and the players stand around in the air-conditioning in wet hair and sandals and employ about forty languages and wait for results of matches to go up on the board and for their own next matches' schedules to get posted. Some of them listen to headphones; none seem to read. They all have the unhappy and self-enclosed look of people who spend huge amounts of time on planes and in hotel lobbies, waiting around — the look of people who must create an envelope of privacy around themselves with just their expressions. A lot of the players seem extremely young — new guys trying to break into the tour — or conspicuously older — like over thirty — with tans that look permanent and faces lined from years in the trenches of tennis's minor leagues.

The Canadian open, one of the ATP Tour's "Super 9" tournaments, which weigh most heavily in the calculations of world ranking, officially starts on Monday, July 24. What's going on for the two days right before it is the qualies. This is essentially a competition to determine who will occupy the seven slots in the Canadian Open's main draw designated for "qualifiers." A qualifying tourney precedes just about every big-money ATP event, and money and prestige and lucrative careers are often at stake in qualie matches, and often they feature the best matches of the whole tournament, and it's a good bet you've never heard of qualies.

The realities of the men's professional tennis tour bear about as much resemblance to the lush finals you see on TV as a slaughterhouse does to a well-presented cut of restaurant sirloin. For every Sampras–Agassi final we watch, there's been a weeklong tournament, a pyramidical single-elimination battle between 32, 64, or 128 players, of whom the finalists are the last men standing. But a player has to be eligible to enter that tournament in the first place. Eligibility is determined by ATP computer ranking. Each tournament has a cutoff, a minimum ranking required to be entered automatically in the main draw. Players below that ranking who want to get in have to compete in a kind of pretournament tournament. That's the easiest way to describe qualies. In actual practice, the whole thing's quite a bit messier, and I'll try to describe the logistics of the Canadian Open's qualies in just enough detail to communicate the complexity without boring you mindless.

The du Maurier Omnium Ltée has a draw of sixty-four. The sixteen entrants with the highest ATP rankings get "seeded," which means their names are strategically dispersed in the draw so that, barring upsets, they won't have to meet one another until the latter rounds. Of the seeds, the top eight — here, Andre Agassi, Pete Sampras, Michael Chang, the Russian Yevgeny Kafelnikov, Croatia's Goran Ivanisevic, South Africa's Wayne Ferreira, Germany's Michael Stich, and Switzerland's Marc Rosset, respectively — get "byes," or automatic passes, into the tournament's second round. This means that there is actually room for fifty-six players in the main draw. The cutoff for the 1995 Canadian Open isn't fifty-six, however, because not all of the top fifty-six players in the world are here.[6]

Here, the cutoff is eighty-five. You'd think that this would mean that anybody with an ATP ranking of eighty-six or lower would have to play the qualies, but here, too, there are exceptions. The du Maurier Omnium Ltée, like most other big tournaments, has five "wild card" entries into the main draw. These are special places given either to high-ranked players who entered after the six-week deadline but are desirable to have in the tournament because they're big stars (like Ivanisevic, number six in the world but a notorious flakeroo who supposedly "forgot" to enter till a week ago) or to players ranked lower than eighty-fifth whom the tournament wants because they are judged "uniquely deserving."

*

By the way, if you're interested, the ATP Tour updates and publishes its world rankings weekly, and the rankings constitute a nomological orgy that makes for truly first-rate bathroom reading. As of this writing, Mahesh Bhupathi is 284th, Luis Lobo 411th. There's Martin Sinner and Guy Forget. There's Adolf Musil and Jonathan Venison and Javier Frana and Leander Paes. There's — no kidding — Cyril Suk. Rodolfo Ramos-Paganini is 337th, Alex Lopez-Moron is 174th. Gilad Bloom is 228th and Zoltan Nagy is 414th. Names out of some postmodern Dickens: Udo Riglewski and Louis Gloria and Francisco Roig and Alexander Mronz. The twenty-ninth-best player in the world is named Slava Dosedel. There's Claude N'Goran and Han-Cheol Shin (276th but falling fast) and Horacio de la Pena and Marcus Barbosa and Amos Mansdorf and Mariano Hood. Andres Zingman is currently ranked two places above Sander Groen. Horst Skoff and Kris Goossens and Thomas Hogstedt are all ranked higher than Martin Zumpft. One reason the industry sort of hates upsets is that the ATP press liaisons have to go around teaching journalists how to spell and pronounce new names.

The Canadian qualies themselves have a draw of fifty-six world-class players; the cutoff for qualifying for the qualies is an ATP ranking of 350th.[7]

The qualies won't go all the way through to the finals, only to the quarterfinals: the seven quarterfinalists of the qualies will receive first-round slots in the Canadian Open.[8]

This means that a player in the qualies will need to win three rounds — round of fifty-six, round of twenty-eight, round of fourteen — in two days to get into the first round of the main draw.[9]

The eight seeds in the qualies are the eight players whom the Canadian Open officials consider most likely to make the quarters and thus get into the main draw. The top seed this weekend is Richard Krajicek,[10] a six-foot five-inch Dutchman who wears a tiny white billed hat in the sun and rushes the net like it owes him money and in general plays like a rabid crane. Both his knees are bandaged. He's in the top twenty and hasn't had to play qualies for years, but for this tournament he missed the entry deadline, found all the wild cards already given to uniquely deserving Canadians, and with phlegmatic Low Country cheer decided to go ahead and play the weekend qualies for the match practice. The qualies' eighth seed is Jamie Morgan, an Australian journeyman, around one hundredth in the world, whom Michael Joyce beat in straight sets last week in the second round of the main draw at the Legg Mason Tennis Classic in Washington, D.C. Michael Joyce is seeded third.

If you're wondering why Joyce, who's ranked above the number-eighty-five cutoff, is having to play the Canadian Open qualies, gird yourself for one more smidgen of complication. The fact is that six weeks before, Joyce's ranking was not above the cutoff, and that's when the Canadian entry deadline was, and that's the ranking the tournament used when it made up the main draw. Joyce's ranking jumped from 119th to 88th after Wimbledon 1995, where he beat Marc Rosset (ranked 11th in the world) and reached the round of sixteen.

The qualie circuit is to professional tennis sort of what AAA baseball is to the major leagues: somebody playing the qualies in Montreal is an undeniably world-class tennis player, but he's not quite at the level where the serious TV and money are. In the main draw of the du Maurier Omnium Ltée, a first-round loser will earn $5,400, and a second-round loser $10,300. In the Montreal qualies, a player will receive $560 for losing in the second round and an even $0.00 for losing in the first. This might not be so bad if a lot of the entrants for the qualies hadn't flown thousands of miles to get here. Plus, there's the matter of supporting themselves in Montreal. The tournament pays the hotel and meal expenses of players in the main draw but not of those in the qualies. The seven survivors of the qualies, however, will get their hotel expenses retroactively picked up by the tournament. So there's rather a lot at stake — some of the players in the qualies are literally playing for their supper or for the money to make airfare home or to the site of the next qualie.

You could think of Michael Joyce's career as now kind of on the cusp between the majors and AAA ball. He still has to qualify for some tournaments, but more and more often he gets straight into the main draw. The move from qualifier to main-draw player is a huge boost, both financially and psychically, but it's still a couple of plateaus away from true fame and fortune. The main draw's 64 or 128 players are still mostly the supporting cast for the stars we see in televised finals. But they are also the pool from which superstars are

drawn. McEnroe, Sampras, and even Agassi had to play qualies at
the start of their careers, and Sampras spent a couple of years losing
in the early rounds of main draws before he suddenly erupted in
the early nineties and started beating everybody.

Still, even most main-draw players are obscure and unknown. An
example is Jakob Hlasek,[11] a Czech who is working out with Marc
Rosset on one of the practice courts this morning when I first
arrive at Stade Jarry. I notice them and go over to watch only because Hlasek and Rosset are so beautiful to see — at this point, I
have no idea who they are. They are practicing ground strokes
down the line — Rosset's forehand and Hlasek's backhand — each
ball plumb-line straight and within centimeters of the corner, the
players moving with the compact nonchalance I've since come to
recognize in pros when they're working out: the suggestion is of a
very powerful engine in low gear. Jakob Hlasek is six foot two and
built like a halfback, his blond hair in a short square Eastern European cut, with icy eyes and cheekbones out to here: he looks like
either a Nazi male model or a lifeguard in hell and seems in general
just way too scary ever to try to talk to. His backhand is a one-
hander, rather like Ivan Lendl's, and watching him practice it is like
watching a great artist casually sketch something. I keep having to
remember to blink. There are a million little ways you can tell that
somebody's a great player — details in his posture, in the way he
bounces the ball with his racket head to pick it up, in the way he
twirls the racket casually while waiting for the ball.

Hlasek wears a plain gray T-shirt and some kind of very white
European shoes. It's midmorning and already at least 90 degrees,
and he isn't sweating. Hlasek turned pro in 1983, six years later had
one year in the top ten, and for the last few years has been ranked
in the sixties and seventies, getting straight into the main draw of all
the tournaments and usually losing in the first couple of rounds.

Watching Hlasek practice is probably the first time it really strikes
me how good these professionals are, because even just fucking
around, Hlasek is the most impressive tennis player I've ever seen.[12]
I'd be surprised if anybody reading this article has ever heard of
Jakob Hlasek. By the distorted standards of TV's obsession with
Grand Slam finals and the world's top five, Hlasek is merely an
also-ran. But last year, he made $300,000 on the tour (that's just
in prize money, not counting exhibitions and endorsement con-

tracts), and his career winnings are more than $4 million, and it turns out his home base was for a time Monte Carlo, where lots of European players with tax issues end up living.

Michael Joyce, 22, is listed in the *ATP Tour Player Guide* as five eleven and 165 pounds, but in person he's more like five nine. On the Stadium Court, he looks compact and stocky. The quickest way to describe him would be to say that he looks like a young and slightly buff David Caruso. He is fair-skinned and has reddish hair and the kind of patchy, vaguely pubic goatee of somebody who isn't quite old enough yet to grow real facial hair. When he plays in the heat, he wears a hat.[13]

He wears Fila clothes and uses Yonex rackets and is paid to do so. His face is childishly full, and though it isn't freckled, it somehow looks like it ought to be freckled. A lot of professional tennis players look like lifeguards — with that kind of extreme tan that looks like it's penetrated to the subdermal layer and will be retained to the grave — but Joyce's fair skin doesn't tan or even burn, though he does get red in the face when he plays, from effort.[14]

His on-court expression is grim without being unpleasant; it communicates the sense that Joyce's attentions on-court have become very narrow and focused and intense — it's the same pleasantly grim expression you see on, say, working surgeons or jewelers. On the Stadium Court, Joyce seems boyish and extremely adult at the same time. And in contrast to his Canadian opponent, who has the varnished good looks and Pepsodent smile of the stereotypical tennis player, Joyce looks terribly real out there playing: he sweats through his shirt,[15] gets flushed, whoops for breath after a long point. He wears little elastic braces on both ankles, but it turns out they're mostly prophylactic.

It's 1:30 P.M. Joyce has broken Brakus's serve once and is up 3–1 in the first set and is receiving. Brakus is in the multibrand clothes of somebody without an endorsement contract. He's well over six feet tall, and, as with many large male college stars, his game is built around his serve.[16]

With the score at 0–15, his first serve is flat and 118 miles per hour and way out to Joyce's backhand, which is a two-hander and hard to lunge effectively with, but Joyce lunges plenty effectively and sends the ball back down the line to the Canadian's forehand, deep in the court and with such flat pace that Brakus has to stutter-step a little and backpedal to get set up — clearly, he's used to playing guys for whom 118 mumps out wide would be an outright ace or at least produce such a weak return that he could move up easily and put the ball away — and Brakus now sends the ball back up the line, high over the net, loopy with topspin — not all that bad a shot, considering the fierceness of the return, and a topspin shot that'd back most tennis players up and put them on the defensive. But Michael Joyce's level of tennis is such that he moves in on balls hit with topspin and hits them on the rise,[17] moves in and takes the ball on the rise and hits a backhand cross so tightly angled that nobody alive could get to it. This is kind of a typical Joyce–Brakus point.

The match is carnage of a particularly high-level sort: it's like watching an extremely large and powerful predator get torn to pieces by an even larger and more powerful predator. Brakus looks pissed off after Joyce's winner and makes some berating-himself-type noises, but the anger seems kind of pro forma — it's not like there's anything Brakus could have done much better, not given what he and the seventy-ninth-best player in the world have in their respective arsenals.

Michael Joyce will later say that Brakus "had a big serve, but the guy didn't belong on a pro court." Joyce didn't mean this in an unkind way. Nor did he mean it in a kind way. It turns out that what Michael Joyce says rarely has any kind of spin or slant on it; he mostly just reports what he sees, rather like a camera. You couldn't even call him sincere, because it's not like it seems ever to occur to him to try to be sincere or nonsincere. For a while, I thought that Joyce's rather bland candor was a function of his not being very bright. This judgment was partly informed by the fact that Joyce didn't go to college and was only marginally involved in his high school academics (stuff I know because he told me it right away).[18]

What I discovered as the tournament wore on was that I can be kind of a snob and an asshole and that Michael Joyce's affectless openness is not a sign of stupidity but of something else.

Advances in racket technology and conditioning methods over the last decade have dramatically altered men's professional tennis. For much of the twentieth century, there were two basic styles of top-level tennis. The "offensive"[19] style is based on the serve and the net game and is ideally suited to slick, or "fast," surfaces like grass and cement. The "defensive," or "baseline," style is built around foot speed, consistency, and ground strokes accurate enough to hit effective passing shots against a serve-and-volleyer; this style is most effective on "slow" surfaces like clay and Har-Tru composite. John McEnroe and Bjorn Borg are probably the modern era's greatest exponents of the offensive and defensive styles, respectively.

There is now a third way to play, and it tends to be called the "power baseline" style. As far as I can determine, Jimmy Connors[20] more or less invented the power-baseline game back in the seventies, and in the eighties Ivan Lendl raised it to a kind of brutal art. In the nineties, the majority of young players on the ATP Tour have a power-baseline-type game.

This game's cornerstone is ground strokes, but ground strokes hit with incredible pace, such that winners from the baseline are not unusual.[21]

A power-baseliner's net game tends to be solid but uninspired — a PBer is more apt to hit a winner on the approach shot and not need to volley at all. His serve is usually competent and reasonably forceful, but the really inspired part of a PBer's game is usually his return of serve.[22]

He often has incredible reflexes and can hit winners right off the return. The PBer's game requires both the power and aggression of an offensive style and the speed and calculated patience of a defensive style. It is adjustable both to slick grass and to slow clay, but its most congenial surface is DecoTurf II,[23] the type of abrasive hard-court surface now used at the U.S. Open and at all the broiling North American tune-ups for it, including the Canadian Open.

Boris Becker and Stefan Edberg are contemporary examples of the classic offensive style. Serve-and-volleyers are often tall,[24] and tall Americans like Pete Sampras and Todd Martin and David Wheaton are also offensive players.

Michael Chang is a pure exponent of the defensive style, as are Mats Wilander, Carlos Costa, and a lot of the tour's Western Europeans and South Americans, many of whom grew up exclusively on clay and now stick primarily to the overseas clay-court circuits. Americans Jimmy Arias, Aaron Krickstein, and Jim Courier all play a power-baseline game. So does just about every new young male

player on the tour. But its most famous and effective post-Lendl
avatar is Andre Agassi, who on 1995's hard-court circuit was simply
kicking everyone's ass.[25]

Michael Joyce's style is power baseline in the Agassi mold: Joyce is
short and right-handed and has a two-handed backhand, a serve
that's just good enough to set up a baseline attack, and a great
return of serve that is the linchpin of his game. Like Agassi, Joyce
takes the ball early, on the rise, so he always looks like he's moving
forward in the court even though he rarely comes to net. Joyce's
first serve usually comes in around ninety-five miles per hour[26] and
his second serve is in the low eighties but has so much spin on it
that the ball turns topological shapes in the air and bounces high
and wide to the first-round Canadian's backhand. Brakus has to
stretch to float a slice return, the sort of weak return that a serve-
and-volleyer would be rushing up to the net to put away on the fly.
Joyce does move up, but only halfway, right around his own service
line, where he lets the floater land and bounce up all ripe, and he
winds up his forehand and hits a winner crosscourt into the deuce
corner, very flat and hard, so that the ball makes an emphatic
sound as it hits the scarlet tarp behind Brakus's side of the court.
Ball boys move for the ball and reconfigure complexly as Joyce
walks back to serve another point. The applause of a tiny crowd is
so small and sad and tattered-sounding that it'd almost be better if
people didn't clap at all.

Like those of Lendl and Agassi and Courier and many PBers,
Joyce's strongest shot is his forehand, a weapon of near-Wagnerian
aggression and power. Joyce's forehand is particularly lovely to
watch. It's sparer and more textbook than Lendl's whip-crack forehand or Borg's great swooping loop; by way of decoration, there's
only a small loop of flourish[27] on the backswing. The stroke itself is
completely horizontal, so Joyce can hit through the ball while it's
still well out in front of him. As with all great players, Joyce's side is
so emphatically to the net as the ball approaches that his posture is
a classic contrapposto.

As Joyce on the forehand makes contact with the tennis ball, his
left hand behind him opens up, as if he were releasing something,
a decorative gesture that has nothing to do with the mechanics of
the stroke. Michael Joyce doesn't know that his left hand opens up
at impact on forehands: it is unconscious, some aesthetic tic that

started when he was a child and is now inextricably hardwired into a stroke that is itself, now, unconscious for Joyce, after years of his hitting more forehands over and over and over than anyone could ever count.[28]

Agassi, who is 25, is kind of Michael Joyce's hero. Just the week before this match, at the Legg Mason Tennis Classic in Washington, in wet-mitten heat that had players vomiting on-court and defaulting all over the place, Agassi beat Joyce in the third round of the main draw, 6–2, 6–2. Every once in a while now, Joyce will look over at his coach next to me in the player-guest section of the Grandstand and grin and say something like, "Agassi'd have killed me on that shot." Joyce's coach will adjust the set of his sunglasses and not say anything — coaches are forbidden to say anything to their players during a match.

Joyce's coach, Sam Aparicio,[29] a protégé of Pancho Gonzalez's, is based in Las Vegas, which is also Agassi's hometown, and Joyce has several times been flown to Las Vegas at Agassi's request to practice with him and is apparently regarded by Agassi as a friend and peer — these are facts Michael Joyce will mention with as much pride as he evinces in speaking of victories and world ranking.

There are differences between Agassi's and Joyce's games, however. Though Joyce and Agassi both use the western forehand grip and two-handed backhand that are distinctive of topspinners, Joyce's ground strokes are very flat — i.e., spinless, passing low over the net, driven rather than brushed — because the actual motion of his strokes is so levelly horizontal. Joyce's balls actually look more like Jimmy Connors's balls than like Agassi's.[30] Some of Joyce's ground strokes look like knuckleballs going over the net and you can actually see the ball's seams just hanging there not spinning. Joyce also has a slight hitch in his backhand that makes it look stiff and slightly awkward, though his pace and placement are lethal; Agassi's own backhand is flowing and hitchless.[31]

And while Joyce is far from slow, he lacks Agassi's otherworldly foot speed. Agassi is every bit as fast as Michael Chang.[32]

Watch him on TV sometime as he's walking between points: he takes the tiny, violently pigeon-toed steps of a man whose feet weigh basically nothing.

Michael Joyce — also in his own coach's opinion — doesn't "see" the ball in the same magical way that Andre Agassi does, and so

Joyce can't take the ball quite so early or generate quite the same amount of pace off his ground strokes. The business of "seeing" is important enough to explain. Except for the serve, power in tennis is not a matter of strength but of timing. This is one reason why so few top tennis players look muscular.[33]

Any normal adult male can hit a tennis ball with pro pace; the trick is being able to hit the ball both hard and accurately. If you can get your body in just the right position and time your stroke so you hit the ball in just the right spot — waist-level, just slightly out in front of you, with your own weight moving from your back leg to your front leg as you make contact — you can both cream the ball and direct it. Since ". . . just the right . . ." is a matter of millimeters and microseconds, a certain kind of vision is crucial.[34]

Agassi's vision is literally one in a billion, and it allows him to hit his ground strokes as hard as he can just about every time. Joyce, whose hand-eye coordination is superlative, in the top 1 percent of all athletes everywhere (he's been exhaustively tested), still has to take some incremental bit of steam off most of his ground strokes if he wants to direct them.

I submit that tennis is the most beautiful sport there is,[35] and also the most demanding.

It requires body control, hand-eye coordination, quickness, flat-out speed, endurance, and that weird mix of caution and abandon we call courage. It also requires smarts. Just one single shot in one exchange in one point of a high-level match is a nightmare of mechanical variables. Given a net that's three feet high (at the center) and two players in (unrealistically) fixed positions, the efficacy of one single shot is determined by its angle, depth, pace, and spin. And each of these determinants is itself determined by still other variables — i.e., a shot's depth is determined by the height at which the ball passes over the net combined with some integrated function of pace and spin, with the ball's height over the net itself determined by the player's body position, grip on the racket, height of backswing, and angle of racket face, as well as the 3-D coordinates through which the racket face moves during that interval in which the ball is actually on the strings. The tree of variables and determinants branches out and out, on and on, and then on much further when the opponent's own position and predilections and the ballistic features of the ball he's sent you to hit are factored in.[36]

No silicon-based RAM yet existent could compute the expansion of variables for even a single exchange; smoke would come out of the mainframe. The sort of thinking involved is the sort that can be done only by a living and highly conscious entity, and then it can *really* be done only unconsciously, i.e., by fusing talent with repetition to such an extent that the variables are combined and controlled without conscious thought. In other words, serious tennis is a kind of art.

If you've played tennis at least a little, you probably have some idea how hard a game it is to play really well. I submit to you that you really have no idea at all. I know I didn't. And television doesn't really allow you to appreciate what real top-level players can do — how hard they're actually hitting the ball, and with what control and tactical imagination and artistry. I got to watch Michael Joyce practice several times, right up close, like six feet and a chain-link fence away. This is a man who, at full run, can hit a fast-moving tennis ball into a one-foot-square area seventy-eight feet away over a net, hard. He can do this something like more than 90 percent of the time. And this is the world's seventy-ninth-best player, one who has to play the Montreal qualies.

It's not just the athletic artistry that compels interest in tennis at the professional level. It's also what this level requires — what it's taken for the one-hundredth-ranked player in the world to get there, what it takes to stay, what it would take to rise even higher against other men who've paid the same price number one hundred has paid.

Americans revere athletic excellence, competitive success, and it's more than lip service we pay; we vote with our wallets. We'll pay large sums to watch a truly great athlete; we'll reward him with celebrity and adulation and will even go so far as to buy products and services he endorses.

But it's better for us not to know the kinds of sacrifices the professional-grade athlete has made to get so very good at one particular thing. Oh, we'll invoke lush clichés about the lonely heroism of Olympic athletes, the pain and analgesia of football, the early rising and hours of practice and restricted diets, the prefight celibacy, et cetera. But the actual facts of the sacrifices repel us when we see them: basketball geniuses who cannot read, sprinters who dope themselves, defensive tackles who shoot up with bovine hormones until they collapse or explode. We prefer not to consider closely the shockingly vapid and primitive comments uttered by athletes in postcontest interviews or to consider what impoverishments in one's mental life would allow people actually to think the way great athletes seem to think. Note the way "up close and personal" profiles of professional athletes strain so hard to find evidence of a rounded human life — outside interests and activities, values beyond the sport. We ignore what's obvious, that most of this straining is farce. It's farce because the realities of top-level athletics today require an early and total commitment to one area of excellence. An ascetic focus.[37] A subsumption of almost all other features of human life to one chosen talent and pursuit. A consent to live in a world that, like a child's world, is very small.

Playing two professional singles matches on the same day is almost unheard-of, except in qualies. Michael Joyce's second qualifying round is at 7:30 on Saturday night. He's playing an Austrian named Julian Knowle, a tall and cadaverous guy with pointy Kafkan ears. Knowle uses two hands off both sides[38] and throws his racket when he's mad. The match takes place on Stade Jarry's Grandstand Court. The smaller Grandstand is more intimate: the box seats start just a few yards from the court surface, and you're close enough to see a welt on Joyce's cheek or the abacus of sweat on Herr Knowle's forehead. The Grandstand could hold maybe forty-eight hundred people, and tonight there are exactly four human beings in the audience as Michael Joyce basically beats the ever-living shit out of Julian Knowle, who will be at the Montreal airport tonight at 1:30 to board a red-eye for a minor league day tournament in Poznan, Poland.

During this afternoon's match, Joyce wore a white Fila shirt with different-colored sleeves. Onto his sleeve is sewn a patch that says POWERBAR; Joyce is paid $1,000 each time he appears in the media wearing this patch. For tonight's match, Joyce wears a pinstripe Jim Courier–model Fila shirt with one red sleeve and one blue sleeve. He has a red bandanna around his head, and as he begins to perspire in the humidity, his face turns the same color as the bandanna. It is hard not to find this endearing. Julian Knowle has on an abstract pastel shirt whose brand is unrecognizable. He has very tall hair, Knowle does, that towers over his head at near-Beavis altitude and doesn't diminish or lose its gelled integrity as he perspires.[39]

Knowle's shirt, too, has sleeves of different colors. This seems to be the fashion constant this year among the qualifiers: sleeve-color asymmetry.

The Joyce–Knowle match takes only slightly more than an hour. This is including delays caused when Knowle throws his racket and has to go retrieve it or when Knowle walks around in aimless circles, muttering blackly to himself in some High German dialect. Knowle's tantrums seem a little contrived and insincere to me, though, because he rarely loses a point as a result of doing anything particularly wrong. Here's a typical point in this match: it's 1–4 and 15–30 in the sixth game. Knowle hits a respectable 110-mile-an-hour slice serve to Joyce's forehand. Joyce returns a very flat, penetrating drive crosscourt so that Knowle has to stretch and hit his forehand on the run, something that's not particularly easy to do with a two-handed forehand. Knowle gets to the forehand and hits a thoroughly respectable shot, heavy with topspin and landing maybe only a little bit short a few feet behind the service line, whereupon he reverses direction and starts scrambling back to get in the middle of the baseline to get ready for his next shot. Joyce, as is SOP, has moved in on the slightly short ball and takes it on the rise just after it's bounced, driving a backhand even flatter and harder in the exact same place he hit his last shot, the spot Knowle is scrambling away from. Knowle is now forced to reverse direction and get back to where he was. This he does, and he gets his racket on the ball, but only barely, sending back a weak little USDA Prime loblet that Joyce, now in the vicinity of the net, has little trouble blocking into the open court for a winner. The four people clap, Knowle's racket goes spinning into the blood-colored tarp, and Joyce walks expressionlessly back to the deuce court to receive again whenever Knowle gets around to serving. Knowle has slightly more firepower than the first round's Brakus: his ground strokes are formidable, probably even lethal if he has sufficient time to get to the ball and get set up. Joyce simply denies him that time. Joyce will later admit that he wasn't working all that hard in this match, and he doesn't need to. He hits few spectacular winners, but he also makes very few unforced errors, and his shots are designed to make

the somewhat clumsy Knowle move a lot and to deny him the time
and the peace ever to set up his game. This strategy is one that
Knowle cannot solve or interdict: he has the firepower but not the
speed to do so. This may be one reason why Joyce is unaffronted by
having to play the qualies for Montreal. Barring some kind of major
injury or neurological seizure, he's not going to lose to somebody
like Austria's Julian Knowle — Joyce is simply on a different plane
than the mass of these qualie players.

The idea that there can be wholly distinct levels to competitive
tennis — levels so distinct that what's being played is in essence a
whole different game — might seem to you weird and hyperbolic. I
have played probably just enough tennis to understand that it's
true. I have played against men who were on a whole different,
higher plateau than I, and I have understood on the deepest and
most humbling level the impossibility of beating them, of "solving
their game." Knowle is technically entitled to be called a professional, but he is playing a fundamentally different grade of tennis
from Michael Joyce's, one constrained by limitations Joyce does not
have. I feel like I could get on a tennis court with Julian Knowle. He
would beat me, perhaps handily, but I don't feel like it would be
absurd for me to occupy the same seventy-eight-by-twenty-seven-
foot rectangle as he. The idea of me playing Joyce — or even hitting around with him, which was one of the ideas I was entertaining
on the flight to Montreal — is now revealed to me to be in a certain
way obscene, and I resolve not even to let Joyce[40] know that I used
to play competitive tennis, and (I'd presumed) rather well. This
makes me sad.

This article is about Michael Joyce and the realities of the tour, not
me. But since a big part of my experience of the Canadian Open
and its players was one of sadness, it might be worthwhile to spend
a little time letting you know where I'm coming from vis-à-vis these
players. As a young person, I played competitive junior tennis,
traveling to tournaments all over the Midwest, the region that the
United States Tennis Association has in its East Coast wisdom designated the "western" region.

Most of my best friends were also tennis players, and on a regional level we were successful, and we thought of ourselves as
extremely good players. Tennis and our proficiency at it were tre-

mendously important to us — a serious junior gives up a lot of his time and freedom to develop his game,[41] and it can very easily come to constitute a big part of his identity and self-worth.

The other 14-year-old Midwest hotshots and I knew that our fishpond was somehow limited; we knew that there was a national level of play and that there were hotshots and champions at that level. But levels and plateaus beyond our own seemed abstract, somehow unreal — those of us who were the best in our region literally could not imagine players our own age who were substantially better than we.

A child's world tends to be very small. If I'd been just a little bit better, an actual regional champion, I would have gotten to see that there were fourteen-year-olds in the United States playing a level of tennis unlike anything I knew about.

My own game as a junior was a particular type of the classic defensive style, a strategy Martin Amis once described as "craven retrieval." I didn't hit the ball all that hard, but I rarely made unforced errors, and I was fast, and my general approach was simply to keep hitting the ball back to my opponent until my opponent fucked up and either made an unforced error or hit a ball so short and juicy that even I could hit a winner off it. It doesn't look like a very glorious or even interesting way to play, now that I see it here in bald retrospective print, but it was interesting to me, and you'd be surprised how effective it was (on the level at which I was competing, at least). At age 12, a good competitive player will still generally miss after four or five balls (mostly because he'll get impatient or grandiose). At age 16, a good player will generally keep the ball in play for more like seven or eight shots before he misses. At the collegiate level, too, opponents were stronger than junior players but not markedly more consistent, and if I could keep a rally going to seven or eight shots, I could usually win the point on the other guy's mistake.[42]

I still play — not competitively, but seriously — and I should confess that deep down inside, I still consider myself an extremely good tennis player, very hard to beat. Before coming to Montreal to watch Michael Joyce, I'd seen professional tennis only on television, which, as has been noted, does not give the viewer a very accurate picture of how good pros are. I thus further confess that I arrived in Montreal with some dim unconscious expectation that these professionals — at least the obscure ones, the nonstars — wouldn't be all that much better than I. I don't mean to imply that I'm insane: I was ready to concede that age, a nasty ankle injury in 1988, and a penchant for nicotine (and worse) meant that I wouldn't be able to compete physically with a young unhurt professional, but on TV (while eating junk and smoking), I'd seen pros whacking balls at each other that didn't look to be moving substantially faster than the balls I'd hit. In other words, I arrived at my first professional tournament with the pathetic deluded pride that attends ignorance. And I have been brought up sharply. I do not play and never have played even the same game as these qualifiers.

The craven game I'd spent so much of my youth perfecting would not work against these guys. For one thing, pros simply do not make unforced errors — or, at any rate they make them so rarely that there's no way they are going to make the four unforced errors in seven points necessary for me to win a game. For another thing, they will take any ball that doesn't have simply ferocious depth and pace on it and — given even a fractional moment to line up a shot — hit a winner off it. For yet another thing, their own shots have such ferocious depth and pace that there's no way I'd be able to hit more than a couple of them back at any one time. I could not meaningfully exist on the same court with these obscure, hungry players. Nor could you. And it's not just a matter of talent or practice. There's something else.

Once the main draw starts, you get to look up close and live at name tennis players you're used to seeing only as arrays of pixels. One of the highlights of Tuesday's second round of the main draw is getting to watch Agassi play MaliVai Washington. Washington, the most successful U.S. black man on the tour since Arthur Ashe, is unseeded at the Canadian Open but has been ranked as high as number eleven in the world and is dangerous, and since I loathe Agassi with a passion, it's an exciting match. Agassi looks scrawny and faggy and, with his shaved skull and beret-ish hat and black shoes and socks and patchy goatee, like somebody just released from reform school (a look you can tell he's carefully decided on with the help of various paid image consultants). Washington, who's in dark-green shorts and a shirt with dark-green sleeves, was a couple of years ago voted by *People* magazine one of the Fifty Prettiest Human Beings or something, and on TV is real pretty but in person is awesome. From twenty yards away, he looks less like a human being than like a Michelangelo anatomy sketch: his upper body the V of serious weightlifting, his leg muscles standing out even in repose, his biceps little cannonballs of fierce-looking veins. He's beautiful and doomed, because the slowness of the Stadium Court makes it impractical for anybody but a world-class net man to rush the net against Agassi, and Washington is not a net man but a power-baseliner. He stays back and trades ground strokes with Agassi, and even though the first set goes to a tiebreaker, you can tell it's a mismatch. Agassi has less mass and flat-out speed than Washington, but he has timing and vision that give his ground strokes way more pace. He can stay back and hit nuclear ground strokes and force Washington until Washington eventually makes a fatal error. There are two ways to make an error against Agassi: the first is the standard way, hitting it out or into the net; the second is to hit anything shorter than a couple of feet inside the baseline, because anything that Agassi can move up on, he can hit for a winner. Agassi's facial expression is the slightly smug self-aware one of somebody who's used to being looked at and who automatically assumes the minute he shows up anywhere that everybody's looking at him. He's incredible to see play in person, but his domination of Washington doesn't make me like him any better; it's more like it chills me, as if I'm watching the devil play.

Television tends to level everybody out and make everyone seem kind of blandly good-looking, but at Montreal it turns out that a lot of the pros and stars are interesting- or even downright funny-looking. Jim Courier, former number one but now waning and seeded tenth here,[43] looks like Howdy Doody in a hat on TV but here turns out to be a very big boy — the "Guide Média" lists him at 175 pounds, but he's way more than that, with big smooth muscles and the gait and expression of a Mafia enforcer. Michael Chang, aged 23 and ranked number five in the world, sort of looks like two different people stitched crudely together: a normal upper body perched atop hugely muscular and totally hairless legs. He has a mushroom-shaped head, inky-black hair, and an expression of deep and intractable unhappiness, as unhappy a face as I've seen outside a graduate creative-writing program.[44]

Pete Sampras is mostly teeth and eyebrows in person and has

unbelievably hairy legs and forearms — hair in the sort of abundance that allows me confidently to bet that he has hair on his back and is thus at least not 100 percent blessed and graced by the universe.

Goran Ivanisevic is large and tan and surprisingly good-looking, at least for a Croat; I always imagine Croats looking ravaged and emaciated, like somebody out of a Munch lithograph — except for an incongruous and wholly absurd bowl haircut that makes him look like somebody in a Beatles tribute band. It's Ivanisevic who will beat Joyce in three sets in the main draw's second round. Czech former top-ten Petr Korda is another clastic-looking mismatch: at six three and 160, he has the body of an upright greyhound and the face of — eerily, uncannily — a freshly hatched chicken (plus soulless eyes that reflect no light and seem to see only in the way that fishes' and birds' eyes see).

And Wilander is here — Mats Wilander, Borg's heir and top-ten at 18, number one at 24, now 30 and basically unranked and trying to come back after years off the tour, here cast in the role of the wily mariner, winning on smarts. Tuesday's best big-name match is between Wilander and Stefan Edberg, 28 and Wilander's *own* heir[45] and now married to Annette Olsen, Wilander's SO during his glory days, which adds a delicious personal cast to the match, which Wilander wins 6–4 in the third. Wilander ends up getting all the way to the semifinals before Agassi beats him as badly as I have ever seen one professional beat another professional, the score being 6–2, 6–0, and the match not nearly as close as the score would indicate.

Even more illuminating than watching pro tennis live is watching it with Sam Aparicio. Watching tennis with him is like watching a movie with somebody who knows a lot about the technical aspects of film: he helps you see things you can't see alone. It turns out, for example, that there are whole geometric sublevels of strategy in a power-baseline game, all dictated by various PBers' strengths and weaknesses. A PBer depends on being able to hit winners from the baseline. But, as Sam teaches me to see, Michael Chang can hit winners only at an acute angle from either corner. An "inside-out" player like Jim Courier, though, can hit winners only at obtuse angles from the center out. Hence, wily and well-coached players tend to play Chang "down the middle" and Courier "out wide." One of the things that makes Agassi so good is that he's capable of hitting winners from anywhere on the court — he has no geometric restriction. Joyce, too, according to Sam, can hit a winner at any angle. He just doesn't do it quite as well as Agassi, or as often.

Michael Joyce in close-up, viewed eating supper or riding in a courtesy car, looks slighter and younger than he does on-court. Close-up, he looks his age, which to me is basically that of a fetus. Michael Joyce's interests outside tennis consist mostly of big-budget movies and genre novels of the commercial-paperback sort that one reads on airplanes. He has a tight and long-standing group of friends back home in L.A., but one senses that most of his personal connections have been made via tennis. He's dated some. It's impossible to tell whether he's a virgin. It seems staggering and impossible, but my sense is that he might be. Then again, I tend to idealize and distort him, I know, because of how I feel about what he can do on a tennis court. His most revealing sexual comment was made in the context of explaining the odd type of confidence that keeps him from freezing up in a match in front of large crowds or choking on a point when there's lots of money at stake.[46]

Joyce, who usually needs to pause about five beats to think before he answers a question, thinks the confidence is partly a matter of temperament and partly a function of hard work and practice.

"If I'm in like a bar, and there's a really good-looking girl, I might be kind of nervous. But if there's like a thousand gorgeous girls in the stands when I'm playing, it's a different story. I'm not nervous then, when I play, because I know what I'm doing. I know what to do out there." Maybe it's good to let these be his last quoted words.

Whether or not he ends up in the top ten and a name anybody will know, Michael Joyce will remain a paradox. The restrictions on his life have been, in my opinion, grotesque; and in certain ways Joyce himself is a grotesque. But the radical compression of his attention and sense of himself have allowed him to become a transcendent practitioner of an art — something few of us get to be. They've allowed him to visit and test parts of his psychic reserves most of us do not even know for sure we have (courage, playing with violent nausea, not choking, et cetera).

Joyce is, in other words, a complete man, though in a grotesquely limited way. But he wants more. He wants to be the best, to have his name known, to hold professional trophies over his head as he patiently turns in all four directions for the media. He wants this and will pay to have it — to pursue it, let it define him — and will pay up with the regretless cheer of a man for whom issues of choice became irrelevant a long time ago. Already, for Joyce, at 22, it's too late for anything else; he's invested too much, is in too deep. I think he's both lucky and unlucky. He will say he is happy and mean it. Wish him well.

Notes

1. Comprising Washington, D.C., Montreal, Los Angeles, Cincinnati, Indianapolis, New Haven, and Long Island, this is possibly the most grueling part of the yearly ATP Tour (as the erstwhile Association of Tennis Professionals Tour is now officially known), with three-digit temperatures and the cement courts shimmering like Moroccan horizons and everyone wearing a hat and even the spectators carrying sweat towels.

2. Joyce lost that final to Thomas Enqvist, now ranked in the ATP's top twenty and a potential superstar and in high-profile attendance here in Montreal.

3. Tarango, 27, who completed three years at Stanford, is regarded as something of a scholar by Joyce and the other young Americans on tour. His little bio in the 1995 ATP Tour Player Guide lists his interests as including "philosophy, creative writing, and bridge," and his slight build and receding hairline do in fact make him look more like an academic or a tax attorney than a world-class tennis player. Also a native Californian, he's a friend and something of a mentor to Michael Joyce, whom he practices with regularly and addresses as "Grasshopper." Joyce — who seems to like pretty much everybody — likes Jeff Tarango and won't comment on his on-court explosion at Wimbledon except to say that Tarango is "a very intense guy, very intellectual, that gets kind of paranoid sometimes."

4. An economical way to be a tournament sponsor: supply free stuff to the tournament and put your name on it in really big letters. All the courts' tall umpire chairs have signs that say TROPICANA; all the bins for fresh and unfresh towels say WAMSUTTA; the dunk coolers at courtside (the size of trash barrels, with clear plastic lids) say TROPICANA and EVIAN. Those players who don't individually endorse a certain brand of drink tend, as a rule, to drink Evian, orange juice being a bit heavy for on-court rehydration.

5. Most of the girlfriends have something indefinable about them that

suggests extremely wealthy parents whom the girls are pissing off by hooking up with an obscure professional tennis player.

6. Except for the four in the Grand Slam — Wimbledon and the U.S., French, and Australian opens — no tournament draws all the top players, although every tournament would obviously like to, since the more top players are entered, the better the paid attendance and the more media exposure the tournament gets for itself and its sponsors. Players in the top twenty or so, though, tend to play a comparatively light schedule of tournaments, taking time off not only for rest and training but to compete in wildly lucrative exhibitions that don't affect ATP ranking. (We're talking *wildly* lucrative, like millions of dollars per annum for the top stars.) Given the sharp divergence of interests between tournaments and players, it's not surprising that there are Kafkanly complex rules for how many ATP tournaments a player must enter each year to avoid financial or ranking-related penalties, and commensurately complex and crafty ways players have for getting around these rules and doing pretty much what they want. These will be passed over. The thing to realize is that players of Michael Joyce's station tend to take way less time off; they play just about every tournament they can squeeze in and get to unless they're forced by injury or exhaustion to sit out a couple of weeks. This is because they need to, not just financially but because under the ATP's (very complex) set of algorithms for determining ranking, most players fare better the more tournaments they enter.

7. There is here no qualifying tournament for the qualies themselves, though some particularly huge tournaments have metaqualies. The qualies also have a number of wild-card berths, most of which here are given to Canadian players, like the collegiate legend whom Michael Joyce is beating the shit out of right now in the first round.

8. These places are usually right near the top seeds, which is the reason why in the televised first rounds of major tournaments you usually see Agassi or Sampras beating the shit out of some totally obscure guy — that guy's usually a qualifier. It's also part of why it's so hard for somebody low-ranked enough to have to play the qualies to move up in the rankings enough that he doesn't have to play the qualies anymore — he usually meets a high-ranked player in the very first round and gets smeared.

9. Another reason qualifiers usually get smeared by the top players they face in the early rounds is that the qualifier is playing his fourth or fifth match in three days, while the top player usually has had a couple of days with his masseur or creative-visualization consultant to get ready for the first round. Michael Joyce details all these asymmetries and stacked odds the way a farmer speaks of weather, with an absence of emotion that seems deep instead of blank.

10. pronounced *kry*-chek

11. pronounced *ya*-kob h*la*-sick, if that helps

12. Joyce is even more impressive, but I hadn't seen Joyce yet. And Enqvist is even more impressive than Joyce, and Agassi is even more impressive than Enqvist. After the week was over, I truly understood why Charlton Heston looks gray and ravaged on his descent from Sinai: past a certain point, impressiveness is corrosive to the psyche.

13. During his two daily one-hour practice sessions, he wears the hat backward and also wears boxy plaid shorts that look for all the world like swim trunks. His favorite practice T-shirt has FEAR: THE ENEMY OF DREAMS on the chest. He laughs a lot when he practices. You can tell just by looking at him out there that he's totally likable and cool.

14. If you've played only casually, it is probably hard to understand how physically demanding really serious tennis is. Realizing that these pros can move one another from one end of the twenty-seven-foot baseline to the other pretty much at will and that they hardly ever end a point early by making an unforced error might help your imagination. A close best-of-three-set match is probably equivalent in its demands to a couple of hours of full court basketball, but we're talking *serious* basketball.

15. Something else you don't get a good sense of on television: tennis is a very sweaty game. On ESPN or whatever, when you see a player walk over to the ball boy after a point and request a towel and quickly wipe his arm and hand off and toss the wet towel back to the (rather luckless) ball boy, most of the time the towel thing isn't a stall or a meditative pause — it's done because sweat is running down the inside of the player's arm in such volume that it's getting all over his hand and making the racket slippery. Especially on the sizzling North American summer junket, players sweat through their shirts early on and sometimes also their shorts. And they drink enormous amounts of water — staggering amounts. I thought I was seeing things at first, watching matches, as players seemed to go through one of those skinny half-lifer Evian bottles every second side change, but Michael Joyce confirmed it. Pro-grade tennis players seem to have evolved a metabolic system that allows rapid absorption of water and its transformation into sweat. (Most players I spoke with confirmed, by the way, that Gatorade and All-Sport and Boost and all those pricey sports drinks are mostly bullshit, that salt and carbs at table and small lakes of daily H_2O are the way to go. The players who didn't confirm this turned out to be players who had endorsement deals with some pricey-sports-drink manufacturer, but I personally saw at least one such player dumping out his bottled pricey electrolytic contents and replacing them with good old water for his match.

16. The taller you are, the harder you can serve (get a protractor and

figure it out), but the less able to bend and reverse direction you are. Tall guys tend to be serve-and-volleyers, and they live and die by their serves. Bill Tilden, Stan Smith, Arthur Ashe, Roscoe Tanner, and Goran Ivanisevic were/are all tall guys with serve-dependent games. And so on.

17. This is mind-bogglingly hard to do when the ball's hit hard. If we can assume you've played Little League or sandlot ball or something, imagine the hardest-hit grounder of all time coming at you at shortstop, and you not standing and waiting to try to knock it down but actually of your own free will running forward toward the grounder, then trying not just to catch it in a big glove but to strike it hard and reverse its direction and send it someplace frightfully specific and very far away — this comes close.

18. Joyce could have gone to college, but if he'd gone to college, it would have been primarily to play tennis. Coaches at major universities apparently offered Joyce inducements to come play for them so literally outrageous and incredible that I wouldn't repeat them here even if Joyce hadn't asked me not to.

The reason Michael Joyce would have gone to college primarily to play tennis is that the academic and social aspects of collegiate life interest him about as much as hitting twenty-five hundred crosscourt forehands while a coach yells at you in foreign languages would interest you. Tennis is what Michael Joyce loves and lives for and *is*. He sees little point in telling anybody anything different. It's the only thing he's devoted himself to, and he's devoted massive amounts of himself to it, and, as far as he understands it, it's all he wants to do or be involved in. Because he started playing at age 2 and playing competitively at age 7 and had the first half-dozen years of his career directed rather, shall we say, forcefully and enthusiastically by his father (who Joyce estimates spent probably around $250,000 on lessons and court time and equipment and travel during Michael's junior career), it's perhaps reasonable to ask Joyce to what extent he *chose* to devote himself to tennis. Can you *choose* something when you are forcefully and enthusiastically immersed in it at an age when the resources and information necessary for choosing are not yet yours?

Joyce's response to this line of inquiry strikes me as both unsatisfactory and totally satisfactory. Because of course the question is unanswerable, or at least it's unanswerable by a person who's already — as far as he understands it — chosen. Joyce's answer is that it doesn't really matter much to him whether he originally "chose" serious tennis or not; all he knows is that he loves it. He tries to explain the U.S. juniors, which he won in 1991: "You get there and look at the draw; it's a 128 draw — there's so many guys you have to beat. And then it's all over and you've won, you're the national champion — there's nothing like it. I get chills even talking about it." Or just the previous week in Washington: "I'm playing Agassi, and it's great tennis, and there's like thousands of fans going nuts. I can't describe the feeling. Where else could I get that?"

What he says is understandable, but it's not the satisfactory part of the answer. The satisfactory part is the way Joyce's face looks when he talks about what tennis means to him. He loves it — you can see this in his face when he talks about it: his eyes normally have a kind of Asiatic cast because of the slight epicanthic fold common to ethnic Irishmen, but when he speaks of tennis and his career, the eyes get round and the pupils dilate and the look in them is one of love. The love is not the love one feels for a job or a lover or any of the loci of intensity that most of us choose to call the things we love. It's the sort of love you see in the eyes of really old people who've been married for an incredibly long time or in religious people who are so religious, they've devoted their whole lives to religious stuff. It's the sort of love whose measure is what it's cost, what one's given up for it. Whether there's "choice" involved is, at a certain point, of no interest . . . since it's the surrender of choice and self that informs the love in the first place.

19. a.k.a. serve-and-volley; see immediately *supra*.

20. I don't know whether you know this, but Connors had one of the most eccentric games in the history of tennis — he was an aggressive "power" player who rarely came to net, had the serve of an ectomorphic girl, and hit everything totally spinless and flat (which is inadvisable on ground strokes because the absence of spin makes the ball so hard to control). His game was all the more strange because the racket he generated all his firepower from the baseline with was a Wilson T2000, a weird steel thing that's one of the single shittiest tennis rackets ever made and is regarded by most serious players as useful only for home defense or prying large rocks out of your backyard or something. Connors was addicted to this racket and kept using it long after Wilson stopped even making it, and he forfeited millions in potential endorsement money by doing so. Connors was also eccentric (and kind of repulsive) in lots of other ways, too, none of which are germane to this article.

21. In the yore days before wide-body ceramic rackets and scientific strength mining, the only two venues for hitting winners used to be the volley — where your decreased distance from the net allowed for greatly increased angle (get that protractor out) — and the defensive passing shot, i.e., in the tactical language of boxing, "punch" versus "counterpunch." The new power-baseline game allows a player, in effect, to punch his opponent all the way from his stool in the corner; it changes absolutely everything, and the analytic geometry of these changes would look like the worst calculus final you ever had in your life.

22. This is one reason why the phenomenon of "breaking serve" in a set

is so much less important when a match involves power-baseliners. It is one reason why so many older players and fans no longer like to watch pro tennis as much: the structural tactics of the game are now ineluctably different from when they played.

23. a trademark of the Wichita, Kansas, Koch Materials Company, "a leader in asphalt-emulsions technology"

24. John McEnroe wasn't all that tall, and he was arguably the best serve-and-volley man of all time, but then McEnroe was an exception to pretty much every predictive norm there was. At his peak (say 1980 to 1984), he was the greatest tennis player who ever lived — the most talented, the most beautiful, the most tormented: a genius. For me, watching McEnroe don a blue polyester blazer and do stiff lame truistic color commentary for TV is like watching Faulkner do a Gap ad.

25. One answer to why public interest in men's tennis has been on the wane in recent years is an essential and unpretty *thugishness* about the power-baseline style that's become dominant on the tour. Watch Agassi closely sometime — for so small a man and so great a player, he's amazingly absent of finesse, with movements that look more like a heavy-metal musician's than an athlete's. The power-baseline game itself has been compared to metal or grunge. But what a top PBer really resembles is film of the old Soviet Union putting down a rebellion. It's awesome, but brutally so, with a grinding, faceless quality about its power that renders that power curiously dull and empty.

26. Compare Ivanisevic's at 136 miles per hour or Sampras's at 132 or even this Brakus kid's at 118.

27. The loop in a pro's backswing is kind of the trademark flourish of excellence and consciousness of same, not unlike the five-star chef's quick kiss of his own fingertips as he presents a piece or the magician's hand making a French curl in the air as he directs our attention to his vanished assistant.

28. All serious players have these little extraneous tics, stylistic fingerprints, and the pros even more so because of years of repetition and ingraining. Pros' tics have always been fun to note and chart, even just e.g. on the serve. Watch the way Sampras's lead foot rises from the heel on his toss, as if his left foot's toes got suddenly hot. The odd Tourettic way Gerulaitis used to whip his head from side to side while bouncing the ball before his toss, as if he were having a small seizure. McEnroe's weird splayed stiff-armed service stance, both feet parallel to the baseline and his side so severely to the net that he looked like a figure on an Egyptian frieze. The odd sudden shrug Lendl gives before releasing his toss. The way Agassi shifts his weight several times from foot to foot as he bounces before the toss like he needs desperately to pee. Or, here at the Canadian

Open, the way the young star Thomas Enqvist's body bends queerly back as he tosses, limboing away from the toss, as if for a moment the ball smelled very bad. This tic derives from Enqvist's predecessor Edberg's own weird spinal arch and twist on the toss. Edberg also has this strange sudden way of switching his hold on the racket in mid-toss, changing from an eastern forehand to an extreme backhand grip, as if the racket were a skillet.

29. Who looks a bit like a Hispanic Dustin Hoffman and is an almost unbelievably nice guy, with the sort of inward self-sufficiency of truly great teachers and coaches everywhere, with the Zen-like blend of focus and calm developed by people who have to spend enormous amounts of time sitting in one place watching closely while somebody else does something. Sam gets a percent of Joyce's gross revenues and spends his time in airports reading gigantic tomes on Mayan architecture and is one of the coolest people I've ever met either inside the tennis world or outside it (so cool I'm kind of scared of him and haven't called him once since the assignment ended, if that makes sense). In return, Sam travels with Joyce, rooms with him, coaches him, supervises his training, analyzes matches with him, and attends him in practice, even to the extent of picking up errant balls so that Joyce doesn't have to spend part of his tightly organized practice time picking up errant balls. The stress and weird loneliness of pro tennis, where everybody's in the same community and sees one another every week but is constantly on the diasporic move and is one another's rival, with enormous amounts of money at stake and life essentially a montage of airports and bland hotels and non-home-cooked food and courtesy cars and nagging injuries and staggering long-distance bills, and with people's families back home tending to be wackos, since only wackos would make the financial and temporal sacrifices necessary to let their offspring become good enough at something to turn pro at it — all this means that most players lean heavily on their coaches for emotional support and friendship as well as technical counsel. Sam's role with Joyce looks to me to approximate what in the latter century was called that of "companion," those older ladies who traveled with nubile women when they traveled abroad.

30. Agassi's balls look more like Borg's balls would have looked if Borg had been on a yearlong regimen of both steroids and methamphetamines and was hitting every single fucking ball just as hard as he could. Agassi hits his ground strokes as hard as anybody who's ever played tennis — so hard you almost can't believe it in person.

31. But Agassi does have this exaggerated follow-through in which he keeps both hands on the racket and follows through almost like a hitter in baseball, which causes his shirtfront to lift and his hairy tummy to be

exposed to public view — in Montreal I find this repellent, though the females in the stands around me seem ready to live and die for a glimpse of Agassi's tummy. Agassi's significant other, Brooke Shields, is in Montreal, by the way, and will end up highly visible in the player-guest box for all Agassi's matches, wearing big sunglasses and what look to be multiple hats. This may be the place to insert that Brooke Shields is rather a lot taller than Agassi and considerably less hairy, and that seeing them standing together in person is rather like seeing Sigourney Weaver on the arm of Danny DeVito. The effect is especially surreal when Brooke is wearing one of the plain, classy sundresses that make her look like a deb summering in the Hamptons and Agassi's wearing his new Nike on-court ensemble, a blue-black horizontally striped outfit that together with his black sneakers makes him look like somebody's idea of a French Resistance fighter. (Since we all enjoy celeb stuff, this might also be the place to insert an unkind but true observation. Up close in person, Brooke Shields is in fact extremely pretty, but she is not at all sexy. Her eyebrows are actually not nearly as thick and bushy as Groucho's or Brezhnev's, but she's incredibly tall, and her posture's not all that great, and her prettiness is that sort of computer-enhanced-looking prettiness that is resoundingly unsexy. To find somebody sexy, I think you actually have to be able to imagine having sex with them, and something intrinsically remote and artificial about Brooke Shields makes it possible to imagine jacking off to a picture of her but not to imagine actually having sex with her.)

32. Some tennis writer somewhere observed of Michael Chang that whereas all pros up at net will run back to retrieve a lob placed over their heads, Chang is the only pro known sometimes to run back and retrieve *passing shots.*

33. Though note that very few of them wear eyeglasses, either.

34. A whole other kind of vision — the kind attributed to Larry Bird in basketball, sometimes, when he's made those incredible surgical passes to people who nobody else could even see were open — is required when you're hitting: this involves seeing the other side of the court — where your opponent is and which direction he's moving in and what possible angles are open to you in consequence of where he's going. The schizoid thing about tennis is that you have to use both kinds of vision — ball and court — at the same time.

35. Basketball comes close, but it's a team sport and lacks tennis's primal mano a mano intensity. Boxing might come close — at least at the lighter weight divisions — but the actual physical damage the fighters inflict on each other makes it too concretely brutal to be really beautiful — a level of abstraction and formality (i.e., "play") is necessary for a sport to possess true metaphysical beauty (in my opinion).

36. For those of you into business stats, the calculus of a shot in tennis

would be rather like establishing a running compound-interest expansion in a case in which not only is the rate of interest itself variable and not only are the determinants of that rate variable and not only is the amount of time during which the determinants influence the interest rate variable, but the principal itself is variable.

37. Sex and substance issues notwithstanding, professional athletes are our culture's holy men: they give themselves over to a pursuit, endure great privation and pain to actualize themselves at it, and enjoy a relationship to "excellence" and "perfection" that we admire and reward (the monk's begging bowl, the RBI guru's eight-figure contract) and like to watch, even though we have no inclination to walk that road ourselves. In other words, they do it for us, sacrifice themselves for our redemption.

38. Meaning a two-handed forehand, whose pioneer was a South African named Frew McMillan and whose most famous practitioner today is Monica Seles.

39. The idea of what it would be like to perspire heavily with huge amounts of gel in your hair is sufficiently horrific to me that I approached Knowle after the match to ask him about it, only to discover that neither he nor his coach spoke enough English — or even French — to be able to determine who I was, and the whole sweat-and-gel issue will, I'm afraid, remain a matter for your own imagination.

40. Who is clearly such a fundamentally nice guy that he would probably hit around with me for a little while just out of politeness, since for him it would be at worst a little bit dull. For me, though, it would be, as I said, a little obscene.

41. The example of Michael Joyce's childhood, though, shows me that we were comparative sluggards, dilettantes. He described his daily schedule: "I'd be in school till 2:00. Then, after, I'd go [driven by father] to the [West End Racquet] Club [in Torrance, California] and have a lesson with [legendary, wildly expensive, and unbelievably hard-ass Robert] Lansdorp [former childhood coach of, among others, Tracy Austin] from 3:00 to 4:00. Then I'd have drills from 4:00 to 6:00, then we'd drive all the way home — it's like half an hour — and I'm like, 'Thank God, I can finally watch TV or go up and talk with [my friends] on the phone or something,' but Dad is like, 'You didn't practice your serve yet.' At 12 or 13 [years old], you're not going to want to do it. [No lie, since two hours of serious drills alone were enough to put me in a fetal position for the rest of the day.] You need somebody to make you do it. But then, after like a hundred or so serves, I start to get into it [standing by himself out in the Joyces' tennis court in their back yard with a huge bucket of balls and hitting serve after serve to no one in the gathering twilight], I like it — I'm glad I'm doing it."

42. An important variable I'm skipping is that children are (not surpris-

ingly) immature and tend to get angry with themselves when they fuck up, and so a key part of my strategy involved putting the opponent in a position where he made a lot of unforced errors and got madder and madder at himself, which would ruin his game: feelings of self-disgust at his errors or (even better for me) bitter grievance at the universe for making him have "bad luck" or an "off day" would mount until, usually by sometime in the second set, he'd sink into a kind of enraged torpor and expect to miss or occasionally even have a kind of grand Learesque tantrum, complete with racket hurling and screamed obscenities and sometimes tears. This happened less and less as I got older and opponents got more mature, and by the time I was in college, only genuine head cases could be counted on to get so mad that they'd basically make themselves lose to an inferior player. It's something of a shock, then, to watch Joyce do to his third-round opponent what I used to do to 12-year-old rich kids, which is essentially to retrieve and avoid errors and wait for this opponent to have a temper tantrum. Because Sunday was a rainout, Joyce's third round is played Monday at 10:00 A.M., at the same time that some of the main draw's first rounds are beginning. Joyce's opponent is a guy named Mark Knowles, 23, a 1986 U.S. junior indoor champion, a native of the Bahamas, now known primarily as a doubles player but still a serious opponent, ranked in the world's top two hundred, somebody on Joyce's plateau.

Knowles is tall and thin — muscular in the corded way tall, thin people are muscular — and has an amazing tan and tight blond curls and from a distance is an impressive-looking guy, though up close he has a kind of squished buggy face and the slightly bulging eyes of a player who is spring-loaded on a tantrum. There's a chance to see Knowles up close because he and Joyce play their match on one of the minor courts, where spectators stand and lean over a low fence only a few yards from the court. I and Joyce's coach and Knowles's coach and beautiful girlfriend are the only people really seriously standing and watching, though a lot of spectators on their way to more high-profile matches pass by and stop and watch a few points before moving on. The constant movement of civilians past the court aggrieves Knowles no end, and sometimes he shouts caustic things to people who've started walking away while a point is still in progress.

"Don't worry about it!" is one thing Knowles shouted at somebody who moved. "We're only playing for money! We're only professionals! Don't give it a second thought!" Joyce, preparing to serve, will stare affectlessly straight ahead while he waits for Knowles to finish yelling, his expression sort of the one Vegas dealers have when a player they're cleaning out is rude or abusive: a patient and unjudging look whose expression is informed by the fact that they're being extremely well compensated for being patient and unjudging.

Joyce's coach describes Knowles as "brilliant but kind of erratic," and I think the coach is being kind, because Knowles seems to me to belong on a locked ward for people with serious emotional and personality disorders. He rants and throws and screams scatological curses I haven't heard since junior high. If one of his shots hits the top of the net cord and bounces back, Knowles will scream, "I must be the luckiest guy in the world!" — his eyes protruding and mouth twisted. For me, he's an eerie echo of all the rich and well-instructed Midwest kids I used to play and beat because they'd be unable to eat the frustration when things didn't go their way. He seems not to notice that Joyce gets as many bad breaks and weird bounces as he, or that passing spectators are equally distracting to both players. I have a hard time believing that someone this off-the-wall could rise to a serious pro plateau, though it's true that when Knowles isn't letting his attention get scattered, he's a gorgeous player, with fluid strokes and marvelous touch and control over spin and pace. His read on Joyce is that Joyce is a slugger (which is true), and his tactic is to try to junk him up — change pace, vary spins, hit drop shots to draw Joyce in, deny Joyce pace or routine — and because he's Joyce's equal in firepower, the tactic is sound, Joyce wins the first set in a tiebreaker. But three times in the tiebreaker, Knowles yells at migratory spectators: "Don't worry! It's only a tiebreaker in a professional match!" and is basically a wreck by the time the first set is over, and the second set is perfunctory, a formality that Joyce concludes as fast as possible before he hurries back to the players' tent to pack carbohydrates and find out whether he has to play his first round in the main draw later this same day.

43. He will lose badly to Michael Stich in the round of sixteen here, the same Stich Michael Joyce beat at the Lipton Championships in Key Biscayne four months before; in fact, Joyce will himself beat Courier in straight sets the next week, at the Infiniti Open in Los Angeles, in front of family and friends, for one of the biggest wins of his career.

44. Chang's mother is here — one of the most infamous of the dreaded Tennis Parents of the men's and women's tours, a woman who's reliably rumored to have reached down her child's shorts in public to check his underwear — and her attendance (she's seated hierophantically in the player-guest boxes courtside) may have something to do with the staggering woe of Chang's mien and play. Thomas Enqvist ends up beating him badly in the quarterfinals on Friday. (Enqvist, by the way, looks eerily like a young Richard Chamberlain — the Richard Chamberlain of *The Towering Inferno*, say, with that narrow, sort of rodentially patrician quality. The best thing about him is his girlfriend, who wears glasses and, when applauding a good point, sort of hops up and down in her seat with refreshing uncoolness.)

45. As Enqvist appears to be Edberg's . . . Swedish tennis tends to be like

monarchic succession: the Swedes tend to have only one really great player at a time, and this player is always male, and he almost always ends up best in the world for a while. This is one reason marketers and endorsement consultants are circling Enqvist like sharks all through the summer.

46. Nerves and choking are a huge issue in a precision-and-timing sport like tennis, and a "bad head" washes more juniors and collegians out of the competitive life than any sort of deficit in talent or drive.

JACK McCALLUM

Ace Venture

FROM SPORTS ILLUSTRATED

THERE ARE SIX OF US standing behind the tee box on the 17th hole of the Seaview Resort's Bay Course in Absecon, New Jersey. The flag is about 120 yards away, on the left side of the green, twenty feet behind a large sand trap. We are firing wedges, nine-irons, eight irons, and even a seven-wood or two into the early-morning mist, the idea being for one of us to hit the ball into the cup off the tee. Technically, of course, it would not count as a hole in one, because regulation aces have to be scored during regulation rounds. There is the story of one Lew Cullum of Largo, Florida, who in 1966 hit his tee shot into the lake on the 145-yard 11th hole at Yacht Club Estates Golf Club, near St. Petersburg, and followed it by depositing three more tee shots in the same place. His fifth shot, however, found the cup, thus earning him a 9 on the hole.

But I'm not expecting an ace anyway. Although two members of my group — Seaview head pro Matt Gillogly and assistant pro Andrew Rogers — each have had a hole in one (though not on the Bay 17th), I am positive it will not happen over the three-hour period set aside for our seemingly pointless endeavor. I have nothing to prove with this hole-in-one experiment except that I am not hole-in-one lucky. I've never gotten a hole in one, I never expect to, and I've never played a round in a group with anybody who did get one.

But I'm convinced there is a parallel universe out there, one in which holes in one are as common as mulligans: Hole in One World. Aces reported to *Golf Digest,* the hole-in-one clearinghouse since 1952 (the year the magazine began sending out report forms to every clubhouse in the country), range from about 38,000 to

42,000 per year. Newspapers regularly run reports of 80-year-old grandmothers and 10-year-old grandsons who "aced the 110-yard 12th with a three-wood." A number of insurance agencies make good money by providing hole-in-one insurance to tournaments in which cash prizes, automobiles, golf vacations or, in the case of the National Funeral Directors Association tournament, a casket is given away for aces. Indeed, there is nothing in sports that seems at once so remarkable and yet so pedestrian as the hole in one.

There's even one man who makes a living off his hole-in-one reputation: Mancil Davis, a fast-talking, wisecracking former club pro, who is now the director of event management for the National Hole In One Association. Davis, 42, played junior golf in Texas against Ben Crenshaw and Tom Kite and, in 1975, briefly tried the PGA Tour. He quit because, he says, "my caddie made more money than I did." Davis can't drive and can't putt, but what he can do is find the hole from the tee. The self-proclaimed King of Aces puts his hole-in-one total at 50, and that does not include, he says, the 10 or so he has made at corporate outings, in which he stays at one par-3 and fires tee shots at the flag all day, in much the same way my companions and I are doing right now. Davis's career path was set early. He had eight aces in 1966, when he was only 12, and earned an appearance on *I've Got a Secret,* where he stumped the formidable mixed foursome of Bill Cullen, Henry Morgan, Bess Myerson, and Betsy Palmer.

But no matter how I analyze it, 50 holes in one by one man (and that's not even the record; more on that later) — not to mention 40,000 per year in a country that produces more duffers than dentists — seems like an unnatural conquest of the odds, which, by the way, are about 13,500 to 1 for an amateur golfer, about half that for a club pro, and about 3,500 to 1 for a touring pro.

Now, there are hole-in-one parameters. For an ace to be official, it must be witnessed by at least one person willing to sign the scorecard and must be scored on a golf course with no more than six par-3s. But there's a lot of gray area. Touring pros usually count only the holes in one that they score in competition — there have been 26 in 38 men's and women's Tour events so far this season — yet among the 46 holes in one credited to Art Wall Jr., the hole-in-one king of Tour golfers, are many that he scored in casual play at his home course in Honesdale, Pennsylvania.

As for the thousands and thousands of aces by amateurs, well, let's think about it. In golf a 95 becomes an 89 with a few conceded putts; a snowman becomes a 5 if those white stakes near the woods are considered decorative landscaping and not out-of-bounds markers. Is there any reason to believe that hole-in-one claims are an island of probity in this confounding game, in which otherwise honest souls routinely compromise their integrity over a $2 Nassau? Tom Weiskopf, who has made sixteen aces (in both practice and competitive rounds), says there were snickers about Wall's holes in one even among the pros. "I don't care if you're standing on the same 90-yard hole, hitting a wedge into a green shaped like a punch bowl," says Weiskopf. "Thirty or forty aces is a helluva lot."

Still, there's no doubt that some golfers just seem to have a knack for aces. Davis says that psychologists have done tests on him and found that "my brain waves are different, much more positive, when I'm hitting a six-iron on a par-3 tee than when I'm hitting a six-iron from the fairway." Well, it figures that brain waves would be involved when you hit a ball that measures at least 1.68 inches in diameter into a hole that measures 4.25 inches in diameter from distances of 100 to 496 yards. (Oh, yes, there has been a 496-yard ace; more on that later, too.) Or, as Mac O'Grady, the Tour's only certifiable spaceman, once said: "A hole in one is amazing when you think of the different universes this white mass of molecules has to pass through on its way to the hole."

I ask my hole-in-one partners if they think much about brain waves or different universes when they're on a par-3. "Right now I'm thinking about blisters," says my friend Bob Fink as he hits his fiftieth shot of the morning. It passes through several universes before landing in a sandy one in front of the green.

The first hole in one, according to *The Golfer's Handbook,* a British publication, was scored by one of the sport's earliest notables, "Young" Tom Morris, in the first round of the 1868 British Open. It happened on the 8th hole at Prestwick in Scotland, which, with classic British precision, was measured at 166 yards, four inches. In *Prestwick,* a volume that sits among thousands in the library of the U.S. Golf Association in Far Hills, New Jersey, Morris's scorecard from that round is reproduced. It bears a single vertical slash at number 8. Rounds were twelve holes in those days — boy, there's an idea that deserves reconsideration — and Morris went 50-55-52 to win the Open.

It's impossible to say how common holes in one were before the turn of the century. There was no *Golf Digest,* after all, and the Brits have never celebrated the ace as much as Americans have. During a practice round at Scotland's Carnoustie the week before the 1975 British Open, Weiskopf was amazed when his windblown ace at number 8 received so little reaction from the gallery.

"Didn't you see my ball go in?" he asked two elderly Scots who were camped at the back of the green on sit sticks.

"Aye, laddie," said one.

"And you didn't even clap?" said Weiskopf.

"Boot laddie," said the other, "it didn't coont now, did it?"

Weiskopf's sixteen career aces are sixteen more than the immortal Bobby Jones scored, at least according to the record books. However, Jones, who died in 1971, said he had two unofficial holes in one, the first on the 11th at East Lake in Atlanta and the other at the Augusta Country Club, not to be confused with Augusta National, which he cofounded. Jones also made a number of eagles and double eagles. "All these things, of course, were nothing but luck," he wrote more than thirty years ago to Ian Woolridge of the London *Daily Mail.* "I got a bigger kick when the ball stopped close."

That sounds like something Ben Hogan, who had four holes in one (none in competition) during his legendary career, would say. "I would've had more," Hogan once said, "but I rarely aimed at the flag. I aimed at the spot where I had the best birdie opportunity." The best Hogan hole-in-one story is from the 1947 Masters, at which he was paired with Claude Harmon during a practice round. On the celebrated 145-yard 12th, Harmon knocked his tee shot into the cup. As the crowd cheered wildly, Hogan remained stoic and put his tee shot eight feet from the cup. The roar for Harmon's feat increased as the players approached the green, but Hogan still said nothing. When Harmon lifted his ball from the cup, there was another cheer. Hogan studied his line. After he had made the putt for a birdie, and after he had hit his drive on 13, Hogan finally spoke.

"You know back there on the 12th hole. . . ."

"Yes?" said Harmon.

"I've been thinking. I believe that's the first time I ever birdied that hole."

Even friendly pros, aware of the unwashed masses of double-digit handicappers who have holes in one, don't like to dwell on the ace. "I mean, some people skull it along the ground and get one, don't they?" says Laura Davies, a dominant LPGA player.

Davis Love III, who like Davies has made only two holes in one, remembers sitting at Kapalua with an amateur golfer after Fred Couples scored the only hole in one of his career a few years ago. "I can't believe Freddy's had only one," the amateur said.

"Well, how many have *you* had?" Love asked.

"Nineteen," the guy answered.

"Nineteen!" Love exclaimed. "Jeez, who keeps track of that for you?"

That's the question, isn't it?

It's unlikely that a pro standing on the tee is thinking about a hole in one, although the TV mikes picked up Nick Faldo's famous "called shot" in the 1993 Ryder Cup at the Belfry in Sutton Cold-field, England. "This would be a good time to hole one," said Faldo right before hitting a six-iron into the cup at the 14th to help him halve his match with Paul Azinger. Then again, Mancil Davis says he *always* aims directly at the hole on a par-3. His only other tip is not to use a tee. "Beyond that, if you want me to explain why I have 50," says Davis, "I plumb cain't." Others plumb cain't either. The ace is golf's parlor trick, and to probe serious-minded golfers about it is like asking Yo-Yo Ma if he plays "She'll Be Comin' 'Round the Mountain."

Double eagles — now *that's* a fun subject for the pros. "I get much more excited about a double eagle, because, man, that's three shots [under par]," says John Daly. He has only three aces, but he has five double eagles. Making a double eagle almost always involves following a monster drive with a monster fairway wood, which accounts for the fact that only 200 to 250 double eagles are recorded each year. (The King of Aces, incidentally, says he has brain-waved ten double eagles into the cup too.) But precisely because they're so rare, double eagles lack the populist allure, the tantalizing attainability, the catch-lightning-in-a-bottle magic of the hole in one.

*

Within a three-hour span during the second round of the 1989 U.S. Open, Doug Weaver, Mark Wiebe, Jerry Pate, and Nick Price all aced the 167-yard 6th hole at Oak Hill Country Club in Rochester, New York. The odds of that happening, according to USGA number crunchers, were 2.4 million to 1. Before our morning session at Seaview, Gillogly and Rogers figured that it would take about 250 to 300 balls for one of us — more likely, one of them — to get an ace. "In this kind of situation, it's like mortar practice," says Gillogly. "It takes a while to get the coordinates, but after that, you should be able to do it." I don't agree. It's not going to happen as long as I am here. As I said, I'm not hole-in-one lucky.

The morning rolls on. Two hours, two and a half hours. Five hundred balls, seven hundred balls. Gillogly hits the pin on the fly, and the ball comes down about eighteen inches behind the hole. There is a five-minute span in which Rogers puts a half-dozen drives within the leather. But none drops. I start one toward the pin and shout, absurdly, "Get in the hole!" It gets within three feet. No doubt I would've missed the birdie putt.

"I got an idea," says Joe Cirigliano, one of my buddies. "Let's try it blindfolded." We all take a crack at swinging with our eyes closed. Rogers actually finds the green. Elwood Williams, a friend and the final member of our sixsome, finds the rain shelter, which is located behind a clump of trees just to the left of the tee.

Cirigliano's idea is not so crazy, though. In 1970 Charlie Boswell, the famous blind champion, aced the 141-yard 14th at Vestavia Country Club in Birmingham with a six-iron. And in May 1994 an 82-year-old gentleman named Philip Lopiano used a five-wood to ace the 136-yard 17th hole at Glen Brook Country Club in Stroudsburg, Pennsylvania, even though a condition known as macular degeneration has left him nearly blind. "I can see the ball when I look down on it directly," says Lopiano, "but I can't see it once I hit it." As he lined up his tee shot on 17, one of his playing partners, Ray Cook, directed him toward the green and told him that the pin was set on the left side, just behind a trap.

"It went in!" exclaimed Cook after Lopiano tagged the yellow ball he uses to increase his chances of seeing it.

"In the trap?" asked Lopiano.

"In the hole!" said Cook.

The story went out on the AP wire, and Lopiano, who had two

previous aces, heard from golfers all over the world. "I even did a radio interview from Japan, and they sent me one of those screens that, you know, people stand behind when they're changing clothes," says Lopiano. "It's a beautiful thing."

I wondered to what extent the joy of scoring a hole in one was moderated by not being able to see it go in the hole. "Well, when I go to the hospital for my eyes, I see dozens of children who will never see," says Lopiano, "so I'm sure not going to complain about not seeing a hole in one."

Holes in one have been scored on drives that bounced off trees and bridges, off rakes and sprinklers, off frozen ponds, off wires strung above the greens and snow fences set up behind them, off farm implements and farm animals. Last March, while playing the Felixstowe Ferry Golf Club course in Suffolk, England, Neville Rowlandson, 56, skulled his tee shot at number 1 along the ground. It struck a marker in front of the tee, caromed to the right, traveled twenty-five yards, struck the pin on the 18th green and dropped into the cup. *Golf World* called the miracle shot a "course in one."

Holes in one have been scored by one-armed golfers and golfers in wheelchairs, by right-handed golfers hitting lefty, by left-handed golfers hitting righty, by joking golfers hitting from their knees, by golfers too drunk to know what they had done. Davis says he once hit a three-iron off the tee and watched it go dead right, strike a small mesquite tree ("Hitting a tree in west Texas is stranger than getting a hole in one," says the King), kick left, hit a sprinkler and roll in the hole. "Just no rhyme nor reason for that kinda thing," Davis drawls.

There are countless tales of husbands and wives acing the same hole, of brothers and sisters acing different holes on different courses on the same day, of mothers and daughters acing the same hole one year apart. (And they say the family structure has disintegrated!) You want parallelism? During the Skins Game on November 29, 1987, Lee Trevino aced the 17th at PGA West in La Quinta, California (it was only his second hole in one, and he has had only one since), to win $175,000. Amazingly, that same week another Lee Trevino, a female amateur and no relation, aced the 119-yard 13th at Caloosa Golf and Country Club in Sun City Center, Florida.

Two years ago a 73-year-old golfer named Eric Johnson achieved

a lifetime dream by scoring an ace at the Queen's Park Golf Club in Southland, New Zealand. He died a few hours later. A fellow named Bill Higginbotham of Terre Haute, Indiana, didn't have to wait nearly that long for his ace. One March day in 1963 Higginbotham, then 25, and his buddy Jerry Rice were sitting in Bill Griffith's barbershop when Rice and Griffith decided to play nine holes at nearby Linton Municipal. Higginbotham tagged along and was coaxed into giving the game a try. He picked up a borrowed seven-iron, knocked his tee shot on number 1 into a hill near the green and watched it bounce a few times and roll into the cup. It was not only the first hole of golf he ever played; it was the first time he ever took a *swing*.

Almost as lucky as Higginbotham was one David Terpoilli of West Norristown, Pennsylvania, who, during an October 1994 corporate outing at Whitemarsh Country Club, fired a 123-over 193 that included an ace on the 128-yard 16th. Here was Terpoilli's back nine: 9-21-9-16-11-13-1-11-9–100. "I haven't picked up a club since," says Terpoilli. "How could I ever top that?"

Speaking of topping, consider the peculiar tale of Charles Mellanakos and John Bariahtaris at the Nabnasset Lake (Massachusetts) Country Club in 1960. At the 125-yard 2nd, Mellanakos hit his tee shot into the cup. Bariahtaris then did the same, except that his ball bounced out because it hit Mellanakos's ball. That's no weirder than what happened to Dean Colbert and his brother Ken on the 9th hole at River View Golf Course in Santa Ana, California, in 1977. Dean left his ball a few inches from the hole. Ken hit next, and his well-struck drive nudged Dean's ball into the cup. According to match-play rules in effect at the time, Dean could play the ball where it stopped or replace it. Guess which he chose. That rule was changed in 1984, and now, in stroke and match play, the ball must be replaced.

One amateur, Joe Lucius, has made a record thirteen aces at one hole, the fifteenth at the Mohawk Golf Club in Tiffin, Ohio; there's even a plaque at the tee to commemorate the feat. But my partners and I are eight hundred balls into our experiment at Seaview's 17th, and we have no holes in one. I am prepared for this, but it's starting to frustrate the pros, who are now trying to "ugly in" an ace, hitting cut nine-irons and even pounding eight-irons into the bank

in front of the green to get a roll. It shouldn't be this hard, they believe. Sam Snead claims to have made a hole in one with every club except the putter. That contrasts with the experience of Faldo, who scored all five of his aces with a six-iron, and LPGA veteran Debbie Massey, who made her six with a five-iron.

If Larry Nishi were at the tee with us, I bet we would have a hole in one. Two summers ago at the Mid-Pacific Country Club of Honolulu, the 69-year-old Nishi hit a five-iron into the cup on the 145-yard 4th hole. Two holes later, on the 186-yard, into-the-wind 6th, Nishi pulled out a five-wood and holed out again. "Funny thing is," says Nishi, a 14 handicapper who had two previous aces, "I clipped the pin on 11, the next par-3." Nishi came out ahead on the deal, incidentally: The traditional buy-for-the-house punishment for aces cost him about $350, but he collected a $500 pro-shop gift certificate from a fund to which members at Mid-Pacific kick in $2 each. Or maybe we need Idaho State golfer Shane Langstaff. On the second day of practice two years ago, Langstaff, who is from Columbus, Montana, used an eight-iron to ace the 162-yard 2nd hole at the Riverside Golf Course in Pocatello. Shortly afterward he pulled out a wedge and aced the 147-yard 4th. After the round Langstaff bought $5 worth of state lottery tickets. He didn't win.

Holes in one have been hit by mechanical golfers, such as the USGA's Iron Byron (five in 1985) and Ping's Pingman (one in 1993), and by mechanical crooners, such as Perry Como and Vic Damone. Bing Crosby scored an ace, and so did Alice Cooper, without face paint. Bob Hope has six holes in one; that's five more than Couples.

On May 15, 1960, Gummo Marx used a three-iron to ace the 155-yard 2nd at Tamarisk Country Club in Palm Springs, California, a feat witnessed by his brothers Harpo and Zeppo. The mind reels at what that scene might have been: Harpo dancing around and waving that silly hat while Gummo shakes his head and smiles.

Joe DiMaggio donated a TV set as a hole-in-one prize at a 1966 tournament at the Sharp Park Golf Course in Pacifica, California, and then hit an eight-iron into the cup on the 140-yard 15th for the only ace of the competition. There is no report on whether he reclaimed the set.

Though politicians are most frequently seen conking spectators in the head with right-angle duck hooks, several have had holes in one. The September 5, 1961, issue of *Golf Digest* includes the Official Hole-in-One Clearinghouse Application Form filled out and sent in by Richard Nixon after he aced the 2nd hole at the Bel Air Country Club on September 4. *Age: 44. Address: Los Angeles. Handicap: 18. Right-handed. Spalding club, five-iron; Spalding ball.* Nixon later called it "the greatest thrill in my life — even better than being elected." Can't you just see the Trickster striding up the fairway in a pair of garish red pants, an awkward grin on his face, waving to or saluting an imaginary crowd and thinking, Take *that,* JFK! Nixon finished with a 91 that day and said he lost three bucks. Six-and-a-half years later, Senator Edmund Muskie of Maine had a hole in one at the 153-yard 11th hole at Webhannet Golf Club in Kennebunk Beach, a course later played by President George Bush. Muskie's ace was hardly a harbinger of political luck: eight months later he and Hubert Humphrey lost the presidential election to Nixon and Spiro Agnew.

One of the most talented golfer-politicos, John F. Kennedy, was actually relieved once when he *didn't* get a hole in one. Playing at Cypress Point in California shortly before the 1960 election to succeed Dwight Eisenhower, an avid golfer, JFK sent a seven-iron toward the pin on the 143-yard 15th. "Go in! Go in!" yelled one of his playing partners, Paul B. Fay Jr., later undersecretary of the Navy. Kennedy had "a look of horror on his face," says Fay. The ball hit the pin and kicked to the side, stopping about six inches from the cup, and Kennedy breathed a sigh of relief. "If that ball had gone into that hole," Kennedy told Fay, "in less than an hour the word would be out to the nation that another golfer was trying to get in the White House."

Less secretive about his golfing prowess is Kim Jong Il, president of North Korea. In October '94 Kim scored five aces in a round at the Pyongyang Golf Club en route to a, ahem, 38-under 34. That obliterated the previous low round of 59, shot by Al Geiberger at the Memphis Classic in 1977 and Chip Beck at the '91 Las Vegas Invitational. That was the report, anyway, from Pyongyang pro Park Young Nam, who added, "Dear Leader comrade general Kim Jong Il, whom I respect from the bottom of my heart, is an excellent golfer." We should say so. Incidentally, according to his biography Kim, 54, also can produce bumper rice crops at will, so this golf thing is kind of a sideline.

Far more interesting are the hole-in-one tales of unknowns, those whom Fate tapped on the shoulder and put on *Golf Digest*'s all-time hole-in-one list. Four names in particular intrigued me: Rose Montgomery, the oldest woman to score a hole in one; Robert Mitera, the man with the longest straightaway hole in one in history; Norman Manley, who has the all-time record number of holes in one (59); and Dr. Joseph Boydstone, who scored three aces in one round and finished one incredible year with 11. Well, maybe.

The Rose Montgomery story is bittersweet. On June 2, 1992, Montgomery pulled out a club, probably a five-wood, and knocked her drive on the 100-yard 7th hole at Canyon Country Club in Palm Springs into the cup for her tenth career ace. She was 96 years old. "There's no doubt it happened," says Jack Koennecker, golf director emeritus at the club, where Montgomery frequently won the women's championship. "Everybody around the club heard about it right away." Koennecker speaks approvingly of Montgomery's competitiveness and determination. "Rose used to spit on her gloves and say, 'Let's get after it,'" he says. "Some people thought that was kind of crude. But I thought it was great. She was one of the few women I ever heard of who shot her age." Indeed, on the day she recorded that tenth ace, Montgomery shot a 92. Shortly after that historic round, however, she became ill, and last year she died.

On October 7, 1965, Mitera, a Creighton University golfer, stepped to the tee at the 447-yard 10th hole at the appropriately named Miracle Hills Golf Club in Omaha. It was an extremely blustery day, and the wind was behind him. Mitera let it rip. The ball got into the wind, landed near the green, bounced a few times and presumably rolled into the hole, though no one saw it do so. That broke the previous long-ball record on a straightaway hole by twenty yards. (The record on a dogleg is a 496-yard ace by Shaun Lynch of Devon, England, on the 17th at the Teign Valley Club in Christow, England, last year.)

I wondered how this singular feat had sat with Mitera over the years and whether it had propelled him to a successful amateur career. After numerous phone calls to Omaha, I finally located him. "What do you want with me?" he asked impatiently.

"I'd like to talk about your hole in one," I said.

"I don't want to," said Mitera. "Goodbye." And he hung up.

*

"Yes, I've been called a liar many times," says Norman Manley, who claims he, not Mancil Davis, is the *real* King of Aces. Well, you won't hear him called a liar here. No one but Manley can say whether he truly has fifty-nine holes in one, amassed over thirty years on courses from Lake Tahoe to Mexico and all marked down in a book he keeps at his home in Long Beach, California. But does it not strain credulity that Manley, a talented amateur to be sure (his handicap in his prime ranged between six and eight, and he was a seven-time champion at Del Valle Country Club in Saugus, California) but no Hogan, put it into the cup from the tee fifty-nine times? And, on one record-breaking occasion — August 4, 1964 — did it on *consecutive par-4s* at Del Valle?

"I've always been both lucky and good in sports," says Manley, 73, who played two or three times a week despite punching a clock as an aeronautics worker and a movie projectionist. "Before I knew how to play, I went to take a lesson, and the pro told me, 'You don't need it. You're a natural.' Anything I did in sports I was good at.

"Witnesses? Well, a friend who died of cancer, Les Elliott, saw sixteen of my holes in one."

Manley's hole-in-one days may be over. He's just now getting back to the game after a series of painful operations that have left him with two artificial knees, one artificial hip, and, he says, "a ruined swing." And one has the feeling that his record has been a mixed blessing. He's dealt with skepticism and downright hostility; he's never won a red cent on his aces; and he's never gotten, he believes, proper credit.

"The PGA won't recognize me, because I'm an amateur," he complains. "It's always, 'Mancil Davis, King of Aces.' Well, I'm the real king. I know it, and the people who played with me know it."

Well, there are no ace kings in our group. We have hit 999 balls at the blasted number 17 stick. We have a couple of Jimmies, our term for drives that have sliced onto heavily traveled Jimmie Leeds Road, which runs along the course. (We've heard no screeching of tires.) And we have a couple of Roberts, our term for misstruck drives that have threatened the health and welfare of Robert Clark, a Seaview intern who has been assigned the mind-numbing task of green repair, ball collection, trap raking, and, if necessary, ace witnessing. It has not been necessary.

"This is it," says Gillogly as he addresses number 1,000. He reaches over and touches fingers with Rogers for luck. His wedge shot is perfect. Just not perfect enough.

"If Joe Boydstone were here," I tell the group, "I bet we would've gotten one."

They look at me in confusion.

Around his hometown of Bakersfield, California, Doc Boydstone, the former physician for Kern County Jail, has a bit of a, well, reputation. "He's a phony," says Babe Lazane, the retired pro at Bakersfield Country Club, where Boydstone claims to have holed out a few times during his unbelievable eleven-ace year of '62. "I used to come in in the morning, and there would be a scorecard from Boydstone shoved under the door with a 1 circled, like he got a hole in one at 6 A.M. Hell, I threw away forty holes in one he turned in." But could Boydstone play? "Ah, he couldn't hit it from here to there," scoffs Lazane. Obviously Lazane is not from the Park Young Nam school of golf-pro diplomacy.

In 1967 Larry Press, then sports editor at the *Bakersfield Californian,* got Boydstone's hole-in-one feats deleted from *The World Almanac.* "There were just too many reports that the holes in one were bogus," says Press, now a *Californian* columnist. "It became such a joke that one day there was a message for Boydstone tacked to the bulletin board at the country club that read DR. BOYDSTONE — PLEASE CALL ED SULLIVAN. It was a cruel joke, I guess, but that's how people felt about his alleged records."

Still, Boydstone's feats earned him a two-page feature and large photo in the February 1963 issue of *Golf Digest.* The hole-in-one bible referred to him as "the deeply-tanned, mustachioed Bakersfield sharpshooter," and his two alleged records — three aces in one round and eleven in one year — are still on the magazine's All-Time Holes-in-One list. Were they possible?

"I'm not going to say yes or no for sure," says Eddie Nowak, who was owner and pro at the Bakersfield Public Golf Course, where Boydstone supposedly had the ace hat-trick round. "I took Joe down to a pro-am around L.A. one time and, well, I'm not sure he even put it on the green on any of the par-3s. He was maybe an 85 shooter on his good days. He was also, you know, a great hypnotist."

Hypnotist?

"That's right," says Nowak. "He could put you under in about ten seconds. I remember a friend of my son's stuttered real bad, and Boydstone hypnotized him out of stuttering. It worked for a few months. So, I don't know, maybe he hypnotized some of his playing partners into thinking he got all those holes in one. That's one theory. Joe really played it to the hilt, though. One day he called me up and told me to meet him downtown. He had bought this trophy — I swear, it was taller than me — and he had somebody take a picture of me presenting it to him as the hole-in-one champion."

On March 11, 1972, Boydstone and five friends from Bakersfield were on a fishing trip in Morro Bay on California's central coast, near Hearst Castle at San Simeon. Their twenty-eight-foot cabin cruiser ran aground and capsized in heavy morning fog. Three survived. Boydstone and two others drowned.

The story was big news in Bakersfield, and the *Californian* ran several articles about it. One noted the following: "Dr. Boydstone was once acclaimed the golf world's 'hole-in-one champion.'" May he rest in peace.

GARY SMITH

The Chosen One

FROM SPORTS ILLUSTRATED

IT WAS ORDINARY. It was oh so ordinary. It was a salad, a dinner roll, a steak, a half potato, a slice of cake, a clinking fork, a podium joke, a ballroom full of white-linen-tablecloth conversation. Then a thick man with tufts of white hair rose from the head table. His voice trembled and his eyes teared and his throat gulped down sobs between words, and everything ordinary was cast out of the room.

He said, "Please forgive me . . . but sometimes I get very emotional . . . when I talk about my son. . . . My heart . . . fills with so . . . much . . . joy . . . when I realize . . . that this young man . . . is going to be able . . . to help so many people. . . . He will transcend this game . . . and bring to the world . . . a humanitarianism . . . which has never been known before. The world will be a better place to live in . . . by virtue of his existence . . . and his presence. . . . I acknowledge only a small part in that . . . in that I know that I was personally selected by God himself . . . to nurture this young man . . . and bring him to the point where he can make his contribution to humanity. . . . This is my treasure. . . . Please accept it . . . and use it wisely. . . . Thank you."

Blinking tears, the man found himself inside the arms of his son and the applause of the people, all up on their feet.

In the history of American celebrity, no father has ever spoken this way. Too many dads have deserted or died before their offspring reached this realm, but mostly they have fallen mute, the father's vision exceeded by the child's, leaving the child to wander, lost, through the sad and silly wilderness of modern fame.

So let us stand amidst this audience at last month's Fred Haskins

Award dinner to honor America's outstanding college golfer of 1996, and take note as Tiger and Earl Woods embrace, for a new manner of celebrity is taking form before our eyes. Regard the 64-year-old African-American father, arm upon the superstar's shoulder, right where the chip is so often found, declaring that this boy will do more good for the world than any man who ever walked it. Gaze at the 20-year-old son, with the blood of four races in his veins, not flinching an inch from the yoke of his father's prophecy but already beginning to scent the complications. The son who stormed from behind to win a record third straight U.S. Amateur last August, turned pro and rang up scores in the 60s in 21 of his first 27 rounds, winning two PGA Tour events as he doubled and tripled the usual crowds and dramatically changed their look and age.

Now turn. Turn and look at us, the audience, standing in anticipation of something different, something pure. Quiet. Just below the applause, or within it, can you hear the grinding? That's the relentless chewing mechanism of fame, girding to grind the purity and the promise to dust. Not the promise of talent, but the bigger promise, the father's promise, the one that stakes everything on the boy's not becoming separated from his own humanity and from all the humanity crowding around him.

It's a fitting moment, while he's up there at the head table with the audience on its feet, to anoint Eldrick (Tiger) Woods — the rare athlete to establish himself immediately as the dominant figure in his sport — as *Sports Illustrated*'s 1996 Sportsman of the Year. And to pose a question: Who will win? The machine . . . or the youth who has just entered its maw?

Tiger Woods will win. He'll fulfill his father's vision because of his mind, one that grows more still, more willful, more efficient, the greater the pressure upon him grows.

The machine will win because it has no mind. It flattens even as it lifts, trivializes even as it exalts, spreads a man so wide and thin that he becomes margarine soon enough.

Tiger will win because of God's mind. Can't you see the pattern? Earl Woods asks. Can't you see the signs? "Tiger will do more than any other man in history to change the course of humanity," Earl says.

Sports history, Mr. Woods? Do you mean more than Joe Louis

and Jackie Robinson, more than Muhammad Ali and Arthur Ashe? "More than any of them because he's more charismatic, more educated, more prepared for this than anyone."

Anyone, Mr. Woods? Your son will have more impact than Nelson Mandela, more than Gandhi, more than Buddha?

"Yes, because he has a larger forum than any of them. Because he's playing a sport that's international. Because he's qualified through his ethnicity to accomplish miracles. He's the bridge between the East and the West. There is no limit because he has the guidance. I don't know yet exactly what form this will take. But he is the Chosen One. He'll have the power to impact nations. Not people. Nations. The world is just getting a taste of his power."

Surely this is lunacy. Or are we just too myopic to see? One thing is certain: we are witnessing the first volley of an epic encounter, the machine at its mightiest confronting the individual groomed all his life to conquer it and turn it to his use. The youth who has been exposed to its power since he toddled onto *The Mike Douglas Show* at 9, the set of *That's Incredible!* at 5, the boy who has been steeled against the silky seduction to which so many before him have succumbed. The one who, by all appearances, brings more psychological balance, more sense of self, more consciousness of possibility to the battlefield than any of his predecessors.

This is war, so let's start with war. Remove the images of pretty putting greens from the movie screen standing near the ballroom's head table. Jungle is what's needed here, foliage up to a man's armpits, sweat trickling down his thighs, leeches crawling up them. Lieut. Col. Earl Woods, moving through the night with his rifle ready, wondering why a U.S. Army public information officer stationed in Brooklyn decided in his mid-30s that he belonged in the Green Berets and ended up doing two tours of duty in Vietnam. Wondering why his first marriage has died and why the three children from it have ended up without a dad around when it's dark like this and it's time for bed — just as Earl ended up as a boy after his own father died. Wondering why he keeps plotting ways to return to the line of fire — "creative soldiering," he calls it — to eyeball death once more. To learn once again about his dark and cold side, the side that enables Earl, as Tiger will remark years later, "to slit your throat and then sit down and eat his dinner."

Oh, yes, Earl is one hell of a cocktail. A little Chinese, a little

Cherokee, a few shots of African-American; don't get finicky about measurements, we're making a vat here. Pour in some gruffness and a little intimidation, then some tenderness and some warmth and a few jiggers of old anger. Don't hold back on intelligence. And stoicism. Add lots of stoicism, and even more of responsibility — "the most responsible son of a bitch you've ever seen in your life" is how Earl himself puts it. Top it all with "a bucket of whiskey," which is what he has been known to order when he saunters into a bar and he's in the mood. Add a dash of hyperbole, maybe two, and to hell with the ice, just whir. This is one of those concoctions you're going to remember when morning comes.

Somewhere in there, until a good fifteen years ago, there was one other ingredient, the existential Tabasco, the smoldering why? The Thai secretary in the U.S. Army office in Bangkok smelled it soon after she met Earl, in 1967. "He couldn't relax," says Kultida (Tida) Woods. "Searching for something, always searching, never satisfied. I think because both his parents died when he was young, and he didn't have Mom and Dad to make him warm. Sometimes he stayed awake till three or four in the morning, just thinking."

In a man so accustomed to exuding command and control, in a Green Beret lieutenant colonel, *why?* has a way of building up power like a river dammed. Why did the Vietcong sniper bracket him that day (first bullet a few inches left of one ear, second bullet a few inches right of the other) but never fire the third bullet? Why did Earl's South Vietnamese combat buddy, Nguyen Phong — the one Earl nicknamed Tiger, and in whose memory he would nickname his son — stir one night just in time to awaken Earl and warn him not to budge because a viper was poised inches from his right eye? What about that road Earl's jeep rolled down one night, the same road on which two friends had just been mutilated, the road that took him through a village so silent and dark that his scalp tingled, and then, just beyond it . . . hell turned inside-out over his shoulder, the sky lighting up and all the huts he had just passed spewing Vietcong machine-gun and artillery fire? He never understands what is the purpose of Lieutenant Colonel Woods's surviving again and again. He never quite comprehends what is the point of his life, until . . .

Until the boy is born. He will get all the time that Earl was unable to devote to the three children from his first marriage. He will be the only child from Earl's second marriage, to the Thai woman he brought back to America, and right away there are signs. What other 6-month-old, Earl asks, has the balance to stand in the palm of his father's hand and remain there even as Daddy strolls around the house? Was there another 11-month-old, ever, who could pick up a sawed-off club, imitate his father's golf swing so fluidly, and drive the ball so wickedly into the nylon net across the garage? Another 4-year-old who could be dropped off at the golf course at 9 A.M. on a Saturday and picked up at 5 P.M., pockets bulging with money he had won from disbelievers ten and twenty years older, until Pop said, "Tiger, you can't do that"? Earl starts to get a glimmer. He is to be the father of the world's most gifted golfer.

But why? What for? Not long after Tiger's birth, when Earl has left the military to become a purchaser for McDonnell Douglas, he finds himself in a long discussion with a woman he knows. She senses the power pooling inside him, the friction. "You have so much to give," she tells him, "but you're not giving it. You haven't even scratched the surface of your potential." She suggests he try EST, Erhard Seminars Training, an intensive self-discovery and self-actualizing technique, and it hits Earl hard, direct mortar fire to the heart. What he learns is that his overmuscular sense of responsibility for others has choked his potential.

"To the point," says Earl, "that I wouldn't even buy a handkerchief for myself. It went all the way back to the day my father died, when I was 11, and my mother put her arm around me after the funeral and said, 'You're the man of the house now.' I became the father that young, looking out for everyone else, and then she died two years later.

"What I learned through EST was that by doing more for myself, I could do much more for others. Yes, be responsible, but love life, and give people the space to be in your life, and allow yourself room to give to others. That caring and sharing is what's most important, not being responsible for everyone else. Which is where Tiger comes in. What I learned led me to give so much time to Tiger, and to give him the space to be himself, and not to smother him with dos and don'ts. I took out the authority aspect and turned it into companionship. I made myself vulnerable as a parent. When you have to earn respect from your child, rather than demanding it because it's owed to you as the father, miracles happen. I realized that, through him, the giving could take a quantum leap. What I could do on a limited scale, he could do on a global scale."

At last, the river is undammed, and Earl's whole life makes sense. At last, he sees what he was searching for, a pattern. No more volunteering for missions — he has his. Not simply to be a great golfer's father. To be destiny's father. His son will change the world.

"What the hell had I been doing in public information in the army, posted in Brooklyn?" he asks. "Why, of course, what greater training can there be than three years of dealing with the New York media to prepare me to teach Tiger the importance of public relations and how to handle the media?"

Father: Where were you born, Tiger?

Son, age 3: I was born on December 30, 1975, in Long Beach, California.

Father: No, Tiger, only answer the question you were asked. It's important to prepare yourself for this. Try again.

Son: I was born in Long Beach, California.

Father: Good, Tiger, good.

The late leap into the Green Berets? "What the hell was that for?" Earl says. "Of course, to prepare me to teach Tiger mental toughness."

The three children by the first marriage? "Not just one boy the first time," says Earl, "but two, along with a girl, as if God was saying, 'I want this son of a bitch to really have previous training.'"

The Buddhist wife, the one who grew up in a boarding school after her parents separated when she was 5, the girl who then vowed that her child would know nothing but love and attention? The one who will preach inner calm to Tiger simply by turning to him with that face — still awaiting its first wrinkle at 52? Whose eyes close when she speaks, so he can almost see her gathering and sifting the thoughts? The mother who will walk every hole and keep score for Tiger at children's tournaments, adding a stroke or two if his calm cracks? "Look at this stuff!" cries Earl. "Over and over you can see the plan being orchestrated by someone other than me because I'm not this damn good! I tried to get out of that combat assignment to Thailand. But Tida was meant to bring in the influence of the Orient, to introduce Tiger to Buddhism and inner peace, so he would have the best of two different worlds. And so he would have the knowledge that there were two people whose lives were totally committed to him."

What of the heart attack Earl suffered when Tiger was 10 and the way the retired lieutenant colonel felt himself floating down the gray tunnel toward the light before he was wrenched back? "To prepare me to teach Tiger that life is short," Earl says, "and to live each day to the maximum, and not worry about the future. There's only now. You must understand that time is just a linear measurement of successive increments of now. Anyplace you go on that line is now, and that's how you have to live it."

No need to wonder about the appearance of the perfect childhood coach, John Anselmo; the perfect sports psychologist, Jay Brunza; the perfect agent, Hughes Norton; the perfect attorney, John Merchant; and the perfect pro swing instructor, Butch Harmon. Or about the great tangle of fate that leads them all to Tiger at just the right junctures in his development. "Everything," says Earl, "right there when he needs it. Everything. There can't be this much coincidence in the world. This is a directed scenario, and none of us involved in the scenario has failed to accept the responsibility. This is all destined to be."

His wife ratifies this, in her own way. She takes the boy's astrological chart to a Buddhist temple in Los Angeles and to another in Bangkok and is told by monks at both places that the child has wondrous powers. "If he becomes a politician, he will be either a president or a prime minister," she is told. "If he enters the military, he will be a general."

Tida comes to a conclusion. "Tiger has Thai, African, Chinese, American Indian, and European blood," she says. "He can hold everyone together. He is the Universal Child."

This is in the air the boy breathes for twenty years, and it becomes bone fact for him, marrow knowledge. When asked about it, he merely nods in acknowledgment of it, assents to it; of course he believes it's true. So failure, in the rare visits it pays him, is not failure. It's just life pausing to teach him a lesson he needs in order to go where he's inevitably going. And success, no matter how much sooner than expected it comes to the door, always finds him dressed and ready to welcome it. "Did you ever see yourself doing this so soon?" a commentator breathlessly asks him seconds after his first pro victory, on October 6 in Las Vegas, trying to elicit wonder and awe on live TV. "Yeah," Tiger responds. "I kind of did." And sleep comes to him so easily: in the midst of conversation, in a car, in a plane, off he goes, into the slumber of the destined. "I don't see any of this as scary or a burden," Tiger says. "I see it as fortunate. I've always known where I wanted to go in life. I've never let anything deter me. This is my purpose. It will unfold."

No sports star in the history of American celebrity has spoken this way. Maybe, somehow, Tiger can win.

The machine will win. It must win because it too is destiny, 5 billion destinies leaning against one. There are ways to keep the hordes back, a media expert at Nike tells Tiger. Make broad gestures when you speak. Keep a club in your hands and take practice swings, or stand with one foot well out in front of the other, in almost a karate stance. That will give you room to breathe. Two weeks later, surrounded by a pen-wielding mob in La Quinta, California, in late November, just before the Skins Game, the instruction fails. Tiger survives, but his shirt and slacks are ruined, felt-tip-dotted to death.

The machine will win because it will wear the young man down, cloud his judgment, steal his sweetness, the way it does just before the Buick Challenge in Pine Mountain, Georgia, at the end of September. It will make his eyes drop when the fans' gaze reaches for his, his voice growl at their clawing hands, his body sag onto a sofa after a practice round and then rise and walk across the room and suddenly stop in bewilderment. "I couldn't even remember what I'd just gotten off the couch for, two seconds before," he says. "I was like mashed potatoes. Total mush."

So he walks. Pulls out on the eve of the Buick Challenge, pulls out of the Fred Haskins Award dinner to honor him, and goes home. See, maybe Tiger can win. He can just turn his back on the machine and walk. Awards? Awards to Tiger are like echoes, voices bouncing off the walls, repeating what a truly confident man has already heard inside his own head. The Jack Nicklaus Award, the one Jack himself was supposed to present to Tiger live on ABC during the Memorial tournament last spring? Tiger would have blown it off if Wally Goodwin, his coach at Stanford during the two years he played there before turning pro, hadn't insisted that he show up.

The instant Tiger walks away from the Buick Challenge and the Haskins dinner, the hounds start yapping. See, that's why the machine will win. It's got all those damn heel-nippers. Little mutts on the PGA Tour resenting how swiftly the 20-year-old was ordained, how hastily he was invited to play practice rounds with Nicklaus and Arnold Palmer, with Greg Norman and Ray Floyd and Nick Faldo and Fred Couples. And big dogs snapping too. Tom Kite quoted as saying, "I can't ever remember being tired when I was twenty," and Peter Jacobsen quoted, "You can't compare Tiger to Nicklaus and Palmer anymore because they never [walked out]."

He rests for a week, stunned by the criticism — "I thought those people were my friends," he says. He never second-guesses his decision to turn pro, but he sees what he surrendered. "I miss college," he says. "I miss hanging out with my friends, getting in a little trouble. I have to be so guarded now. I miss sitting around drinking beer and talking half the night. There's no one my own age to hang out with anymore because almost everyone my age is in college. I'm a target for everybody now, and there's nothing I can do about it. My mother was right when she said that turning pro would take away my youth. But golfwise, there was nothing left for me in college."

He reemerges after the week's rest and rushes from four shots off the lead on the final day to win the Las Vegas Invitational in sudden death. The world's waiting for him again, this time with reinforcements. Letterman and Leno want him as a guest; *GQ* calls about a cover; Cosby, along with almost every other sitcom you can think of, offers to write an episode revolving around Tiger, if only he'll appear. Kids dress up as Tiger for Halloween — did anyone ever dress up as Arnie or Jack? — and Michael Jordan declares that his only hero on earth is Tiger Woods. Pepsi is dying to have him cut a commercial for one of its soft drinks aimed at Generation Xers; Nike and Titleist call in chits for the $40 million and $20 million contracts he signed; money managers are eager to know how he wants his millions invested; women walk onto the course during a practice round and ask for his hand in marriage; kids stampede over and under ropes and chase him from the 18th hole to the clubhouse; piles of phone messages await him when he returns to his hotel room. "Why," Tiger asks, "do so many people want a piece of me?"

Because something deeper than conventional stardom is at work here, something so spontaneous and subconscious that words have trouble going there. It's a communal craving, a public aching for a superstar free of anger and arrogance and obsession with self. It's a hollow place that chimes each time Tiger and his parents strike the theme of father and mother and child love, each time Tiger stands at a press conference and declares, "They have raised me well, and I truly believe they have taught me to accept full responsibility for all aspects of my life." During the making of a Titleist commercial in November, a makeup woman is so moved listening to Earl describe his bond with Tiger that she decides to contact her long-estranged father. "See what I mean?" cries Earl. "Did you affect someone that way today? Did anyone else there? It's destiny, man. It's something bigger than me."

What makes it so vivid is context. The white canvas that the colors are being painted on — the moneyed, mature, and almost minority-less world of golf — makes Tiger an emblem of youth overcoming age, have-not overcoming have, outsider overcoming insider, to the delight not only of the 18-year-olds in the gallery wearing nose rings and cornrows, but also — of all people — of the aging insider haves.

So Tiger finds himself, just a few weeks after turning pro at the end of August, trying to clutch a bolt of lightning with one hand and steer an all-at-once corporation — himself — with the other, and before this he has never worked a day in his life. Never mowed a neighbor's lawn, never flung a folded newspaper, never stocked a grocery shelf; Mozarts just don't, you know. And he has to act as if none of this is new or vexing because he has this characteristic — perhaps from all those years of hanging out with his dad at tournaments, all those years of mixing with and mauling golfers five, ten, twenty, thirty years older than he is — of never permitting himself to appear confused, surprised, or just generally a little squirt. "His favorite expression," Earl says, "is, 'I knew that.'" Of course Pop, who is just as irreverent with Tiger as he is reverent, can say, "No, you didn't know that, you little s—." But Earl, who has always been the filter for Tiger, decides to take a few steps back during his son's first few months as a pro because he wishes to encourage Tiger's independence and because he is uncertain of his own role now that the International Management Group (IMG) is managing Tiger's career.

Nobody notices it, but the inner calm is beginning to dissolve. Earl enters Tiger's hotel room during the Texas Open in mid-October to ask him about his schedule, and Tiger does something he has never done in his twenty years. He bites the old man's head off.

Earl blinks. "I understand how you must feel," he says.

"No, you don't," snaps Tiger.

"And I realized," Earl says later, "that I'd spent twenty years planning for this, but the one thing I didn't do was educate Tiger to be the boss of a corporation. There was just no vehicle for that, and I thought it would develop more slowly. I wasn't presumptuous enough to anticipate this. For the first time in his life, the training was behind the reality. I could see on his face that he was going through hell."

The kid is fluid, though. Just watch him walk. He's quick to flow into the new form, to fit the contour of necessity. A few hours after the outburst he's apologizing to his father and hugging him. A few days later he's giving Pop the O.K. to call a meeting of the key members of Tiger's new corporation and establish a system, Lieutenant Colonel Woods in command, chairing a two-and-a-half-hour teleconference with the team each week to sift through all the demands, weed out all the chaff, and present Tiger five decisions to make instead of five hundred. A few days after that, the weight forklifted off his shoulders, at least temporarily, Tiger wins the Walt Disney World/Oldsmobile Classic. And a few weeks later, at the Fred Haskins Award dinner, which has been rescheduled at his request, Tiger stands at the podium and says, "I should've attended the dinner [the first time]. I admit I was wrong, and I'm sorry for any inconvenience I may have caused. But I have learned from that, and I will never make that mistake again. I'm very honored to be part of this select group, and I'll always remember, for both good and bad, this Haskins Award; for what I did and what I learned, for the company I'm now in and I'll always be in. Thank you very much." The crowd surges to its feet, cheering once more.

See, maybe Tiger can win. He's got the touch. He's got the feel. He never writes down a word before he gives a speech. When he needs to remember a phone number, he doesn't search his memory or a little black book; he picks up a phone and watches what number his fingers go to. When he needs a 120-yard shot to go under an oak branch and over a pond, he doesn't visualize the shot, as most golfers would. He looks at the flag and pulls everything from the hole back, back, back . . . not back into his mind's eye, but into his hands and forearms and hips, so they'll do it by feel. Explain how he made that preposterous shot? He can't. Better you interview his knuckles and metacarpals.

"His handicap," says Earl, "is that he has such a powerful creative mind. His imagination is too vivid. If he uses visualization, the ball goes nuts. So we piped into his creative side even deeper, into his incredible sense of feel."

"I've learned to trust the subconscious," says Tiger. "My instincts have never lied to me."

The mother radiates this: the Eastern proclivity to let life happen, rather than the Western one to make it happen. The father comes to it in his own way, through fire. To kill a man, to conduct oneself calmly and efficiently when one's own death is imminent — a skill Earl learns in Green Beret psychological training and then again and again in jungles and rice paddies — one removes the conscious mind from the task and yields to the subconscious. "It's the more powerful of the two minds," Earl says. "It works faster than the conscious mind, yet it's patterned enough to handle routine tasks over and over, like driving a car or making a putt. It knows what to do.

"Allow yourself the freedom of emotion and feeling. Don't try to control them and trap them. Acknowledge them and become the beneficiary of them. Let it all outflow."

Let it all because it's all there: the stability, almost freakish for a close-of-the-millennium California child — same two parents, same house all his twenty years, same best friends, one since second grade, one since eighth. The kid, for god's sake, never once had a baby-sitter. The conditioning is there as well, the two years of psychological boot camp during which Earl dropped golf bags and pumped cart brakes during Tiger's backswings, jingled change and rolled balls across his line of vision to test his nerves, promising him at the outset that he only had to say "Enough" and Earl would cut off the blowtorch, but promising too that if Tiger graduated, no man he ever faced would be mentally stronger than he. "I am the toughest golfer mentally," Tiger says.

The bedrock is so wide that opposites can dance upon it: the cautious man can be instinctive, the careful man can be carefree. The bedrock is so wide that it has enticed Tiger into the habit of falling behind — as he did in the final matches of all three U.S. Junior Amateur and all three U.S. Amateur victories — knowing in his tissue and bones that danger will unleash his greatest power. "Allow success and fame to happen," the old man says. "Let the legend grow."

To hell with the Tao. The machine will win, it has to win, because it makes everything happen before a man knows it. Before he knows it, a veil descends over his eyes when another stranger approaches. Before he knows it, he's living in a walled community with an electronic gate and a security guard, where the children trick-or-treat in golf carts, a place like the one Tiger just moved into in Orlando to preserve some scrap of sanity. Each day there, even with all the best intentions, how can he help but be a little more removed from the world he's supposed to change, and from his truest self?

Which is . . . who? The poised, polite, opaque sage we see on TV? No, no, no; his friends hoot and haze him when they see that Tiger on the screen, and he can barely help grinning himself. The Tiger they know is perfectly a fast food freak who never remembers to ask if anyone else is hungry before he bolts to Taco Bell or McDonald's for the tenth time of the week. The one who loves riding roller coasters, spinning out golf carts, and winning at cards no matter how often his father accuses him of "reckless eyeballing." The one who loves delivering the dirty joke, who owns a salty barracks tongue just a rank or two beneath his father's. The one who's flip, who's downright cocky. When a suit walks up to him before the Haskins Award dinner and says, "I think you're going to be the next great one, but those are mighty big shoes to fill," Tiger replies, "Got big feet."

A typical exchange between Tiger and his agent, Norton:

"Tiger, they want to know when you can do that interview."

"Tell them to kiss my ass!"

"All right, and after that, what should I tell them?"

"Tell them to kiss my ass again!"

"O.K., and after that . . ."

But it's a cockiness cut with humility, the paradox pounded into his skull by a father who in one breath speaks of his son with religious awe and in the next grunts, "You weren't s— then, Tiger. You ain't s— now. You ain't never gonna be s—."

"That's why I know I can handle all this," Tiger says, "no matter how big it gets. I grew up in the media's eye, but I was taught never to lose sight of where I came from. Athletes aren't as gentlemanly as they used to be. I don't like that change. I like the idea of being a role model. It's an honor. People took the time to help me as a kid, and they impacted my life. I want to do the same for kids."

So, if it's a clinic for children instead of an interview or an endorsement for adults, the cynic in Tiger gives way to the child who grew up immersed in his father's vision of an earth-altering compassion, the 7-year-old boy who watched scenes from the Ethiopian famine on the evening news, went right to his bedroom and returned with a $20 bill to contribute from his piggy bank. Last spring busloads of inner-city kids would arrive at golf courses where Tiger was playing for Stanford, spilling out to watch the Earl and Tiger show in wonder. Earl would talk about the dangers of drugs, then proclaim, "Here's Tiger Woods on drugs," and Tiger would stagger to the tee, topping the ball so it bounced crazily to the side. And then, presto, with a wave of his arms Earl would remove the drugs from Tiger's body, and his son would stride to the ball and launch a 330-yard rocket across the sky. Then Earl would talk about respect and trust and hard work and demonstrate what they can all lead to by standing ten feet in front of his son, raising his arms and telling Tiger to smash the ball between them — and, *whoosh*, Tiger would part not only the old man's arms but his haircut too.

They've got plans, the two of them, big plans, for a Tiger Woods Foundation that will fund scholarships across the country, set up clinics and coaches and access to golf courses for inner-city children. "I throw those visions out there in front of him," Earl says, "and it's like reeling in a fish. He goes for the bait, takes it, and away he goes. This is nothing new. It's been working this way for a long time."

"That's the difference," says Merchant, Tiger's attorney and a family friend. "Other athletes who have risen to this level just didn't have this kind of guidance. With a father and mother like Tiger's, he has to be real. It's such a rare quality in celebrities nowadays. There hasn't been a politician since John Kennedy whom people have wanted to touch. But watch Tiger. He has it. He actually listens to people when they stop him in an airport. He looks them in the eye. I can't ever envision Tiger Woods selling his autograph."

See, maybe Tiger can win.

Let's be honest. The machine will win because you can't work both sides of this street. The machine will win because you can't transcend wearing sixteen Nike swooshes, you can't move human hearts while you're busy pushing sneakers. Gandhi didn't hawk golf balls, did he? Jackie Robinson was spared that fate because he came and went while Madison Avenue was still teething. Ali became a symbol instead of a logo because of boxing's disrepute and because of the attrition of cells in the basal ganglia of his brain. Who or what will save Tiger Woods?

Did someone say Buddha?

Every year near his birthday, Tiger goes with his mother to a Buddhist temple and makes a gift of rice, sugar, and salt to the monks there who have renounced all material goods. A mother-of-pearl Buddha given to Tiger by his Thai grandfather watches over him while he sleeps, and a gold Buddha hangs from the chain on his neck. "I like Buddhism because it's a whole way of being and living," Tiger says. "It's based on discipline and respect and personal responsibility. I like Asian culture better than ours because of that. Asians are much more disciplined than we are. Look how well behaved their children are. It's how my mother raised me. You can question, but talk back? Never. In Thailand, once you've earned people's respect, you have it for life. Here it's, What have you done for me lately? So here you can never rest easy. In this country I have to be very careful. I'm easygoing, but I won't let you in completely. There, I'm Thai, and it feels very different. In many ways I consider that home.

"I believe in Buddhism. Not every aspect, but most of it. So I take bits and pieces. I don't believe that human beings can achieve ultimate enlightenment, because humans have flaws. I don't want to get rid of all my wants and desires. I can enjoy material things, but that doesn't mean I need them. It doesn't matter to me whether I live in a place like this" — the golf club in his hand makes a sweep of the Orlando villa — "or in a shack. I'd be fine in a shack, as long as I could play some golf. I'll do the commercials for Nike and for Titleist, but there won't be much more than that. I have no desire to be the king of endorsement money."

On the morning after he decides to turn pro, there's a knock on his hotel room door. It's Norton, bleary-eyed but exhilarated after a late-night round of negotiations with Nike. He explains to Tiger and Earl that the benchmark for contract endorsements in golf is Norman's reported $2½ million-a-year deal with Reebok. Then, gulping down hard on the yabba-dabba-doo rising up his throat, Norton announces Nike's offer: $40 million for five years, 8 mil a year. "Over three times what Norman gets!" Norton exults.

Silence.

"Guys, do you realize this is more than Nike pays any athlete in salary, even Jordan?"

Silence.

"Finally," Norton says now, recalling that morning, "Tiger says, 'Mmmm-hmmm,' and I say, 'That's it? Mmmm-hmmm?' No 'Omigod.' No slapping five or 'Ya-hooo!' So I say, 'Let me go through this again, guys.' Finally Tiger says, 'Guess that's pretty amazing.' That's it. When I made the deal with Titleist a day later, I went back to them saying, 'I'm almost embarrassed to tell you this one. Titleist is offering a little more than $20 million over five years.'"

On the Monday morning after his first pro tournament, a week after the two megadeals, Tiger scans the tiny print on the sports page under Milwaukee Open money earnings and finds his name. Tiger Woods: $2,544. "That's my money," he exclaims. "I earned this!"

See, maybe Tiger can win.

How? How can he win when there are so many insects under so many rocks? Several more death threats arrive just before the Skins Game, prompting an increase in his plainclothes security force, which is already larger than anyone knows. His agent's first instinct is to trash every piece of hate mail delivered to IMG, but Tiger won't permit it. Every piece of racist filth must be saved and given to him. At Stanford he kept one letter taped to his wall. Fuel comes in the oddest forms.

The audience, in its hunger for goodness, swallows hard over the Nike ad that heralds Tiger's entrance into the professional ranks. The words that flash on the screen over images of Tiger — "There are still courses in the United States I am not allowed to play because of the color of my skin. I've heard I'm not ready for you. Are you ready for me?" — ooze the very attitude from which many in the audience are seeking relief. The media backlash is swift: the Tiger Woods who used to tell the press "The only time I think about race is when the media ask me" — whoa, what happened to him?

What happened to him was a steady accretion of experiences, also known as a life. What happened, just weeks before he was born, was a fusillade of limes and BBs rattling the Woods house in Cypress, California, one of the limes shattering the kitchen window, splashing glass all around the pregnant Tida, to welcome the middle-class subdivision's first non-Caucasian family.

What happened was a gang of older kids seizing Tiger on his first day of kindergarten, tying him to a tree, hurling rocks at him, calling him monkey and nigger. And Tiger, at age 5, telling no one what happened for several days, trying to absorb what this meant about himself and his world.

What happened was the Look, as Tiger and Earl came to call it, the uneasy, silent stare they received in countless country-club locker rooms and restaurants. "Something a white person could never understand," says Tiger, "unless he went to Africa and suddenly found himself in the middle of a tribe." What happened was Tiger's feeling pressured to leave a driving range just two years ago, not far from his family's California home, because a resident watching Tiger's drives rocket into the nearby protective netting reported that a black teenager was trying to bombard his house.

What happened was the cold shoulder Earl got when he took his tyke to play at the Navy Golf Course in Cypress — "a club," Earl says, "composed mostly of retired naval personnel who knew blacks only as cooks and servers, and along comes me, a retired lieutenant colonel outranking 99 percent of them, and I have the nerve to take up golf at 42 and immediately become a low handicap and beat them, and then I have the audacity to have this kid. Well, they had to do something. They took away Tiger's playing privileges twice, said he was too young, even though there were other kids too young who they let play. The second time it happened, I went up to the pro who had done it and made a bet. I said, 'If you'll spot my 3-year-old just one stroke a hole, nine holes, playing off the same tees, and he beats you, will you certify him?' The pro started laughing and said, 'Sure.' Tiger beat him by two strokes, got certified, then the members went over the pro's head and kicked him out again. That's when we switched him to another course."

Beat them. That was his parents' solution for each banishment, each Look. Hold your tongue, hew to every rule, and beat them. Tiger Woods is the son of the first black baseball player in the Big Seven, a catcher back in the early '50s, before the conference became the Big Eight. A man who had to leave his Kansas State teammates on road trips and travel miles to stay in motels for blacks; who had to go to the back door of restaurant kitchens to be fed while his teammates dined inside; who says, "This is the most racist society in the world — I know that." A man who learned neither to extinguish his anger nor spray it but to quietly convert it into animus, the determination to enter the system and overcome it by turning its own tools against it. A Green Beret explosives expert whose mind naturally ran that way, whose response, upon hearing Tiger rave about the security in his new walled community, was, "I could get in. I could blow up the clubhouse and be gone before they ever knew what hit them." A father who saw his son, from the beginning, as the one who would enter one of America's last Caucasian bastions, the PGA Tour, and overthrow it from within in a manner that would make it smile and ask for more. "Been planning that one for twenty years," says Earl. "See, you don't turn it into hatred. You turn it into something positive. So many athletes who reach the top now had things happen to them as children that created hostility, and they bring that hostility with them. But that hostility uses up energy. If you can do it without the chip on the shoulder, it frees up all that energy to create."

It's not until Stanford, where Tiger takes an African-American history course and stays up half the night in dormitories talking with people of every shade of skin, that his experiences begin to crystallize. "What I realized is that even though I'm mathematically Asian — if anything — if you have one drop of black blood in the United States, you're black," says Tiger. "And how important it is for this country to talk about this subject. It's not me to blow my horn, the way I come across in that Nike ad, or to say things quite that way. But I felt it was worth it because the message needed to be said. You can't say something like that in a polite way. Golf has shied away from this for too long. Some clubs have brought in tokens, but nothing has really changed. I hope what I'm doing can change that."

But don't overestimate race's proportion in the fuel that propels Tiger Woods. Don't look for traces of race in the astonishing rubble at his feet on the Sunday after he lost the Texas Open by two strokes and returned to his hotel room and snapped a putter in two with one violent lift of his knee. Then another putter. And another. And another and another — eight in all before his rage was spent and he was ready to begin considering the loss's philosophical lesson. "That volcano of competitive fire, that comes from me," says Earl. A volcano that's mostly an elite athlete's need to win, a need far more immediate than that of changing the world.

No, don't overestimate race, but don't overlook it, either. When

Tiger is asked about racism, about the effect it has on him when he senses it in the air, he has a golf club in his hands. He takes the club by the neck, his eyes flashing hot and cold at once, and gives it a short upward thrust. He says, "It makes me want to stick it right up their asses." Pause. "On the golf course."

The machine will win because there is so much of the old man's breath in the boy . . . and how long can the old man keep breathing? At 2 A.M., hours before the second round of the Tour Championship in Tulsa on October 25, the phone rings in Tiger's hotel room. It's Mom. Pop's in an ambulance, on his way to a Tulsa hospital. He's just had his second heart attack.

The Tour Championship? The future of humanity? The hell with 'em. Tiger's at the old man's bedside in no time, awake most of the night. Tiger's out of contention in the Tour Championship by dinnertime, with a second-round 78, his worst till then as a pro. "There are things more important than golf," he says.

The old man survives   and sees the pattern at work, of course. He's got to throw away the cigarettes. He's got to quit ordering the cholesterol special for breakfast. "I've got to shape up now, God's telling me," Earl says, "or I won't be around for the last push, the last lesson." The one about how to ride the tsunami of runaway fame.

The machine will win because no matter how complicated it all seems now, it is simpler than it will ever be. The boy will marry one day, and the happiness of two people will lie in his hands. Children will follow, and it will become his job to protect three or four or five people from the molars of the machine. Imagine the din of the grinding in five, ten, fifteen years, when the boy reaches his golfing prime.

The machine will win because the whole notion is so ludicrous to begin with, a kid clutching an eight-iron changing the course of humanity. No, of course not, there won't be thousands of people sitting in front of tanks because of Tiger Woods. He won't bring about the overthrow of a tyranny or spawn a religion that one day will number 300 million devotees.

But maybe Pop is onto something without quite seeing what it is. Maybe it has to do with timing: the appearance of his son when America is turning the corner to a century in which the country's faces of color will nearly equal those that are white. Maybe, every now and then, a man gets swallowed by the machine, but the machine is changed more than he is.

For when we swallow Tiger Woods, the yellow-black-red-white man, we swallow something much more significant than Jordan or Charles Barkley. We swallow hope in the American experiment, in the pell-mell jumbling of genes. We swallow the belief that the face of the future is not necessarily a bitter or bewildered face; that it might even, one day, be something like Tiger Woods's face: handsome and smiling and ready to kick all comers' asses.

We see a woman, 50-ish and Caucasian, well-coiffed and tailored — the woman we see at every country club — walk up to Tiger Woods before he receives the Haskins Award and say, "When I watch you taking on all those other players, Tiger, I feel like I'm watching my own son" . . . and we feel the quivering of the cosmic compass that occurs when human beings look into the eyes of someone of another color and see their own flesh and blood.

Biographical Notes

ROGER ANGELL is a writer and editor for *The New Yorker.*

TOM BOSWELL has covered baseball for the *Washington Post* for nearly thirty years. A sports commentator on National Public Radio since 1984, he served as guest editor for *The Best American Sports Writing 1994.*

JEFF COPLON was a contributor to the first edition of *The Best American Sports Writing.* His stories have appeared in a number of publications, including *Playboy, Rolling Stone,* and *The New York Times Magazine.* His latest book is *Gold Buckle.*

A native of Jackson, Mississippi, RICHARD FORD now lives in New Orleans. Formerly a writer for *Inside Sports* magazine, Ford is best known for his novels and short stories. His most recent novel, *Independence Day,* won the Pulitzer Prize and PEN/Faulkner Award for fiction.

IAN FRAZIER is the author of *Family, Great Plains,* and *Coyote V. Acme.* His work has appeared in a wide variety of publications.

KEN FUSON was an award-winning feature writer for *The Des Moines Register.* He is now a reporter for *The Baltimore Sun.*

DAVID HALBERSTAM served as guest editor for the inaugural edition of *The Best American Sports Writing.* His reportage of the Vietnam War earned him a Pulitzer Prize. His latest sports title is *October 1964,* an account of the 1964 World Series between the St. Louis Cardinals and the New York Yankees.

Writer and humorist TONY HENDRA lives in New York. A former editor of *Spy Magazine,* Hendra played the character of Ian Faith, the band manager in the Rob Reiner film *This Is Spinal Tap.* He is a frequent contributor to *Harper's* and *Esquire.*

JON KRAKAUER won a National Magazine Award for his story "Into Thin Air" for *Outside.* He is also the author of *Into the Wild.*

A screenwriter and contributing editor of *Esquire,* MARK KRAM'S work has previously been featured in *The Best American Sports Writing 1993* and *1995.*

JACK MCCALLUM has been on the staff of *Sports Illustrated* since 1981, where he edits the weekly "Scorecard" column. He lives in Bethlehem, Pennsylvania, and is a graduate of Muhlenberg College.

THOMAS MCGUANE is the author of *Nothing But Blue Skies* and *Ninety-two Degrees in the Shade.* His essays on sports appear in the collection *Outside Chance.* He served as guest editor for *The Best American Sports Writing 1992.*

University of Florida creative writing professor PADGETT POWELL's work has appeared in *Esquire, The New York Times,* and *The New Yorker.* He is the author of *Edisto Revisited.*

A four-time winner of the Sportswriter of the Year Award from the National Association of Sportscasters and Sportswriters, RICK REILLY covers professional golf for CNN/*SI.* The author of *Missing Links,* a golf novel, he is currently at work on a screenplay about the early days of the NFL.

DAVID REMNICK is a staff writer for *The New Yorker* and the author of *Lenin's Tomb: The Last Days of the Soviet Empire,* which won the Pulitzer Prize in 1993.

LINDA ROBERTSON is a reporter for the *Miami Herald* and former president of the Association for Women in Sports Media. Her work has appeared in *A Twentieth-Century Treasury of Sports* and *A Kind of Grace.* She was a contributor to *The Best American Sports Writing 1991* and *1993.*

A native of Bloomington, Minnesota, STEVE RUSHIN is a graduate of Marquette University and a senior writer for *Sports Illustrated.*

GARY SMITH is a past winner of the National Magazine Award for feature writing. A four-time contributor to *The Best American Sports Writing,* Smith is a senior writer for *Sports Illustrated.*

GAY TALESE is the author of *Thy Neighbor's Wife, Honor Thy Father,* and *Unto the Sons.* He is a contributing editor for *Esquire.*

As a teenager, DAVID FOSTER WALLACE was a nationally ranked tennis player. He teaches at Illinois State University and is the author of *The Broom of the System, Infinite Jest, A Supposedly Fun Thing I'll Never Do Again,* and a collection of short stories, *The Girl with Curious Hair.*

Notable Sports Writing of 1996

SELECTED BY GLENN STOUT